## What Doctors Are Saying About
### *Your Pregnancy Week by Week*

"*Your Pregnancy Week by Week* is the primary book I recommend to patients during pregnancy. I know I can trust it. It's organized, up to date, and provides women with terrific information."

—ELIZABETH D. WARNER, M.D., OB/GYN,
ROCHESTER GYNECOLOGIC
AND OBSTETRIC ASSOCIATES

"*Your Pregnancy Week by Week* is an extraordinarily well-written and accessible book. Dr. Glade Curtis' years of practice make him familiar with what really concerns patients and with what they most want to know. *Your Pregnancy* covers not only the specific issues every pregnant woman experiences, but deals with the whole wide array of potential concerns that can arise in pregnancy. All this, together with the elegant side-bars and skillful drawings, make *Your Pregnancy* not only the most comprehensive of the pregnancy books available for the lay public but also the most readable."

—HENRY M. LERNER, M.D., OB/GYN,
NEWTON-WELLESLEY HOSPITAL,
CLINICAL INSTRUCTOR IN
OBSTETRICS AND GYNECOLOGY AT
HARVARD MEDICAL SCHOOL

"Regular contact with an obstetrician is an important part of a healthy pregnancy. And that's why I can so strongly recommend *Your Pregnancy Week by Week* to patients who want to have a doctor's advice in addition to my own. It's written by a doctor, it's full of trustworthy and up-to-date information and its 'bedside manor' is excellent."

—HENRY HESS, M.D., ASSOCIATE CLINICAL
PROFESSOR OF OBSTETRICS AND GYNECOLOGY,
UNIVERSITY OF ROCHESTER SCHOOL OF MEDICINE

# What Other Women Are Saying About
## *Your Pregnancy Week by Week*

"Most books only give you a month by month breakdown of what's going on with baby and mom. I like how this one gives you week by week information. I look forward to reading it each week." —RACHEL M., OHIO

"*Your Pregnancy Week by Week* has been a good friend. Reading each week and knowing what changes my baby was going through was important to me." —ANITA A., CALIFORNIA

"I have other pregnancy books but when I started reading *Your Pregnancy Week by Week*, I put the others down. This book is excellent. I highly recommend it to all new mothers." —CRYSTAL L., VIRGINIA

"The week by week style is wonderful. It lets you know what to expect as it happens." —HEATHER H., LOUISIANA

"I liked how it went week by week because that is how my doctor thinks, too." —REBECCA C., VIRGINIA

"The detailed week by week information about my and my baby's changing body was excellent. It gave me something to read weekly, not just monthly." —DEANA S., MASSACHUSETTS

"*Your Pregnancy Week by Week* was my second Bible. I used it so much I have almost memorized it! I recommend it to everyone!" —CHRISSY M., ILLINOIS

"*Your Pregnancy Week by Week* was very comforting, it put my mind at ease." —JENNIFER W., KENTUCKY

"This book is full of helpful ideas that both new and experienced mothers-to-be can put to immediate use." —ZENAIDA M., FLORIDA

"This book is the 'A, B, C book to pregnancy'" —DORIS H., INDIANA

"Reading this book is like talking to your mom about how it was being pregnant." —AMANDA S., KENTUCKY

"All the information on a weekly basis is wonderful. I highly recommend this book to every woman expecting." —THERESA C., CALIFORNIA

"This book should be read by every mother-to-be. It gives you information week by week instead of month by month and it helped me so much." —KRISTI C., GEORGIA

# your
# pregnancy™
## week by week

Also by Glade B. Curtis, M.D., M.P.H., OB/GYN, and Judith Schuler, M.S.

*Your Baby's First Year Week by Week*
*Your Pregnancy Questions and Answers*
*Your Pregnancy After 35*
*Your Pregnancy for the Father-to-Be*
*Your Pregnancy Journal Week by Week*
*Bouncing Back After Your Pregnancy*
*Your Pregnancy—Every Woman's Guide*

5TH EDITION

# your
# pregnancy™
## week by week

**Glade B. Curtis, M.D., M.P.H., OB/GYN**

**Judith Schuler, M.S.**

Da Capo
LIFE
LONG

A Member of the Perseus Books Group

Your Pregnancy is a trademark of Da Capo Press

Illustrations by David Fischer
Designed by Lisa Kreinbrink
Set in 11.5 point Minion by the Perseus Books Group

Cataloging-in-Publication data for this book is available from the Library of Congress.

First Da Capo Press printing 2004
ISBN 1–55561–346–2 (pbk.); 1-55561-347-0 (hardcover)

Published by Da Capo Press
A Member of the Perseus Books Group
http://www.dacapopress.com

Da Capo Press books are available at special discounts for bulk purchases in the U.S. by corporations, institutions, and other organizations. For more information, please contact the Special Markets Department at the Perseus Books Group, 11 Cambridge Center, Cambridge, MA 02142, or call (800) 255-1514 or (617) 252-5298, or e-mail special.markets@perseusbooks.com.

9—08   07   06

# About the Authors

*Glade B. Curtis, M.D., M.P.H., F.A.C.O.G.*, is board-certified by the American Board of Obstetrics and Gynecology and a Fellow of the American College of Obstetricians and Gynecologists. He is in practice in Salt Lake City, Utah, is a Medical Consultant to the State of Utah Department of Health and a Medical Director of The Health Clinics of Utah.

One of Dr. Curtis's goals as a doctor has been to provide patients with information about gynecological and obstetrical conditions they may have, problems they may encounter and procedures they may undergo. In pursuit of that goal, he and Ms. Schuler have co-authored several additional books for pregnant women and their partners, including *Your Pregnancy for the Father-to-Be*, *Your Pregnancy Questions and Answers*, *Your Pregnancy after 35*, *Your Pregnancy—Every Woman's Guide*, *Your Pregnancy Journal Week by Week* and *Bouncing Back after Your Pregnancy*. He and Ms. Schuler have also written a book dealing with baby's health and development after birth titled *Your Baby's First Year Week by Week*.

Dr. Curtis is a graduate of the University of Utah with a Bachelor of Science and a Master's Degree in Public Health (M.P.H.). He attended the University of Rochester School of Medicine and Dentistry in New York. He interned and was a resident and chief resident in Obstetrics and Gynecology at the University of Rochester Strong Memorial Hospital, Rochester, New York.

*Judith Schuler, M.S.*, has worked with Dr. Curtis for more than 22 years, as his co-author and editor. They have collaborated together on 12 books dealing with pregnancy, women's health and children's health. Ms. Schuler earned a Master of Science degree in Family Studies from the University of Arizona in Tucson.

Before becoming an editor for HPBooks, where she and Dr. Curtis first began working together, Ms. Schuler taught at the university level in California and Arizona. She has one grown son. She divides her time between Tucson, Arizona, and Laramie, Wyoming.

# Acknowledgments

We would both like to take this opportunity to thank Marnie Cochran, senior editor at Da Capo Press and our editor for nearly 5 years, for her hard work on our behalf on so many fronts. She has made our association a happier experience for us all.

***Glade B. Curtis.*** In this, the 5th edition of *Your Pregnancy Week by Week*, I have continued to draw upon the many questions from discussions with my patients and their partners, and my professional colleagues. Nearly every day brings new insights and greater understanding of the joy and anticipation of impending parenthood. I rejoice in my patients' happiness and thank all of them for allowing me to be part of this miraculous process.

Credit must also be given to my understanding and generous wife, Debbie, and our family, who support me in a profession that requires much of them. Beyond that commitment, they have supported and encouraged me to pursue the challenge of this project. And my parents have always offered their unconditional love and support.

***Judith Schuler.*** I wish to thank all of my friends and family members who have shared with me their questions and concerns about the journey through pregnancy. They have helped me immensely in our efforts to provide for all readers the pregnancy information they seek.

To my parents, Bob and Kay Gordon, I appreciate your love and continued support. To my son, Ian, thank you for your interest, friendship and love. And thanks to Bob Rucinski for helping me in so many ways—for your professionalism, your expertise and your encouragement.

# Contents

# *Preparing for Pregnancy*

Nothing compares with the miracle and magic of pregnancy. It's your chance to be involved in life's creative process. Planning ahead for this experience can improve your chances of doing well yourself and of having a healthy baby.

Your lifestyle affects your baby's health. By planning ahead, you can ensure you and your baby are exposed to good things and avoid harmful things during your pregnancy.

By the time most women realize they are pregnant, they are 1 to 2 months into their pregnancy. By the time they see their doctor, they are 2 or 3 months along. The first 12 weeks of pregnancy are extremely important because this is when the baby forms its major organ systems. Many important things can happen before you realize you are pregnant or before you see your doctor. Getting in shape for pregnancy means physical and mental preparation.

Pregnancy is a condition, not an illness; a pregnant woman is not sick. However, you will experience major changes during the course of your pregnancy. Having good general health before pregnancy can help you deal with the physical and emotional stresses of pregnancy, labor and delivery. It can help you prepare to take care of a newborn baby.

## Your General Health

In recent years, an explosion of technology has resulted in new medications, medical advances and new medical treatments. Through these advances, we have learned that your health at the beginning of pregnancy and during pregnancy can have a major effect on you and your developing baby.

In the past, the emphasis was on being healthy during pregnancy. Today, most doctors suggest looking at pregnancy as lasting 12 months instead of just 9 months. This includes at least a 3-month period of preparation. Preparing your body with good general health can help you prepare for a healthy pregnancy and a healthy baby.

## Preparing for Pregnancy

The following are important actions to take before you get pregnant. If you have any questions or concerns, discuss them with your doctor.

• Achieve your ideal weight at least 3 months before you conceive. Your baby's health is tied to *your* body weight when you get pregnant. Overweight pregnant women run the risk of high blood pressure and gestational diabetes; they also have a higher rate of Cesarean delivery. Underweight women may have a harder time conceiving; babies born to underweight women are more often premature and have a lower birthweight.

• *Start* taking prenatal vitamins, and *stop* taking your daily multivitamin. *More is not better* in this situation!

• Start a regular exercise program, and stick with it. Exercising moderately before you get pregnant and continuing throughout your pregnancy can help you a great deal.

• Discuss any medications you take on a regular basis with your physician.

• Be sure any chronic medical conditions you have are under control.

- Stop smoking. Avoid secondhand smoke.
- Stop drinking alcohol.
- Have your immunity to rubella and chicken pox checked. If you need vaccinations, find out how long you have to wait after you have them before you can start trying to get pregnant.
- Schedule any necessary medical tests, such as X-rays, before you stop your contraception method.
- Keep a record of your fertility cycle by using charts. Or check your fertility cycle with an ovulation-predictor kit or a saliva-testing kit.
- Be careful about taking dietary supplements and botanicals. Some herbs, such as St. John's wort, saw palmetto and echinacea, may interfere with conception.
- Start taking folic acid—400mcg/day is recommended. Folic acid can help prevent birth defects of the brain and spinal cord, called *neural-tube defects*. It has also been shown that low levels may increase your risk of miscarriage. You need to start taking folic acid *before* you get pregnant because folic acid protects you the most during the first 28 days of pregnancy. Because you may not know when you get pregnant, begin taking it when you stop contraception and while you're trying to conceive.
- Ask your physician to check your iron levels. You don't want to have an iron deficiency before pregnancy—this situation could make you feel even more fatigued than is normal during pregnancy.
- Check your cholesterol level; decrease high cholesterol levels with a high-fiber nutrition plan that is also low in saturated fat. High cholesterol levels may contribute to high blood pressure during pregnancy.
- Stay healthy; try to avoid infections. Wash hands frequently, have someone else change the kitty litter, eat foods that are well prepared and avoid situations where you might be exposed to infection.
- Avoid hazardous chemicals at work and at home.
- Try to lessen any unnecessary stress in your life.

- Have a dental checkup; periodontal disease should be under control. Periodontal disease during pregnancy increases the risk of having a low-birthweight baby.
- Find out your HIV status.
- Know your blood type and the blood type of your baby's father.
- Together with your partner, write down your family medical histories.
- Consider how pregnancy fits into your future plans (education, career, travel).
- Check your health insurance to see what maternity coverage it provides.

Some of the above actions may be harder to begin *during* a pregnancy. Deal with these issues before pregnancy, know you are healthy and you won't have to worry about the risks they may pose while you're pregnant. It makes sense to continue birth control until you've achieved the above.

## Seeking Medical Advice

Seeing a doctor before you get pregnant is good preparation for pregnancy. Arrange for a checkup and to discuss your pregnancy plans. Then you'll know that when you do get pregnant, you are in the best possible health.

You may have a medical condition that requires attention before pregnancy. If you don't take care of it before trying to conceive, it may affect your ability to get pregnant. You may need to change medications you are taking, or you may need to make lifestyle changes.

### ∾ Tests for You
A general physical exam before you get pregnant helps ensure you won't have to deal with new medical problems during pregnancy. A Pap smear and a breast exam should be included in this physical. Lab tests to consider before pregnancy include tests for rubella, blood

type and Rh-factor. If you are 35 or older, a mammogram is also a good idea.

If you have been exposed to HIV or hepatitis, ask your doctor to conduct tests for these. If you have a family history of other medical problems, such as diabetes, ask whether you should have any tests to rule them out. If you have other chronic medical problems, such as anemia or recurrent miscarriages, your physician may suggest other specific tests.

### ✌ X-rays and Other Imaging Tests

If you are trying to conceive, ask for a pregnancy test before having any diagnostic test involving radiation, including dental work. Tests that involve radiation include *X-rays, CT scans* and *MRIs*. Use reliable contraception before these tests to make sure you are not pregnant. If you schedule these tests right after the end of your period, you can be sure you are not pregnant. If you must receive a series of these tests, continue to use contraception.

### ✌ Possible Prepregnancy Tests

Your doctor may conduct many tests before you become pregnant, depending on your current medical problems and your family history. Some tests you may have include:

- a physical exam
- a Pap smear
- breast exam (and mammogram if you are at least 35)
- rubella titers
- blood type and Rh-factor
- HIV (if you have been exposed to risk factors)
- hepatitis (if you have been exposed to risk factors)
- cystic fibrosis screening

Another test that is done before you become pregnant is *preimplantation genetic diagnosis (PGD)*; it is often done if you have in vitro fertilization. With in vitro fertilization, an embryo is created outside the womb (in vitro) by mixing an egg and sperm, then it is implanted in the woman.

With PGD, a few cells are removed for genetic testing *before* the embryo is implanted to identify genes that may be responsible for some severe hereditary diseases. The goal is to select healthy embryos for implantation to avoid serious genetic disease. The technique has been used to diagnose cystic fibrosis, Down syndrome, Duchenne muscular dystrophy, hemophilia, Tay–Sachs disease and Turner syndrome. A normal (unaffected) embryo is implanted in the uterus and allowed to develop to term (birth).

## Medical History

A prepregnancy visit with your doctor is the best time to discuss your medical history and any problems you may have had in previous pregnancies. Ask what you can do to eliminate or to decrease chances of the same problems recurring in your next pregnancy. Past problems include ectopic pregnancy, miscarriage, previous C-sections (Cesarean deliveries) or other pregnancy complications.

This is also a good time to talk about exposure to, and problems with, sexually transmitted diseases or other infections. If you have had major surgery or any female surgery in the past, discuss it now. If you are being treated for other medical problems, discuss them with your doctor. Make plans to take medications that are safe to use during a pregnancy *before* you try to get pregnant.

## Discontinuing Contraception

It's important to continue using some form of contraception until you are ready to get pregnant. If you are in the middle of treatment for a medical problem or if you are undergoing tests, finish the course of treatment or tests before trying to conceive. (If you're not using some form of birth control, you're basically trying to get pregnant.) After discontinuing your regular contraceptive, use some other birth-control method until your periods become normal. You can choose from condoms, spermicides, the sponge or a diaphragm.

### ᵜ *Birth-Control Pills or Patches*
Most doctors recommend you have two or three normal periods after you stop using birth-control pills or the patch before you get pregnant. If you get pregnant immediately after stopping these contraceptives, it may be difficult to determine when you conceived. This can make it harder to determine your due date. This may not seem important now, but it will be very important to you during pregnancy and at the end of your pregnancy.

### ✑ *IUDs*

If you have an IUD (intrauterine device), you must have it removed before you try to conceive. However, pregnancy can occur while an IUD is in place. If you have any sign of infection with an IUD, take care of it before trying to get pregnant. The best time to remove an IUD is during a menstrual period.

### ✑ *Norplant*

If you use Norplant, you should have at least two or three normal menstrual cycles after it is removed before trying to get pregnant. It may take a few months for your periods to return to normal after Norplant is removed. If you get pregnant immediately after removing Norplant, it may be difficult to determine when you got pregnant and what your due date is.

### ✑ *Depo Provera*

Depo provera, a hormone injection used for birth control, should be discontinued for at least 3 to 6 months before trying to conceive. Wait until you have had at least two or three normal periods.

## Current Medical Problems

Before you become pregnant, examine your lifestyle, diet, physical activity and any chronic medical problems you have, such as high blood pressure or diabetes. You may require extra care before and during pregnancy. Tell your doctor about any medications you currently take. Discuss any tests you may be planning to have, such as X-rays, and cover all medical problems you are being treated for. It's easier to answer questions about these problems, their treatment and their complications before you get pregnant rather than after you are pregnant.

### ✑ *Anemia*

*Anemia* means you do not have enough hemoglobin to carry oxygen to your body's cells. Symptoms include weakness, fatigue, shortness of breath and pale skin. *It is possible to develop anemia during pregnancy, even if you are not anemic before you get pregnant.* While you are pregnant, the baby makes great demands on your body for iron and iron stores. If you have low iron levels at the beginning of pregnancy, pregnancy can tip the balance and make you anemic. Ask for a CBC (complete blood count) as a part of your prepregnancy physical.

If you have a family history of anemia (such as sickle-cell anemia or thalassemia), discuss these with your doctor *before* you get pregnant. (See Week 22 for more information on different types of anemia.) If you take hydroxyurea to treat your sickle-cell disease, discuss whether you should continue using it while trying to conceive. We do not know whether this medication is safe during pregnancy.

### ᘓ Asthma

Asthma affects about 1% of all pregnant women. Half of those women with asthma see no change in their condition during pregnancy. For about 25%, asthma improves, and for the other 25%, the condition worsens.

Most asthma medications are safe to take during pregnancy, but talk to your doctor about taking any medication. Most people with asthma know what triggers attacks. While you're trying to get pregnant and during pregnancy, be especially careful to avoid things that trigger attacks. Try to get asthma under good control before trying to become pregnant. (Read more about how asthma affects pregnancy in Week 28.)

### ᘓ Bladder or Kidney Problems

Bladder infections, commonly called *urinary-tract infections* or *UTIs*, may occur more often during pregnancy. If a urinary-tract infection is not treated, it can cause an infection of the kidneys, called *pyelonephritis*.

Urinary-tract infections and pyelonephritis are associated with premature delivery. If you have a history of pyelonephritis or repeated urinary-tract infections, you should be evaluated before you begin pregnancy.

Kidney stones may also create problems during pregnancy. Because they cause pain, it may be difficult to differentiate between kidney stones and other problems that can occur during pregnancy. Kidney stones can also cause an increased chance of urinary-tract infections and pyelonephritis.

If you have had kidney or bladder surgery, any major kidney problems or if you know your kidney function is less than normal, tell your doctor. It may be necessary to evaluate your kidney function with tests before you become pregnant.

If you have had an occasional bladder infection, don't be alarmed. Your doctor will decide whether further testing is necessary before you become pregnant. (See Week 18 for more information.)

### ‿ *Cancer*

If you have had any type of cancer in the past, tell your doctor when planning your pregnancy or as soon as you discover you are pregnant. He or she may need to make decisions about individualized care for you during this pregnancy. (See Week 30 for more information about cancer and pregnancy.)

### ‿ *Diabetes*

Diabetes is a medical problem that can have serious effects during pregnancy. Historically, women with diabetes have had problems with pregnancy, but with good control, a diabetic woman today is usually able to have a healthy pregnancy. If diabetes is *not* under control when you get pregnant, your risk of having a child with a birth defect increases 5 *times!*

If you have diabetes, it may be harder for you to become pregnant. It can also increase the chance of miscarriage, stillbirth and birth defects. These risks can be decreased by good control of blood sugar during pregnancy.

If your diabetes is not controlled, the combination of pregnancy and diabetes can be dangerous for you and your baby. Many of the problems and damage caused by diabetes occur during the first trimester (the first 13 weeks of pregnancy); poor control, however, can affect the entire pregnancy.

Pregnancy may affect diabetes by increasing your body's need for insulin. Insulin makes it possible for the body to use sugar. Most doctors recommend you have diabetes under control for at least 2 to 3 months before pregnancy begins. Controlling your diabetes may require checking your blood sugar several times a day.

If you have a family history of diabetes or suspect you might have diabetes, have it checked before getting pregnant. This will help you lower the risk of miscarriage and other problems. If you haven't had diabetes before and develop it during pregnancy, it is called *gestational diabetes*. (See Week 23.)

### ᨔ *Epilepsy and Seizures*

*Epilepsy* includes several different problems; however, seizures are the most severe. There are two kinds of epileptic seizures—*grand mal* and *petit mal*. A mother-to-be with epilepsy has a 1 in 30 chance of having a baby with a seizure disorder. Babies also have a higher chance of birth defects, perhaps related to medications taken to control epilepsy during pregnancy.

If you take medication for epilepsy, it is important to consult your doctor before you become pregnant. Discuss the amounts and the types of medication you take. Some medications are safe during pregnancy. Most doctors will have you switch to phenobarbital during the time you are trying to conceive and while you are pregnant.

Seizures can be dangerous to the mother and fetus. It is important for you to take your medication regularly and as prescribed by your doctor. Do not decrease or discontinue any medication on your own!

### ᨔ *Heart Disease*

During pregnancy, the workload on your heart increases by about 50%. If you have any kind of heart condition, tell your physician about it before you get pregnant. Some heart problems, such as *mitral-valve prolapse*, may be serious during pregnancy and may require antibiotics at the time of delivery. Other heart problems, such as congenital heart problems, may seriously affect your health. Your doctor may advise against pregnancy in these cases. Consult your physician about any heart condition so it can be dealt with before you become pregnant.

### ✌ *Hypertension*

*Hypertension*, or high blood pressure, can cause problems for a pregnant woman and her unborn baby. For the woman, these problems may include headaches, kidney damage or stroke. For a developing baby, high blood pressure in a mother-to-be can cause decreased blood flow to the placenta, resulting in a smaller baby or intrauterine-growth restriction (IUGR).

If you have high blood pressure before pregnancy, you must closely monitor your blood pressure during pregnancy. Your doctor may ask you to see an internist who will help you control your blood pressure.

Some high-blood-pressure medications are safe to take during pregnancy; others are not. *Do not stop or decrease any medication on your own!* This can be dangerous. If you're planning a pregnancy, ask your doctor about the medication you take for high blood pressure and its safety during conception and pregnancy.

### ✌ *Lupus*

*Systemic lupus erythematosus* (SLE) is an autoimmune disease. This means you produce antibodies to your own organs, which may destroy or damage those organs and their function. Lupus can affect many parts of the body, including joints, kidneys, lungs and the heart.

This problem can be difficult to diagnose. Lupus occurs in about 1 in 700 women between 15 and 64 years of age. In black women, it occurs once in 254 women. Lupus is found more often in women than in men, especially between the ages of 20 and 40.

There is no cure for lupus at present. Treatment is individual and usually involves taking steroids. It is best not to become pregnant while you are experiencing a flare-up. There is an increased risk of miscarriage and stillbirths in women with lupus, which requires extra care during pregnancy.

Babies born to women with lupus may have a rash, heart block and heart defects. These babies may be born prematurely or experience intrauterine-growth restriction. Talk to your doctor before you become pregnant if you have lupus. (See Week 27 for more information on lupus in pregnancy.)

### ✺ Migraine Headaches

About 15 to 20% of all pregnant women suffer from migraine headaches. Many women notice an improvement in their headaches while they are pregnant. If you must take medication for headaches during pregnancy, check with your doctor ahead of time so you'll know whether the one you take is safe to use.

### ✺ Thyroid Problems

Thyroid problems can appear as either too much or too little thyroid hormone. Too much thyroid hormone, *hyperthyroidism*, results in a faster metabolism; it is usually caused by Graves' disease. The problem is often treated by surgery or medication to reduce the amount of thyroid hormone in your system. If left untreated during pregnancy, there is a higher risk of premature delivery and low birthweight. If treatment is necessary during pregnancy, there are safe medications you can take.

Too little thyroid hormone, *hypothyroidism*, is usually caused by autoimmune problems; the thyroid gland is damaged by your own antibodies. Doctors treat this problem with thyroid hormones. If left untreated, you may suffer from infertility or have a miscarriage.

If you have either thyroid problem, you should be tested before pregnancy to determine the correct amount of medication for you. Pregnancy can change medication requirements, so you will also need to be checked during pregnancy.

### ✌ Other Medical Problems

Many other specific chronic illnesses can affect a pregnancy. If you have any chronic problem or take any medication on a regular basis, talk it over with your doctor.

## Current Medications

It's important for you and your doctor to consider the possibility of pregnancy each time you are given a prescription or advised to take a medication. When you are pregnant, everything changes with regard to medications.

Medications that are safe when you are not pregnant may have harmful effects when you are pregnant. Whether a medication is safe during pregnancy is not always known. Ask your doctor before changing any medication. (Some effects of medications and chemicals are discussed in Week 4.)

Most organ development in the baby occurs in the first 13 weeks of pregnancy. This is an important time to avoid exposing your baby to unnecessary medications. You'll feel better and do better during pregnancy if you have medication use under control before you try to get pregnant.

Some medications are intended for short-term use, such as antibiotics for infections. Others are for chronic or long-lasting problems, such as high blood pressure or diabetes. Some medications are OK to

### Be Careful with Medications

During pregnancy, play it safe. Some general guidelines for medication use while you are trying to get pregnant include the following.

- Do not stop birth control unless you want to be pregnant.
- Take prescriptions exactly as they are prescribed.
- Tell your doctor if you think you might be pregnant or if you are not using birth control when a medication is prescribed.
- Do not self-treat or use medications you were given in the past for other problems.
- Never use someone else's medications.
- If you are unsure about a medication, consult your doctor *before* you use it.

take while you are pregnant and might even help make your pregnancy successful. Other medications may not be safe to take during pregnancy.

## Vaccinations

The same rule applies to vaccinations as to X-ray tests—when you have a vaccination, use reliable contraception. Some vaccines are safe during pregnancy; some are not. A good rule of thumb is to complete vaccinations at least 3 months before trying to get pregnant.

Vaccinations are usually most harmful to a pregnancy in the first trimester. If you need a vaccination for rubella or MMR (measles, mumps, rubella) or chicken pox before you get pregnant, the Centers for Disease Control (CDC) now recommends you wait at least 4 weeks after receiving it before you try to conceive.

An exception to this rule is the flu vaccine. The flu vaccine *should* be taken by a pregnant woman who will be past the 3rd month of pregnancy during the flu season. If you are advised to take the flu vaccine because of your job or for some other reason, go ahead. It's considered safe during pregnancy and while you are trying to conceive.

## Fertility Monitors May Help in Achieving Pregnancy

Today we are fortunate to have many valuable tests available to predict when ovulation occurs to help a woman conceive. These tests can be done at home, and most are easy to use.

The *Clear-Plan Easy Fertility Monitor* helps you track where you are in your menstrual cycle. All you have to do is press a button at the start of a new menstrual period to begin tracking your cycle. For 10 days during the cycle, you use a urine sample for testing hormone levels. The monitor judges where you are in your fertility cycle. This monitor costs about $220.

Another ovulation test is the *Donna Saliva Ovulation Tester*, which uses your saliva to predict ovulation. In the 1940s, researchers found the salt content of a woman's saliva is the same as the woman's cervical fluid when she ovulates. Using this information, this test was developed to help predict ovulation. Saliva is placed on the microscope lens, and the crystallized pattern is examined after it dries. When a woman is *not* ovulating, random dots appear; however, 1 to 3 days before ovulation, short hairlike structures can be seen. On the day of ovulation, a fernlike pattern appears, which makes it easy to distinguish from the other patterns. Cost of this test runs about $60.

## Genetic Counseling

If you're planning your first pregnancy, you are probably not considering genetic counseling. However, there may be circumstances in which genetic counseling could help you and your partner make informed decisions about childbearing. There are more than 13,000 inherited gene disorders that we know about. Each year in the United States, about 150,000 babies are born with some type of birth defect. Certain ethnic groups have a higher incidence of specific genetic defects. In addition, certain medications, chemicals and pesticides can put a couple at risk.

Genetic counseling is an information session between you and your partner and a genetic counselor or group of counselors. Any information you share with or receive from a genetic counselor is confidential. It may involve one visit or several visits. Genetic counseling is available at most major universities. Your physician can advise you.

Through genetic counseling, you and your partner hope to understand the possibilities or probabilities of what might affect your ability to get pregnant or your future offspring. The information you receive is not precise. Counselors may speak in terms of "chances" or "odds" of a problem.

A genetic counselor will not make a decision for you. He or she will provide information on tests you might take and what the results of those tests may indicate. When speaking with a genetic counselor, don't hide information you feel is embarrassing or hard to talk about. It is important to give him or her as much information as possible.

Ask your doctor if you should seek genetic counseling. Most couples who need genetic counseling do not find out they needed it until after they have a child born with a birth defect. You might consider genetic counseling if any of the following apply to you.

- You will be at least 35 years old at the time of delivery.
- You have delivered a child with a birth defect.
- You or your partner has a birth defect.
- You or your partner has a family history of Down syndrome, mental retardation, cystic fibrosis, spina bifida, muscular dystrophy, bleeding disorders, skeletal or bone problems, dwarfism, epilepsy, congenital heart defects or blindness.
- You or your partner has a family history of inherited deafness (prenatal testing can identify congenital deafness caused by the Connexin–26 gene, allowing parents and medical personnel the opportunity to manage the problem immediately).
- You and your partner are related (consanguinity).
- You have had recurrent miscarriages (usually three or more).
- You *and* your partner are descended from Ashkenazi Jews (risk of Tay–Sachs disease or Canavan's disease).
- You or your partner are African American (risk of sickle-cell anemia).
- Your partner is at least 40 years old. (Medical information shows a father in his forties may have an increased chance of fathering a child with a birth defect. See page 19 for more information.)

Some of the information you need may be difficult to gather, especially if you or your partner was adopted. You may know little or nothing of your family's medical history. Discuss this with your doctor before you become pregnant. If you learn about the chances of problems before getting pregnant, you won't be forced to make difficult choices after becoming pregnant. The primary goal in genetic counseling is the same as other goals in pregnancy—early diagnosis and prevention of problems.

## Pregnancy after 35

More women are choosing to marry after they have established their career, and more couples are choosing to start their families at a later age. Today, physicians are seeing more older first-time mothers, and more of these mothers are having safe, healthy pregnancies than women their age did in the past.

We have found that an older woman considering pregnancy has two major concerns. She wants to know how the pregnancy will affect her and how her age will affect her pregnancy. There is a slight increase in the possibility of complications for the mother and baby when the mother is older. You may also want to read our book, *Your Pregnancy after 35*, which focuses primarily on pregnancy in older women.

A pregnant woman older than 35 may be more likely to face increased risks of the following:

- a baby born with Down syndrome
- high blood pressure
- pelvic pressure or pelvic pain
- pre-eclampsia
- Cesarean delivery
- multiple births
- placental abruption
- bleeding and other complications
- premature labor

An older pregnant woman must also deal with problems a younger woman might not face. A broad simplification of this is that it is easier to be pregnant when you are 20 than it is when you are 40. Chances are, by age 40 you have a job or other children making demands on your time. You may find it harder to rest, exercise and eat right.

Maternal problems associated with increasing age include most of the chronic illnesses that tend to appear as age increases. High blood pressure is one of the more common pregnancy complications in women over 35 (see Week 31). There is also a higher incidence of pre-eclampsia (see Week 31). Older women who give birth have a slightly higher risk of abnormalities and problems, including premature labor, pelvic pressure and pelvic pain.

The chance of diabetes, as well as complications of diabetes, increases with age. Researchers cite figures showing that twice as many women over age 35 have complications with diabetes. In the past, hypertension (high blood pressure) and diabetes were major complications in any pregnancy. With today's advances, we can manage these complications of pregnancy quite well.

### ෴ *Down Syndrome*

Through medical research, we know older women are at higher risk of giving birth to a child with Down syndrome, although many of these pregnancies end in miscarriage or stillbirth. Various tests are offered to an older woman during pregnancy to determine whether a baby will have Down syndrome. It is the most common chromosomal defect detected by amniocentesis. (See Week 16 for more information on amniocentesis.)

The risk of delivering a baby with Down syndrome increases as you get older. Look at the following statistics:

- at age 25 the risk is 1 in 1300 births
- at 30 it is 1 in 965 births
- at 35 it is 1 in 365 births
- at 40 it is 1 in 109 births
- at 45 it is 1 in 32 births
- at 49 it is 1 in 12 births

But there is also a positive way to look at these statistics. If you're 45, you have a 97% chance of *not* having a baby with Down syndrome. If you're 49, you have a 92% chance of delivering a child without Down syndrome. If you are concerned about the risk of Down syndrome because of your age or family history, discuss it with your doctor.

### ᔍ *Father's Age*

Research shows a father's age may also be important to a pregnancy. Chromosomal abnormalities that cause birth defects occur more often in older women and in men over 40. Men over 55 have twice the normal risk of fathering a child with Down syndrome. The chance of chromosomal problems increases with the increase in the age of the father. Some researchers recommend that men father their children before age 40. However, there is still some controversy about this.

### ᔍ *Your General Health*

Important questions to consider before getting pregnant when you are older include those about your general health. Are you fit for pregnancy? If you are older, you can maximize your chances of having a successful pregnancy by being as healthy as possible *before* you become pregnant.

Most researchers recommend a baseline mammogram be done at age 35. Have this test before you become pregnant. Paying attention to general recommendations for your diet and your health care are also important in preparing for pregnancy.

## Your Nutrition before Pregnancy

Most people feel better and work better when they eat a well-balanced diet. Planning and following a good diet before pregnancy ensures that your developing fetus receives good nutrition during the first few weeks or months of pregnancy.

Usually a woman takes good care of herself once she knows she is pregnant. By planning ahead, you will guarantee that your baby has a healthy environment for the entire 9 months of pregnancy, not for just the 6 or 7 months after you discover you truly are pregnant. When you make your nutrition plan, you are preparing the environment in which your baby will be conceived and will develop and grow.

## ✑ Weight Management

Before trying to get pregnant, pay attention to your weight; you don't want to be too overweight or too underweight. Either condition can make pregnancy more difficult for you.

Do *not* diet during pregnancy or while you are trying to conceive. Don't take diet pills, unless you're using reliable contraception. Consult your doctor if you are considering a special diet for weight reduction or weight gain before you try to get pregnant. Dieting may cause temporary deficiencies in vitamins and minerals that both you and your developing baby need.

## ✑ Be Careful with Vitamins, Minerals and Herbs

Don't self-medicate with large amounts or unusual combinations of vitamins, minerals or herbs. You *can* overdo it. Certain vitamins, such as vitamin A, can cause birth defects if used in excessive amounts.

As a general rule, stop all extra supplementation at least 3 months before pregnancy. Eat a well-balanced diet and take one multivitamin or one prenatal vitamin a day. Most doctors are happy to prescribe prenatal vitamins if you are planning a pregnancy.

## ✑ Folic Acid

Folic acid is a B vitamin ($B_9$) that can contribute to a healthy pregnancy. If a mother-to-be takes 0.4mg (400 micrograms) of folic acid each day, starting 3 or 4 months *before* pregnancy begins, it may protect her developing baby against various birth defects of the spine and brain, called *neural-tube defects*.

One of these defects, *spina bifida*, afflicts nearly 4000 babies born in the United States every year. It develops in the first few weeks of pregnancy. Studies have shown that about 75% of all cases can be prevented if a mother-to-be takes folic acid. As you plan your pregnancy, ask your physician about supplementation.

In 1998, the U.S. government ordered that some grain products, such as flour, breakfast cereals and pasta, be fortified with folic acid. It is found in many other foods, too. A varied diet can help you reach your goal. Many common foods contain folic acid, including:

asparagus • avocados • bananas • black beans • broccoli • citrus fruits and juices • egg yolks • fortified breads and cereals • green beans • leafy green vegetables • lentils • liver • peas • plantains • spinach • strawberries • tuna • wheat germ • yogurt

## ✎ Begin Good Eating Habits

Often, a woman carries her prepregnancy eating habits into her pregnancy. Many women eat on the run and pay little attention to what they eat most of the day. Before pregnancy, you may be able to get away with this. However, because of the increased demands on you and the requirements of your developing baby, this won't work when you do become pregnant.

The key to good nutrition is balance. Eat a balanced diet. Going to extremes with vitamins or fad diets can be harmful to you and your growing baby. It could even make you feel run-down during pregnancy.

## ✎ Specific Considerations

Specific factors to consider before getting pregnant include whether you follow a vegetarian diet, the amount of exercise you do, whether you skip meals, your diet plan (are you trying to lose or gain weight?) and any special dietary needs you might have.

If you eat a special diet because of medical problems, consult your doctor about it. Much information is available through your doctor or your local hospital about good diets and healthful nutrition.

Many diets go to extremes that you may be able to tolerate, but these extremes can

### Can You Help Avoid Morning Sickness in Pregnancy?

A recent study showed that women who ate high amounts of saturated fat—the kind found in cheese and red meat—in the year *before* they got pregnant had a higher risk of suffering severe morning sickness during pregnancy. If you're planning a pregnancy, you may want to cut down on these foods.

be harmful to a developing baby. It is important to discuss dieting with your doctor ahead of time. You don't want to find out when you are 8 weeks pregnant that you are malnourished because of dieting.

## Exercise before Pregnancy

Exercise is good for you—before you become pregnant and during pregnancy. Benefits may include weight control, a feeling of well-being and increased stamina or endurance, which will become important later in pregnancy.

Begin exercising regularly before you become pregnant. Making adjustments in your lifestyle to include regular exercise will benefit you now and make it easier to stay in shape throughout pregnancy.

Exercise can be carried to extremes, however, which can cause problems. While you are trying to get pregnant, avoid intense training. Don't try to increase your exercise program. This is not a good time to play competitive sports that involve pushing yourself to the maximum.

It's important to find exercise you enjoy and will continue on a regular basis, in any kind of weather. Concentrate on improving strength in your lower back and abdominal muscles to help during your pregnancy.

If you have concerns about exercise before or during pregnancy, discuss them with your doctor. Exercise you tolerate well and can do easily before pregnancy may be more difficult for you during pregnancy.

The American College of Obstetricians and Gynecologists (ACOG) has proposed guidelines for exercise before pregnancy and during pregnancy. Many hospitals and health clubs or spas have exercise programs for pregnant women. ACOG has videotapes available on exercising during pregnancy and after pregnancy. Ask your doctor how to obtain these tapes or the guidelines. See Week 3 for more information about exercise, including guidelines, suggestions and possible problems.

The best approach to exercise is a balanced one. Regular exercise that is enjoyable helps you feel better and enjoy your pregnancy more. It will also provide your developing baby with a healthier environment.

## Substance Use before Pregnancy

In the past, little was understood about drug or alcohol abuse, and not a lot could be done to help a person with these problems. Today healthcare providers are able to give suggestions and provide care for those who use or abuse drugs, alcohol or other substances. Don't be embarrassed to confide in your doctor about substance use. Your doctor's concern is for you and your baby.

*Tip for Prepregnancy*

Even though you know you aren't pregnant, treat your body as if you were during your preparation period. When you do get pregnant, you'll be on the right track for eating, exercising and avoiding harmful substances.

We have learned much about drug and alcohol use and the effect on pregnancy in recent years. We now believe the safest approach to drug or alcohol use during pregnancy is *no use at all.*

It makes sense to solve these problems before pregnancy. By the time you realize you're pregnant, you may already be 8 or 10 weeks along. Your baby goes through some of its most important developmental stages in the first 13 weeks of pregnancy. You might use drugs and not realize you are pregnant. Few women would take these substances if they knew they were pregnant. Stop using any substance you don't need at least 3 months before trying to conceive!

Research into these problems continues, showing that use of drugs or alcohol during pregnancy may affect a child's IQ, attention span and learning ability. To date, no safe level of these substances has been determined.

Drug use before pregnancy is serious business. Fortunately, there is help for those who use drugs. Get help before you become pregnant. Preparing for pregnancy may be a good reason for you and your partner to change your lifestyle.

### ⌒ *Common Substances of Abuse*
**Tobacco**. We have known for a long time that smoking affects fetal development. Mothers who smoke during pregnancy are more likely to have low-birthweight babies or babies with intrauterine-growth restriction. Ask for help to stop smoking before you become pregnant. Your doctor should be receptive to this request. (See Weeks 1 & 2 for tips on quitting.)

**Alcohol.** In the past, some believed a small amount of alcohol during pregnancy was OK. Today, we believe *no amount* of alcohol is safe to drink during pregnancy. Alcohol crosses the placenta and directly affects your baby. Heavy drinking during pregnancy can cause fetal alcohol syndrome (FAS) or fetal alcohol exposure (FAE), discussed in Weeks 1 & 2.

**Cocaine.** Cocaine has been shown to affect the baby throughout pregnancy, not just during the first trimester. If you use cocaine during the first 12 weeks of pregnancy, you run a higher risk of miscarriage. Cocaine can also cause severe deformities in a fetus. The type of defect it causes depends on the point at which cocaine is used in the pregnancy.

*Dad Tip* If your partner is making lifestyle changes to prepare for pregnancy, such as giving up smoking or not drinking alcohol, support her in her efforts. Quit these habits, too, if you share them.

Infants born to mothers who use cocaine during pregnancy have been found to have long-term mental deficiencies. Sudden infant death syndrome (SIDS) is also more common in these babies. Many babies born to women who use cocaine are stillborn.

Cocaine affects the mother-to-be, too. It is a stimulant and increases the user's heart rate and blood pressure. Women who use the drug during pregnancy have a higher rate of placental abruption, which is the premature separation of the placenta from the uterus.

In some parts of the United States, more than 10% of all pregnant women use cocaine at some time during their pregnancy. Stop using cocaine before you stop using birth control. Damage to the embryo (later the fetus) can occur as early as 3 days after conception!

**Marijuana.** Marijuana (hashish) is dangerous during pregnancy because it crosses the placenta and enters the baby's system. It can have long-lasting effects on babies exposed before birth. Research has shown that a mother's marijuana use during pregnancy can affect cognitive function, decision-making ability and future-planning ability in her child. Use can also affect a child's verbal reasoning and memory.

If your partner smokes marijuana, encourage him to stop. One study showed that the risk of SIDS was twice the average for children if their father smoked marijuana. The risk is present if the male smokes before conception. Researchers believe the THC in marijuana may adversely affect sperm and the growing fetus.

## Work and Pregnancy

You may need to consider your job when you plan a pregnancy. Many women do not know they are pregnant until the early stages of the pregnancy are already behind them. It's wise to plan ahead. Learn about things you are exposed to at work.

### *Are You in the Military?*

Are you currently serving in the U.S. Armed Forces or planning to enter one of the services soon? If so, as you prepare for your pregnancy, there are some things to keep in mind.

Studies have shown that women who get pregnant while they are on active duty may face many challenges, including some risks to their developing fetuses. The pressure to meet military body-weight standards can have an effect on a mother-to-be's health. Many women also have low iron stores and lower-than-normal folic acid levels due to poor dietary habits. As we discuss on page 20, folic acid is extremely important early in pregnancy, and you must have adequate iron stores throughout pregnancy. In addition, some aspects of a job may pose hazards, such as standing for prolonged periods, heavy lifting and exposure to toxic chemicals. All of these factors can impact on your pregnancy.

If you're planning on getting pregnant during your service commitment, work hard to reach your ideal weight a few months before you conceive, then maintain that weight. Be sure your folic-acid intake is adequate and your iron stores are at an acceptable level by following a well-balanced food plan and eating foods high in these substances. You may also want to take prenatal vitamins. If you are concerned about hazards related to your work, discuss it with a superior. Find out if you're pregnant before receiving any vaccinations or inoculations.

It's important to take care of yourself and your baby. Start by making plans now to have a healthy pregnancy. Also see the discussion of *Pregnancy in the Military* in Week 14.

Some jobs might be considered harmful during pregnancy. Some substances you might be exposed to at work, such as chemicals, inhalants, radiation or solvents, could be a problem while you're pregnant. Much of this chapter has discussed your lifestyle and how you take care of yourself. It is important to consider things you are exposed to at work as part of your lifestyle. Continue reliable contraception until you know the environment at work is safe.

Other important work-related considerations are the types of benefits or insurance coverage you have and your company's maternity-leave program. Most programs allow some time off work. It makes sense to check into this before getting pregnant. With the expense of medical care and having a baby, it could cost you several thousand dollars if you don't plan ahead.

Women who stand for long periods have smaller babies. If you have had a premature delivery in the past or if you have had an incompetent cervix, a job that requires you to stand a great deal may not be the wisest choice for you during pregnancy. Talk to your doctor about your work situation.

## Sexually Transmitted Diseases

Infections or diseases passed from one person to another by sexual contact are called *sexually transmitted diseases* (STDs). These infections can affect your ability to get pregnant and can harm your developing baby. The type of contraception you use may have an effect on the likelihood of your contracting an STD. Condoms and spermicides can lower the risk of getting an STD. You are more likely to get a sexually transmitted disease if you have more than one sexual partner.

Some STD infections can cause *pelvic inflammatory disease* (PID). PID is serious because it can spread from the vagina and cervix through the uterus and involve the Fallopian tubes and ovaries. The result can be scarring and blockage of the tubes, making it difficult or impossible for you to become pregnant or making you more susceptible to an ectopic pregnancy (see Week 5).

## ◌ *Protecting Yourself from STDs*

Part of planning and preparing for pregnancy includes protecting yourself against STDs. Take the following actions.

- Use a condom (regardless of what other type of contraception you might be using).
- Limit the number of sexual partners you have.
- Have sexual contact only with those you are sure do not have multiple sexual partners.

Ask for treatment if you think you have a sexually transmitted disease. Get tested if you have any chance of having an STD, even if you haven't had any symptoms.

# Weeks 1 & 2

## *Pregnancy Begins*

*T*his is an exciting time for you—having a baby growing inside you is an incredible experience! This book will help you understand and enjoy your pregnancy. You will learn what is going on in your body and how your baby is growing and changing.

You are not alone in your pregnancy. Millions of women successfully complete a pregnancy every year. In fact, the average number of babies born every day in the United States is 11,120. Over 4 million babies are born each year in the United States alone!

One focus of this book is to help you see how your actions and activities affect your health and well-being and that of your growing baby. If you're aware of how a particular test at a particular time, such as an X-ray, will affect the developing fetus, you may decide on another course of action. If you understand how taking a certain drug can harm your baby or cause long-lasting effects, you may decide not to use it. If you know a poor diet can cause heartburn or nausea in you or delayed growth in your baby, you may choose to eat nutritiously. If you are aware of how much your actions affect your pregnancy, you may be able to choose wisely, free yourself from worry and enjoy your pregnancy a great deal more.

Material in this book is divided into weeks of pregnancy. Illustrations help you see clearly how you and your baby are changing and growing each week. General topics each week cover areas of special concern as well as how big your baby is, how big you are and how your actions affect your baby.

The information in this book is *not* meant to take the place of any discussion with your doctor. Be sure you discuss any and all concerns with him or her. Use this material as a starting place in your dialogue. It may help you put your concerns or interests into words.

## Signs and Symptoms of Pregnancy

Many changes in your body can indicate pregnancy. If you have one or more of the following symptoms and you believe you could be pregnant, contact your physician:

- missed menstrual period
- nausea, with or without vomiting
- food aversions or food cravings
- fatigue
- frequent urination
- breast changes and breast tenderness
- new sensitivity or feelings in your pelvic area
- metallic taste in your mouth

What will you notice first? It's different for every woman. When your expected menstrual period does not begin, it may be the first sign of pregnancy.

## When Is Your Baby Due?

The beginning of a pregnancy is actually figured from the beginning of your last menstrual period. That means, for your doctor's computational purposes, you are pregnant 2 weeks before you actually conceive! This can be confusing, so let's examine it more closely.

## Definitions of Time

**Gestational age (menstrual age)**—Begins from the first day of your last period, which is actually about 2 weeks *before* you conceive. This is the age most doctors use to discuss your pregnancy. Average length of pregnancy is 40 weeks.

**Ovulatory age (fertilization age)**—Begins the day you conceive. Average length of pregnancy is 38 weeks.

**Trimester**—Each trimester lasts about 13 weeks. There are three trimesters in a pregnancy.

**Lunar months**—A pregnancy lasts an average of 10 lunar months (28 days each).

### ～ Figuring Your Due Date

Most women don't know the exact date of conception, but they are usually aware of the beginning of their last period. This is the point from which a pregnancy is dated. A due date is important in pregnancy because it helps your doctor determine when to perform certain tests or procedures. It also helps estimate the baby's growth and may indicate whether you are overdue. For most women, the fertile time of the month (ovulation) is around the middle of their monthly cycle or about 2 weeks before the beginning of their next period.

Pregnancy lasts about 280 days, or 40 weeks, from the beginning of the last menstrual period. You can calculate your due date by counting 280 days from the first day of bleeding of your last period. Or count back 3 months from the date of your last period and add 7 days. This also gives you the approximate date of delivery. For example, if your last period began on February 20, your due date is November 27.

Calculating a pregnancy this way gives the gestational age (menstrual age). This is how most doctors and nurses keep track of time during pregnancy. It is different from ovulatory age (fertilization age), which is 2 weeks shorter and dates from the actual date of conception.

Some medical experts are now suggesting that instead of a "due date," women be given a "due week"—a 7-day window of time during which delivery may occur. This time period would fall between 39½ and 40½ weeks. Because so few women (only 5%) deliver on their actual due date, this 7-day period could conceivably help ease a mom-to-be's anxiety about when her baby will be born.

Many people count the time during pregnancy using weeks. It's really the easiest way. But it can be confusing to remember to begin counting from when your period starts and that you don't become pregnant until about 2 weeks later. For example, if your doctor says you're 10 weeks pregnant (from your last period), conception occurred 8 weeks ago.

You may hear references to your stage of pregnancy by trimester. *Trimesters* divide pregnancy into three periods, each about 13 weeks long. This helps group together developmental stages. For example, your baby's body structure is largely formed and his or her organ systems develop during the first trimester. Most miscarriages occur during the first trimester. During the third trimester, most maternal problems with pregnancy-induced hypertension or pre-eclampsia occur.

You may even hear about lunar months, referring to a complete cycle of the moon, which is 28 days. Because pregnancy is 280 days from the beginning of your period to your due date, pregnancy lasts 10 lunar months.

### ᴥ 40-Week Timetable

In this book, pregnancy is based on a 40-week timetable. Using this method, you actually become pregnant during the third week. Details of your pregnancy are discussed week by week beginning with Week 3. Your due date is the end of the 40th week.

Each weekly discussion includes the actual age of your growing baby. For example, in Week 8, you'll see the following:

Week 8 *(gestational age)*
Age of Fetus—6 Weeks *(fertilization age)*

In this way, you'll know how old your developing baby is at any point in your pregnancy.

It's important to understand a due date is only an estimate, not an exact date. As we've already said, only 1 out of 20 women delivers on her due date. It's a mistake to count on a particular day (your due date or an earlier date). You may see that day come and go and still not have your baby. Think of your due date as a goal—a time to look forward to and to prepare for. It's helpful to know you're making progress.

No matter how you count the time of your pregnancy, it's going to last as long as it's going to last. But a miracle is happening—a living human being is growing and developing inside you! Enjoy this wonderful time in your life.

### ᧞ Your Menstrual Cycle

Menstruation is the normal periodic discharge of blood, mucus and cellular debris from the cavity of the uterus. The usual interval for menstruation is 28 days, but this can vary widely and still be considered normal. The duration and amount of menstrual flow can vary; the usual duration is 4 to 6 days.

Two important cycles actually occur at the same time—the ovarian cycle and the endometrial cycle. The *ovarian cycle* provides an egg for fertilization. The *endometrial cycle* provides a suitable site for implantation of the fertilized egg inside your uterus. Because endometrial changes are regulated by hormones made in the ovary, the two cycles are intimately related.

## Tip for Weeks 1 & 2

Over-the-counter pregnancy tests are reliable and can be positive (indicate pregnancy) as early as 10 days after conception.

The ovarian cycle produces an egg (ovum) for fertilization. There are about 2 million eggs in a newborn girl at birth. This decreases to about 400,000 in girls just before puberty. The maximum number of eggs is actually present *before* birth. When a female fetus is about 5 months old (4 months before birth), she has about 6.8 million eggs!

Some women (about 25%) experience lower abdominal pain or discomfort on or about the day of ovulation, called *mittelschmerz*. It is believed to be caused by irritation from fluid or blood from the follicle when it ruptures. The presence or absence of this symptom is not considered proof that ovulation did or did not occur.

## Your Health Affects Your Pregnancy

Your health is one of the most important factors in your pregnancy. Good nutrition, proper exercise, sufficient rest and attention to how you care for yourself all affect your pregnancy. Throughout this book, we provide information about medications you may take, medical tests you may need, over-the-counter substances you might use and many other topics that may concern you. This information is necessary for you to be aware of how your actions affect your health and the health of your developing baby.

The health care you receive can also affect your pregnancy and how well you tolerate being pregnant. Good health care is important to the development and well-being of your baby.

### ✎ *Your Healthcare Provider*
You have many choices when it comes time to choose your healthcare provider. An *obstetrician* is a doctor who specializes in the care of pregnant women, including delivering babies. Obstetricians are M.D.s (medical doctors who have graduated from an accredited medical school and have fulfilled the requirements for a medical license) or D.O.s (doctors of osteopathic medicine who have graduated from an accredited school of osteopathic medicine and have fulfilled the requirements for a medical license). Both have completed further training after medical school (residency).

Obstetricians who specialize in high-risk pregnancies are *perinatologists*. Few women require a perinatologist (only 1 out of 10). Ask your doctor if you need to see a specialist, if you're concerned about past health problems.

Some women choose a *family practitioner* because he or she is the family doctor. In some cases, an obstetrician may not be available because a community is small or in a remote area. The family practitioner often serves as your internist, obstetrician/gynecologist and pediatrician. Many family practitioners are experienced at delivering babies. If problems arise, a family practitioner may need to refer you to an obstetrician for your prenatal care. This may also be the case if a Cesarean section is required for delivery of your baby.

Pregnant women sometimes choose *certified nurse-midwives* for their care. A certified nurse-midwife is a trained professional who delivers low-risk, uncomplicated pregnancies. These professionals are registered nurses with additional training and certification in nurse-midwifery. They require the immediate availability of a physician, in case complications arise.

**Communication Is Important.**   It's important to be able to communicate well with your healthcare provider. Pregnancy and delivery are individual experiences. You need to be able to ask any questions you have, such as those listed below.

- Do you believe in natural childbirth?
- Are there routines you perform on every patient? Does everyone "get" an enema, fetal monitor or more?
- Who covers patient care for you when you are away?
- Are there other doctors I will meet or who will take care of me?

Express your concerns and talk about whatever is important to you. Your doctor has experience involving hundreds or thousands of deliveries and is drawing on this for your well-being. He or she has to consider what is best for you and your baby while trying to honor any "special" requests you may have.

Don't be afraid to ask any question; your doctor has probably already heard it. It may be that a request is unwise or risky for you, but it's important to ask about it ahead of time. If a request is possible, then you can plan for it together, barring unforeseen developments.

**Finding the "Right" Caregiver for You.** How do you find someone who "fits the bill"? If you already have an obstetrician you're happy with, you may be all set. If you don't, call your local medical society. Ask for references to professionals who are taking new patients for pregnancy.

An added credential is *board certification*. Not all doctors who deliver babies are board-certified. It is not a requirement. "Board certification" means your doctor has put in extra time preparing for and taking exams to qualify him or her to care for pregnant women and to deliver their babies.

Board certification is administered by the American Board of Obstetrics and Gynecology, under the direction of the American College of Obstetricians and Gynecologists. If your doctor has passed his or her boards, it is often indicated by the initials *F.A.C.O.G.* after the doctor's name. This means he or she is a Fellow of the American College of Obstetricians and Gynecologists. Your local medical society can also give you this information.

There are other ways to find a doctor you'll be happy with. Ask friends who have recently had a baby about their experiences. Ask the opinion of a labor-delivery nurse at your local hospital. Various publications, such as the *Directory of Medical Specialties* or the *Directory of the American Medical Association*, are available at most U. S. libraries. In Canada, refer to the *Canadian Medical Directory*. Another doctor, such as a pediatrician or internist, may also provide a reference.

When you pick a doctor, you usually also pick a hospital. Keep the following in mind when choosing where to have your baby.

• Is the facility close by?
• What are the policies regarding your partner and his participation?
• Can he be present if you have a Cesarean section?
• Can you have an epidural?
• Is it a birthing center (if that's what you want)?
• Does your HMO (health maintenance organization) or your insurance cover the doctor *and* the hospital?

## How Your Actions
## Affect Your Baby's Development

It's never too early to start thinking about how your activities and actions can affect your growing baby. Many substances you normally use may have adverse effects on the baby you carry. These substances include drugs, tobacco, alcohol and caffeine. Below are discussions of cigarette smoking and alcohol use. Either of these activities can harm a developing baby. Other substances are discussed throughout the book.

### ৵ *Cigarette Smoking*

Smoking cigarettes has harmful effects on a pregnancy. A pregnant woman who smokes 20 cigarettes a day (one pack) inhales tobacco smoke more than 11,000 times during an average pregnancy! And when you smoke, your baby does, too. What we mean by that is cigarette smoke crosses the placenta to your baby. A recent study showed that when this occurs, a baby is exposed to *much higher concentrations of nicotine* than its mother. This higher concentration could lead to nicotine withdrawal in baby after his or her birth.

Tobacco smoke contains many harmful substances, such as nicotine, carbon monoxide, hydrogen cyanide, tars, resins and some cancer-causing agents (carcinogens). These substances may be responsible singly or together for damaging your developing baby.

Scientific evidence has shown smoking during pregnancy increases the risk of fetal death or fetal damage. Smoking interferes with a woman's absorption of vitamins B and C and folic acid. Lack of folic acid can result in neural-tube defects and increases the risk of pregnancy-related complications in a mother-to-be.

For more than 30 years, we have known infants born to mothers who smoke weigh less by about 7 ounces (200g). That is why cigarette packages carry a warning to women about smoking during pregnancy. Decreased birthweight is directly related to the number of cigarettes the expectant mother smoked. These effects don't appear in her other babies if the mother doesn't smoke with other pregnancies. There is a direct relationship between smoking and impaired fetal growth.

A growing baby is greatly affected by its mother's smoking. Smoking causes narrowing of the capillaries in the placenta; the capillaries carry blood, oxygen and other nutrients to the baby. This narrowing can lead to a reduction in the nourishment baby receives from you, which can lead to low birthweight and smaller-in-stature (shorter) babies.

Children born to mothers who smoked during pregnancy have been observed to have lower IQ scores and increased incidence of reading disorders than children of nonsmokers. The incidence of minimal-brain-dysfunction syndrome (hyperactivity) has also been reported to be higher among children of mothers who smoked during pregnancy.

Cigarette smoking during pregnancy increases the risk of miscarriage and fetal death or death of a

## Nicoderm Patch, Nicorette Gum and Zyban

Many studies have shown the harmful effects of cigarette smoking during pregnancy. You may be wondering if you can use an aid to help you stop smoking, such as the patch, gum or the stop-smoking pill. The specific effects on fetal development of these three devices are unknown.

Nicotrol, available as an inhaler, a nasal spray, gum or patch, is a popular aid used for smoking cessation. Nicotrol is sold under the brand names *Nicoderm* and *Nicorette;* it is also sold generically. All Nicotrol preparations contain nicotine and are *not* recommended for use during pregnancy.

Zyban (bupropion hydrochloride) is an oral medication that is a nonnicotine aid to help with smoking cessation. This medication is also marketed as the antidepressant Wellbutrin or Wellbutrin SR. Zyban is not recommended for use by pregnant women.

If you are pregnant, researchers advise avoiding gum, the patch and the pill. Discuss the situation with your physician if you have questions.

baby soon after birth. The risk is also directly related to the number of cigarettes the pregnant woman smokes. The risk may increase as much as 35% in a woman who smokes more than one pack of cigarettes a day.

Smoking also increases the incidence of serious complications in a mother-to-be. An example of this is placental abruption, discussed in detail in Week 33. The risk of developing placental abruption increases by almost 25% in moderate smokers and more than 65% in heavy smokers.

Placenta previa (discussed in Week 35) also occurs more frequently among smokers. The rate of occurrence increases by 25% in moderate smokers and 90% in heavy smokers.

What can you do? The answer sounds simple but isn't—quit smoking. In more realistic terms, a woman who smokes during pregnancy will benefit from reducing or stopping cigarette use before or during pregnancy—and so will her developing baby. Some studies indicate that a nonsmoker and her unborn baby exposed to secondary smoke (cigarette smoke in the environment) are exposed to nicotine and other harmful substances. Perhaps pregnancy can serve as good motivation for everyone in the family to stop smoking!

## *Tips for Stopping Smoking*

- Make a list of things you can do instead of smoking, especially activities that involve using your hands, such as puzzles or needlework.
- List things you'd like to buy for yourself or your baby. Set aside the money you normally spend on cigarettes to buy these items.
- Identify all your "triggers"—what brings on an urge to smoke. Make plans to avoid them or to handle them differently.
- Instead of smoking after meals, brush your teeth, wash dishes or go for a walk.
- If you always smoke while driving, clean your car inside and out, and use an air freshener. Sing along with the radio or a cassette tape. Listen to an audiobook. Take a bus or carpool for a while.
- Drink lots of water.

If you continue to have trouble stopping, a recent study determined that using a "quitter's hotline" for help is twice as effective as going it alone. You can talk directly to someone who has been through the same experience. If you're interested, call the National Partnership to Help Pregnant Women Quit Great Start Quitline, at (866) 66-START.

### ᔓ *Alcohol Use*

Alcohol use by a pregnant woman carries risk. Moderate drinking has been linked to an increased chance of miscarriage. Excessive alcohol consumption during pregnancy often results in fetal abnormalities. Chronic use of alcohol in pregnancy can lead to abnormal fetal development called *fetal alcohol syndrome (FAS)*.

FAS is characterized by growth restriction before and after birth, and defects in limbs, the heart and facial characteristics of children are also seen. Facial characteristics are recognizable—the nose is upturned and short, the upper jawbone is flat and the eyes look "different." An FAS child may also have behavioral problems.

FAS children often have impaired speech, and their fine and gross motor functions are impaired. The infant mortality rate is 15 to 20%.

### Alcohol in Cooking

Most pregnant women know they should avoid alcohol during pregnancy but what about recipes that call for alcohol? A good rule of thumb is it's probably OK to eat a food that contains alcohol if it has been baked or simmered for at least 1 hour. Cooking for that length of time evaporates most of the alcohol content.

Most studies indicate women would have to drink four to five drinks a day for FAS to occur. But mild abnormalities have been associated with two drinks a day (1 ounce of alcohol). These milder birth defects are the result of *fetal alcohol exposure* (FAE), a condition that can result from very little alcohol. This has led many researchers to conclude there is *no safe level of alcohol consumption* during pregnancy. For this reason, all alcoholic beverages in the United States carry warning labels similar to those on cigarette packages. The warning advises women to avoid alcohol during pregnancy because of the possibility of fetal problems, including fetal alcohol exposure and fetal alcohol syndrome.

Taking drugs with alcohol increases the chances of damage to a baby. Analgesics, antidepressants and anticonvulsants cause the most concern. Some researchers have suggested the father's heavy alcohol consumption before conception may also result in fetal alcohol syndrome. Alcohol intake by the father has been cited as one possible cause of intrauterine-growth restriction.

As a precaution, be very careful about over-the-counter cough and cold remedies you may use. Many contain alcohol—some as much as 25%!

Some women want to know if they can drink socially. There is a great deal of disagreement about it because there is no known safe level of alcohol consumption during pregnancy. Why take chances? For the health and well-being of your developing baby, abstain from alcohol during pregnancy. Responsibility for preventing these problems rests squarely on your shoulders!

## Your Nutrition

If your weight is normal before pregnancy, you need to increase your caloric intake during pregnancy. During the first trimester (first 13 weeks), you should eat a total of about 2200 calories a day. During the second and third trimesters, you probably need an additional 300 calories each day.

Extra calories provide the energy your body needs for you and your growing baby. Your baby uses the energy to create and to store protein, fat and carbohydrates. It needs energy for fetal body processes to function. The extra calories also support changes your body is going through. Your uterus increases in size, and your blood volume increases by about 50%.

*Dad Tip* Give your partner a lot of hugs. Many women enjoy more hugging and cuddling during this very special time.

You can meet most of your nutritional needs by eating a well-balanced, varied diet. The *quality* of your calories is important, too. If a food grows in the ground or on a tree (meaning it's fresh), it's probably better for you than if it comes out of a box or can.

Be cautious about adding the extra 300 calories to your nutrition plan—it doesn't mean doubling your portions. A medium apple and a cup of low-fat yogurt add up to 300 calories!

## You Should Also Know

### ᴧ *Hepatitis in Pregnancy*
Hepatitis is a viral infection of the liver. It is one of the most serious infections that can occur during pregnancy. Hepatitis B is responsible

for nearly half the cases of hepatitis in the United States. It is transmitted by sexual contact or reuse of hypodermic needles.

Those at risk for contracting hepatitis B include people with a history of intravenous drug use, a history of sexually transmitted diseases or exposure to people or blood products that contain hepatitis B. The B type can be transmitted to the developing fetus of a pregnant woman.

Hepatitis symptoms include the following:

Although this book is designed to take you through your pregnancy by examining one week at a time, you may seek specific information. Because the book cannot include *everything* you need *before* you know you're looking for it, check the index, beginning on page 460, for a particular topic. For example, if you're searching for information early in your pregnancy on ways to snack healthfully, check the index for various page references. We may not cover the subject until a later week.

- nausea
- flulike symptoms
- jaundice (yellow skin)
- dark urine
- pain in or around the liver or upper-right abdomen

Hepatitis B is diagnosed by blood tests. In most areas, women are tested for hepatitis B at the beginning of pregnancy. If you test positive, your baby may receive *immune globulin* (antibodies to fight hepatitis) after delivery. It is now recommended that all newborns receive hepatitis vaccine shortly after birth. Ask your pediatrician if it is available in your area.

If you want to chart your pregnancy weight gain, we've provided a chart on the following page just for that purpose. The weeks listed are weeks when you may have a prenatal appointment. If your appointment doesn't fall on that exact week, cross out the week number that we have listed and mark down which week you made your visit to the doctor.

# Chart Your
# Pregnancy Weight Gain

*Weight Before Pregnancy Begins* _____115_____

| Week | Weight at Prenatal Appointment | Weight Gain |
|------|-------------------------------|-------------|
| 8    | _____ | _____ |
| 12   | _____ | _____ |
| 16   | _____ | _____ |
| 20   | _____ | _____ |
| 24   | _____ | _____ |
| 28   | _____ | _____ |
| 30   | _____ | _____ |
| 32   | _____ | _____ |
| 34   | _____ | _____ |
| 36   | _____ | _____ |
| 37   | _____ | _____ |
| 38   | _____ | _____ |
| 39   | _____ | _____ |
| 40   | _____ | _____ |

*Total pregnancy weight gain* _____

# Week 3

*Age of Fetus—1 Week*

## How Big Is Your Baby?

The embryo growing inside you is very small. At this point, it is only a group of cells, but it is multiplying and growing rapidly. The embryo is the size of the head of a pin and would be visible to the naked eye if it weren't inside you. The group of cells doesn't look like a fetus or baby; it looks like the illustration on page 45. During this first week, the embryo is about 0.006 inch (0.150mm) long.

## How Big Are You?

In this third week of pregnancy, you won't notice any changes. It's too soon! Few women know they have conceived. Remember, you haven't even missed a period yet.

## How Your Baby Is Growing and Developing

A great deal is happening, even though your pregnancy is in its earliest stage. Ovaries lie free in your pelvis (or peritoneal cavity). They are close to the uterus and Fallopian tube. At the time of ovulation, the end of the tube (called the *fimbria*) lies close to the ovary. Some researchers believe this tube opening covers the area on the ovary where the egg (ovum) is released at the time of ovulation. The release site on the ovary is called the *stigma*.

During intercourse, an average of 0.06 to 0.15 ounce (2 to 5ml) of semen is deposited in the vagina. Each milliliter contains an average of 70 million sperm; each ejaculation contains 140 to 350 million sperm. Only about 200 sperm actually reach the egg in the tube. *Fertilization* is the joining together of one sperm and an egg.

### ᴧ Fertilization of the Egg

Fertilization is believed to occur in the middle part of the tube, called the *ampulla*, not inside the uterus. Sperm travel through the uterine cavity and out into the tube to meet the egg.

When the sperm and egg join, the sperm must pass through the outer layer of the ovum, the *corona radiata*. The sperm then digests its way through another layer of the ovum, the *zona pellucida*. Although several sperm may penetrate the outer layers of the ovum, usually only one sperm enters the ovum and fertilizes it.

> ### Boy or Girl?
>
> Your baby's sex is determined at the time of fertilization by the type of sperm (male or female) that fertilizes the egg. A Y-chromosome-bearing sperm produces a boy, and an X-chromosome-bearing sperm produces a girl.

After the sperm penetrates the ovum, the sperm head attaches to its surface. The membranes of the sperm and ovum unite, enclosing them in the same membrane or sac. The ovum reacts to this contact with the sperm by making changes in the outer layers so no other sperm can enter.

Once the sperm gets inside the ovum, it loses its tail. The head of the sperm enlarges and is called the *male pronucleus*; the ovum is called the *female pronucleus*. The chromosomes of the male and female pronuclei intermingle. When this happens, extremely small bits of information and characteristics from each partner unite. This

**Blastomere**

Nine-cell embryo 3 days after fertilization. The embryo is made up of many blastomeres; together they form a blastocyst.

chromosomal information gives each of us our particular characteristics. The usual number of chromosomes in each human is 46. Each parent supplies 23 chromosomes. Your baby is a combination of chromosomal information from you and your partner.

### ᑐ Embryonic Development Begins

The developing ball of cells is called a *zygote*. The zygote passes through the uterine tube on its way to the uterus as the division of cells continues. These cells are called a *blastomere*. As the blastomere continues to divide, a solid ball of cells is formed, called a *morula*. The gradual accumulation of fluid within the morula results in the formation of a *blastocyst*, which is tiny.

During the next week, the blastocyst travels through the uterine tube to the cavity of the uterus (3 to 7 days after fertilization in the tube). The blastocyst lies free in the uterine cavity as it continues to grow and to develop. About a week after fertilization, it attaches to the uterine cavity (implantation), and cells burrow into the lining of the uterus.

## Changes in You

Some women can tell when they ovulate. They may feel mild cramping or pain, or they may have an increased vaginal discharge. Occasionally at the time of implantation of the fertilized egg into the uterine cavity, a woman may notice a small amount of bleeding.

It's too early for you to notice many changes. Your breasts haven't started to enlarge and you aren't starting to "show." That lies ahead! (See the discussion in Weeks 1 & 2 for signs and symptoms of pregnancy.)

## How Your Actions Affect Your Baby's Development

Exercise is an important part of life for many women. The more we learn about health, the more the advantages of regular exercise become evident. Regular exercise may decrease your risk of developing several medical problems, including cardiovascular disease, osteoporosis (softening of bones), depression, premenstrual syndrome (PMS) and obesity.

There are many types of exercise to choose from before, during and after pregnancy. Each offers its own advantages. Aerobic exercise is very popular with women who want to keep in shape. Muscle-building exercises are also a popular way to tone and to increase strength. Many women combine the two. Good exercise choices for pregnant women include brisk walking, stationary bicycling, swimming and aerobic exercise designed especially for pregnant women.

### ᔥ *Aerobic Exercise*

For cardiovascular fitness, aerobic exercise is the best. You must exercise at least 3 times a week at a sustained heart rate of 110 to 120 beats a minute, maintained for at least 15 continuous minutes. The rate of 110 to 120 beats a minute is an approximate target for people of different ages.

If you exercised aerobically before pregnancy, you can probably continue aerobic exercise at a somewhat lower rate. If you have any problems, such as bleeding or premature labor, you and your doctor will have to choose another program.

It is unwise to start a strenuous aerobic exercise program or to increase training during

### Target Heart Rates

| Age (years) | Target heart rate (beats/minute) | Max. heart rate (beats/minute) |
|---|---|---|
| 20 | 150 | 200 |
| 25 | 117–146 | 195 |
| 30 | 114–146 | 190 |
| 35 | 111–138 | 185 |
| 40 | 108–135 | 180 |
| 45 | 105–131 | 175 |
| 50 | 102–131 | 170 |

*(U.S. Department of Health and Human Services)*

pregnancy. If you haven't been involved in regular, strenuous exercise before pregnancy, walking and swimming are probably about as involved as you should get with exercise.

**Before you begin any exercise program, discuss it with your doctor.** Together you can develop a program consistent with your current level of conditioning and your exercise habits.

### ॐ *Muscle Strength*

Some women exercise for muscle strength. To strengthen a muscle, there has to be resistance against it. There are three different kinds of muscle contractions—isotonic, isometric and isokinetic. *Isotonic exercise* involves shortening the muscle as tension is developed, such as when you lift a weight. *Isometric exercise* causes the muscle to develop tension but doesn't change its length, such as when you push against a stationary wall. *Isokinetic exercise* occurs when the muscle moves at a constant speed, such as when you swim.

Cardiac and skeletal muscles cannot usually be strengthened at the same time. Strengthening skeletal muscles requires lifting heavy weights, but you can't lift these heavy weights long enough to strengthen the cardiac muscle.

Weight-bearing exercise is the most effective way of promoting increased bone density to help avoid osteoporosis. Other advantages of exercise include flexibility, coordination, improvement in mood and alertness. Stretching and warming up muscles before and after exercise help you improve flexibility and avoid injury.

### ॐ *Should You Exercise during Pregnancy?*

As a pregnant woman, you are probably concerned about the risks of exercise. Can you or should you exercise when you're pregnant?

Pregnant women need cardiovascular fitness. Women who are physically fit are better able to perform the hard work of labor and delivery. Exercise during pregnancy is not without some risk, however. Risks to the developing baby can include any of the following:

• increased body temperature
• decreased blood flow to the uterus
• possible injury to the mother's abdominal area

You can exercise during pregnancy if you do it wisely. Avoid raising your body temperature above 102F (38.9C). Aerobic exercise can raise your body temperature higher than this, so be careful. A rise in body temperature can be increased by dehydration. Avoid prolonged aerobic exercise, particularly during hot weather.

While exercising aerobically, blood can be diverted to the exercising muscle or skin and away from other organs, such as the uterus, liver or kidneys. A lower workload during pregnancy is advised to avoid potential problems. Now is *not* the time to try to set new records or to train for an upcoming marathon! During pregnancy, keep your heart rate below 140 beats a minute.

### ✎ *General Exercise Guidelines*
Before beginning any exercise program, consult your doctor about any medical problems or pregnancy problems.

- Begin any exercise program before you become pregnant.
- Begin exercising gradually. Start with 15-minute workout sessions, with 5-minute rest periods in between.
- Check your heart rate every 15 minutes. Don't let it exceed 140 beats a minute (bpm). An easy way to calculate your pulse is to count the number of heartbeats by feeling the pulse in your neck or wrist for 15 seconds. Multiply by 4. If your pulse exceeds 140 bpm, rest until your pulse drops below 90.
- Allow enough time to warm up and to cool down.
- Wear comfortable clothing during exercise, including clothing that is warm enough or cool enough, and good, comfortable athletic shoes that offer maximum support.
- Do not allow yourself to become overheated.
- Exercise on a regular basis.
- Avoid risky sports, such as horseback riding or water skiing.
- Increase the number of calories you consume.
- When you're pregnant, be careful about getting up and lying down.
- After the 4th month of pregnancy (16 weeks), don't lie on your back while exercising. This can decrease blood flow to the uterus and placenta.
- When you finish exercising, lie on your left side for 15 to 20 minutes.

*Dad Tip* Bring home flowers for no special occasion.

### ᴥ Possible Problems

Stop exercising and consult your doctor if you experience bleeding or loss of fluid from the vagina while exercising, shortness of breath, dizziness, severe abdominal pain or any other pain or discomfort. Consult your doctor, and exercise only under his or her supervision, if you experience (or know you have) an irregular heartbeat, high blood pressure, diabetes, thyroid disease, anemia or any other chronic medical problem.

*Tip for Week 3* Talk with your doctor before starting an exercise program during pregnancy. If you have been exercising, cut back your level of exercise to no more than 80% of your prepregnancy level.

Talk to your doctor about exercise if you have a history of three or more miscarriages, an incompetent cervix, intrauterine-growth restriction, premature labor or any abnormal bleeding during pregnancy.

## How Your Actions
## Affect Your Baby's Development

### ᴥ Aspirin Use

Almost any medication taken during pregnancy can have some effect on your baby. The reason there are warnings about aspirin is because aspirin use can increase bleeding. It causes changes in the platelet function; platelets are important in blood clotting. This is particularly important to know if you are bleeding during pregnancy or if you are at the end of your pregnancy and close to delivery. Small doses of aspirin may be acceptable during pregnancy; see the box on page 51. **Note:** Do *not* take any amount of aspirin without discussing it with your doctor first!

Read labels on any medication you take to see if it contains aspirin. Avoid using aspirin or any products that contain aspirin unless you first discuss it with your doctor.

If you need a pain reliever or a medication to reduce fever, and you cannot reach your physician for advice, acetaminophen is one over-the-counter medication you can use for a short while with little fear of complications or problems for you or your baby. For further information about over-the-counter medication use during pregnancy, see Week 7.

## Your Nutrition

Folic acid, also referred to as *folate, folacin* or *vitamin B₉*, is important to you during pregnancy. Studies indicate taking folic acid during pregnancy may help prevent or decrease the incidence of neural-tube defects, which are defective closures of the neural tube during early pregnancy. Some of these defects include *spina bifida*, when the base of the spine remains open, exposing the spinal cord and nerves; *anencephaly*, congenital (present at birth) absence of the brain and spinal cord; and *encephalocele*, a protrusion of the brain through an opening in the skull.

> ### Taking Baby Aspirin during Pregnancy
>
> Even though you have heard warnings about taking aspirin during pregnancy, research has shown there may be situations in which aspirin use is beneficial. Researchers now believe that taking a *very low dose* of aspirin in the evening may be good insurance against some pregnancy complications, such as premature labor and high blood pressure. Discuss it with your doctor. Baby aspirin, which contain 81½mg of aspirin, may be prescribed. A woman who takes low doses of aspirin is advised to begin taking it *before* week 16 because the protective effect is not as evident if she begins taking it later.

A folic acid deficiency can also result in anemia in the mother-to-be. Additional folic acid may be necessary with multiple fetuses or when the mother suffers from Crohn's disease or alcoholism.

A prenatal vitamin contains 0.8mg to 1mg of folic acid. This is usually sufficient for a woman with a normal pregnancy. Researchers believe spina bifida may be prevented if the mother-to-be takes 0.4mg of folic acid a day, beginning before pregnancy and continuing through the first 13 weeks. This is suggested for all pregnant women. A pregnant woman's body excretes four or five times the normal amount of folic acid. Because folic acid is not stored in the body for very long, it must be replaced every day.

Beginning in 1998, the U.S. government ordered that some grain products, including flour, breakfast cereals and pasta, be fortified with folic acid. Eating 1 cup of fortified breakfast cereal, with milk, and drinking a glass of orange juice supplies about half of your folic-acid requirement for one day. Folic acid is found naturally in many other foods, too, such as fruits, legumes, brewer's yeast, soybeans, whole-grain products and dark, leafy vegetables. A well-balanced diet can help you reach your folic-acid-intake goal. Also see the list of foods that are good folic-acid sources in Preparing for Pregnancy.

## You Should Also Know

### ✂ *Bleeding during Pregnancy*

Bleeding during pregnancy causes concern. In the first trimester, bleeding can make you worry about the well-being of your baby and the possibility of a miscarriage. (We discuss miscarriage in Week 8.)

Bleeding during pregnancy is *not* unusual. Some researchers estimate that 1 in 5 pregnant women bleeds during the first trimester. Although it makes you worry about possible problems, not all women who bleed have a miscarriage.

Bleeding at the time of implantation is mentioned on page 46. This can occur as the blastocyst burrows into the uterine lining. At this point, you won't know you are pregnant because you haven't missed a period. If this happens, you may just think your period is starting.

As your uterus grows, the placenta forms and vascular connections are made. Bleeding may occur at this time. Strenuous exercise or intercourse may also cause some bleeding. If this occurs, stop your activities and check with your doctor, who will advise you what to do.

If bleeding causes your physician concern, he or she may order an ultrasound exam. Sometimes ultrasound can show a reason for bleeding, but during this early part of pregnancy, there may be no discernible reason for it.

Most doctors suggest resting, decreasing activity and avoiding intercourse when bleeding occurs. Surgery or medication are not helpful and are unlikely to make a difference. Call your doctor if you experience any bleeding. He or she will advise you what to do.

## Benefits of Pregnancy

- Allergy and asthma sufferers may feel better during pregnancy because the natural steroids produced during pregnancy help reduce their symptoms.
- Pregnancy may help protect against breast cancer and ovarian cancer. The younger a woman is when she starts having babies, and the more pregnancies she has, the greater the benefit.
- Migraine headaches often disappear during the second and third trimesters of pregnancy.
- Menstrual cramps are a thing of the past during pregnancy. An added benefit—they may not return after your baby is born!
- Endometriosis (when endometrial tissue attaches to parts of the ovaries and other sites outside the uterus) causes pelvic pain, heavy bleeding and other problems during menstruation for some women. Pregnancy can stop growth of endometriosis.

# Week 4

*Age of Fetus—2 Weeks*

If you've just found out you're pregnant, you might
want to begin by reading the previous chapters.

## How Big Is Your Baby?

Your developing baby is still tiny. Its size varies from 0.014 inch to
about 0.04 inch (0.36mm to about 1mm) in length. One millimeter is
half the size of a letter "o" on this page.

## How Big Are You?

At this point, your pregnancy doesn't show at all. You haven't gained
weight, and your figure hasn't changed. The illustration on page 55
gives you an idea of how small your baby is, so you can see why you
won't notice any changes yet.

Uterus

Pregnancy at around 4 weeks (fetal age—2 weeks).

# How Your Baby Is
# Growing and Developing

Fetal development is still in the very early stages, but many great changes are taking place! The implanted blastocyst is embedded more deeply into the lining of your uterus, and the amniotic cavity, which will be filled with amniotic fluid, is starting to form. The placenta is forming; it plays an important role in hormone production and transport of oxygen and nutrients. Vascular networks that contain maternal blood are becoming established.

### ✎ Germ Layers

Different layers of cells are developing. They are called *germ layers* and develop into specialized parts of your baby's body, such as various organs. There are three germ layers—the *ectoderm, endoderm* and *mesoderm.*

The ectoderm will become the nervous system (including the brain), the skin and the hair. The endoderm develops into the lining of the gastrointestinal tract, the liver, pancreas and thyroid. From the mesoderm comes the skeleton, connective tissues, blood system, urogenital system and most of the muscles.

## Changes in You

You are probably expecting a period around the end of this week. When it doesn't occur, pregnancy may be one of the first things you think of!

### ✎ The Corpus Luteum

When you ovulate, the egg leaves the ovary. The area on the ovary where the egg comes from is called the *corpus luteum*. If you become pregnant, it is called the *corpus luteum of pregnancy*. The corpus luteum forms immediately after ovulation at the site of the ruptured follicle where the egg is released. It looks like a small sac of fluid on the ovary. It undergoes rapid blood-vessel development in preparation for producing hormones, such as progesterone, to support a pregnancy before the placenta takes over.

The importance of the corpus luteum is the subject of much debate. It is believed to be essential in the early weeks of pregnancy because it produces progesterone. The placenta takes over this function between 8 and 12 weeks of pregnancy. The corpus luteum lasts until about the 6th month of pregnancy, when it shrinks, although normal corpus lutea have been found with full-term pregnancies. Successful pregnancies have also occurred when the corpus luteum was removed because of a ruptured cyst as early as the 20th day after a menstrual period or about the time of implantation.

## How Your Actions Affect Your Baby's Development

During pregnancy, nearly every parent worries whether their baby will be perfect. Most parents worry unnecessarily. Major birth defects are apparent in only about 3% of all newborns at birth. Of those 3%, are causes of these abnormalities known? Could they have been prevented?

### ❧ Abnormal Fetal Development

*Teratology* is the study of abnormal fetal development. An exact cause or reason for a birth defect is found in less than half of all cases. Obstetricians and other doctors providing care to pregnant women are often asked about substances (teratogens) that may be harmful. A *teratogen* is a substance that can produce birth defects, including major and minor structural deformities and abnormalities in the way organs function. Researchers have been unable to prove the danger of some agents we believe are harmful. They *have* proved the harm of other agents.

Some agents cause major defects if exposure occurs at a specific, critical time in fetal development. But they may not be harmful at other times. Once the fetus has completed major development, usually by the 13th week, the effect of a certain substance may be only growth restriction or smaller organ size rather than large structural defects. One example is rubella. It can cause many anatomical defects, such as heart malformations, if the fetus is infected during the first trimester of pregnancy. A rubella infection occurring later is less serious.

### ∿ *Individual Response to Exposure*

Individual responses to particular agents and to different doses of agents vary greatly. Alcohol is a good example. Large amounts appear to have no effect on some fetuses, while other fetuses may be harmed by low amounts.

Animal studies provide much of our information about possible harmful agents. This information can be helpful but cannot always be applied directly to humans. Other information comes from situations in which women were exposed who did not know they were pregnant or that a particular substance could be harmful. Information gathered from these instances is difficult to apply directly to a particular pregnancy.

*Tip for Week 4*

Secondary smoke may harm a nonsmoking woman and her developing baby. Ask those who smoke to refrain from smoking around you during your pregnancy.

A list of known teratogens and the effects they may have on an embryo or fetus appears on page 60. If you have taken any of these substances, discuss them as soon as possible with your doctor for your peace of mind. If testing or follow-up is necessary, he or she will advise you.

### ∿ *Drug Use*

Information about the effects of a specific drug on a human pregnancy comes from cases of exposure before the pregnancy is discovered. These "case reports" help researchers understand possible harmful effects but leave gaps in our knowledge. For this reason, it can be difficult or impossible to make exact statements about particular drugs and their effects. The charts on pages 59 and 60 list possible effects of various substances.

If you use drugs, be honest with your doctor. Ask questions about drugs and drug use. Tell your doctor about anything you take or have taken that may affect your baby. The victim of drug use is your baby. A

# Effects of Various Substances on Fetal Development

Many substances can affect your baby's early development. Below is a list of substances and their effects on a developing fetus. This list is of common prescription drugs and chemicals. A second list, which contains other substances, can be found on page 60.

## Common Prescription Drugs and Other Chemicals

| Drug or Chemical | Possible Effects on Your Baby |
| --- | --- |
| **Androgens** (male hormones) | ambiguous genital development (depends on dose given and when given) |
| **Angiotensin-converting enzyme (ACE) inhibitors** (enalapril, captopril) | fetal and neonatal death |
| **Anticoagulants** | bone and hand abnormalities, intrauterine-growth restriction (IUGR), central-nervous-system and eye abnormalities |
| **Antithyroid drugs** (propylthiouracil, iodide, methimazole) | hypothyroidism, fetal goiter |
| **Carbamazepine** | birth defects, spina bifida |
| **Chemotherapeutic drugs** (methotrexate, aminopterin) | increased risk of miscarriage, fetal death and birth defects |
| **Coumadin derivatives** (warfarin) | hemorrhage (bleeding), birth defects, an increase in miscarriage and stillbirth |
| **Diethylstilbestrol** (DES) | abnormalities of female reproductive organs (in females and males), infertility |
| **Folic-acid antagonists** (methotrexate, aminopterin) | increased risk of miscarriage, fetal death and birth defects |
| **Isotretinoin** (Accutane) | increased miscarriage rate, nervous-system defects, facial defects, cleft palate |
| **Lead** | increased miscarriage and stillbirth rates |
| **Lithium** | congenital heart disease |
| **Organic mercury** | cerebral atrophy, mental retardation, spasticity, seizures, blindness |
| **Phenytoin** (Dilantin) | IUGR, microcephaly |
| **Streptomycin** | hearing loss, cranial-nerve damage |
| **Tetracycline** | hypoplasia of tooth enamel, discoloration of permanent teeth |
| **Thalidomide** | severe limb defects |
| **Trimethadione** | cleft lip, cleft palate, IUGR, miscarriage |
| **Valproic acid** | neural-tube defects |
| **Vitamin A and derivatives** (etritinate, retinoids) | fetal death and birth defects |
| **X-ray therapy** | microcephaly, mental retardation, leukemia |

(Modified from A.C.O.G. Technical Bulletin 84, Teratology, February, 1985, American College of Obstetricians and Gynecologists)

## Drugs and Other Substances to Avoid

| Drug | Possible Effects on Your Baby |
| --- | --- |
| Alcohol | fetal abnormalities, fetal alcohol syndrome (FAS), fetal alcohol exposure (FAE), IUGR |
| Amphetamines | placental abruption, IUGR, fetal death |
| Barbiturates | possible birth defects, withdrawal symptoms, poor eating habits, seizures |
| Benzodiazepines (including Valium and Librium) | increased chance of congenital malformations |
| Caffeine | decreased birthweight, smaller head size, breathing problems, sleeplessness, irritability, jitters, poor calcium metabolism, IUGR, mental retardation, microcephaly, various major malformations |
| Cocaine/crack | miscarriage, stillbirth, congenital defects, severe deformities in a fetus, long-term mental deficiencies, sudden infant death syndrome (SIDS) |
| Ecstasy | long-term learning problems, memory problems |
| Glues and solvents | shortened stature, low birthweight, small head, joint and limb problems, abnormal facial features, heart defects |
| Ketamine | behavioral problems, learning problems |
| Marijuana and hashish | attention-deficit disorder (ADD), attention-deficit hyperactivity disorder (ADHD), memory problems, impaired decision-making ability |
| Methamphetamines | IUGR, difficulty bonding, tremors, extreme fussiness |
| Nicotine | miscarriage, stillbirth, neural-tube defects, low birthweight, lower IQ, reading disorders, minimal-brain dysfunction syndrome (hyperactivity) |
| Opioids such as morphine, heroin, Demerol | congenital abnormalities, premature birth, IUGR, withdrawal symptoms in baby |

drug problem may have serious consequences that your physician can best deal with if he or she knows about your drug use in advance.

If your partner uses marijuana, it's a good idea for him to stop, too. Researchers have found that children born to men who smoke marijuana have twice the risk of experiencing SIDS (sudden infant death syndrome) after birth. This occurred whether the father smoked before pregnancy, during pregnancy or after the baby's birth.

## Your Nutrition

You must be prepared to gain weight during your pregnancy. It's necessary for your health and the health of your growing baby. Getting on the scale and seeing your weight rise may be very hard for you. Acknowledge now that it's OK to gain weight. You don't have to let yourself go—you can control your weight by eating carefully and nutritiously. But you *need* to gain enough weight to meet the needs of your pregnancy.

Many years ago, women were not allowed to gain much weight—sometimes only 12 to 15 pounds for their entire pregnancy! Today, we know that restricting weight gain to this extent is not healthy for the baby or the mother-to-be. However, the American Association for Cancer Research has demonstrated an important reason to watch your weight during pregnancy. They found that normal-weight women who gained more than 38 pounds during a singleton pregnancy were at higher risk for developing breast cancer after menopause. Not shedding those extra pounds after pregnancy also contributed to higher risk.

Gain weight slowly. Don't let yourself go, just because you're pregnant. You may be eating for two, but you don't have to eat twice as much! The amount of weight you gain during the first trimester is important. The amount you gain in the *first 13 weeks* has been found to correlate more closely with your baby's birth weight than the amount of weight you put on later in pregnancy. If you gain a lot of weight during the first trimester, your baby may be large. Conversely, if you don't gain very much weight in early pregnancy, you may have a lower-birthweight baby.

You probably won't be able to eat all you want during pregnancy, unless you are one of the lucky women who doesn't have a problem with calories. Even then, you must pay strict attention to the foods you choose, and eat healthfully. Eat nutritious foods. Avoid those with empty calories (lots of sugar and fat). Choose fresh fruits and vegetables. Avoid caffeine when possible. We discuss many of these subjects in later weeks.

## You Should Also Know

### ⌖ *Environmental Pollutants and Pregnancy*

Some environmental pollutants may be harmful to a developing baby. Avoiding exposure to these pollutants is important for a mother-to-be. The box on the opposite page provides information on specific pollutants.

**What Can You Do?** There is a lack of clear information on the safety of many chemicals in our environment. The safest course of action is to avoid exposure when possible, whether by oral ingestion or through the air you breathe. It may not be possible to eliminate all contact with every possible chemical. If you know you will be around various chemicals, wash your hands well before eating. Not smoking cigarettes also helps.

One reassuring fact is that most of the chemicals tested have produced illness in the mother-to-be before damage to her growing baby occurred. An environment that is healthful for you will be healthful for your developing baby.

**Ðad Tip** Make it a habit to pull out your favorite pregnancy book, such as *Your Pregnancy Week by Week*, and read together about what is happening each week in your pregnancy.

### ⌖ *Health of the Baby's Father*

Can the father's health and drug or alcohol use affect the health of the developing baby?

In recent years, more attention has been given to the father's contribution in pregnancy. We now believe if a father is over 40, it may increase the risk of Down syndrome, although there is not a great deal of evidence to support this theory. A father's drug habit at the time of conception may influence the outcome of a pregnancy. Evidence is scanty, but there does appear to be an effect. Why take the chance?

### ⌖ *Do You Take Paxil?*

If you take the antidepressant Paxil, discuss its use with your doctor. Research has shown that taking the medication during your third

## Some Pollutants to Avoid during Pregnancy

### Lead

The toxicity of lead has been known for centuries. In the past, most lead exposure came from the atmosphere. Today, exposure may come from many sources, including some gasoline (now regulated), water pipes, solders, storage batteries, construction materials, paints, dyes and wood preservatives.

Lead is easily transported across the placenta to the baby. Toxicity can occur as early as the 12th week of pregnancy, which could result in lead poisoning in the baby. Avoid exposure to lead. If you might be exposed in your workplace, discuss it with your physician.

### Mercury

Mercury has a long history as a potential poison to a pregnant woman. Reports of fish contaminated with mercury have been linked to cerebral palsy and microcephaly.

### PCBs

Our environment has been significantly contaminated with polychlorinated biphenyls (PCBs). PCBs are mixtures of several chemical compounds.

Most fish, birds and humans now have measurable amounts of PCBs in their tissues. Some experts have suggested that pregnant women limit their intake of fish (to avoid exposure to mercury and PCBs), particularly if a woman is exposed to PCBs where she works. See the discussion of fish in Week 26.

### Pesticides

Pesticides cover a large number of agents used to control unwanted plants and animals. Human exposure is common because pesticides are used extensively. Those of most concern contain several agents—DDT, chlordane, heptachlor, lindane and others.

trimester could expose your baby to potential problems, including respiratory distress, jaundice and low blood sugar. Although these problems are usually temporary, why take the risk? Other treatment options may be available, so ask your doctor about them. You may need to start other treatment options early in pregnancy.

# Week 5

*Age of Fetus—3 Weeks*

If you've just found out you're pregnant, you might
want to begin by reading the previous chapters.

## How Big Is Your Baby?

Your developing baby hasn't grown a great deal. It's about 0.05 inch (1.25mm) long.

## How Big Are You?

At this point, there are still no big changes in you. Even if you are aware you're pregnant, it will be awhile before others notice your changing figure.

## How Your Baby Is Growing and Developing

As early as this week, a plate that will later become the heart has developed. The central nervous system (brain and spinal cord), and muscle and bone formation are beginning to take shape. During this time, your baby's skeleton is also starting to form.

## Changes in You

Many changes are occurring now. You may be aware of some of them; others will be evident only after some kind of test.

### ᘯ *Pregnancy Tests*

Home pregnancy tests have become more sensitive, which makes early diagnosis of pregnancy more common. Tests detect the presence of *human chorionic gonadotropin* (HCG), a hormone of early pregnancy. A pregnancy test can be positive before you have even missed a period!

Many tests can provide positive results (you are pregnant) 10 days after you become pregnant. You might want to wait until you have missed a period before investing money and emotional energy in pregnancy tests, whether done at a hospital, in a clinic or at home. The best time to take a home pregnancy test is the first day *after your missed period* or any time thereafter. If you take the test too early, you may get a false-negative result, meaning you are really pregnant when the test says you're not! False-negative results occur for 50% of the women who take the test *too early.*

**Dad Tip** Clean or vacuum the house without being asked.

Most home tests range in price from $12 to $30. They vary in how effective they are in helping you "diagnose" your pregnancy. Many hospitals or clinics offer free pregnancy testing, which can save you some money.

### ᘯ *Nausea and Vomiting*

An early symptom of pregnancy for some women is nausea, with or without vomiting; it is often called *morning sickness.* The condition affects nearly 70% of all pregnant women. Whether it occurs in the morning or later in the day, it usually starts early and improves throughout the day as you become active. Morning sickness can begin around the 6th week of pregnancy. Take heart—morning sickness usually improves and disappears around the end of the first trimester (week 13). Hang in there, and keep in mind that this condition is temporary.

Many women have nausea. It doesn't usually cause enough trouble to require medical attention. However, a condition called *hyperemesis gravidarum* (severe nausea and vomiting) causes a great deal of vomiting, which results in loss of nutrients and fluid. The pregnant woman is often treated in the hospital with intravenous fluids and medications. Hypnosis has also been used successfully in treating the problem.

If you experience severe nausea and vomiting, if you cannot eat or drink anything or if you feel so ill that you cannot carry on your daily activities, call your physician. Your first prenatal appointment may not be scheduled for a while, but there's no reason you should suffer. There may be some simple suggestions your doctor can offer that will help. Or your doctor may offer a prescription for Bendectin. (See discussion below.) Reassurances that this situation is normal and your baby is OK can be comforting.

There is no completely successful treatment for the normal nausea and vomiting of pregnancy. A pill to help relieve the symptoms of morning sickness is available once again in the United States. Sold under the trade name Bendectin, it was removed in the early 1980s because some claimed it caused birth defects. However, studies have not supported these claims and have actually proved it is safe to use during pregnancy. The FDA reexamined the studies and research data and deemed the drug "safe." A prescription is required for Bendectin.

*Tip for Week 5*

Precaution: Be careful about using over-the-counter cough and cold remedies. Many contain alcohol—some as much as 25%.

Acupressure, acupuncture and massage may also prove helpful in dealing with nausea and vomiting. Acupressure wristbands, worn for motion and seasickness, help some women feel better. There's also an FDA-approved device that may help you deal with nausea. See the box on the opposite page.

You may have heard about acupressure wrist bands that can help some women with nausea. Another device has been approved by the FDA that goes beyond acupressure. This band has been on the market since 1997 and has been used to relieve motion sickness and the nausea and vomiting many people experience with chemotherapy. A new study shows it also works to help relieve morning sickness.

Patented and sold under the name *ReliefBand*, it is about the size of a large watch and worn like a wristwatch on the inside of your wrist. Using gentle electrical signals, it stimulates the nerves in the wrist; this stimulation is believed to interfere with messages between the brain and stomach that cause nausea. It has various stimulation levels that allow you to adjust signals for maximum control for your individual comfort. It can be used when nausea begins, or you can wear it before you feel ill. This device does not interfere with eating or drinking. It is water resistant and shock resistant, so you can wear it just about any time!

This is an extremely important period in the development of your baby. Don't expose your unborn baby to herbs, over-the-counter treatments or any other "remedies" for nausea that are not known to be safe during pregnancy. Discuss different ways to deal with nausea with your doctor.

**Some Actions You Can Take.** Eat small meals more frequently to help you feel better. Experts agree that you should eat what appeals to you—foods that are appealing may be the ones you can keep down more easily right now. If that means sourdough bread and lemon-lime soda, go for it! Some women find that protein foods settle more easily in their stomachs; these foods include cheese, eggs, peanut butter and nonfatty meats. Also see the discussion in the Nutrition section.

Be sure you keep up your fluid intake, even if you can't keep food down. Dehydration is a lot more serious than not eating for a while. If you vomit a great deal, you may want to choose fluids that contain electrolytes to help replace those you lose when you vomit. Ask your doctor what fluids he or she recommends.

If you experience nausea and vomiting, there's an on-the-go solution that might provide some help for you. Check to see if *Preggie Pops* are available at your local store. They are lollipops that come in a variety of flavors that you can suck on to help relieve nausea. Ask

about them at your grocery store or pharmacy. Or call the company at
1-866-PREGGIE.

---

## Be Prepared for Morning Sickness!

It may be a good idea to carry your own "morning sickness" emergency
traveling bag. You may find it comes in handy, especially if you suffer from
nausea and vomiting throughout the day. In a sturdy bag, pack along some
opaque plastic bags (plastic grocery sacks are a good choice) without
holes, wet wipes, tissue or napkins to wipe your face and mouth, a small
bottle of water to rinse your mouth and teeth, a toothbrush and toothpaste
to brush away stomach acids and a small bottle of breath spray or breath
mints. With your emergency bag along, you'll feel confident you can handle this temporary side effect of pregnancy, no matter where you are.

---

**If You're Absent from Work.** If morning sickness causes you to be absent from your job, you may be interested to know that the Family and
Medical Leave Act (FMLA) states you do *not* need a doctor's note veri-
fying the problem. Nausea and vomiting of pregnancy is classified as a
"chronic condition" and may require you to be out occasionally, but
you don't need a doctor's treatment.

## Other Changes You May Notice

In early pregnancy, you may need to urinate frequently. It can continue
during most of your pregnancy and become particularly annoying near
delivery, as your uterus enlarges and puts pressure on your bladder.

You may notice changes in your breasts. Tingling or soreness in the
breasts or nipples is common. You may also see a darkening of the areola or an elevation of the glands around the nipple. See Week 13 for
more information on how your breasts are affected by pregnancy.

Another early symptom of pregnancy is fatigue or tiring easily. This
common symptom may continue throughout pregnancy. Be sure to
take your prenatal vitamins and any other medications prescribed by

your doctor, and get enough rest. If you experience fatigue, avoid sugar and caffeine; either can make the problem worse.

## How Your Actions
## Affect Your Baby's Development

### ᔕ *When Should You Visit the Doctor?*

One of the first questions you may ask yourself when you suspect you're pregnant is, "When should I see my doctor?"

Good prenatal care is necessary for the health of the baby and mother-to-be. Make an appointment to see your physician as soon as you are reasonably sure you're pregnant. This could be as early as a few days after a missed period.

### ᔕ *Getting Pregnant while Using Birth Control*

If you have been using some type of birth control, tell your doctor. No method is 100% effective. Occasionally a method fails, even oral contraceptives. If you are sure you're pregnant, stop taking the pill and set up an appointment as soon as possible. Don't become overly alarmed if this happens to you; talk to your doctor about it.

Pregnancy can also occur with an intrauterine device (IUD) in place. If this happens, see your doctor immediately. Discuss whether the IUD should be removed or left in place. In most cases, an attempt is made to remove the IUD. If left in place, the risk of miscarriage increases slightly.

Spermicides used alone, or with a condom, sponge or diaphragm, may be in use when pregnancy occurs. They have not been shown to be harmful to a developing baby.

## Your Nutrition

As discussed previously, you may have to deal with nausea and vomiting during pregnancy. Not every woman suffers from it, but many women do. The same hormone—HCG (human chorionic gonadotropin)—that makes a home pregnancy test change color causes morning sickness. If you suffer this discomfort, you may be happy to know that HCG levels taper off near the end of the first trimester, so your nausea and vomiting should improve then. If you experience morning sickness, try some of the following suggestions.

- Eat small meals frequently to keep your stomach from being over-full.
- Drink lots of fluid.
- Find out what foods, smells or situations make you nauseated. Avoid them when possible.
- Avoid coffee because it stimulates stomach acid.
- A high-protein snack before bed may help stabilize blood sugar.
- Sometimes a high-carbohydrate snack before bed helps.
- Ask your partner to make you some dry toast in the morning before you get up; eat it in bed. Or keep crackers or dry cereal near the bed to nibble on before you get up in the morning. They help absorb stomach acid.
- Keep your bedroom cool at night, and air it out often. Cool, fresh air may help you feel better.
- Get out of bed slowly.
- If you take an iron supplement, take it an hour before meals or 2 hours after a meal.
- Nibble on raw ginger, or pour boiling water over it and sip the "tea."
- Salty foods help some women with nausea.
- Lemonade and watermelon may help alleviate symptoms.

## ᔛ *Weight Gain during Pregnancy*

The amount of weight women gain during pregnancy varies greatly. It may actually range from weight loss to a total gain of 50 pounds or more.

We know complications increase at the extremes of these weight changes. Because of this, it's difficult to set one figure as an "ideal" weight gain during pregnancy. How much weight you gain is affected by your weight before you became pregnant. Many experts quote a weight-gain figure of ⅔ of a pound (10 ounces) a week until 20 weeks, then 1 pound a week from 20 to 40 weeks.

Other researchers have suggested weight-gain amounts acceptable for underweight, normal weight and overweight women. See the box to the right.

If you have any questions about your weight gain during pregnancy, discuss them with your physician. He or she will advise you on how much weight you should gain during your pregnancy.

Dieting while you're preg-

| Average Pregnancy Weight Gain | |
|---|---|
| Body Type | Acceptable Gain (pounds) |
| Underweight | 28 to 40 |
| Normal weight | 25 to 35 |
| Overweight | 15 to 25 |

nant is not a wise idea, but that doesn't mean you shouldn't watch your caloric intake. You should! It's important for your baby to get proper nutrition from the foods you eat. Choose foods for the nutrition they provide for you and your growing baby.

## You Should Also Know

### ✑ What Sex Will Your Baby Be?
You can guess the sex of your child as well as your doctor—often better! As we've mentioned, the sex of your baby is determined when the egg is fertilized by the baby's father's sperm.

Many couples ask for ways to "get a boy" or "get a girl" before they try to get pregnant. In a few cases, sperm separation is used. Male and female sperm are separated, and artificial insemination deposits the selected sperm in the woman. It's not a foolproof method, and it is expensive. This procedure may be done when there is a sex-specific problem, such as a family history of hemophilia or Duchenne muscular dystrophy.

### ✑ Ectopic Pregnancy
As described in Weeks 1 & 2, fertilization occurs in the Fallopian tube. The fertilized egg travels through the tube to the uterus, where

it implants on the cavity wall. An *ectopic pregnancy* occurs when the egg implants outside the uterine cavity, usually in the tube itself. Ninety-five percent of all ectopic pregnancies occur in the tube (hence the term *tubal pregnancy*). Other possible sites of implantation are the ovary, cervix or other places in the abdomen. The illustration on the opposite page shows some possible locations of an ectopic pregnancy.

In the past 10 years, ectopic pregnancies have almost tripled in number—rising from 55,000 in the early 1990s to over 150,000 in 2001. The reason for the increase? Researchers believe STDs (sexually transmitted diseases) are the cause, especially chlamydia and gonorrhea. If you have had an STD in the past, tell your doctor at your first prenatal visit. And be sure to tell him or her if you have had a previous ectopic pregnancy.

Ectopic pregnancy occurs in 1 of every 100 pregnancies. Chances of an ectopic pregnancy occurring increase with damage to the Fallopian tubes from pelvic inflammatory disease (PID), from other infections, such as a ruptured appendix, from infertility, endometriosis, sexually transmitted diseases and prior tubal or abdominal surgery. Other factors that contribute to an increased risk of ectopic pregnancy include smoking, exposure to DES (diethylstilbestrol) during your mother's pregnancy and increase in a mother-to-be's age. If you have had a previous ectopic pregnancy, there is a 12% chance of recurrence. Use of an intrauterine device (IUD) also increases the chance of ectopic pregnancy.

### ✐ Symptoms of an Ectopic Pregnancy
Symptoms of ectopic pregnancy, which occur in the first 12 weeks of pregnancy, include:

- cramps
- tenderness in the lower abdomen
- bleeding or brown spotting
- shoulder pain, caused by blood from the ruptured tube irritating the peritoneum in the area between the chest and stomach
- weakness, dizziness or fainting, caused by blood loss
- nausea

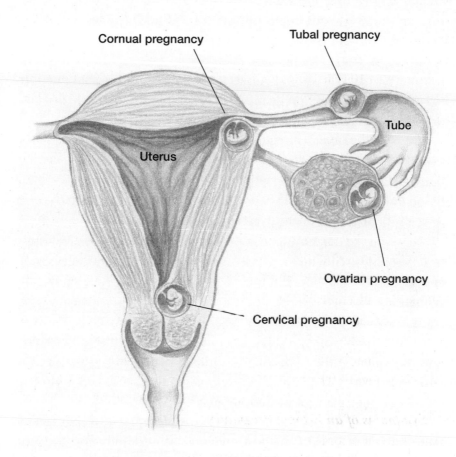

**Cornual pregnancy**

**Tubal pregnancy**

**Tube**

**Uterus**

**Ovarian pregnancy**

**Cervical pregnancy**

Possible locations of an ectopic (tubal) pregnancy.

It may be difficult for your doctor to diagnose an ectopic pregnancy because many of these symptoms can be present in a normal pregnancy.

**Diagnosing Ectopic Pregnancy.** To test for an ectopic pregnancy, human chorionic gonadotropin (HCG) is measured. The test is called a *quantitative HCG.* The level of HCG increases rapidly in a normal pregnancy and doubles in value about every 2 days. If HCG levels do not increase as they should, an abnormal pregnancy is suspected. In the case of an ectopic pregnancy, the woman may have a high HCG level with no sign by ultrasound of a pregnancy inside the uterus.

Ultrasound testing is helpful in diagnosing an ectopic pregnancy. (We discuss ultrasound in detail in Week 11.) A tubal pregnancy may be visible in the tube during ultrasound examination. Doctors may see blood in the abdomen from rupture and bleeding or a mass in the area of the Fallopian tube or the ovary.

Our ability to diagnose an ectopic pregnancy has improved with use of laparoscopy. Tiny incisions are made in the area of the bellybutton and in the lower-abdominal area. Doctors view the inside of the abdomen and the pelvic organs with a small instrument called a *laparoscope*. They can see an ectopic pregnancy if one is present.

An attempt is made to diagnose a tubal pregnancy before it ruptures and damages the tube, which could make it necessary to remove the entire tube. Early diagnosis also attempts to avoid the risk of internal bleeding from a ruptured, bleeding tube.

Most ectopic pregnancies are detected around 6 to 8 weeks of pregnancy. The key in early diagnosis involves communication between you and your doctor about any symptoms and their severity.

**Treatment for Ectopic Pregnancy.** With an ectopic pregnancy, the doctor's goal is to remove the pregnancy while preserving fertility. Surgical treatment requires general anesthesia, laparoscopy or laparotomy (a larger incision and no scope) and recovery from surgery. In many instances, it is necessary to remove the Fallopian tube, which affects future fertility.

A nonsurgical treatment of an unruptured ectopic pregnancy involves the use of a cancer drug, methotrexate. Methotrexate is given by an I.V. in the hospital or at an outpatient clinic. Methotrexate is cytotoxic; it terminates the pregnancy. HCG levels should decrease after this treatment, which indicates the pregnancy has been terminated. Symptoms should improve.

# Week 6

## Age of Fetus—4 Weeks

If you've just found out you're pregnant, you might
want to begin by reading the previous chapters.

## How Big Is Your Baby?

The crown-to-rump length of your growing baby is 0.08 to 0.16 inch
(2 to 4mm). *Crown-to-rump* is the sitting height or distance from the
top of the baby's head to its rump or buttocks. This measurement is
used more often than crown-to-heel length because the baby's legs are
most often bent, making that determination difficult.

Occasionally, with the proper equipment, a heartbeat can be seen
on ultrasound by the 6th week. Ultrasound is discussed in detail in
Week 11.

## How Big Are You?

You may have gained a few pounds by now. If you have been nauseated
and not eating well, you may have lost weight. You have been pregnant
for 1 month, which is enough time to notice some changes in your

body. If this is your first pregnancy, your abdomen may not have changed much. Or you may notice your clothes are getting a little tighter around the waist. You may be gaining weight in your legs or other places, such as your breasts. If you have a pelvic exam, your doctor can usually feel your uterus and note some change in its size.

## How Your Baby Is Growing and Developing

This is the beginning of the *embryonic period* (from conception to week 10 of pregnancy; or from conception to week 8 of fetal development). It is a period of extremely important development in your baby! At this time, the embryo is most susceptible to factors that can interfere with its development. Most malformations originate during this critical period.

As the illustration on page 78 shows, the result of this growth is a body form showing the head and tail area. Around this time, the neural groove closes and early brain chambers form. The eyes are also forming, and limb buds appear. The heart tubes fuse, and heart contractions begin. This can be seen on ultrasound.

## Changes in You

### ✐ *Heartburn*

Heartburn discomfort *(pyrosis)* is one of the most common complaints of pregnancy. It may begin early, although generally it becomes more severe later in pregnancy. It is usually caused by the backing up *(reflux)* of gastric and duodenal contents into the esophagus. This occurs more frequently during pregnancy for two reasons—food moves more slowly through the intestines and the stomach is compressed as the uterus enlarges and moves up into the abdomen.

Symptoms are not severe for most women. Eat small, frequent meals, and avoid some positions, such as bending over or lying flat.

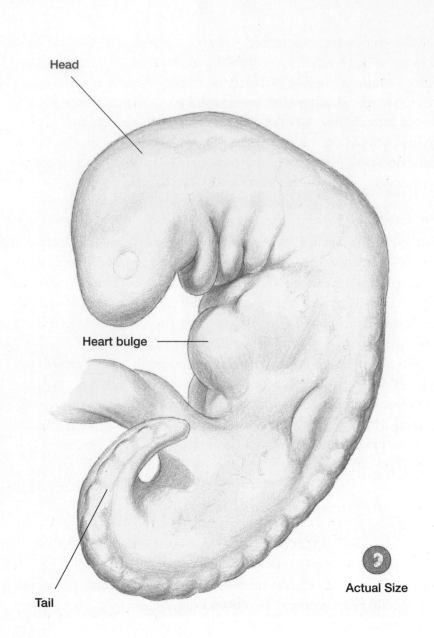

Head

Heart bulge

Tail

Actual Size

Embryo at 6 weeks of pregnancy (fetal age—4 weeks). It is growing rapidly.

One sure way to get heartburn is to eat a large meal, then lie down! (This is true for anyone, not just pregnant women.)

Some antacids provide considerable relief, including aluminum hydroxide, magnesium trisilicate and magnesium hydroxide (Amphojel, Gelusil, milk of magnesia and Maalox). Follow your doctor's advice or the instructions on the package relating to pregnancy. Don't overdo taking antacids! Avoid sodium bicarbonate because it contains excessive amounts of sodium that may cause you to retain water.

### ᘑ *Constipation*
Your bowel habits will probably change during pregnancy. Most women notice some constipation, often accompanied by irregular bowel movements. Hemorrhoids may occur more often (see Week 14).

You can help avoid constipation problems during pregnancy. Increase your fluid intake. Exercise also helps. Many doctors suggest a mild laxative, such as milk of magnesia or prune juice, if you have problems. Certain foods, such as bran and prunes, can increase the bulk in your diet, which may help relieve constipation.

Do not use laxatives, other than those mentioned, without your doctor's OK. If constipation is a continuing problem, discuss treatment at a prenatal visit. Try not to strain when you have a bowel movement, if you are constipated. Straining can lead to hemorrhoids.

## How Your Actions Affect Your Baby's Development

During pregnancy, a sexually transmitted disease can harm your growing baby. Take care of any STD as soon as possible!

### ᘑ *Genital Herpes Simplex Infection*
Often a herpes infection during pregnancy is a reinfection, not a primary infection. Infection in the mother is associated with higher risks of premature delivery and low-birthweight infants. We believe an infant can be infected when traveling through the birth canal.

When membranes rupture, the infection may also travel upward to the uterus.

There is no safe treatment during pregnancy for genital herpes. When a woman has an active herpes infection late in pregnancy, a Cesarean section may be done to deliver the baby.

### ✎ *Yeast Infections (Monilial Vulvovaginitis)*

Yeast (monilial) infections are more common in pregnant women than in nonpregnant women. They have no major negative effect on pregnancy, but they may cause you discomfort and anxiety.

Yeast infections are sometimes harder to control when you're pregnant. They may require frequent retreatment or longer treatment (10 to 14 days instead of 3 to 7 days). Creams used for treatment are usually safe during pregnancy. Your partner does not need to be treated.

A newborn infant can get thrush after passing through a birth canal infected with monilial vulvovaginitis. Treatment with nystatin is effective. Avoid the use of fluconazole (Diflucan); it may not be safe to use during pregnancy.

### ✎ *Trichomonal Vaginitis*

This infection has no major effects on pregnancy. However, a problem in treatment may arise because some doctors believe metronidazole, the drug of choice, shouldn't be taken in the first trimester of pregnancy. Most doctors will prescribe metronidazole for a bad infection after the first trimester.

### ✎ *HPV—Human Papillomavirus (Condyloma Acuminata)*

Human papillomavirus (HPV) is the virus that causes venereal warts, also called *condyloma acuminata*. Some strains of HPV cause genital warts; some strains of genital warts can lead to cancer of the cervix and cancer of the genitals.

The Pap smear that is done at one of your first prenatal visits can reassure you that you do not have this problem. HPV is one of the main causes of abnormal Pap smears.

If you do have genital warts, tell your doctor at your first prenatal appointment. During pregnancy, certain treatments, such as laser ablation or acids, should be avoided. Discuss the problem with your physician.

If you have extensive venereal warts, a Cesarean delivery may be necessary to avoid heavy bleeding. Warty skin tags often enlarge during pregnancy. In rare instances, they have blocked the vagina at the time of delivery. Infants have also been known to get *laryngeal papillomas* (small benign tumors on the vocal cords) after delivery.

### ↬ Gonorrhea

Gonorrhea presents risks to a woman and her partner, and to her baby when it passes through the birth canal. The baby may contract *gonorrheal ophthalmia*, a severe eye infection. Eye drops are used in newborns to prevent this problem. Other infections may also result. Gonorrheal infections in the mother are treated with penicillin or other medications that are safe to use during pregnancy.

### ↬ Syphilis

Detection of a syphilis infection is important for you, your partner and your growing baby. Fortunately this rare infection is also treatable. If you notice any open sore on your genitals during pregnancy, have your doctor check it. Syphilis can be treated effectively with penicillin and other medications that are safe to use in pregnancy.

### ↬ Chlamydia

You may have heard or read about chlamydia. It is a common sexually transmitted disease; between 3 and 5 million people are infected every year. It may be difficult to determine if you have a chlamydial infection because you may not have symptoms. Infection is caused by a germ that invades certain types of healthy cells. Infection may be passed through sexual activity, including oral sex.

Between 20 and 40% of all sexually active women have probably been exposed to chlamydia at some time. Infection can cause serious problems if left untreated, but these problems can be avoided with treatment.

Chlamydia is most likely to occur in young people who have more than one sexual partner. It may also occur in women who have other sexually transmitted diseases. Some doctors believe chlamydia occurs more commonly in women who take oral contraceptives. Barrier methods of contraception, such as diaphragms and condoms used with spermicides, may offer protection from infection.

*Tip for Week 6* If you have questions between your prenatal visits, call your doctor's office. It's OK to call; as a matter of fact, your doctor *wants* you to call to get correct medical information. You'll probably feel more comfortable when your questions are answered.

One of the most significant complications of chlamydia is pelvic inflammatory disease (PID), a severe infection of the upper genital organs involving the uterus, the Fallopian tubes and even the ovaries. There may be pelvic pain, or there may be no symptoms at all. PID can result from an untreated infection that spreads throughout the pelvic area. Chlamydia is one of the main causes of PID. If a PID infection is prolonged or recurrent, the reproductive organs, Fallopian tubes and uterus may be damaged, with formation of adhesions. Surgery may be required to repair them. If tubes are damaged, scar tissue can increase the risk of ectopic (tubal) pregnancy and may make it harder to get pregnant (infertility).

**Chlamydia in Pregnancy.** During pregnancy, a mother-to-be can pass the infection to her baby as it comes through the birth canal and vagina. The baby has a 20 to 50% chance of getting chlamydia if the mother has it. It may cause an eye infection, but that is easily treated. Complications that are more serious include pneumonia, which may require hospitalization of the baby.

Research has shown that chlamydial infection may be linked to ectopic pregnancy. One study showed 70% of the women studied who had an ectopic pregnancy also had chlamydia. If a woman is trying to get pregnant, she may want to be screened for this STD, which can be treated easily.

**Testing for Chlamydia.** Chlamydia can be detected by a cell culture, but as we've said, more than half of those infected have no symptoms. Symptoms that may appear include burning or itching in the genital area, discharge from the vagina, painful or frequent urination, or pain in the pelvic area. Men may also experience symptoms. Rapid diagnostic tests can be done in the doctor's office. They can provide a result quickly, possibly even before you go home.

Chlamydia is usually treated with tetracycline, but this drug should not be given to a pregnant woman. During pregnancy, erythromycin may be the drug of choice. After treatment, your doctor may want to do another culture to make sure the infection is gone. If you're concerned about a possible chlamydial infection, discuss it at a prenatal visit. Your doctor will advise you.

### ❧ *HIV and AIDS*

HIV (human immunodeficiency virus) is the virus that causes AIDS (acquired immune deficiency syndrome); 2 out of every 1000 women who enter pregnancy are HIV positive. Research has shown that an infected woman can pass the virus to her baby as early as the 8th week of pregnancy. It is important to tell your doctor if you are HIV positive or think you might be.

The exact number of people infected with HIV is unknown. Currently it is estimated that up to 2 million people in the United States alone may be infected. The AIDS epidemic among women has grown to 20% of all reported cases. AIDS can leave an individual susceptible to, and unable to fight, various infections.

Women at greatest risk include current or former intravenous drug users and women whose sexual partners have used drugs intravenously or engaged in bisexual activities. Women with sexually transmitted diseases, those who engage in prostitution or those who received blood transfusions before screening began are also at higher risk. If you are unsure about your risk, seek counseling about testing for the AIDS virus.

A woman infected with HIV may not have symptoms. There may be a period of weeks or months when tests do not reveal the presence of the virus. In most cases, antibodies can be detected 6 to 12 weeks after exposure. In some cases, this latent period can be as long as 18 months. Once the test is positive, a person may remain free of symptoms for a variable amount of time. For every patient with AIDS, we believe there are 20 to 30 infected individuals who have no symptoms.

There is no evidence of transmission through casual contact with water, food or environmental surfaces. There is no evidence the virus can be transmitted with RhoGAM. (See Week 16.) A mother can pass HIV to her baby before birth or during its birth. We know that 90% of all cases of HIV in children are due to transmission related to pregnancy—mother to baby during pregnancy, childbirth or breastfeeding.

Pregnancy may hide some AIDS symptoms, which makes the disease harder to discover. Because the illness can be a serious threat to an unborn child, counseling and psychological support are critical.

There is some positive news for women who suffer from AIDS. We know if a woman is in the early course of the illness, she may have an uneventful pregnancy, labor and delivery. Her baby has a risk of being infected during pregnancy, birth or breastfeeding. However, research shows that the risk of a woman infected with HIV passing the virus to her baby can now be greatly reduced and nearly eliminated. If she takes AZT during pregnancy and has a Cesarean delivery, she reduces the risk of passing the virus to about 2%! Studies have not found any birth defects linked to the use of these medications. However, if an infection is left untreated, there's a 25% chance her baby will be born with the virus.

**Testing for AIDS.** Testing comprises two tests—the ELISA test and the Western Blot test. The ELISA is a screening test. If positive, it should be confirmed by the Western Blot test. Both tests involve testing blood to measure antibodies to the virus, not the virus itself. No test should be considered positive until the Western Blot test is done. It is believed to be more than 99% sensitive and specific.

**HIV/AIDS and Pregnancy.** If you are HIV positive, expect more blood tests during pregnancy. These tests help your doctor assess how well you are doing as a pregnant woman. Breastfeeding is not recommended for women who are HIV positive.

## Your Nutrition

To get the nutrition you need during your pregnancy, you must be selective in your food choices. You *cannot* eat whatever you want. Eating the right foods, in the correct amounts, takes planning. Eat foods high in vitamins and minerals, especially iron, calcium, magnesium, folic acid and zinc. You also need fiber and fluids to help alleviate any constipation problems.

Some of the foods you should eat, and the amounts of each, are listed below. You should try to eat these foods every day. Ways to get enough of each food group are discussed in the following weeks. Check out each weekly discussion for nutrition tips. Foods to help your baby grow and develop include:

> ### *Understanding Serving Portions of the Food Pyramid*
>
> Many people today overeat because they do not understand what constitutes a "portion" or "serving," as determined by the USDA's Food Pyramid. You may believe it will be difficult for you to eat all the portions you need for the health of your growing baby.
>
> To learn the *correct* serving size for each of the food groups, as listed here, check out the USDA's website, www.cnpp.usda.gov, which lists actual serving portions. For example, a large bagel can actually be *four* to *five* grain servings! If you don't have access to a computer, ask your physician for some guidelines. He or she probably has some nutrition handouts for you.

- bread, cereal, pasta and rice—at least 6 servings/day
- fruits—3 to 4 servings/day
- vegetables—4 servings/day
- meat and other protein sources—2 to 3 servings/day
- dairy products—3 to 4 servings/day
- fats, sweets and other "empty" calorie foods—2 to 3 servings/day

## You Should Also Know

### ☞ Your First Visit to the Doctor

Your first prenatal visit may be one of your longest. There's a lot to accomplish. If you saw your doctor before you got pregnant, you may have already discussed some of your concerns.

Feel free to ask questions to get an idea of how your doctor will relate to you and your needs. This is important as your pregnancy progresses. During pregnancy, there should be an exchange of ideas. Consider what your doctor suggests and why. It's important to share your feelings and ideas. Your doctor has experience that can be valuable to you during pregnancy.

**What Will Happen?** What should you expect at this first visit? First, your doctor will ask for a history of your medical health. This includes general medical problems and any problems relating to your gynecological and obstetrical history. He or she will ask about your periods and recent birth-control methods. If you've had an abortion or a miscarriage, or if you've been in the hospital for surgery or for some other reason, it's important information. If you have old medical records, bring them with you.

Your doctor needs to know about any medication you take or any medication you are allergic to. Your family's medical history may also be important, such as the occurrence of diabetes or other chronic illness.

**Dad Tip** Bring home her favorite dinner, or cook it yourself, if she's not suffering a lot of nausea and/or vomiting.

You will have a physical exam, including a pelvic exam and Pap smear. This exam determines if your uterus is the appropriate size for how far along you are in your pregnancy.

Laboratory tests may be done at this first visit or on a subsequent visit. If you have questions, ask them. If you think you may have a "high-risk" pregnancy, discuss it with your doctor.

In most cases, you will be asked to return every 4 weeks for the first 7 months, then every 2 weeks until the last month, then every week. If problems arise, you may be scheduled for more frequent visits.

# Ways to Have a Great Pregnancy

Every woman wants to have a happy, healthy pregnancy. Start now to help ensure that yours will be the best it can be! Try the following.

**Prioritize**—Examine what you need to do to help yourself and your growing baby. Do what you need to do, decide what else you can do and let the rest go.

**Involve others in your pregnancy**—When you include your partner, other family members and friends in your pregnancy, it helps them understand what you are going through so they can be more understanding and supportive.

**Treat others with respect and love**—You may be having a hard time, especially at the beginning of your pregnancy. You may have morning sickness. You may find adjusting to the role of "mom-to-be" difficult. People will understand if you take the time to let them know how you feel. Show respect and appreciation for their concern. Treat them with kindness and love, and they will respond in kind.

**Create memories**—It takes some planning, but it is definitely worth it. When you're pregnant, it seems like it will go on forever. However, speaking from experience, we can tell you it passes very quickly and is soon a memory. Take steps to document the many changes that are occurring in your life right now. Include your partner in all this. Have him jot down some of his thoughts and feelings. Take his picture, too! You'll be able to look back and share the highs and lows with him, and in the years ahead, you and your kids will be glad you did.

**Relax when you can**—Easing the stress in your life is very important now. Do things that help you relax and focus on what is important in your lives right now.

**Enjoy this time of preparation**—All too soon your pregnancy will be over, and you'll be a new mother, with all the responsibilities of being a mom and a partner! You may have other responsibilities, too, in your professional or personal life. This is a time to concentrate on your couple relationship and on the many changes you will be experiencing in the near future.

**Focus on the positive**—You may hear negative things from friends or family members, such as scary stories or sad tales. Ignore them. Most pregnancies work out great!

**Don't be afraid to ask for help**—Your pregnancy is important to others, too. Friends and family will be pleased if you ask them to be involved.

**Get information**—There are many sources today, such as books, magazine articles, television programs, radio interviews and the Internet.

**Smile**—You're part of a very special miracle that is happening to you and your partner!

# Week 7

*Age of Fetus—5 Weeks*

If you've just found out you're pregnant, you might
want to begin by reading the previous chapters.

## How Big Is Your Baby?

Your baby goes through an incredible growth spurt this week! At the
beginning of the 7th week, the crown-to-rump length of your growing
baby is 0.16 to 0.2 inch (4 to 5mm). This is about the size of a BB pel-
let. By the end of the week, your baby has more than doubled in size, to
about ½ inch (1.1 to 1.3cm).

## How Big Are You?

Although you are probably quite anxious to show the world you're
pregnant, there still may be little noticeable change. Changes will come
soon, though.

## How Your Baby Is
## Growing and Developing

Leg buds are beginning to appear as short fins. As you can see on page 90, arm buds have grown longer; they have divided into a hand segment and an arm-shoulder segment. The hand and foot have a digital plate where the fingers and toes will develop.

The heart bulges from the body. By this time, it has divided into right and left heart chambers. The primary *bronchi* are present in the lungs; bronchi are air passages in the lungs. The cerebral hemispheres, which make up the brain, are also growing. Eyes and nostrils are developing.

Intestines are developing, and the appendix is present. The pancreas, which produces the hormone insulin, is also present. Part of the intestine bulges into the umbilical cord. Later in your baby's development, it will return to the abdomen.

## Changes in You

Changes are occurring gradually. You still probably won't "show," and people won't be able to tell you're pregnant unless you tell them. You may be gaining weight throughout your body, but you should have gained only a couple of pounds this early in your pregnancy.

If you haven't gained weight or if you have lost a couple of pounds, it isn't unusual. It will go the other direction in the weeks to come. You may still be experiencing morning sickness and other symptoms of early pregnancy.

## How Your Actions
## Affect Your Baby's Development

### ⌁ *Using Over-the-Counter Medications and Preparations*
Many people don't consider over-the-counter (OTC) preparations as medication, and they take them at will, pregnant or not. Some

Head

Actual Size

Arm Bud

Tail

Leg Bud

Your baby's brain is growing and developing. The heart has divided into right and left chambers.

researchers believe nonprescription, or over-the-counter, medication usage actually *increases* during pregnancy.

OTC medications and preparations may not be safe during pregnancy. Use them with as much caution as any other drug! Many over-the-counter preparations are combinations of medications. For example, pain medication can contain aspirin, caffeine and phenacetin. Cough syrups or sleep medications can contain as much as 25% alcohol. This is no different than drinking wine or beer during pregnancy.

There are quite a few OTC medications to be careful with during pregnancy, including ibuprofen (Advil, Motrin, Rufen),

*Tip for Week 7* Don't take any over-the-counter medications for longer than 48 hours without consulting your doctor. If a problem doesn't resolve, your physician may have another treatment plan for you.

naproxen (Aleve), ketoprofen (Orudis), famotidine (Pepcid AC), cimetidine (Tagamet HB), hydrocortisone and any medication containing iodine. Because experience with use of these medications during pregnancy is limited, it's best to avoid them. Take them *only* under the supervision of your doctor.

Read package labels and package inserts about safety during pregnancy—nearly all medications contain this information. Some antacids contain sodium bicarbonate, which increases your intake of sodium (this can be important to avoid if you have water-retention problems). Antacids can also cause constipation and increased gas. Some antacids contain aluminum, which can cause constipation and affect the metabolism of other minerals (phosphate). Others contain magnesium; excessive use of these may cause magnesium poisoning.

Some over-the-counter medications and preparations can be used safely during pregnancy, if you use them wisely. Check the list below:

• analgesics and pain relievers—acetaminophen (Tylenol)
• decongestants—chlorpheniramine (Chlor-Trimeton)
• nasal spray decongestants—oxymetazoline (Afrin, Dristan Long-Lasting)

- cough medicine—dextromethorphan (Robitussin; Vicks Formula 44)
- stomach relief—antacids (Amphojel, Gelusil, Maalox, milk of magnesia)
- throat relief—throat lozenges (Sucrets)
- laxatives—bulk-fiber laxatives (Metamucil, Fiberall)

If you think your symptoms or discomfort are more severe than they should be, call your doctor. Follow his or her advice. In addition, take good care of yourself. Exercise, eat right and keep a positive mental attitude about your pregnancy.

---

### Using Acetaminophen

Most physicians and researchers believe acetaminophen is OK to use during pregnancy. It's hard to avoid because the drug is in over 200 products! However, recent studies have found that it is easy to overdose on the medication because it *is* in so many medications. You may not be aware that acetaminophen is contained in various products you may take to treat a single problem. Taking multiple products to treat a condition or illness could be dangerous. *Always read labels* if you are thinking about taking more than one product to help relieve your symptoms. For example, take only *one* medication to treat a cold or flu symptoms, and always take the correct dose!

---

## Your Nutrition

Dairy products can be very important to you during pregnancy. They contain calcium, which is important to you and your baby. They also contain vitamin D, which aids in calcium absorption.

Calcium helps keep your bones healthy, and baby needs it to develop strong bones and teeth. During pregnancy, you need about 1200mg of calcium a day. Other important reasons to get enough calcium in your diet are it may help prevent high blood pressure, and it may also lower your risk of pre-eclampsia. In addition, your body stores calcium in the latter part of pregnancy to draw on if you breastfeed.

### ✎ *How Much Calcium Do You Need?*

How much calcium should you take in each day? Recommended for pregnant women is 1200mg a day (1½ times the recommended amount for nonpregnant women). Your prenatal vitamin supplies about 300mg, so be sure you eat enough of the right foods to get the other 900mg.

Read food labels for information on the calcium content of packaged foods. Keep track of the number of milligrams (mg) of calcium in the foods you eat. Every day, write down the amount of calcium in each of the foods you consume, and keep a running total to be sure you're getting 1200mg each day.

### ✎ *Some Good Sources of Calcium*

Milk, cheese, yogurt and ice cream are good calcium sources. Other foods that contain calcium include broccoli, bok choy, collards, spinach, salmon, sardines, garbanzo beans (chickpeas), sesame seeds, almonds, cooked dried beans, tofu and trout. Some foods are now calcium fortified, such as orange juice, breads, cereals and grains. Check your grocery shelves.

Some dairy foods you may choose, and their serving sizes, include the following:

- cottage cheese—¾ cup
- processed cheese (American)—2 ounces
- hard cheese (Parmesan or Romano)—1 ounce
- custard or pudding—1 cup
- milk (whole, 2%, 1%, skim)—8 ounces
- natural cheese (cheddar)—1½ ounces
- yogurt (plain or flavored)—1 cup

If you want to keep your calorie intake low, choose low-fat dairy products. Some choices include skim milk, low-fat yogurt and low-fat cheese. Calcium content is unaffected in low-fat dairy products.

### ᔓ *Other Ways to Get Calcium*

You can increase the amount of calcium in your diet in other ways. Add powdered nonfat milk to recipes, such as soup, mashed potatoes and meat loaf. Make fruit shakes with fresh fruit and milk; add a scoop of ice milk, frozen yogurt or ice cream. Cook rice and oatmeal in skim or low-fat milk.

### ᔓ *Some Precautions with Calcium*

Some foods interfere with the body's absorption of calcium. Salt, tea, coffee, protein and unleavened bread decrease the amount of calcium absorbed.

If your doctor decides you need calcium supplementation, calcium carbonate combined with magnesium (to aid calcium absorption) is a good choice. Avoid any supplement derived from animal bones, oyster shells or dolomite because it may contain lead.

**Note:** Your body cannot absorb more than 500mg of calcium at a time, so spread your intake out over the course of the day. At breakfast, if your meal consists of calcium-fortified orange juice, calcium-fortified bread, cereal with milk and a carton of yogurt, you may be taking in a lot more than 500mg, but your body won't be able to absorb it.

**Ɗad Ʈip** Buy a present for your partner and the baby.

### ᔓ *Calcium Supplement*

Some doctors prescribe calcium supplementation. Calcium is important for every pregnant woman. It helps build strong bones and teeth in the baby and helps keep your bones healthy. During pregnancy, you need 1200 to 1500mg a day. That's about 3 to 4 glasses of skim milk a day.

### ᔓ *Lactose Intolerance*

If you're lactose intolerant, there are still many sources of calcium available to you. As mentioned earlier, look for calcium-fortified products. Rice milk and soy milk can provide calcium and vitamin D. If you like cheese, hard cheeses, such as cheddar, gouda, Parmesan and Swiss, contain a lower lactose content.

The over-the-counter medicine *Lactaid* (lactase enzyme) contains a natural enzyme that helps the body break down lactose, the complex sugar found in products and food. When lactose is not properly digested, it can cause gas, bloating, cramps and diarrhea. There are no warnings or precautions for this medication during pregnancy; however, check with your doctor *before* you use it.

---

## A Caution for Listeriosis

Avoid unpasteurized milk and any foods made from unpasteurized milk. Also avoid soft cheeses such as Camembert, Brie, feta and Roquefort. These products are a common source of *listeriosis,* a form of food poisoning. Undercooked poultry, red meat, seafood, deli meats and hot dogs can contain listeriosis. Cook all meat and seafood thoroughly before eating. Thoroughly heat deli meats till steaming. Be careful about cross contamination of foods. If you place raw seafood or hot dogs on a counter or other surface during preparation, thoroughly wash the surface with soap and water or a disinfectant *before* you place any other food on that surface.

---

### ∾ *Do You Need Extra Iron?*

Nearly all diets that supply a sufficient number of calories for appropriate weight gain contain enough minerals (except iron) to prevent mineral deficiency. During pregnancy, your iron requirement increases. Very few women have sufficient iron stores to meet pregnancy demands. During a normal pregnancy, blood volume increases by about 50%. A large amount of iron is required to produce those additional blood cells.

Iron needs are most important in the latter half of pregnancy. Most women don't need to take iron supplements during the first trimester. If prescribed at this time, they can worsen symptoms of nausea and vomiting.

The iron content of prenatal vitamins can irritate your stomach. Iron supplements may also cause constipation. Even if you need them, you may not be able to take iron supplements until after the first trimester.

### Prenatal Vitamins

Prenatal vitamins are usually prescribed for a pregnant woman during pregnancy. Some women begin taking prenatal vitamins while they are trying to get pregnant. Supplements contain the daily amounts of vitamins and minerals recommended for you during pregnancy.

Your prenatal vitamin is different from a regular multivitamin because of its iron and folic-acid content. These are the most important supplements for you in pregnancy. Prenatal vitamins are often best tolerated if you take them with meals or at night before bed.

Prenatal vitamins contain many essential ingredients for the development of your baby and your continued good health. That's why you should take them every day until your baby is born. A typical prenatal vitamin contains the following:

- calcium to build baby's teeth and bones, and to help strengthen your own
- copper to help prevent anemia, and to help baby's bone formation
- folic acid to reduce the risk of neural-tube defects and to help in blood-cell production
- iodine to help control metabolism
- iron to prevent anemia, and to help baby's blood development
- vitamin A for general health and body metabolism
- vitamin $B_1$ for general health and body metabolism
- vitamin $B_2$ for general health and body metabolism
- vitamin $B_3$ for general health and body metabolism
- vitamin $B_6$ for general health and body metabolism
- vitamin $B_{12}$ to promote blood formation
- vitamin C to aid in your body's absorption of iron
- vitamin D to strengthen baby's bones and teeth, and to help your body use phosphorus and calcium
- vitamin E for general health and body metabolism
- zinc to help balance fluids in your body and to aid nerve and muscle function

## ✑ Zinc

Research has found that zinc may be helpful to a thin or underweight woman during pregnancy. We believe this mineral helps a thin woman increase her chances of giving birth to a bigger, healthier baby.

## ✑ Fluoride Supplementation

The value of fluoride and fluoride supplementation in a pregnant woman is unclear. Some researchers believe fluoride supplementation during pregnancy results in improved teeth in the child; not everyone agrees. Fluoride supplementation in a pregnant woman has not been proved harmful to her baby. Some prenatal vitamins contain fluoride.

## You Should Also Know

### ᴧ *Sexual Intimacy during Pregnancy*

Many couples question whether it is wise or permissible to have sexual intercourse during pregnancy. Sexual relations are usually OK for a healthy pregnant woman and her partner.

Sex doesn't just mean sexual intercourse. There are many ways for couples to be sensual together, including giving each other a massage, bathing together and talking about sex. Whatever you do, be honest with your partner about how you're feeling—and keep a sense of humor!

**Can Sex during Pregnancy Hurt the Baby?**  Many men wonder if sexual activity can harm a growing baby. Neither intercourse nor orgasm should be a problem if you have a low-risk pregnancy.

The baby is well protected by the amniotic sac and amniotic fluid. Uterine muscles are strong, and they protect the baby. A thick mucus plug seals the cervix, which helps protect against infection.

If you have questions, bring them up at a prenatal visit. This may be especially helpful if your partner goes with you to your appointments. If he doesn't, assure him there should be no problems if your doctor gives you the go-ahead.

Frequent sexual activity should not be harmful to a healthy pregnancy. Usually a couple can continue the level of sexual activity they are used to. If you are concerned, discuss it at an office visit.

Some doctors recommend abstinence from intercourse during the last 4 weeks of pregnancy, but not all physicians agree with this. Discuss it with your doctor.

# Week 8

*Age of Fetus—6 Weeks*

If you've just found out you're pregnant, you might want to begin by reading the previous chapters.

## How Big Is Your Baby?

By your 8th week of pregnancy, the crown-to-rump length of your baby is ½ to ¾ inch (1.4 to 2cm). This is about the size of a pinto bean.

## How Big Are You?

Your uterus is getting bigger, but it probably still isn't big enough for you to be showing, especially if this is your first pregnancy. You will notice a gradual change in your waistline and the fit of your clothes. Your doctor will see that your uterus is enlarged, if you have a pelvic exam.

*Tip for Week 8* Wash your hands thoroughly throughout the day, especially after handling raw meat or using the bathroom. This simple activity can help prevent the spread of many bacteria and viruses that cause infection.

# How Your Baby Is
# Growing and Developing

Your baby is continuing to grow and to change rapidly during these early weeks. Compare the illustration on page 100 with the illustration for the 7th week of pregnancy. Can you see the incredible changes?

Eyelid folds are forming on the face and nerve cells in the retina are beginning to develop. The tip of the nose is present. Ears are forming, internally and externally.

In the heart, the aortic and pulmonary valves are present and distinct. Tubes leading from the throat to the functioning part of the lungs are branched, like the branches of a tree. The body's trunk area is getting longer and straightening out.

Elbows are present, and the arms and legs extend forward. Arms have grown longer. They bend at the elbows and curve slightly over the heart. The digital rays, which become fingers, are notched. Toe rays are present on the feet.

## Changes in You

### ∽ *Changes in Your Uterus*

Before pregnancy, your uterus was about the size of your fist. After 6 weeks of growth, it is about the size of a grapefruit. As you progress through pregnancy and your uterus grows, you may feel cramping or even pain in your lower abdomen or your sides. Some women feel tightening or contractions of the uterus.

The uterus tightens or contracts throughout pregnancy. If you don't feel this, don't worry. However, when contractions are accompanied by bleeding from the vagina, call your doctor.

### ∽ *Sciatic-Nerve Pain*

Many women experience an occasional excruciating pain in their buttocks and down the back or side of their legs as pregnancy progresses. This is called *sciatic-nerve pain*. The sciatic nerve runs behind the

**Actual Size**

Eye

Arms

Elbow

Liver bulge

Embryo at 8 weeks (fetal age—6 weeks). Crown-to-rump length is about ¾ inch (20mm). Arms are longer and bend at the elbows.

uterus in the pelvis to the legs. We believe pain is caused by pressure on the nerve from the growing, expanding uterus.

The best treatment for the pain is to lie on your opposite side. This helps relieve pressure on the nerve.

## How Your Actions Affect Your Baby's Development

### ✌ *Avoid Accutane*

Some women notice an improvement in their acne during pregnancy. But this doesn't happen for everyone.

Accutane (isotretinoin) is commonly prescribed for the treatment of acne. **Do not take Accutane during pregnancy!** Taken during the first trimester, Accutane is responsible for a higher frequency of miscarriages and malformations of the fetus.

If you are pregnant or think you might be pregnant, don't take Accutane. Use reliable birth control to avoid pregnancy if you use this product.

### ✌ *Miscarriage*

*Miscarriage* occurs when a pregnancy ends before the embryo or fetus can survive on its own outside the uterus, during the first 20 weeks of pregnancy. After 20 weeks, loss of a pregnancy is called a *stillbirth*. Nearly every pregnant woman thinks about miscarriage during pregnancy, but it occurs in only about 15% of all pregnancies.

Some Common Signs of Miscarriage. Some signs you can be alert for that may indicate a miscarriage may be about to occur include:

- vaginal bleeding
- cramps
- pain that comes and goes
- pain that begins in the small of the back and moves to the lower abdomen
- loss of tissue

**What Causes a Miscarriage?** We don't usually know, and are often unable to find out, what causes a miscarriage. The most common finding in early miscarriages is an abnormality in the development of the embryo. Studies indicate more than half of all early miscarriages have chromosomal abnormalities.

Many factors can affect the embryo and its environment, including radiation, chemicals (drugs or medications) and infections. Called *teratogens*, these adverse factors are discussed in depth in Week 4.

We believe various maternal factors are important in some miscarriages. Unusual infections, such as listeriosis, toxoplasmosis and syphilis, have been implicated in miscarriages.

*Dad Tip* If you have pets, take over their care during your partner's pregnancy. Change the cat's litter box (she should *never* do this while pregnant). Walk the dog (the pull on the leash might hurt her back). Buy food and other pet supplies (to save her back from the strain of lifting big food bags). Make and keep vet appointments.

We have no concrete evidence that deficiency of any particular nutrient or even a moderate deficiency of all nutrients causes a miscarriage. Women who smoke have a higher rate of miscarriage. Alcohol is also blamed for an increase in miscarriages.

The trauma of an accident or major surgery has been related to an increase in miscarriages, although this is difficult to verify. An incompetent cervix (see Week 24) is a cause of pregnancy loss after the first trimester. Many women have blamed emotional upset or trauma for a miscarriage, but this is hard to prove.

Below is a discussion of different types and causes of miscarriage. It is included to alert you about what to watch for if you have any symptoms of a miscarriage. If you have questions, discuss them with your doctor.

**Threatened Miscarriage.** A threatened miscarriage may be presumed when there is a bloody discharge from the vagina during the first half of pregnancy. Bleeding may last for days or even weeks. There may not be any cramping or pain. Pain may feel like a menstrual cramp or a mild backache. Resting in bed is about all you can do, although being active does not cause miscarriage. No procedure or medication can keep a woman from miscarrying.

Threatened miscarriage is a common diagnosis because 20% of all women experience bleeding during early pregnancy but not all miscarry.

**Inevitable Miscarriage.** An inevitable miscarriage occurs with the rupture of membranes, dilatation of the cervix and passage of blood clots and even tissue. Miscarriage is almost certain under these circumstances. The uterus usually contracts, expelling the fetus or products of conception.

**Incomplete Miscarriage.** With an incomplete miscarriage, the entire pregnancy may not be passed at once. Part of the pregnancy is passed while part of it remains in the uterus. Bleeding may be heavy and continues until the uterus is empty.

**Missed Miscarriage.** A missed miscarriage can occur with prolonged retention of an embryo that died earlier. There may be no symptoms or bleeding. The time period from when the pregnancy failed to the time the miscarriage is discovered is usually weeks.

**Habitual Miscarriage.** This term usually refers to three or more consecutive miscarriages.

**If You Have Problems.** If you have problems, notify your doctor immediately! Bleeding often appears first, followed by cramping. Ectopic pregnancy must also be considered. A quantitative HCG may be useful in identifying a normal pregnancy, but a single test report usually won't help. Your doctor needs to repeat the test over a period of several days.

Ultrasound may help if you are more than 5 gestational weeks into your pregnancy. You may continue to bleed, but seeing your baby's heartbeat and a normal-appearing pregnancy may be reassuring. If the first ultrasound is not reassuring, you may be asked to wait a week or 10 days, then repeat the ultrasound.

The longer you bleed and cramp, the more likely you are having a miscarriage. If you pass all of the pregnancy, bleeding stops and cramping goes away, you may be done with it. However, if everything is not expelled, it may be necessary to perform a *dilatation and curettage* (D&C) to empty the uterus. It is preferable to do this so you won't bleed for a long time, risking anemia and infection.

Some women are given the hormone progesterone in an effort to help them keep a pregnancy. The use of progesterone to prevent miscarriage is controversial. Doctors do not agree on its use or its effectiveness.

Rh-Sensitivity and Miscarriage. If you're Rh-negative and you have a miscarriage, you will need to receive RhoGAM. This applies *only* if you are Rh-negative. RhoGAM is given to protect you from making antibodies to Rh-positive blood. (This is discussed in Week 16.)

If You Have a Miscarriage. One miscarriage can be traumatic; two in a row can be very difficult to deal with. Repeated miscarriages occur due to chance or "bad luck" in most cases.

Most doctors don't recommend testing to find a reason for miscarriage unless you have three or more miscarriages. Chromosome analysis can be done, and other tests can be performed to investigate the possibility of infections, diabetes and lupus.

Don't blame yourself or your partner for a miscarriage. It is usually impossible to look back at everything you've done, eaten or been exposed to and find the cause of a miscarriage.

## Your Nutrition

It's hard to eat nutritiously for *every* meal. You may not always get the nutrients you need, in the amounts you need. On the opposite page is a chart showing where you can get the various nutrients you should be eating every day. Your prenatal vitamin is *not* a substitute for food, so don't count on it to supply you with essential vitamins and minerals. Food is important, too!

## *Sources of Food Nutrients*

| Nutrient (Daily Requirement) | Food Sources |
| --- | --- |
| Calcium (1200mg) | dairy products, dark leafy vegetables, dried beans and peas, tofu |
| Folic acid (0.4mg) | liver, dried beans and peas, eggs, broccoli, whole-grain products, oranges, orange juice |
| Iron (30mg) | fish, liver, meat, poultry, egg yolks, nuts, dried beans and peas, dark leafy vegetables, dried fruit |
| Magnesium (320mg) | dried beans and peas, cocoa, seafoods, whole-grain products, nuts |
| Vitamin $B_6$ (2.2mg) | whole-grain products, liver, meat |
| Vitamin E (10mg) | milk, eggs, meat, fish, cereals, leafy vegetables, vegetable oils |
| Zinc (15mg) | seafood, meat, nuts, milk, dried beans and peas |

## You Should Also Know

### ᔧ *Lab Tests Your Doctor May Order*

At your first or second visit, routine lab tests are performed. You will have a pelvic exam, including a Pap smear. Other tests include a CBC (complete blood count), urinalysis and urine culture, a test for syphilis (VDRL or ART) and cervical cultures, as indicated. Many doctors test blood sugar (to look for diabetes); they may also test for your immunity against rubella (German measles). Your blood type and Rh-factor are also checked.

Other tests are done as required. Tests are not performed at each visit; they are done at the beginning of pregnancy and as needed. Tests for hepatitis are now standard.

### ᔧ *Toxoplasmosis*

If you have a cat, you may be concerned about *toxoplasmosis*. The disease is spread by eating raw, infected meat or by contact with infected cat feces. It can cross the placenta to your baby. Usually an infection in the mother has no symptoms.

Infection during pregnancy can lead to miscarriage or an infected infant at birth. Antibiotics, such as pyrimethamine, sulfadiazine and erythromycin, can be used to treat toxoplasmosis, but the best plan is prevention. Hygienic measures prevent transmission of the disease.

Avoid exposure to cat feces (get someone else to change the kitty litter). Wash hands thoroughly after petting your cat, and keep your cat off counters and tables. Wash your hands after contact with meat and soil. Cook all meat thoroughly. Avoid cross contamination of foods while preparing and cooking them.

## Medical Conditions and "Safe" Medications to Use during Pregnancy

| Condition | Drugs of Choice that Are Safe to Use |
| --- | --- |
| Acne | benzoyl peroxide (gel), clindamycin (gel), erythromycin (gel) |
| Asthma | inhalers—beta-adrenergic antagonists, corticosteroids, cromolyn, ipratropium |
| Bacterial infection | cephalosporins, clindamycin, cotrimoxazole, erythromycin, nitrofurantoin |
| Bipolar disorder | chlorpromazine, haloperidol |
| Coughs | cough lozenges, dextromethorphan, diphenhydramine, codeine (short term) |
| Depression | fluoxetine, tricyclic antidepressants |
| Headache | acetaminophen |
| Hypertension | hydralazine, methyldopa |
| Hyperthyroidism | propylthiouracil |
| Migraines | codeine, dimenhydrinate |
| Nausea and vomiting | doxylamine plus pyridoxine |
| Peptic ulcer disease | antacids, rantidine |

# *Week 9*

## *Age of Fetus—7 Weeks*

If you've just found out you're pregnant, you might
want to begin by reading the previous chapters.

## How Big Is Your Baby?

The crown-to-rump length of the embryo is 1 to 1¼ inches (2.2 to 3cm).
This is close to the size of a medium green olive.

## How Big Are You?

Each week your uterus grows larger with the baby growing inside it.
You may begin to see your waistline growing thicker by this time. A
pelvic exam will detect a uterus a little bigger than a grapefruit.

## How Your Baby Is Growing and Developing

If you could look inside your uterus, you'd see many changes in your
baby. The illustration on page 109 shows some of them.

Your baby's arms and legs are longer. Hands are flexed at the wrist and meet over the heart area. They continue to extend in front of the body. Fingers are longer, and the tips are slightly enlarged where touch pads are developing. The feet are approaching the midline of the body and may be long enough to meet in front of the torso.

The head is more erect, and the neck is more developed. The eyelids almost cover the eyes. Up to this time, the eyes have been uncovered. External ears are evident and well formed. Your baby now moves its body and limbs. This movement may be seen during an ultrasound exam.

The baby looks more recognizable as a human being, although it is still extremely small. It is probably impossible to distinguish a male from a female. External organs (external genitalia) of the male and female appear very similar and will not be distinguishable for another few weeks.

## Changes in You

### ∽ Weight Change

Most women are interested in their weight during pregnancy; many watch their weight closely. As strange as it may seem, gaining weight is an important way to monitor the well-being of your developing baby. Even though your weight gain may be small, your body is growing.

### How Is Pregnancy Weight Distributed?

| | |
|---|---|
| 12 pounds | Maternal stores (fat, protein and other nutrients) |
| 4 pounds | Increased fluid volume |
| 2 pounds | Breast enlargement |
| 2 pounds | Uterus |
| 7½ pounds | Baby |
| 2 pounds | Amniotic fluid |
| 1½ pounds | Placenta (connects mother and baby; brings baby nourishment and takes away waste) |

**Actual size**

Eye

Fingers

Toes

Embryo at 9 weeks of pregnancy (fetal age—46 to 49 days). Toes are formed and feet are more recognizable. Crown-to-rump length is about 1 inch (25mm).

### ✍ *Increased Blood Volume*

Your blood system changes dramatically during pregnancy. Your blood volume increases greatly—to about 50% more than before you became pregnant. However, this amount varies from woman to woman.

Increased blood volume is important. It is designed to meet the demands of your growing uterus. This increase does not include the blood in the embryo, whose circulation is separate (fetal blood does not mix with your blood). More blood in your system protects you and your baby from harmful effects when you lie down or stand up. The increase is also a safeguard during labor and delivery, when some blood is lost.

The blood-volume increase begins during the first trimester. The largest increase occurs during the second trimester. It continues to increase but at a slower rate during the third trimester.

Blood is composed of fluid (plasma) and cells (red blood cells and white blood cells). Plasma and cells play an important role in your body's function.

Fluid and cells increase to different degrees. Usually there is an initial rise in plasma volume followed by an increase in red blood cells. The increase in red blood cells increases your body's demand for iron.

Red blood cells and plasma both increase during pregnancy; plasma increases more. This increase in plasma can cause anemia. If you're anemic, especially during pregnancy, you may feel tired, fatigue easily or experience a general feeling of ill health. (See Week 22 for a discussion of anemia.)

## How Your Actions
## Affect Your Baby's Development

### ✍ *Saunas, Hot Tubs and Spas*

Some women are concerned about using saunas, hot tubs and spas during pregnancy. They want to know if it is OK to relax in this way.

We recommend that you don't take a chance with a sauna, hot tub or spa. Your baby relies on you to maintain correct body temperature. If your body temperature is elevated high enough, and stays there for an extended period, it may damage the baby if it occurs at various critical times in its development. Wait until more medical research determines that it is not harmful to your baby.

### ✂ *Electric Blankets*

There has been controversy about using electric blankets to keep you warm during pregnancy. There is still much disagreement and discussion about their safety. Some experts question whether these blankets can cause health problems.

*Tip for Week 9* It's an old wives' tale that your hair won't curl if you have a permanent during pregnancy. Our only precaution is that if odors affect you, the fumes from a permanent or hair coloring could make you feel ill.

Electric blankets produce a low-level electromagnetic field. The developing fetus may be more sensitive than an adult to these electromagnetic fields.

Because researchers are uncertain about "acceptable levels" of exposure for a pregnant woman and her baby, the safest alternative at this time is not to use an electric blanket during pregnancy. There are many other ways to keep warm, such as down comforters and wool blankets. One of these is a better choice.

### ✂ *Microwave Ovens*

Some women wonder about the safety of microwave ovens. Are they exposed to radiation? Microwave ovens are helpful to busy people who prepare meals. However, we don't know if there is danger to you if you use a microwave oven during pregnancy. More research is needed.

Initial research indicates tissues developing in the body, which would include the human fetus, may be particularly sensitive to the effects of microwaves. A microwave oven heats tissues from the inside. Follow the directions provided with your microwave oven, and don't stand next to or directly in front of it while it is in use.

## Your Nutrition

Fruits and vegetables are important during pregnancy. Because different kinds of produce are available in different seasons, you can add variety to your diet quite easily with them. They are excellent sources of vitamins, minerals and fiber. Eating a variety can supply you with iron, folic acid, calcium and vitamin C.

## *Tasty, Low-Cal Sources of Vitamin C*

Five excellent sources of vitamin C are easy to add to your diet, and if you're watching your weight, they're low in calories, too! Try the following:

- strawberries—1 cup contains 94mg of vitamin C
- orange juice—1 cup contains 82mg of vitamin C
- kiwi fruit—1 medium contains 74mg of vitamin C
- broccoli—½ cup, cooked, contains 58mg of vitamin C
- red peppers—¼ of a medium red pepper contains 57mg of vitamin C

### ᴔ *Vitamin C Is Important*

Vitamin C can be very important during pregnancy. It is important for fetal-tissue development and the absorption of iron. Recent research indicates vitamin C may help prevent pre-eclampsia. Deficiencies in the vitamin have also been linked to premature delivery; vitamin C helps build the amniotic sac. The recommended daily dose is 85mg—a bit more than what is contained in a prenatal vitamin. You can get some of the extra vitamin C you need by eating fruits and vegetables rich in the vitamin.

Each day, eat one or two servings of fruit high in vitamin C and at least one dark-green or deep-yellow vegetable for extra iron, fiber and folic acid. Fruits and vegetables you may choose, and their serving sizes, include the following:

- grapes—¾ cup
- banana, orange, apple—1 medium
- dried fruit—¼ cup
- fruit juice—½ cup
- canned or cooked fruit—½ cup
- broccoli, carrots or other vegetable—½ cup
- potato—1 medium
- leafy green vegetables—1 cup
- vegetable juice—¾ cup

Don't take more than the recommended dose of vitamin C; too much may cause you stomach cramps and diarrhea. It can also negatively affect your baby's metabolism.

## You Should Also Know

### ✂ *Having a Baby Costs Money!*

Every couple wants to know what it will cost to have a baby. There are really two answers to that question—it costs a lot, and cost varies from one part of the country to another.

To determine how much it costs to have a baby in your area, you need to consider several different factors. Insurance makes a big difference. If you don't have it, you will pay for everything. If you do have insurance, you need to check out some things. Ask your employer the following questions.

- What type of coverage do I have?
- Are there maternity benefits? What are they?
- Do maternity benefits cover Cesarean deliveries?
- What kind of coverage is there for a high-risk pregnancy?
- Do I have to pay a deductible? If so, how much is it?
- If my pregnancy lasts into a new year, will I have to pay 2 years' worth of deductibles?
- How do I submit claims?
- Is there a cap (limit) on total coverage?
- What percentage of my costs are covered?
- Is the cost of taking childbirth-education classes covered?
- Does my coverage restrict the kind of hospital accommodations I may choose, such as a birthing center or a birthing room?
- What procedures must I follow before entering the hospital?
- Does my policy cover a nurse-midwife (if this is of interest to you)?
- Does coverage include medications?
- What tests during pregnancy are covered?

- What tests during labor and delivery are covered?
- What types of anesthesia are covered during labor and delivery?
- How long can I stay in the hospital?
- Does payment go directly to my doctor or to me?
- What conditions or services are not covered?
- What kind of coverage is there for the baby after it is born?
- How long can the baby stay in the hospital?
- Is there an additional cost to add the baby to the policy?
- How do I add the baby to the policy?
- Can we collect a percentage of a fee from my husband's policy and the rest from mine?

Your insurance dictates a lot of the costs and decisions for you. Having a baby generates different costs. One is the hospital. Much of the covered amount for the hospital is determined by the length of stay and the "services" you use. In some cases, having an epidural or Cesarean delivery adds to this bill. Your doctor's bill is separate from this, except under some plans. A pediatrician usually examines the baby, does a physical and sees the baby each day in the hospital. This is another cost.

**Ðad Tip** Ask your partner which visits to the doctor she'd like you to attend. Some couples attend every visit together, when possible. Ask her to let you know the date and time of each appointment.

It would be nice to think about costs before pregnancy and be sure to have insurance to help out. However, many pregnancies are surprises.

What can you do? First, find the answers to your questions. Talk to your insurance carrier, then talk to someone in your doctor's office who handles insurance claims. This person may have answers or know of resources you haven't thought about. Don't be embarrassed to ask questions. You will be happier if you get these issues resolved early. Pregnancy is not the time to cut corners to save money.

Call around so you can compare hospitals and prices. Sometimes it's worth spending a little more money to get what you want. When you call, ask for specifics about what is included in the prices you are quoted. You may get a price that seems lower and better than others but really doesn't cover everything you will want and need.

Today, some hospitals and medical centers offer "pregnancy packages." A package can cover many services for one fee. Ask about it in your area.

You want to be prepared well in advance. The last thing you need at this time is an unpleasant surprise about what is covered or how much you will have to pay for medical services.

### ∾ *Costs of Having a Baby in Canada*
The Canadian health-care system is different from that in the United States. Canadians pay a premium on a monthly basis. Cost varies depending on which province you live in. The doctor who delivers your baby is paid by the government. He or she submits the bill to the government, not you.

# Week 10

## Age of Fetus—8 Weeks

*If you've just found out you're pregnant, you might
want to begin by reading the previous chapters.*

## How Big Is Your Baby?

By the 10th week of pregnancy, the crown-to-rump length of your
growing baby is about 1¼ to 1¾ inches (3.1 to 4.2cm). At this time, we
can start measuring how much the baby weighs. Before this week,
weight was too small to measure weekly differences. Now that the
baby is starting to put on a little weight, weight is included in this section. The baby weighs close to 0.18 ounce (5g) and is the size of a
small plum.

## How Big Are You?

Changes are gradual, and you still may not show much. You may be
thinking about and looking at maternity clothes, but you probably
don't need them just yet.

### ∽ *Molar Pregnancy*

A condition that can make you grow too big too fast is a molar pregnancy, sometimes called *gestational trophoblastic neoplasia* (GTN) or *hydatidiform mole*. The occurrence of GTN is easily monitored by checking HCG levels (see Week 5). Molar pregnancy is treated with surgery.

When a molar pregnancy occurs, an embryo does not usually develop. Other tissue grows, which is abnormal placental tissue. The most common symptom is bleeding during the first trimester. Another symptom is the discrepancy between the size of the mother-to-be and how far along she is supposed to be in pregnancy. Half the time, a woman is too large. Twenty-five percent of the time, she is too small. Excessive nausea and vomiting are other symptoms. Cysts may occur on the ovaries.

The most effective way to diagnose a molar pregnancy is by ultrasound. The ultrasound picture has a "snowflake" appearance. A molar pregnancy is usually found when ultrasound is done early in pregnancy to determine the cause of bleeding or rapid growth of the uterus.

When a molar pregnancy is diagnosed, a dilatation and curettage (D&C) is usually done as soon as possible. After a molar pregnancy occurs, effective birth control is important to be sure the molar pregnancy is completely gone. Most doctors recommend using reliable birth control for at least 1 year before attempting pregnancy again.

## How Your Baby Is
## Growing and Developing

The end of week 10 is the end of the embryonic period. At this time, the fetal period begins. It is characterized by rapid growth of the fetus when the three germ layers are established. (See Week 4 for further information.) During the embryonic period, the embryo is most susceptible to things that could interfere with its development. Most congenital malformations occur before the end of week 10. It is encouraging to know that a critical part of your baby's development is safely behind you.

Few malformations occur during the fetal period. However, drugs and other harmful exposures, such as severe stress or radiation (X-ray), can destroy fetal cells at any time during pregnancy. Continue to avoid them.

By the end of week 10, development of fetal organ systems and the body are well under way. Your baby is beginning to look more human.

## Changes in You

### ✎ Emotional Changes

When your pregnancy is confirmed by an exam or a pregnancy test, you may be affected in many ways. Pregnancy can change many of your expectations. Some women see pregnancy as a sign of womanhood. Some consider it a blessing. Still others feel it is a problem to be dealt with.

You will experience many changes in your body. You may wonder if you are still attractive. Will your partner still find you desirable? (Many men believe pregnant women are beautiful.) Will your partner help you? Clothing may become an issue. Will you look attractive? Can you learn to adapt?

If you aren't immediately excited about pregnancy, don't feel alone. You may question your condition—that's common. Some of this reaction is because you're not sure of what lies ahead.

When and how you begin to regard the fetus as a person is different for everyone. Some women say it is when their pregnancy test is positive. Others say it occurs when they hear the fetal heartbeat, usually at around 12 weeks. For still others, it happens when they first feel their baby move, at between 16 and 20 weeks.

You may find you are emotional about many things. You may feel moody, cry at the slightest thing or drift off in daydreams. Emotional swings are normal and continue to some degree throughout your pregnancy.

How can you help yourself deal with emotional changes? One of the most important things you can do is get good prenatal care. Follow

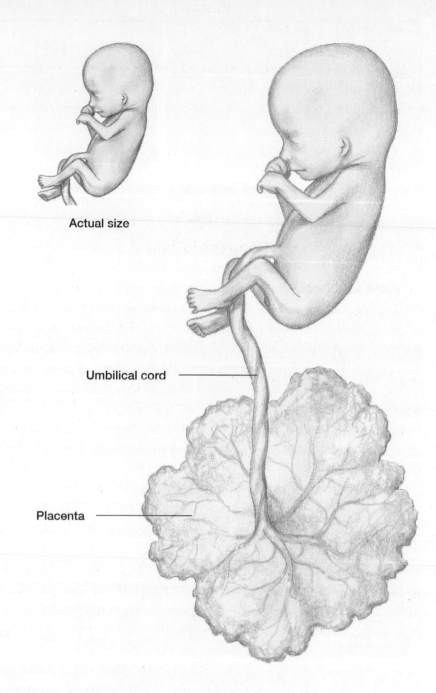

**Actual size**

Umbilical cord ———

Placenta ———

Baby is shown attached to the placenta by its umbilical cord. Eyelids
are fused and remain closed until week 27 (fetal age—25 weeks).

your doctor's recommendations. Keep all your prenatal appointments. Establish good communication with your doctor and his or her office staff. Ask questions. If something bothers you or worries you, discuss it with someone reliable.

## How Your Actions Affect Your Baby's Development

### ⌁ *Vaccinations and Immunizations*

Many vaccines are available to help prevent illness. A vaccine is given to provide you with protection against infection and is usually given by injection or taken orally.

Many women of childbearing age in the United States and Canada have been immunized against measles, mumps, rubella, tetanus and diphtheria. Most people born before 1957 were exposed to and infected naturally with measles, mumps and rubella, and can be considered immune. They have antibodies and therefore are protected.

For those women born after 1957, the situation may not be quite so clear. A blood test for measles is necessary to determine immunity. The diagnosis of rubella is difficult without a blood test because many other illnesses may have similar symptoms. Physician-diagnosed mumps or mumps vaccination is necessary evidence of immunity.

Vaccination for measles, mumps and rubella (MMR) should be administered *only* when a woman is practicing birth control. She must continue to use contraception for at least 4 weeks after receiving this immunization. Other vaccinations are also important, such as the tetanus or DPT (diphtheria, pertussis [whooping cough], tetanus) vaccine.

Risk of Exposure. It's important to consider your risk of exposure to various diseases when you are deciding whether to have a particular vaccination. During pregnancy, try to decrease your chance of exposure to disease and illness. Avoid visiting areas known to have prevalent diseases. Avoid people (usually children) with known illnesses.

It's impossible to avoid all exposure to all diseases. If you have been exposed, or if exposure is unavoidable, the risk of the disease must be balanced against the potential harmful effects of vaccination.

Then the vaccine must be evaluated in terms of its effectiveness and its potential for complicating pregnancy. There is little information available on harmful effects on the developing fetus from vaccines. In general, killed vaccines are safe. Live-measles vaccine should *never* be given to a pregnant woman.

The only immunizing agents recommended for use during pregnancy are the DPT vaccine and the flu vaccine. The flu vaccine is one you can take during pregnancy. If there are no contraindications, it should be taken by every pregnant woman who will be past the 3rd month of pregnancy during the flu season. This is usually from November through March, although the season has gone beyond March in some years. Talk to your doctor about it.

MMR vaccine should be given before pregnancy or after delivery. In October 2001, the Centers for Disease Control (CDC) changed the recommendation concerning how long a woman should wait to get pregnant after receiving rubella vaccine. The waiting time was reduced from 3 months to 1 month. The safe interval for measles and mumps vaccination was already set at 1 month.

A pregnant woman should receive primary vaccination against polio only if her risk of exposure to the disease is high. Only inactivated polio vaccine should be used.

### ↗ Rubella during Pregnancy

It's a good idea to be checked for immunity to rubella before you get pregnant. Rubella (German measles) during pregnancy can be responsible for miscarriage or fetal malformation. Because there is no known treatment for rubella, the best approach is prevention.

If you're not immune, you can receive a vaccination while you take reliable birth control. Do not have a vaccination shortly before or during pregnancy because of the possibility of exposing the baby to the rubella virus.

## ✍ Chicken Pox during Pregnancy

Did you have chicken pox when you were a child? If not, you may be one of the 1 in 2000 women who will develop the infection during pregnancy. Chicken pox is a childhood disease; only 2% of cases occur in the 15-to-49 age group. The CDC, the American Academy of Pediatrics and the American Academy of Family Physicians all recommend that healthy children age 1 year and older receive the chicken-pox vaccine, which is usually given at 12 to 18 months of age.

If you contract chicken pox during pregnancy, take very good care of yourself. In about 15% of those adults who contract chicken pox, a form of pneumonia develops—it can be especially serious for a pregnant woman. If you get chicken pox during pregnancy, just before delivery, your baby may get it, too, which can be serious in a newborn.

If you are exposed to the infection while you are pregnant, contact your doctor immediately! A pregnant woman with a significant exposure to this highly infectious herpes virus should receive varicella-zoster immune globulin (VZIG). If you receive VZIG within 72 hours of exposure, it can help prevent infection or it can lessen the severity of symptoms. If you do contract chicken pox, your physician will probably treat you with acyclovir to lessen symptoms.

If you are exposed during pregnancy, and you're lucky enough not to get this infection, be sure to get vaccinated before your next pregnancy!

## ✍ Effects of Infections on Your Baby

Some infections and illnesses a woman contracts can also affect her baby's development during this growth period. See the box to the left for a list of some infections and diseases and the effects they may have on a developing baby.

| Infections | Effects on Fetus |
|---|---|
| Cytomegalovirus (CMV) | microcephaly, brain damage, hearing loss |
| Rubella (German measles) | cataracts, deafness, heart lesions, can involve all organs |
| Syphilis | fetal death, skin defects |
| Toxoplasmosis | possible effects on all organs |
| Varicella | possible effects on all organs |

## Your Nutrition

Protein supplies you with amino acids,

which are critical for the growth and repair of the embryo/fetus, placenta, uterus and breasts. Pregnancy increases your protein needs. Try to eat 6 ounces of protein each day during the first trimester and 8 ounces a day during the second and third trimesters. However, protein should only make up about 15% of your total calorie intake.

Many protein sources are high in fat. If you need to watch your calories, choose low-fat protein sources. Some protein foods you may choose, and their serving sizes, include the following:

- chickpeas (garbanzo beans)—1 cup
- cheese, mozzarella—1 ounce
- chicken, roasted, skinless—½ breast (about 4 ounces)
- eggs—1
- hamburger, broiled, lean—3½ ounces
- milk—8 ounces
- peanut butter—2 tablespoons
- tuna, canned in water—3 ounces
- yogurt—8 ounces

### ॐ *Brain Builders*

Choline and docosahexaenoic acid (DHA) can help build baby's brain cells during fetal development and after birth, if baby

*Tip for Week 10* It's common for your breasts to tingle and to feel sore early in pregnancy. In fact, it may be one of the first signs of pregnancy.

breastfeeds. Choline is found in milk, eggs, peanuts, whole-wheat bread and beef. DHA is found in fish, egg yolks, poultry, meat, canola oil, walnuts and wheat germ. If you eat these foods during pregnancy and while you're breastfeeding, you can help your baby obtain these important supplements.

### ॐ *You Need to Gain Weight*

You should be gaining weight slowly now; it can be harmful to your baby if you don't. A woman of normal weight can expect to gain between 25 and 35 pounds total while pregnant. Your weight gain gives your doctor an indication of your well-being and that of your baby, too.

Pregnancy is not a time to experiment with different diets or cut down on calories. However, this doesn't mean you have the go-ahead to eat anything you want, any time you want. Exercise and a proper nutrition plan, without "junk food," will help you manage your weight. Be smart about food choices. It's true you're eating for two—however, you must eat wisely for both of you!

## You Should Also Know

### ☞ Chorionic Villus Sampling

*Chorionic villus sampling* (CVS) is a test used to detect genetic abnormalities. Sampling is done early in pregnancy, usually between the 9th and 11th weeks.

CVS is done for many reasons. The test helps identify problems related to genetic defects, such as Down syndrome. This test offers an advantage over amniocentesis because it is done much earlier in pregnancy; results are available in about 1 week. If a pregnancy will be terminated, it can be done earlier and may carry fewer risks to the woman.

Chorionic villus sampling involves placing an instrument through the cervix or abdomen to remove fetal tissue from the placenta. The test should be performed only by someone experienced in the technique.

If your doctor recommends you have CVS, ask about its risks. The risk of miscarriage is small—between 1 and 2%. If you have CVS and are Rh-negative, you should receive RhoGAM after the procedure.

### ☞ Fetoscopy

Fetoscopy provides a view of the baby and placenta inside your uterus. In some cases, abnormalities and problems can be detected and corrected.

The goal of fetoscopy is to correct a defect before the problem worsens, which could prevent a fetus from developing normally. A doctor can see some problems more clearly with fetoscopy than with ultrasound.

The test is done by placing a scope, like the one used in laparoscopy or arthroscopy, through the abdomen. The procedure is similar to amnio-centesis, but the fetoscope is larger than the needle used for amniocentesis.

If your doctor suggests fetoscopy to you, discuss possible risks, advantages and disadvantages of the procedure with him or her. The test should be done only by someone experienced in the technique. Risk of miscarriage is 3 to 4% with this procedure. It is not available everywhere. If you have fetoscopy and are Rh-negative, you should receive RhoGAM after the procedure.

*Ðad Tip* Are you concerned about sex during pregnancy? You both may have questions, so talk about them together and with your partner's doctor. Occasionally during a pregnancy you'll need to avoid intercourse. However, pregnancy is an opportunity for increased closeness and intimacy for you as a couple. Sex can be a positive part of this experience.

# Week 11

*Age of Fetus—9 Weeks*

## How Big Is Your Baby?

By this week, the crown-to-rump length of your baby is 1½ to 2½ inches (4.4 to 6cm). Fetal weight is about 0.3 ounce (8g). Your baby is about the size of a large lime.

## How Big Are You?

While big changes are occurring in your baby, changes are probably happening more slowly with you. You are almost at the end of the first trimester; your uterus has been growing along with the fetus inside it. It is almost big enough to fill your pelvis and may be felt in your lower abdomen, above the middle of your pubic bone.

You won't be able to feel your baby moving yet. If you think you feel your baby move at this time, you either have gas or are further along in your pregnancy than you thought.

## How Your Baby Is Growing and Developing

Fetal growth is rapid now. The crown-to-rump length of your baby doubles in the next 3 weeks. As you can see in the illustration on page 128, the head is almost half the baby's entire length. As the head extends (uncurls or tips backward toward the spine), the chin rises from the chest, and the neck develops and lengthens. Fingernails appear.

External genitalia are beginning to show distinguishing features. Development of the fetus into a male or female is complete in another 3 weeks. If a miscarriage occurs after this point, it may be possible to tell if it is male or female.

All embryos begin life looking the same, as far as outward appearances are concerned. Whether the embryo develops into a male or female is determined by the genetic information contained within the embryo.

## Changes in You

Some women notice changes in their hair, fingernails or toenails during pregnancy. This doesn't happen to everyone, but if it happens to you, don't worry about it. Some fortunate women notice an increase in hair and nail growth during pregnancy. Others find they lose some hair during this time.

Some doctors believe these changes occur during pregnancy because of increased circulation throughout your body. Others credit the hormonal changes occurring in you. Still others

*Dad Tip* Remember that despite morning sickness, headaches and a changing waistline, pregnancy is a miracle! Pregnancy and childbirth happen only a limited number of times in your life. Enjoy this special time together. You'll look back fondly at the challenge of becoming parents and probably even say, "That wasn't so bad." We know that because couples get pregnant again and have more kids!

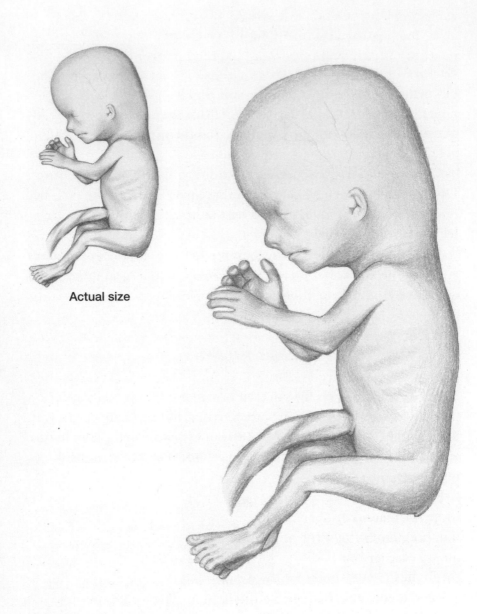

Actual size

By week 11 of gestation (fetal age—9 weeks), fingernails are beginning to appear.

explain these differences with a change in "phase" of the growth cycle of the hair or nails. In any event, these differences are rarely permanent. There is little or nothing you can do about them.

## How Your Actions
## Affect Your Baby's Development

### ✤ *Traveling during Pregnancy*

Pregnant women frequently ask whether travel during pregnancy can hurt their baby. If your pregnancy is uncomplicated and you are not at high risk, travel is usually acceptable. Ask your doctor about any travel you are considering *before* making firm plans or buying tickets.

Whether you travel by car, bus, train or airplane, it's wise to get up and walk at least every hour. Regular visits to the bathroom may take care of this requirement.

The biggest risk of traveling during pregnancy is development of a complication while you are away from those who know your medical and pregnancy history. If you do decide to take a trip, be sensible in your planning. Don't overdo it. Take it easy!

Traveling by Air.  Air travel is safe for most pregnant women. Most U.S. airlines allow women to fly up to 36 weeks of pregnancy. For international travel, the cutoff is 35 weeks of pregnancy.

Pregnant women who are at significant risk for premature labor or who have placental abnormalities should avoid all air travel. You may want to keep the following things in mind if you're considering flying during pregnancy.

- Avoid flights that are high altitude (nonstop overseas or cross-country flights) because they cruise at a higher altitude and oxygen levels are lower. This increases your heartbeat, as well as your baby's; your baby also receives less oxygen.
- If you have problems with swelling, wear loose-fitting shoes and clothes. (This is good advice for every traveler.) Avoid

pantyhose, tight clothes, knee-high socks or stockings, and
tight waistlines.

• You can order special meals, such as low-sodium or vegetarian,
  if you want to avoid some foods that might cause you problems.
• Drink lots of water to keep you hydrated.
• Get up and move around when you can during the flight. Try to
  walk at least 10 minutes every hour. Sometimes just standing up
  helps your circulation.
• Try to get an aisle seat, close to the bathroom. If you have to go
  to the bathroom a lot, it's easier if you don't have to crawl over
  someone to get out.
• Be careful of any X-ray devices in the airport.

### ✌ Auto Safety during Pregnancy

Many women are concerned about driving and using seat belts and
shoulder harnesses during pregnancy. Wearing safety restraints dramatically decreases the incidence of injury in an accident. More than
50,000 deaths and 2 million injuries are directly related to auto accidents every year. Wearing a seat belt and shoulder harness can decrease
these losses. There is no reason not to drive while you're pregnant, if
your pregnancy is normal and you feel OK.

Some women believe using a safety restraint might be harmful
to their pregnancy. Here are some common excuses (and our responses) for not using seat belts and shoulder harnesses in pregnancy.

• *"Using a safety belt will hurt my baby."* There is no evidence that
  seat-belt use will increase the chance of fetal or uterine injury.
  Your chance of survival with a seat belt is better than without
  one. Your survival is important to your unborn baby.
• *"I don't want to be trapped in my car if there is a fire."* Few automobile accidents result in fires. Even if a fire did occur, you
  could probably undo the restraint and escape if you were con-
  scious. Ejection from a car accounts for about 25% of all deaths
  in automobile accidents. Seat-belt use prevents this.

- *"I'm a good driver."* Defensive driving helps, but it doesn't prevent an accident.
- *"I don't need to use a safety belt; I'm just going a short distance."* Most injuries occur within 25 miles of home.

Studies have been done on pregnant women who used seat belts. In one California study, only 14% of all pregnant women used seat belts compared to 30% of nonpregnant women. We know the lap/shoulder seat-belt system is safe to wear during pregnancy, so buckle up for you *and* your baby.

## The Proper Way to Wear a Lap Belt and Shoulder Harness

There is a proper way for you to wear a seat belt during pregnancy. Place the lap-belt portion under your abdomen and across your upper thighs. It should be as snug as is comfortably possible. The shoulder belt should also be snug but comfortable. Adjust your position so the belt crosses your shoulder without cutting into your neck. Position the shoulder belt between your breasts. Do not slip this belt off your shoulder. If it's a long trip, adjust the belt as needed for comfort.

## Your Nutrition

Carbohydrate foods provide the primary source of energy for your developing baby. These foods also ensure that your body uses protein efficiently. Foods from this group are almost interchangeable, so it should be easy to get all the servings you need. Some carbohydrate foods you may choose, and their serving sizes, include the following:

- tortilla—1 large
- pasta, cereal or rice, cooked—½ cup
- cereal, ready-to-eat—1 ounce
- bagel—½ small

• bread—1 slice
• roll—1 medium

## You Should Also Know

### ༄ *Ultrasound in Pregnancy*

By this point, you may have discussed ultrasound with your doctor. Or you may already have had an ultrasound test. Ultrasound (also called *sonography* or *sonogram*) is one of our most valuable methods for evaluating a pregnancy. Although doctors, hospitals and insurance companies (yes, they get involved in this, too) don't agree as to when ultrasound should be done or if every pregnant woman should have an ultrasound test during pregnancy, it definitely has its place. The test has proved useful in improving the outcome in pregnancy. It is a noninvasive test, and there are no known risks associated with it. In the United States, nearly 2.7 million obstetrical ultrasounds are performed each year!

*Tip for Week 11*  You may be able to get a "picture" of your baby before birth from an ultrasound test. Some facilities can even make a videotape for you. Ask about it before the test, if you're scheduled to have one. You may be advised to bring a new, unused videotape.

Ultrasound involves the use of high-frequency sound waves made by applying an alternating current to a transducer. A lubricant is placed on the skin to improve contact with the transducer. The transducer passes over the abdomen above the uterus. Sound waves are projected from the transducer through the abdomen, into the pelvis. As sound waves bounce off tissues, they are directed toward and back to the transducer. The reflection of sound waves can be compared to "radar" used by airplanes or ships.

Different tissues of the body reflect ultrasound signals differently, and we can distinguish among them. Motion can be distinguished, so we can detect motion of the baby or parts of the baby, such as the heart. With ultrasound, a fetal heart can be seen beating as early as 5 or 6 weeks into the pregnancy.

Ultrasound can detect fetal motion. Your baby's body and limbs can be seen moving as early as 4 weeks of embryonic growth (6th week of pregnancy).

Your doctor can use ultrasound in many ways in relation to your pregnancy, such as:

- helping in the early identification of pregnancy
- showing the size and growth rate of the embryo or fetus
- identifying the presence of two or more fetuses
- measuring the fetal head, abdomen or femur to determine the stage of pregnancy
- identifying some fetuses with Down syndrome
- identifying fetal abnormalities, such as hydrocephalus and microcephaly
- identifying abnormalities of internal organs, such as the kidneys or bladder
- measuring the amount of amniotic fluid to help determine fetal well-being
- identifying the location, size and maturity of the placenta
- identifying placental abnormalities
- identifying uterine abnormalities or tumors
- determining the position of an IUD
- differentiating between miscarriage, ectopic pregnancy and normal pregnancy
- in connection with various tests, such as amniocentesis, percutaneous umbilical-cord blood sampling (PUBS) and chorionic villus sampling (CVS), to select a safe place to do each test

You may be asked to drink a lot of water before an ultrasound examination. If you have had an ultrasound exam during a previous pregnancy, one of the main things you may remember is how uncomfortable you were with your bladder full to overflowing!

Your bladder is in front of your uterus. When your bladder is empty, your uterus is harder to see because it is farther down inside the pelvic bones. Bones disrupt ultrasound signals and make the picture harder to interpret. With your bladder full, your uterus rises out of the pelvis and can be seen more easily. The bladder acts as a window to look through to see the uterus and the fetus inside.

**Various Ultrasound Tests.** There's a 3-dimensional ultrasound available in many areas that provides detailed, clear pictures of the fetus in the womb. They're so clear the image almost looks like a picture. For the pregnant woman, the test is almost the same. The difference is that computer software "translates" the picture into a 3-D image. This ultrasound may be used when there is suspicion of fetal abnormalities and the doctor wants to take a closer look. One use of the 3-D ultrasound is to help diagnose and evaluate cleft lip and cleft palate in a developing fetus. It helps medical personnel define the extent of the defect so a treatment program to implement immediately after birth can be planned.

The ultrasound vaginal probe, also called the *transvaginal ultrasound*, can be used in early pregnancy for a better view of the baby and placenta. A probe is placed inside the vagina, and the pregnancy is viewed from this angle. You don't have to have your bladder full for this one!

**Can Ultrasound Determine the Baby's Sex?** Some couples ask for ultrasound to determine whether they are carrying a boy or girl. If the baby is in a good position and it is old enough for the genitals to have developed and they can be seen clearly, determination may be possible. However, many doctors feel this reason alone is not a good reason to do an ultrasound exam. Discuss it with your doctor. Understand ultrasound is a test, and tests can occasionally be wrong.

# Week 12

*Age of Fetus—10 Weeks*

## How Big Is Your Baby?

Your baby weighs between ⅓ and ½ ounce (8 to 14g), and crown-to-rump length is almost 2½ inches (6.1cm). As you can see on page 137, your baby's size has almost doubled in the past 3 weeks! Length of the baby is still a better measure at this time than fetal weight.

## How Big Are You?

By the end of 12 weeks, your uterus is too large to remain completely in your pelvis. You may feel it above your pubic bone (pubic symphysis). The uterus has a remarkable ability to grow while you're pregnant. During pregnancy, it grows upward to fill the pelvis and abdomen, and returns to its normal, prepregnancy size within a few weeks after delivery.

Before pregnancy, your uterus is almost solid. It holds about ⅓ ounce (10ml) or less. The uterus changes during pregnancy into a comparatively thin-walled, muscular container big enough to hold the fetus, placenta and amniotic fluid. The uterus increases its capacity 500 to 1000 times during pregnancy! The weight of the uterus also changes.

When your baby is born, your uterus weighs almost 40 ounces (1.1kg) compared to 2½ ounces (70g) before pregnancy.

The uterine wall grows during the first few months of pregnancy due to hormonal stimulation by estrogen and progesterone. Later in pregnancy, the growth of the baby and the placenta stretch and thin the uterine wall.

## How Your Baby Is Growing and Developing

Few, if any, structures in the baby are formed after this week in pregnancy. However, the structures already formed continue to grow and to develop. At your 12-week visit (or close to that time), you'll probably be able to hear your baby's heartbeat! It can be heard with *doppler*, a special listening machine (not a stethoscope). It magnifies the sound of your baby's heartbeat so you can hear it.

The skeletal system now has centers of bone formation (ossification) in most bones. Fingers and toes have separated, and nails are growing. Scattered rudiments of hair appear on the body. External genitalia are beginning to show distinct signs of male or female sex characteristics.

*Dad Tip* At this doctor's visit, it may be possible to hear the baby's heartbeat. If you can't be there, send a tape recorder with your partner so she can record the baby's heartbeat for you to listen to later.

The digestive system (small intestine) is capable of producing contractions that push food through the bowels. It is also able to absorb glucose (sugar).

At the base of your baby's brain, the pituitary gland is beginning to make many hormones. Hormones are chemicals that are made in one part of the body, but their action is exerted on another part of the body.

Other things are also happening. The fetal nervous system has developed further. Your baby is moving inside your uterus, but you probably won't feel it for a while yet. Stimulating the fetus in certain spots may cause it to squint, open its mouth and move its fingers or toes.

Actual size

Your baby is growing rapidly. It has doubled its length in the past 3 weeks.

The amount of amniotic fluid is increasing. Total volume is now about 1½ ounces (50ml). At this time, the fluid is similar to maternal plasma (the noncellular portion of your blood), except it contains much less protein.

## Changes in You

You are probably starting to feel better than you have for most of your pregnancy. Around this time, morning sickness often begins to improve. You aren't extremely big and are probably still quite comfortable.

If it's your first pregnancy, you may still be wearing regular clothes. If you've had other pregnancies, you may start to show earlier and to feel more comfortable in looser clothing, such as maternity clothes.

You may be getting bigger in places besides your tummy. Your breasts are probably getting larger. They may have been sore for some time. You may also notice weight gain in your hips, legs and at your sides.

### ∾ Skin Changes

Your skin may change in various ways during pregnancy. In many women, skin down the middle of the abdomen becomes markedly darker or pigmented with a brown-black color. It forms a vertical line called the *linea nigra*.

Occasionally irregular brown patches of varying size appear on the face and neck, called *chloasma* or *mask of pregnancy*. These disappear or get lighter after delivery. Oral contraceptives may cause similar pigmentation changes.

Vascular spiders (called *telangiectasias* or *angiomas*) are small red elevations on the skin, with branches extending outward. The condition develops in about 65% of white women and 10% of black women during pregnancy.

A similar condition is redness of the palms, called *palmar erythema*. It is seen in 65% of white women and 35% of black women.

Vascular spiders and palmar erythema often occur together. Symptoms are temporary and disappear shortly after delivery. The occurrence of either condition is probably caused by high levels of estrogen during pregnancy.

### ✧ *Entering Pregnancy with High Blood Pressure*

If you have high blood pressure before you begin your pregnancy, you have an increased risk of pre-eclampsia. If left untreated during your pregnancy, hypertension reduces blood flow to the uterus and increases the risk of intrauterine-growth restriction (IUGR). In the mom-to-be, high blood pressure can cause seizures, kidney disease, liver disease, heart damage and brain damage.

Most blood-pressure medications are safe to use during pregnancy. However, ACE inhibitors should be avoided.

If your blood pressure is high when you begin your pregnancy, you may have more ultrasounds during pregnancy to monitor the baby's growth. Your doctor wants you to avoid IUGR when possible. In addition, you may want to purchase a blood-pressure monitor to use at home so you can check your readings any time.

> *Tip for Week 12* If you have diarrhea that doesn't go away in 24 hours, or if it keeps returning, call your doctor. You can take milk of magnesia for 24 hours to help deal with the problem, but don't self-medicate for longer than this time.

## How Your Actions Affect Your Baby's Development

### ✧ *Physical Injury during Pregnancy*

Trauma (physical injury) occurs in about 6 to 7% of all pregnancies. Accidents involving motor vehicles account for 66% of these cases; falls and assaults account for the remaining 34%. More than 90% of these are minor injuries.

If you experience trauma during pregnancy, you may be taken care of by emergency-medicine personnel, trauma surgeons, general surgeons and your obstetrician. Most experts recommend observing a pregnant woman for a few hours after an accident. This provides adequate time to monitor the baby. Longer monitoring may be necessary in a more serious accident.

## Your Nutrition

Some women misunderstand the concept of increasing their caloric intake during pregnancy. They think they can eat all they want. Don't fall into this trap! It's unhealthy for you and your baby if you gain too much weight during pregnancy, especially early in pregnancy. It makes carrying your baby more uncomfortable, and delivery may be more difficult. It may also be hard to shed the extra pounds after pregnancy. After baby's birth, most women are anxious to return to "normal" clothes and to look the way they did before pregnancy. Having to deal with extra weight can interfere with reaching this goal.

### ᠀ Junk Food
Is junk food your kind of food? Do you eat it several times a day? Pregnancy is the time to break that habit! Now that you're pregnant, your dietary habits affect someone besides just yourself—your growing baby. If you're used to skipping breakfast, getting something "from a machine" for lunch, then eating dinner at a fast-food restaurant, it doesn't help your pregnancy.

What and when you eat become more important when you realize how your actions affect your baby. Proper nutrition takes some planning on your part, but you can do it. Avoid foods that contain a lot of sugar and/or fat. Instead, choose healthful alternatives. If you work, take healthy foods with you for lunches and snacks. Stay away from fast food and junk food.

### ᴦ *Late-Night Snacks*

Late-night nutritious snacks are beneficial for some women. However, for many women, snacking at night is unnecessary. If you're used to ice cream or other goodies before bed, you may pay for it during pregnancy with excessive weight gain. Food in your stomach late at night may also cause you more distress if you suffer from heartburn, indigestion or nausea and vomiting.

### ᴦ *Fats and Sweets*

You may need to be cautious with fats and sweets, unless you're underweight and need to gain some weight. Many of these foods are high in calories and low in nutritional value. Eat them sparingly. Instead of selecting a food with little nutritional value, like potato chips or cookies, choose a piece of fruit, some cheese or a slice of whole-wheat bread with a little peanut butter. You'll satisfy your hunger and your nutritional needs at the same time! Some fats and sweets you may choose, and their serving sizes, include the following:

- sugar or honey—1 tablespoon
- oil—1 tablespoon
- margarine or butter—1 pat
- jam or jelly—1 tablespoon
- salad dressing—1 tablespoon

## You Should Also Know

### ᴦ *Fifth Disease*

Fifth disease, also called *parvo virus B19*, was the fifth disease to be described with a certain kind of rash. (It is *not* related to the parvo virus common in dogs.) Fifth disease is a mild, moderately contagious airborne infection. It spreads easily through groups, such as classrooms or day-care centers.

The rash looks like reddened skin caused by a slap. The reddening fades and recurs, and lasts from 2 to 34 days. There is no treatment.

This virus is important during pregnancy because it interferes with the production of red blood cells in the woman and the fetus. If you believe you have been exposed to fifth disease during pregnancy, contact your doctor. A blood test can determine whether you have previously had the virus. If you haven't, your doctor can monitor you to detect fetal problems. Some fetal problems can be dealt with before the baby is born.

### ✑ *Cystic Fibrosis Screening*

*Cystic fibrosis (CF)* is a genetic disorder that causes digestive and breathing problems. Those with the disorder are usually diagnosed early in life. With modern technology and new screening tests, today we are able to determine whether there is a risk of delivering a child with CF. The screening test uses a blood sample or a saliva sample.

Your chances for carrying the gene are quite low. For a baby to have CF, *both* parents must carry the gene. Whites have a 3% chance of carrying the CF gene; Hispanics have a 2% chance, African Americans a 1½% chance and Asians about a 1% chance. However, a family history of CF increases your chances of carrying the gene.

**Testing for Cystic Fibrosis.** Testing for cystic fibrosis is becoming more widespread. It is often offered to couples before pregnancy, as part of genetic counseling. One test available is called *Cystic Fibrosis (CF) Complete Test;* it can identify more than 1000 mutations of the CF gene. This identification process lets doctors offer accurate detection in carriers, which can lead to prenatal counseling and diagnosis.

If both you and your partner carry the CF gene, your baby will have a 25% chance of having cystic fibrosis, even if you have other children who do not have the problem. Your developing baby can be tested during your pregnancy with chorionic villus sampling (see Week 10) around the 10th or 11th week of pregnancy. Amniocentesis (see pages 174–175) may also be used to test the fetus.

If you believe cystic fibrosis is a serious concern or if you have a family history of the disease, talk to your physician about this test.

Screening is recommended for those at higher risk for CF, such as Caucasians, including Ashkenazi Jews. Testing is a personal decision that you and your partner must make based on the information provided to you by your health-care team.

Many couples choose not to have the test because it would not change what they would do during the pregnancy. In addition, they do not want to expose the mother-to-be or the developing fetus to the risks of CVS or amniocentesis.

# Week 13

*Age of Fetus—11 Weeks*

## How Big Is Your Baby?

Your baby is growing rapidly! Its crown-to-rump length is 2½ to 3 inches (6.5 to 7.8cm), and it weighs between ½ and ¾ ounce (13 to 20g). It is about the size of a peach.

## How Big Are You?

Your uterus has grown quite a bit. You can probably feel its upper edge above the pubic bone in the lowest part of your abdomen, about 4 inches (10cm) below your bellybutton. At 12 to 13 weeks, your uterus fills your pelvis and starts growing upward into your abdomen. It feels like a soft, smooth ball.

*Tip for Week 13* When cutting down on caffeine during pregnancy, read labels. More than 200 foods, beverages and over-the-counter medications contain caffeine!

You have probably gained some weight by now. If morning sickness has been a problem and you've had a hard time eating, you may not have gained much weight. As you feel better and as your baby rapidly starts to gain weight, you'll also gain weight.

# How Your Baby Is
# Growing and Developing

Fetal growth is particularly striking from now through about 24 weeks of pregnancy. The baby has doubled in length since the 7th week. Changes in fetal weight have also been tremendous during the last 8 to 10 weeks of your pregnancy.

One interesting change is the relative slowdown in the growth of your baby's head compared to the rest of its body. In week 13, the head is about half the crown-to-rump length. By week 21, the head is about ⅓ of the baby's body. At birth, your baby's head is only ¼ the size of its body. Fetal body growth accelerates as fetal head growth slows.

Your baby's face is beginning to look more humanlike. Eyes, which started out on the side of the head, move closer together on the face. The ears come to lie in their normal position on the sides of the head. External genitalia have developed enough so a male can be distinguished from a female if examined outside the womb.

Intestines initially develop within a large swelling in the umbilical cord outside the fetal body. About this time, they withdraw into the fetal abdominal cavity. If this doesn't occur and the intestines remain outside the fetal abdomen at birth, a condition called an *omphalocele* occurs. It is rare (occurs in 1 of 10,000 births). The condition can usually be repaired with surgery, and babies do well afterward.

## Changes in You

You are losing your waist! Clothing fits snugly. It's time to start wearing loose-fitting garments.

### ✺ *Stretch Marks*
Stretch marks, called *striae distensae*, are seen often, and in varying degrees, during pregnancy. They may appear early or later in your pregnancy, usually on the abdomen, breasts, and hips or buttocks. After pregnancy, they may fade to the same color as the rest of your skin, but they won't go away. To help avoid the occurrence of stretch marks, gain

weight slowly and steadily. Any large increases in weight can cause stretch marks to appear more readily.

If you use steroid creams, such as hydrocortisone or topicort, to treat stretch marks during pregnancy, you absorb some of the steroid into your system. The substance can then pass to your developing baby. *Don't use steroid creams during pregnancy without first checking with your doctor!*

**Some Actions to Take.** Although the formation of stretch marks may occur during pregnancy, there are some things you can do that may help reduce their severity. Try the following.

- Drink lots of water, and eat healthy foods. Foods high in antioxidants—fruits and vegetables that are bright red, orange or yellow—provide nutrients essential for tissue repair and healing.
- Maintain skin's elasticity by eating adequate amounts of protein and smaller amounts of fats. Flaxseed, flaxseed oil, fish and fish oils are all good sources. Be careful with your fish consumption—you don't want to eat *too* much. See the discussion of fish in Week 26.
- Stay out of the sun!
- Keep up with your exercise program.
- Ask your doctor about using creams with alpha-hydroxy acid, citric acid or lactic acid. Some of these creams and lotions improve the quality of the skin's elastic fibers.

**Treatment after Pregnancy.** Many women want to know what they can do for the stretch marks they develop during pregnancy. After pregnancy, you have quite a few options for treatment. Some new treatments being used today seem to help a lot.

The use of Retin-A or Renova, in combination with glycolic acid, has been shown to be fairly effective. Prescriptions are needed for Retin-A and Renova; you can get glycolic acid from your dermatologist. Cellex-C, with glycolic acid, also improves the appearance of stretch marks. An over-the-counter cream has successfully been used to treat stretch marks. It is called StriVectin-SD and is available directly from the manufacturer. See the Resource section, page 437.

The most effective treatment is laser treatment, but it can be very costly. It is often done in combination with the medication methods described above. With *Nd:YAG laser treatment,* beams of laser light are directed into the collagen in the second layer of skin to help smooth wrinkles. *Pulsed dye laser treatment* can improve new and old stretch marks. However, lasers don't work for everyone.

Massage has proved effective—it increases blood flow to the area to stimulate the healing process and gets rid of dead surface cells. Various creams may also help. Discuss these treatments with your doctor if your stretch marks bother you.

### ∾ *Changes in Your Breasts*

You have probably noticed your breasts are changing. (See the illustration on page 148.) The mammary gland (another name for the breast) got its name from the Latin term for breast—*mamma.*

Your breast is made up of glands, connective tissue to provide support and fatty tissue to provide protection. Milk-producing sacs connect with the ducts leading to the nipple.

Before pregnancy, the average breast weighs about 7 ounces (200g). During pregnancy, breasts increase in size and weight. Near the end of pregnancy, each breast may weigh 14 to 28 ounces (400 to 800g). During nursing, each breast may weigh 28 ounces (800g) or more.

*Dad Tip* Ask the doctor if there is some exercise you can do together on a regular basis during pregnancy, such as walking, swimming or playing golf or tennis.

The size and shape of women's breasts vary greatly. Breast tissue usually projects under the arm. Glands that make up the breast open into ducts in the nipple. Each nipple contains nerve endings, muscle fibers, sebaceous glands, sweat glands and about 20 milk ducts.

The nipple is surrounded by the *areola,* a circular, pigmented area. During pregnancy, the areola darkens and grows larger. A darkened areola may act as a visual signal for the breastfeeding infant.

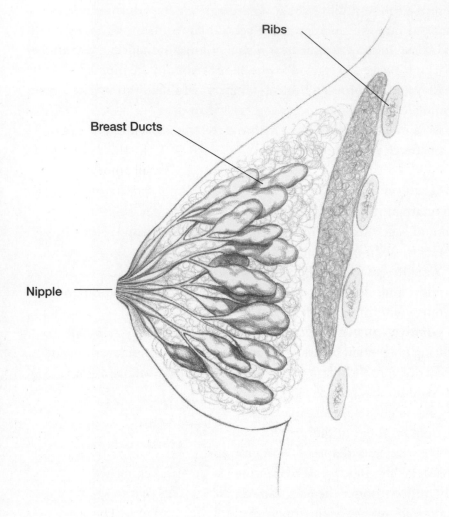

Development of the maternal breast by end of the first trimester (13 weeks of pregnancy).

Breasts undergo many changes during pregnancy. In the early weeks, a common symptom of pregnancy is tingling or soreness of the breasts. After about 8 weeks of pregnancy, your breasts may grow larger and become nodular or lumpy as glands and ducts inside the breasts grow and develop. As your breasts change during pregnancy, you may notice veins appear just beneath the skin.

During the second trimester, a thin yellow fluid called *colostrum* begins to form. It can sometimes be expressed from the nipple by gentle massage. If your breasts have grown, you may notice stretch marks on your breasts similar to those on your abdomen.

Mammary glands begin to develop in the 6-week-old embryo. By the time of birth, milk ducts are present. After birth, a newborn's breasts may be swollen and may even secrete a small amount of milk. This can occur in both male and female infants and is caused by the secretion of estrogen.

## How Your Actions Affect Your Baby's Development

### ᔗ *Working during Pregnancy*

Today, many women work outside the home, and many continue to work during pregnancy. It is common for employers and patients to ask doctors about work and pregnancy.

*"Is it safe to work while I'm pregnant?"*

*"Can I work my entire pregnancy?"*

*"Am I in danger of harming my baby if I work?"*

More than half of all women work or are seeking work. In the United States, more than 1 million babies are born to women who have been employed at some time during pregnancy. These women have understandable concerns about safety and occupational health.

**Legislation that May Affect You.** The *U.S. Pregnancy Discrimination Act* prohibits job discrimination on the basis of pregnancy or childbirth. It states pregnancy and related conditions should be treated the same as any other disability or medical condition. A doctor may be asked to certify that a pregnant woman can work without endangering herself or her pregnancy. Pregnancy-related disability comes from any of the following:

- the pregnancy itself
- complications of pregnancy, such as pre-eclampsia, premature labor or other medical problems
- job situations, such as standing for long periods or exposure to chemicals, inhalants, gases, solvents or radiation

The *Family and Medical Leave Act* was passed in 1993. If you have worked for your present employer for at least 1 year, the law allows a new parent (man or woman) to take up to 12 weeks of unpaid leave in any 12-month period for the birth of a baby. To be eligible, you must work at your job for at least 1250 hours a year (about 60% of a normal 40-hour work week). In addition, if *both parents* work for the same employer, only a *total* of 12 weeks off *between them* is allowed. This act applies only to companies that employ 50 or more people within a 75-mile radius. States may allow an employer to deny job restoration to employees in the top 10% compensation bracket.

Any time taken off *before* the birth of a baby is counted toward the 12 weeks a person is entitled to in any given year. (Taking time before the birth might be necessary in a situation in which a woman is having health/medical problems and needs time off or if her partner must take time off to help her.) Leave may be taken intermittently or all at the same time.

For further information on the Family Medical Leave Act, call their hotline at 800-522-0925.

**State or Provincial Laws and Parental Leave.** About half the states in the United States have passed state legislation that deals with parental leave. Some states provide disability insurance if you have to leave work because of pregnancy or birth.

In Canada, unpaid parental leave is available. The length of time you may take off from work varies from province to province.

State laws about parental leave differ, so check with your state labor office or consult the personnel director in your company's human resources department. A summary of state laws on family leave is also available from:

The Women's Bureau Publications
U.S. Department of Labor
Box EX
200 Constitution Avenue, NW
Washington, D.C. 20210

In Canada, contact the Human Resources office for information. Call the Human Resources Tele-Center of Canada at (416) 730-1211 or (800) 227-9914.

**Some Risks If You Work during Pregnancy.** It may be difficult to know the exact risk of a particular job. In most cases, we don't have enough information to know all the specific substances that can harm a developing baby.

The goal is to minimize the risk to the mother and baby while still enabling a woman to work. A normal woman with a normal job should be able to work throughout her pregnancy. However, she may need to modify her job somewhat. For example, she may need to spend less time standing. Studies show that women who stand in the same position for prolonged periods are more likely to give birth to premature babies and babies with low birthweight.

Work with your doctor and your employer. If problems arise, such as premature labor or bleeding, listen to your doctor. If bed rest at home is suggested, follow that advice. As your pregnancy progresses, you may have to work fewer hours or do lighter work. Be flexible. It doesn't help you or your baby if you wear yourself out and make complications of pregnancy worse.

Take Care of Yourself If You Work.  If you work, you should take some precautions for you and your growing baby.

• Don't participate in anything that is dangerous for you or baby.
• Don't stand for long periods of time.
• Sit up straight at your desk.
• Place a low footstool under your desk to rest your feet on.
• Rest at breaks and during lunch.
• Get up and walk a little every 30 minutes. Going to the bathroom may be a good reason to get up and move around.
• Don't wear clothes that are tight around the waist, especially if you sit most of the day.
• Drink lots of water.
• Listen to soothing music, if you can.
• Bring healthy lunch and snack foods to help you keep tabs on your calorie intake. Fast foods are loaded with empty calories.
• Try to keep stress to a minimum.
• Don't take on new projects or ones that demand a lot of time and attention.

## Your Nutrition

Caffeine is a central-nervous-system stimulant found in many beverages and foods, including coffee, tea, cola drinks and chocolate. Research shows that you may be more sensitive to caffeine during pregnancy. The stimulant is also found in some medications, such as diet aids and headache medications. For over 20 years, the Food and Drug Administration (FDA) has recommended that pregnant women avoid caffeine. To date, no benefits to you or your unborn baby have been found with its use.

---

### A Caffeine Warning

High levels of caffeine in a pregnant woman—400mg a day—may affect a baby's developing respiratory system. One study showed this exposure before birth might be linked to sudden infant death syndrome (SIDS).

High intake of caffeine has been associated with a decreased birth-weight and a smaller head size in newborns. Some researchers also believe there is an association between caffeine use and miscarriage, stillbirth and premature labor.

Cut down on caffeine, or eliminate it from your diet. It crosses the placenta to the baby. It can affect your calcium metabolism and your baby's, too. If you're jittery, your baby may suffer from the same effects. Increased caffeine consumption may increase the chances of breathing problems in a newborn. Caffeine passes to breast milk, which can cause irritability and sleeplessness in a breastfed baby. An infant metabolizes caffeine slower than an adult, and caffeine can collect in the infant.

Effects of caffeine on you during pregnancy may include irritability, headaches, stomach upset, sleeplessness and jitters. Smoking may compound the stimulant effect of caffeine.

Eliminate caffeine from your diet, or limit the amount of caffeine you consume. Read labels on over-the-counter medications for caffeine. Most professionals agree that up to two cups *(not mugs)* of regular coffee or its equivalent each day is probably OK. That's less than 200mg a day.

It may be a good idea to eliminate as much caffeine as you can from your diet. It's healthier for your baby, and you'll probably feel better, too. The list below details the amounts of caffeine from various sources:

- coffee, 5 ounces—from 60 to 140mg and higher
- tea, 5 ounces—from 30 to 65mg
- baking chocolate, 1 ounce—25mg
- chocolate candy, 1 ounce—6mg
- soft drinks, 12 ounces—from 35 to 55mg
- pain relief tablets, standard dose—40mg
- allergy and cold remedies, standard dose—25mg

## You Should Also Know

### ◇ *Lyme Disease*

Lyme disease refers to an infection transmitted to humans by ticks. There are several stages of the illness. About 80% of those bitten have a skin lesion with a distinctive look, called a *bull's eye*. There may be flulike symptoms. After 4 to 6 weeks, symptoms may become more serious.

At the beginning of the illness, blood tests may not diagnose Lyme disease. A blood test done later in the illness can establish the diagnosis.

We know Lyme disease can cross the placenta. However, at this time we don't know if it is dangerous to the baby. Researchers are studying the situation.

Treatment for Lyme disease requires long-term antibiotic therapy and sometimes intravenous antibiotic therapy. Many medications used to treat Lyme disease are safe to use during pregnancy.

Avoid exposure to Lyme disease, if possible. Stay out of areas known to have ticks, especially heavily wooded areas. If you can't avoid these areas, wear long-sleeved shirts, long pants, a hat or scarf, socks and boots or closed shoes. Be sure to check your hair when you come in; ticks often attach themselves there. Check your clothing to make sure no ticks remain in folds, cuffs or pockets.

# Week 14

*Age of Fetus—12 Weeks*

## How Big Is Your Baby?

The crown-to-rump length is 3¼ to 4 inches (8 to 9.3cm). Your baby is about the size of your fist and weighs almost 1 ounce (25g).

## How Big Are You?

Maternity clothes may be a "must" by now. Some women try to get by for a while by not buttoning or zipping their pants all the way or by using rubber bands or safety pins to increase the size of their waistbands. Others wear their partner's clothing, but that usually works for only a short time. You're going to get even bigger. You'll enjoy your pregnancy more and feel better with clothing that fits comfortably and provides you room to grow.

How your body responds to this growth is influenced by any previous pregnancies and the changes your body experienced then. Your skin and muscles stretched to accommodate your uterus, placenta and baby, and that changed them permanently. Skin and muscles may give way faster to accommodate your growing uterus and baby. This means you may show sooner and feel bigger.

# How Your Baby Is
# Growing and Developing

As you can see in the illustration on the opposite page, by this week your baby's ears have moved from the neck to the sides of the head. Eyes have been moving gradually from the side of the head to the front of the face. The neck continues to get longer, and the chin no longer rests on the chest.

> ⋰⋱
>
> If you enjoy listening to your baby's heartbeat, devices are now available so you can listen at home! Some people believe this activity helps a couple bond with their child. If you are interested in a use-at-home doppler device, check with your doctor at an office visit. Or check out these devices on the Internet. See the Resource section, page 436.

Sexual development continues. It is becoming easier to determine male from female by looking at external genitalia, which are more developed.

## Changes in You

### ∽ *Skin Tags and Moles*

Pregnancy can make skin tags and moles change and grow. Skin tags are small tags of skin that may appear for the first time or may grow larger during pregnancy. Moles may appear for the first time during pregnancy, or existing moles may grow larger and darken. If a mole changes, it must be checked. If you notice any change, show it to your doctor!

### ∽ *Do You Have Hemorrhoids?*

*Hemorrhoids*, dilated blood vessels around or inside the anus, are a common problem during or following pregnancy. They are caused during pregnancy by the decreased blood flow in the area around the uterus and the pelvis because of the weight of the uterus, causing congestion or blockage of circulation. Hemorrhoids may worsen toward the end of pregnancy. They may also get worse with each succeeding pregnancy.

Hemorrhoid treatment includes avoiding constipation by eating adequate amounts of fiber and drinking lots of fluid. You may avoid

Your baby continues to change. Ears and eyes move to a more normal position by this week.

hemorrhoids by using stool softeners. Other measures include sitz baths and suppository medications. You can buy suppositories without a prescription. Rarely, hemorrhoids are treated during pregnancy with surgery.

After pregnancy, hemorrhoids usually improve, but they may not go away completely. You can use the treatment methods mentioned above when pregnancy is over.

If hemorrhoids cause you a great deal of discomfort, discuss it with your doctor. He or she will know what treatment method is best for you.

Relieving the Discomfort of Hemorrhoids.  If hemorrhoids are a problem, try any of the following suggestions for relief.

* Rest at least 1 hour every day with your feet and hips elevated.
* Lie with your legs elevated and knees slightly bent (Sims position) when you sleep at night.
* Eat adequate amounts of fiber, and drink lots of fluid.
* Take warm (not hot) baths for relief.
* Suppository medications, available without a prescription, may help.
* Apply ice packs, or cotton balls soaked in witch hazel, to the affected area.
* Don't sit or stand for long periods.

## How Your Actions Affect Your Baby's Development

### ⌁ X-Rays, CT Scans and MRIs during Pregnancy

Some women are concerned about tests that use radiation during pregnancy. Can these tests hurt the baby? Can you have them at any time in pregnancy?

No known amount of radiation is safe for a developing baby. Dangers to your baby include an increased risk of mutations and an increased risk of cancer later in life. Some doctors believe the only safe amount of X-ray during pregnancy is none.

Researchers have become more aware of the potential dangers of radiation to a developing fetus. At present, they believe the fetus is at greatest risk between 8 and 15 weeks gestation (between the fetal age of 6 weeks and 13 weeks).

Problems, such as pneumonia or appendicitis, can and do occur in pregnant women and may require an X-ray for proper diagnosis and treatment. Discuss the need for X-rays with your doctor. It is your responsibility to let your doctor and others involved in your care know you are pregnant or may be pregnant before you undergo any medical test. It's easier to deal with the questions of safety and risk *before* a test is performed.

If you have an X-ray or series of X-rays, then discover you are pregnant, ask your doctor about the possible risk to your baby. He or she will be able to advise you.

Computerized tomographic scans, also called *CT scans,* are a form of specialized X-ray. This technique combines X-ray with computer analysis. Many researchers believe the amount of radiation received by a fetus from a CT scan is much lower than that received from a regular X-ray. However, these tests should be undertaken with caution until we know more about the effects even this small amount of radiation has on a developing fetus.

Magnetic resonance imaging, also called *MRI,* is another diagnostic tool widely used today. At this time, no harmful effects in pregnancy have been reported from the use of MRI. However, it is probably best to avoid MRI during the first trimester of pregnancy.

### ‿ Dental Care

Don't avoid your dentist or ignore your teeth while you're pregnant. See your dentist at least once during pregnancy. Tell your dentist you're pregnant. If you need dental work, postpone it until after the first 12 weeks, if possible. You may not be able to wait if you have an infection. An untreated infection could be harmful to you and your baby.

Antibiotics or pain medications may be necessary. If you need medication, consult your physician before taking anything. Many antibiotics and pain medications are OK to take during pregnancy.

Be careful with regard to anesthesia for dental work during pregnancy. Local anesthesia is OK. Avoid gas and general anesthesia when possible. If general anesthesia is necessary, make sure an experienced anesthesiologist who knows you are pregnant administers it.

**Dental Emergencies.** Dental emergencies do occur. Emergencies you might face include root canal, tooth extraction, a large cavity, an abscessed tooth or problems resulting from an accident or injury. Any of these emergencies can occur during pregnancy. A serious dental problem must be treated. Problems that could result from not treating it are more serious than the risks you might be exposed to with treatment.

*Tip for Week 14* If you must have dental work or diagnostic tests, tell your dentist or your physician you are pregnant so they can take extra care with you. It may be helpful for your dentist and doctor to talk before any decisions are made.

Dental X-rays are sometimes necessary and can be done during pregnancy. Your abdomen must be shielded with a lead apron before X-rays are taken. If possible, wait until after the end of the first trimester to have any dental work done.

## Your Nutrition

Being overweight when pregnancy begins may present special problems for you. Your doctor may advise you to gain less weight than the average 25 to 35 pounds recommended for a normal-weight woman. You will probably have to choose lower-calorie, lower-fat foods to eat. A visit with a nutritionist may be necessary to help you develop a healthful food plan. You will be advised *not* to diet during pregnancy.

Extra weight may cause more problems, including gestational diabetes or high blood pressure. Backaches, varicose veins and fatigue may also be more troublesome. If you gain too much weight during your pregnancy—beyond the amount of weight your physician recommends—you may have a greater chance of needing a Cesarean delivery.

If you're overweight, your doctor may want to see you more often during your pregnancy. Ultrasound may be needed to help establish your due date because it's harder to determine the position and size of the fetus. Extra layers of abdominal fat may make manual examination difficult. Your doctor may order tests for gestational diabetes. Other diagnostic tests may also be necessary as your due date nears.

> **Dad Tip** If you go out of town, call your partner at least once every day. Let her know you are thinking about her and the baby.

## You Should Also Know

### ✄ *Pregnancy in the Military*

Are you pregnant and currently on active duty in the military? If you are, you have made the decision to stay in the Armed Forces. Before 1972, if you were on active duty and became pregnant, you were automatically separated from the military, whether you wanted to be or not!

Today, if you want to stay in the service, you can. Each branch of the service has particular policies regarding pregnancy. Below is a summary of those policies for the Army, Navy, Air Force, Marines and Coast Guard.

**Army Policies.** During pregnancy, you are exempt from body composition and fitness testing. You cannot be deployed overseas. At 20 weeks, you are required to stand at parade rest or attention for no longer than 15 minutes. At 28 weeks, your work week is limited to 40 hours a week, 8 hours a day.

**Navy Policies.** During pregnancy, you are exempt from body composition and fitness testing. You are not allowed to serve on a ship after

20 weeks of pregnancy. You are limited to serving duty in places within 6 hours of medical care. Your work week is limited to 40 hours, and you are required to stand at parade rest or attention for no longer than 20 minutes.

**Air Force Policies.** During pregnancy, you are exempt from body composition and fitness testing. Restrictions are based on your work environment. If you are assigned to an area without OB care, your assignment will be curtailed by week 24.

**Marine Corps Policies.** You will be on full-duty status until a medical doctor certifies that full duty is not medically advised. You may not participate in contingency operations nor may you be deployed aboard a Navy vessel. Flight personnel are grounded, unless cleared by a medical waiver. If a medical doctor deems you are unfit for physical training or you cannot stand in formation, you will be excused from these activities. However, you will remain available for worldwide assignments.

Pregnant Marines will not be detached from Hawaii after their 6th month of pregnancy. If serving aboard a ship, a pregnant woman will be reassigned at the first opportunity but no later than by 20 weeks.

**U.S. Coast Guard.** During pregnancy, you are exempt from body composition and fitness testing. After 28 weeks of pregnancy, your work week will be limited to 40 hours. You will not be assigned overseas. Other duty restrictions are based on your job; however, you will not be assigned to any rescue-swimmer duties during your pregnancy.

You may not be deployed from the 20th week of your pregnancy through 6 months postpartum. You will not be assigned to any flight duties after your second trimester (26 weeks), and you are limited to serving duty in places within 3 hours of medical care.

**Some General Cautions.** We know that women who get pregnant while they are on active duty face many challenges. The pressure to meet military body-weight standards can have an effect on your health; that's the reason these requirements are relaxed during pregnancy. Work hard to eat healthy foods so your iron stores and folic-acid levels are adequate. Examine your job for any hazards you may be exposed to, such as standing for prolonged periods, heavy lifting and exposure to toxic chemicals. Before receiving any vaccinations or inoc-ulations, discuss them with your doctor. All of these factors can impact on your pregnancy.

If you are concerned about any of the above, discuss it with a supe-rior. Changes beyond those described above may have to be made.

### ᠅ *Taking Others to Your Doctor Visits*

Take your partner with you to as many prenatal appointments as pos-sible. It's nice for your partner and doctor to meet before labor begins. Maybe your mother or the other grandmother-to-be would like to go with you to hear their grandchild's heartbeat. Or you may want to take a tape recorder and record the heartbeat for others to hear. Things have changed since your mother carried you; many grandmothers-to-be enjoy this type of visit.

It's a good idea to wait until you have heard your baby's heartbeat before bringing other people. You don't always hear it the first time, and this can be frustrating and disappointing.

Bringing Children to an Office Visit. Some women bring their chil-dren with them to a prenatal appointment. Most office personnel don't mind if you bring your children with you occasionally. They un-derstand it may not always be possible to find someone to watch your children. However, if you are having problems or have a lot to discuss with your doctor, don't bring your child or children.

If a child is sick, has just gotten over chicken pox or is getting a cold, leave him or her at home. Don't expose everyone else in the waiting room.

Some women like to bring one child at a time to a visit if they have more than one. That makes it special for the expectant mom and for them. Crying or complaining children can create a difficult situation, however, so ask your doctor when it's good to bring family members with you before you come in with them.

# Week 15

*Age of Fetus—13 Weeks*

## How Big Is Your Baby?

The fetal crown-to-rump length by this week of pregnancy is 4 to 4½ inches (9.3 to 10.3cm). The fetus weighs about 1¾ ounces (50g). It's close to the size of a softball.

## How Big Are You?

You can easily tell you're pregnant by the changes in your lower abdomen, which change the way your clothes fit. You may be able to feel your uterus about 3 or 4 inches (7.6 to 10cm) below your bellybutton (also called the *umbilicus* or *navel*).

Your pregnancy may not be obvious to other people when you wear regular street clothes. But it may become obvious if you start wearing maternity clothes or put on a swimming suit.

**Dad Tip** When you need to be away or out of touch, ask friends and family members to check on your partner and to be available to help out.

# How Your Baby Is
# Growing and Developing

It's still a little early to feel movement, although you should feel your baby move in the next few weeks!

Your baby's rapid growth continues. Its skin is thin. At this point in its development, you can see blood vessels through the skin. Fine hair, called *lanugo hair,* covers the baby's body.

By this time, your baby may be sucking its thumb. This has been seen with ultrasound examination. Eyes continue to move to the front of the face but are still widely separated.

Ears continue to develop externally. As you can see in the illustration on page 166, they now look more like normal ears. In fact, your baby looks more human with each passing day.

Bones that have already formed are getting harder and retaining calcium (ossifying) rapidly. If an X-ray were done at this time, the baby's skeleton would be visible.

### ✑ Alpha-fetoprotein Testing

As your baby grows inside you, it produces *alpha-fetoprotein.* This protein is found in increasing amounts in the amniotic fluid. Some alpha-fetoprotein crosses fetal membranes and enters your circulation. It is possible to measure the amount of alpha-fetoprotein by drawing your blood.

The level of this protein can be meaningful during pregnancy. An alpha-fetoprotein (AFP) test is usually done between 16 and 18 weeks of gestation. The timing of the test is important and must be correlated to the gestational age of your pregnancy and to your weight.

An elevated level of alpha-fetoprotein can indicate problems with the fetus, such as spina bifida (spinal-cord problem) or anencephaly (serious central-nervous-system defect). Some researchers have even found an association between a low level of alpha-fetoprotein and Down syndrome. In the past, amniocentesis was the only way to test for Down syndrome.

By week 15 of pregnancy (fetal age—13 weeks), your baby may suck its thumb. Eyes are at the front of the face but are still widely separated.

If the level of alpha-fetoprotein is abnormal, a careful ultrasound examination is done to look for spina bifida, anencephaly and Down syndrome. This ultrasound may help determine how far along in pregnancy you are.

The AFP test is not done on all pregnant women, although it is required in some states. It is not used routinely in Canada. If the test isn't offered to you, ask about it. There is relatively little risk, and it tells your doctor how your fetus is growing and developing.

## Changes in You

### ✑ *Pap Smears during Pregnancy*

During your first prenatal visit, you probably had a Pap smear; one is usually done at the beginning of pregnancy. By now, the result is back, and you have discussed it with your doctor, particularly if it was abnormal.

The Pap smear (short for *Papanicolaou smear*) is a screening test done at the time of a pelvic exam. It identifies cancerous or precancerous cells coming from the cervix, which is located at the top of the vagina. This test has contributed to a significant decrease in mortality from cervical cancer because of early detection and treatment.

**An Abnormal Pap Smear.** Pap smears are screening tests. If you have an abnormal Pap smear, your doctor must verify the findings and decide on treatment. Continue to get checked as your doctor advises.

An abnormal Pap smear during pregnancy must be handled individually. When abnormal cells are "not too bad" (premalignant or not as serious), it may be possible to watch them during pregnancy with colposcopy or Pap smears; biopsies are not usually done at this time. The cervix bleeds easily during pregnancy because of changes in circulation. This situation must be handled carefully.

Women who deliver vaginally may see a change in abnormal Pap smears. One study showed that 60% of a group of women who were diagnosed with high-grade squamous intra-epithelial lesions in the cervix before giving birth had normal Pap smears after their baby was born.

**What Is the Next Step?** If your doctor is concerned, he or she may do a *colposcopy*. Colposcopy is a procedure that uses an instrument similar to a pair of binoculars or a microscope to look at the cervix. This enables your doctor to see where abnormal areas are so biopsies can be taken after pregnancy. Most obstetricians/gynecologists can do this procedure in the office.

A biopsy provides a better idea of the nature and extent of the problem. If there is a possibility that abnormal cells could spread to other parts of the body, a *cone biopsy* may need to be done. A cone biopsy precisely determines the extent of more severe disease and removes abnormal tissue. This surgery is done with anesthesia but is not usually performed during pregnancy.

**Treating Abnormal Cells.** There are several ways to treat abnormal cells on the cervix, but most treatment methods cannot be performed during pregnancy. These treatments include surgically removing the abnormal spot (if it can be seen), electric cautery to remove or to "burn" small abnormal spots, cryocautery to freeze small lesions, laser treatment to destroy abnormal areas on the cervix and cone biopsy for more involved lesions.

## How Your Actions Affect Your Baby's Development

### ～ *Change Sleeping Positions Now*

Some women have questions and concerns about their sleeping positions and sleep habits while they're pregnant. Some want to know if they can sleep on their stomachs. Others want to know if they should stop sleeping on their waterbed. (It's OK to continue to sleep on a waterbed.)

As you grow larger during pregnancy, finding comfortable sleeping positions will become more difficult. Don't lie on your back when you sleep. As your uterus gets larger, lying on your back can place the uterus on top of important blood vessels (the aorta and the inferior vena cava) that run down the back of your abdomen. This can decrease circulation to your baby and parts of your body. Some pregnant women also find it harder to breathe when lying on their backs.

*Tip for Week 15* Start now to learn to sleep on your side; it will pay off later as you get bigger. Sometimes it helps to use a few extra pillows. Put one behind you so if you roll onto your back, you won't lie flat. Put another pillow between your legs, or rest your "top" leg on a pillow. Some manufacturers make a "pregnancy pillow" that supports your entire body.

Lying on your stomach puts extra pressure on your growing uterus. This is another reason to learn to sleep on your side. For some women, their favorite thing after delivery is to be able to sleep on their stomach again!

## Your Nutrition

About this time, you'll probably need to start adding an extra 300 calories to your meal plan to meet the needs of your growing fetus and your changing body. Below are some choices of extra food for one day to get those 300 calories. Be careful—300 calories is *not* a lot of food.

- Choice 1—2 thin slices pork, ½ cup cabbage, 1 carrot
- Choice 2—½ cup cooked brown rice, ¾ cup strawberries, 1 cup orange juice, 1 slice fresh pineapple
- Choice 3—4½-ounce salmon steak, 1 cup asparagus, 2 cups Romaine lettuce
- Choice 4—1 cup cooked pasta, 1 slice fresh tomato, 1 cup 1% milk, ½ cup cooked green beans, ¼ cantaloupe
- Choice 5—1 container of yogurt, 1 medium apple

## You Should Also Know

### ~ Getting a Good Night's Sleep

Sleeping soundly may be difficult for you now or later in pregnancy. Try some of the following suggestions to ensure a restful sleep.

- Go to bed and wake up at the same time each day.
- Don't drink too much fluid at night. Slow down after 6pm so you don't have to get up to go to the bathroom all night long.
- Avoid caffeine after late afternoon.
- Get regular exercise.
- Sleep in a cool bedroom; 70F (21.1C) is about the highest temperature for comfortable sleeping.
- If you experience heartburn at night, sleep propped up.

You may experience shortness of breath due to your enlarging abdomen, which can interfere with your sleep. If you do, try lying on your left side. Prop up your head and shoulders with extra pillows. If this measure doesn't provide relief, light exercise followed by a warm shower or a soak in a warm (not hot) tub and a glass of warm milk might be beneficial. If you just can't get comfortable in bed, try sleeping partially sitting up in a recliner.

---

### Were You Hard to Live with When You Had Morning Sickness?

If you suffered with morning sickness and you're starting to feel better, you may want to take stock of your relationship with your partner and others close to you. Were you hard to get along with when you weren't feeling good? Your partner needs your support as your pregnancy progresses, just as you need his support. You may need to make an effort to work very hard at treating each other well—you're both in this together!

# Week 16

*Age of Fetus—14 Weeks*

## How Big Is Your Baby?

The crown-to-rump length of your baby by this week is 4⅓ to 4⅔ inches (10.8 to 11.6cm). Weight is about 2¾ ounces (80g).

## How Big Are You?

As your baby grows, your uterus and placenta are also growing. Six weeks ago, your uterus weighed about 5 ounces (140g). Today, it weighs about 8¾ ounces (250g). The amount of amniotic fluid around the baby is also increasing. There is now about 7½ ounces (250ml) of fluid. You can easily feel your uterus about 3 inches (7.6cm) below your bellybutton.

## How Your Baby Is
## Growing and Developing

Fine lanugo hair covers your baby's head. The umbilical cord is attached to the abdomen; this attachment has moved lower on the body of the fetus.

Fingernails are well formed. The illustration on the opposite page shows soft hair, called *lanugo,* beginning to grow. At this stage, legs are longer than arms, and arms and legs are moving. You can see this movement during an ultrasound examination. You may also be able to feel your baby move at this point in your pregnancy.

Many women describe feelings of movement as a "gas bubble" or "fluttering." Often, it's something you have noticed for a few days or more, but you didn't realize what you were feeling. Then you realize you're feeling the baby moving inside you!

## Changes in You

### ❧ Quickening

If you haven't felt your baby move yet, don't worry. Fetal movement, also called *quickening*, is usually felt between 16 and 20 weeks of pregnancy. The time is different for every woman. It can also be different from one pregnancy to another. One baby may be more active than another and move more. The size of the baby or the number of fetuses can also affect what you feel.

### ❧ Triple-Screen Test

Tests are now available that go beyond alpha-fetoprotein testing in helping your doctor determine if you might be carrying a child with Down syndrome. With the triple-screen test, your alpha-fetoprotein level is checked, along with the amounts of human chorionic gonadotropin (HCG) and unconjugated estriol (a form of estrogen produced by the placenta).

The levels of these three chemicals in your blood may indicate an increased chance your baby has Down syndrome. For older mothers, the detection rate of the problem is better than 60%, with a false-positive rate of nearly 25%.

If you have an abnormal result with a triple-screen test, an ultrasound and amniocentesis may be recommended. An elevated alpha-fetoprotein level can indicate an increased risk of a neural-tube defect (such as spina bifida). HCG and estriol are normal in this case.

By this week, soft lanugo hair covers the baby's body and head.

These blood tests are used to find *possible* problems. They are *screening* tests. A *diagnostic* test will usually be done to confirm any diagnosis.

## How Your Actions
## Affect Your Baby's Development

### ~ Amniocentesis

If it is necessary, an amniocentesis test is usually performed for prenatal evaluation around 16 to 18 weeks of pregnancy. By this point, your uterus is large enough and there is enough fluid surrounding the baby to make the test possible. Doing the procedure at this time allows a woman enough time to make decisions about terminating the pregnancy, if that is what she desires.

With amniocentesis, ultrasound is used to locate a pocket of fluid where the fetus and placenta are not in the way. The part of the abdomen above the uterus is cleaned. Skin is numbed, and a needle is passed through the abdominal wall into the uterus. Fluid is withdrawn from the amniotic cavity (area around the baby) with a syringe. About 1 ounce (30ml) of amniotic fluid is needed to perform various tests.

Fetal cells that float in the amniotic fluid can be grown in cultures and can be used to identify fetal abnormalities. We know of more than 400 abnormalities a child can be born with—amniocentesis identifies about 40 (10%) of them, including the following:

- chromosomal problems, particularly Down syndrome
- fetal sex, if sex-specific problems such as hemophilia or Duchenne muscular dystrophy must be identified
- skeletal diseases, such as osteogenesis imperfecta
- fetal infections, such as herpes or rubella
- central-nervous-system diseases, such as anencephaly
- hematologic (blood) diseases, such as erythroblastosis fetalis
- inborn errors of metabolism (chemical problems or deficiencies of enzymes), such as cystinuria or maple-syrup-urine disease

Risks from amniocentesis include injury to the fetus, placenta or umbilical cord, infection, miscarriage or premature labor. The use of ultrasound to guide the needle helps avoid complications but doesn't eliminate all risk. There can be bleeding from the fetus to the mother, which can be a problem because fetal and maternal blood are separate and may be different types. This is a particular risk to an Rh-negative mother carrying an Rh-positive baby (see the discussion on page 179). This type of bleeding can cause isoimmunization. An Rh-negative woman should receive RhoGAM at the time of amniocentesis to prevent isoimmunization.

Fetal loss from amniocentesis complications is estimated to be less than 3%. The procedure should be done only by someone who has experience doing it.

### ꙮ *Are You an Older Mother-to-Be?*

More women every year are getting pregnant in their 30s or 40s. If you waited to start a family, you are not alone. In the 1980s, births to women in the 35- to 44-year-old age range nearly doubled. First births to women in their 30s in 1990 accounted for about 25% of all births to women in that age group. Every day in the United States, nearly 200 women 35 or older give birth to their first child. Researchers believe that in the 21st century, nearly one in every 10 babies will be born to a mother aged 35 or older.

When you are older, your partner may also be older. You may have married late or you may be in a second marriage and are starting a family together. Some couples have experienced infertility and do not achieve a pregnancy until they have gone through a major workup and testing or even surgery. Or you may be a single mother who has chosen donor insemination to achieve pregnancy.

Today, many healthcare professionals gauge pregnancy risk by the pregnant woman's health status, not her age. Pre-existing medical conditions are the most significant indicator of a woman's well-being during pregnancy. For example, a healthy 39-year-old is less likely to develop pregnancy problems than a woman in her 20s who suffers from diabetes. A woman's fitness can have a greater effect on her pregnancy than her age.

Most women who become pregnant in their 30s and 40s are in good health. A woman in good physical condition who has been exercising regularly may go through pregnancy as easily as a woman 15 to 20 years younger. An exception—women in a first pregnancy who are over 40 may encounter more complications than women the same age who have previously had children. But most healthy women will have a safe delivery.

Some health problems are age related—the risk of developing a condition increases with age. High blood pressure and some forms of diabetes are age related. You may not know you have these conditions unless you see your doctor regularly. Either condition can complicate a pregnancy and should be brought under control before pregnancy, if possible.

**Genetic Counseling May Be a Wise Choice.** If either you or your partner is over 35, genetic counseling may be recommended; this can raise many questions. The risk of chromosome abnormalities exceeds 5% for this age group. The father's age can also impact on a pregnancy.

Genetic counseling brings together a couple and professionals who are trained to deal with the questions and problems associated with the occurrence, or risk of occurrence, of a genetic problem. With genetic counseling, information about human genetics is applied to a particular couple's situation. Information is interpreted so the couple can understand it and make informed decisions about childbearing.

*Tip for Week 16*  Some of the foods you normally love to eat may make you sick to your stomach during pregnancy. You may need to substitute other nutritious foods you tolerate better.

For further information on genetic counseling, see Preparing for Pregnancy.

When a mother is older, the father is often older, too. It can be difficult to determine whose age—the mother's or the father's—matters the most in pregnancy. Some studies have demonstrated that men 55 or older are more likely to father babies with Down syndrome. These studies indicate the risk increases with an older mother. We estimate that at the age of 40, a man's risk of fathering a child with Down syndrome is about 1%; that rate doubles at age 45 but is still only 2%.

Some researchers now recommend that men father children before they are 40. This is a conservative viewpoint, and not everyone agrees with it. More data and research are needed before we can make definitive statements about a father's age and its effect on pregnancy.

**Will Your Pregnancy Be Different If You're Older?**  As an older pregnant woman, your doctor may see you more often or you may have more tests performed. You may be advised to have amniocentesis or CVS, to determine whether your child will have Down syndrome. This may be advisable, even if you would never terminate your pregnancy. Knowing these facts helps you prepare for the birth of your baby.

You may be watched more closely during pregnancy for signs and symptoms of gestational diabetes or hypertension. Both can be troublesome during pregnancy, but with good medical care, they can usually be handled fairly well. Older women are also more likely to have twins.

As far as physical effects, you may gain more weight, see stretch marks where there were none before, notice your breasts sag lower and feel a lack of tone in your muscles. Pregnancy and being older takes its toll. Attention to your lifestyle—nutrition and exercise—can help a great deal.

Because of demands on your time and energy, fatigue may be one of your greatest problems. It's a pregnant woman's most common complaint. Rest is essential to your health and to your baby's. Seize every opportunity to rest and nap. Don't take on more tasks or new roles. Don't volunteer for a big project at work or anywhere else. Learn to say "No." You'll feel better!

Moderate exercise can help boost your energy level and may eliminate or alleviate some discomforts. However, check first with your doctor before starting any exercise program.

Stress can also be a problem. To alleviate feelings of stress, exercise, eat healthfully and get as much rest as possible. Take time for yourself.

Some women find a pregnancy support group is an excellent way to deal with difficulties they may experience. Check with your doctor for further information.

Through research, we know that labor and delivery for an older woman may be different. Your cervix may not dilate as easily as in a younger woman, so labor may last longer. Older women also have a higher rate of Cesarean sections. One cause may be that older women often have larger babies, which may necessitate a C-section. After baby's birth, your uterus may not contract as quickly either. Postpartum bleeding may last longer and be heavier.

For an in-depth look at pregnancy for women over age 35, read our book *Your Pregnancy after 35.*

## Your Nutrition

Good news—pregnant women should snack often, particularly during the second half of pregnancy! You should have three or four snacks a day, in addition to your regular meals. There are a couple of catches, though. First, snacks must be nutritious. Second, meals may need to be smaller so you can eat those snacks. One nutritional goal in pregnancy is to eat enough so important nutrients are always available for your body's use and for use by the growing fetus.

Usually you want a snack to be quick and easy. It may take some planning and effort on your part to make sure nutritious foods are available for snacking. Prepare things in advance. Cut up fresh vegetables for later use in salads and for munching with low-cal dip. Keep some hard-boiled eggs on hand. Peanut butter (reduced-fat or regular), pretzels and plain popcorn are good choices. Low-fat cheese and cottage cheese provide calcium. Fruit juice can replace soda. If juice has more sugar than you need, cut it with water. Herbal teas can be healthful. (See the discussion of herbal teas in Week 30.)

## You Should Also Know

### ᔆ *Don't Lie on Your Back*
Week 16 is the turning point—no more lying flat on your back in bed while resting or sleeping or lying flat on the floor while exercising or

relaxing. This position puts extra pressure on the aorta and vena cava, which can reduce blood flow to your baby.

Blood flow from mother to growing baby supplies the nutrients the fetus needs to develop and to grow. Don't endanger your baby's health and well-being by forgetting this important action.

Reclining in a chair or propped against pillows is OK. Just don't lie flat on your back!

### ✌ *Rh-sensitivity*

The lab tests you've had determined your blood type and Rh-factor. You may know this information by now. Your blood type (such as O, A, B, AB) and the Rh-factor are important. The Rh-factor is a protein in the blood; it is a genetic trait. Rh-positive means you have the factor; Rh-negative means the factor is missing. In the past, an Rh-negative woman who carried an Rh-positive child faced a complicated pregnancy, which could result in a very sick baby.

Your blood is separate from your baby's blood. If you are Rh-positive, you don't have to worry about any of this. If you are Rh-negative, you need to know about it.

If you are Rh-negative and your baby is Rh-positive or if you have had a blood transfusion or received blood products of some kind, there's a risk you could become Rh-sensitized or isoimmunized. *Isoimmunized* means you make antibodies that circulate inside your system, which don't harm you but can attack the Rh-positive blood of your growing baby. (If your baby is Rh negative, there is no problem.) Your antibodies can cross the placenta and attack your baby's blood. This can cause blood disease of the fetus or newborn. It can make your baby anemic while still inside the uterus, and it can be serious. Exposure to antibodies does not cause problems for the mother-to-be.

Fortunately, this reaction is preventable. The use of Rh-immune globulin (RhoGAM) has alleviated many problems. It is given at 28 weeks gestation to prevent sensitization before delivery. Few women today are sensitized. If you are Rh-negative and pregnant, a RhoGAM injection should be part of your pregnancy. RhoGAM is a product that is extracted from human blood. If you have religious, ethical or personal reasons for not using blood or blood products, consult your physician or minister.

An injection of RhoGAM may be given to you if you are exposed to your baby's blood, which is more likely to happen during the last 3 months of pregnancy and at delivery. An injury to the abdomen may expose you to fetal blood. Multiple doses of RhoGAM may also be given following delivery if blood tests show that a larger than normal number of Rh-positive blood cells (from the baby) have entered your bloodstream.

RhoGAM is also given to you within 72 hours after delivery, if your baby is Rh-positive. If your baby is Rh-negative, you don't need RhoGAM after delivery and you didn't need the shot during pregnancy. But it's better not to take that risk and to have the RhoGAM injection during pregnancy.

If you have an ectopic pregnancy and are Rh-negative, you should receive RhoGAM. This applies to miscarriages and abortions as well. If other procedures are performed that can cause the baby's blood and the mother's blood to mix, such as with amniocentesis or CVS, and you are Rh-negative, you should receive RhoGAM.

**Dad Tip** Do you have concerns that you haven't shared with anyone? Are you concerned about your partner's health or the baby's? Do you wonder about your role in labor and delivery? Are you worried about being a good father? Share your thoughts with your partner. You won't burden her. In fact, she'll probably be relieved to know she's not alone in feeling a little overwhelmed by this monumental life change.

# Week 17

## Age of Fetus—15 Weeks

## How Big Is Your Baby?

The crown-to-rump length of your baby is 4½ to 4¾ inches (11 to 12cm). Fetal weight has doubled in 2 weeks and is about 3½ ounces (100g). By this week, your baby is about the size of your hand spread open wide.

## How Big Are You?

Your uterus is 1½ to 2 inches (3.8 to 5cm) below your bellybutton. You are showing more now and have an obvious swelling in your lower abdomen. By this time, expanding or maternity clothing is a must for comfort's sake. When your partner gives you a hug, he may feel the difference in your lower abdomen.

The rest of your body is still changing. A total 5- to 10-pound (2.25- to 4.5-kg) gain by this point in your pregnancy is normal.

## How Your Baby Is
## Growing and Developing

If you look at the illustration on the opposite page and then look at earlier chapters, you'll see the incredible changes that are occurring in your baby. Fat begins to form during this week and the weeks that follow. Also called *adipose tissue,* fat is important to the body's heat production and metabolism.

At 17 weeks of development, water makes up about 3 ounces (89g) of your baby's body. In a baby at term, fat makes up about 5¼ pounds (2.4kg) of the total average weight of 7¾ pounds (3.5kg).

You have felt your baby move, or you will soon. You may not feel it every day. As pregnancy progresses, movements become stronger and probably more frequent.

## Changes in You

Feeling your baby move can reassure you that things are going well with your pregnancy. This is especially true if you've had problems.

As your pregnancy advances, the top of the uterus becomes almost spherical. It increases more rapidly in length (upward into your abdomen) than in width, so the uterus becomes more oval than round. The uterus fills the pelvis and starts to grow into the abdomen. Your intestines are pushed upward and to the sides. The uterus eventually reaches almost to your liver. The uterus doesn't float around, but neither is it firmly attached to one spot.

When you stand, your uterus touches your abdominal wall in the front. You may feel it most easily in this position. When you lie down, it can fall backward onto your spine and blood vessels (vena cava and aorta).

### ‍Round-ligament Pain
Round ligaments are attached to each side of the upper uterus and to the pelvic side wall. During pregnancy and the growth of the uterus, these ligaments are stretched and pulled. They become longer and

Your baby's fingernails are well formed. The baby is beginning to accumulate a little fat.

thicker. Your movements can stretch and pull these ligaments, causing pain or discomfort called *round-ligament pain*. It doesn't signal a problem; it indicates your uterus is growing. Pain may occur on one side only or both sides, or it may be worse on one side than another. This pain does not harm you or the baby.

If you experience this pain, you may feel better if you lie down and rest. Talk to your doctor if pain is severe or if other symptoms arise. Warning signs of serious problems include bleeding from the vagina, loss of fluid from the vagina or severe pain.

## How Your Actions Affect Your Baby's Development

### ✎ *Increased Vaginal Discharge*

During pregnancy, it is normal to have an increase in vaginal discharge or vaginal secretions, called *leukorrhea*. This discharge is usually white or yellow and fairly thick. It is not an infection. We believe it is caused by the increased blood flow to the skin and muscles around the vagina, which causes a violet or blue coloration of the vagina. This appearance, visible to your doctor early in pregnancy, is called *Chadwick's sign*.

You may have to wear sanitary pads if you have a heavy discharge. Avoid wearing pantyhose and nylon underwear; choose underwear with a cotton crotch to allow more air circulation.

Vaginal infections can and do occur during pregnancy. The discharge that accompanies these infections is often foul-smelling. It is yellow or green, and causes irritation or itching around or inside the vagina. If you have any of these symptoms, call your doctor. Many creams and antibiotics used to treat vaginal infections are safe to use during pregnancy.

### ✎ *Douching during Pregnancy*

Most doctors agree you should not douche during pregnancy. Bulb-syringe douches are definitely out!

Using a douche may cause you to bleed or may cause more serious problems, such as an air embolus. An air embolus results when air gets into your bloodstream from the pressure of the douche. It is rare, but it can cause serious problems for you.

*Dad Tip* Offer your partner tension-relieving, muscle-relaxing head, back and foot massages.

## Your Nutrition

Some women choose to eat a vegetarian diet because of personal or religious preferences. Some women are nauseated by meat during pregnancy. Is it safe to eat vegetarian while you're pregnant? It can be, if you pay close attention to the types and combinations of foods you eat.

If you eliminate meat from your diet, you need to eat enough calories to meet your energy needs. These need to be the right kind of calories, such as fresh fruits and vegetables. Avoid empty calories that have little or no nutritional value. Your goal is to eat enough different sources of protein to provide energy for the fetus and for you.

It's important to get the vitamins and minerals you need. If you eat a wide variety of whole grains, dried beans and peas, dried fruit and wheat germ, you should be able to meet your body's demands for iron, zinc and other trace minerals. You must find other sources of calcium and vitamins $B_2$, $B_{12}$ and D.

If you're not eating meat because it makes you ill, ask your physician for a referral to a nutritionist. You'll probably need help developing a good eating plan. If you're a vegetarian by choice, and have been for a while, you may know how to get many of the nutrients you need. However, if you have questions, be sure to discuss them with your doctor.

## You Should Also Know

### ᔆ Quad-screen Test
The quad-screen test can help your physician determine if you might be carrying a baby with Down syndrome. This blood test can also help rule out other problems in your pregnancy, such as neural-tube defects.

The quad-screen test is the same as the triple-screen, with the addition of a fourth measurement—your inhibin-A level. This fourth measurement raises the sensitivity of the standard triple-screen test by 20% in determining whether a fetus has Down syndrome.

The quad-screen test is able to identify 79% of those fetuses with Down syndrome. It has a false-positive result 5% of the time.

### ❧ Are You Thinking about Using a Doula?

You may be wondering if you want a doula to assist you during your baby's birth. A *doula* is a woman who is trained to provide support and assistance to you during labor and delivery of your baby. The doula remains with you from the onset of labor until baby is born.

A doula is different from a midwife because a doula does not *deliver* babies. Her strength comes in the form of physical and emotional support during labor and delivery. This ranges from giving you a massage to helping you focus on your breathing. A doula may even be able to help you begin breastfeeding your baby.

The real strength of a doula is to provide support to a woman who has chosen to have a drug-free labor and delivery. If you've decided you want anesthesia, no matter what, a doula may not be a wise choice for you.

> **Tip for Week 17** If you experience leg cramps during pregnancy, don't stand for long periods. Rest on your side as often as possible. Careful stretching exercises may help. You may also use a heating pad on the cramped area, but don't use it for longer than 15 minutes at a time. Add potassium to your diet to help deal with leg cramps *before* they start—raisins and bananas are excellent sources of potassium.

Although a doula's primary function is to provide support to the expectant mother during labor, she often assists the labor coach. She does not displace a labor coach; she works with him or her. However, in some situations, a doula may *serve* as the labor coach.

The services of a doula may be expensive and can range from $250 to $1500. This covers meetings before the birth, attendance at the labor and delivery, and one or more prenatal visits. She may even meet with you after baby's birth.

## Questions to Ask a Prospective Doula

If you are considering a doula to assist you during labor and delivery, interview more than one before you choose someone. Some questions you may want to ask and some perceptions you might want to analyze after your interview are listed below.

- What are your qualifications and training? Are you certified? By which organization?
- Have you had a baby yourself? What childbirth method did you use?
- What is your childbirth philosophy?
- Are you familiar with the method we have chosen (if you have a particular method you want to use)?
- What kind of plan would you use to help us through our labor?
- How available are you to answer our questions before the birth?
- How often will we meet before the birth?
- How do we contact you when labor begins?
- What happens if you aren't available when we go into labor? Do you work with other doulas? May we meet some of them?
- Are you experienced in helping a new mom with breastfeeding? How available are you after the birth to help with this and other postpartum problems?
- What is your fee?
- Perceptions include how easy the doula is to talk to and to communicate with. Did she listen well and answer your questions? Did you feel comfortable with her?
- If you don't hit it off with one doula, try another!

If you and your partner choose to have a doula present during labor and the birth, talk to your doctor about your decision. He or she may find her presence intrusive and veto the idea. Or the doctor may be able to give you the name of someone he or she often works with.

If you decide to use a doula, begin early to search for someone. Start looking as early as your 4th month of pregnancy—certainly no later than your 6th month. If you wait any longer, you may still be able to find someone, but your choices may be limited. Starting early allows you to relax and to evaluate more critically any women you interview. Look in your local phonebook for the names of doulas in your area, or visit DoulaNetwork.com to find a doula in your area.

# Week 18

## Age of Fetus—16 Weeks

### How Big Is Your Baby?

The crown-to-rump length of your growing baby is 5 to 5½ inches (12.5 to 14cm) by this week. Weight of the fetus is about 5¼ ounces (150g).

### How Big Are You?

You can feel your uterus just below your bellybutton. If you put your fingers sideways and measure, it is about two finger-widths (1 inch) below your bellybutton. Your uterus is the size of a cantaloupe or a little larger.

Your total weight gain to this point should be 10 to 13 pounds (4.5 to 5.8kg). However, this can vary widely. If you have gained more weight than this, talk to your doctor. You may need to see a nutritionist. You still have more than half of your pregnancy ahead of you, and you're going to gain more weight.

Gaining more than the recommended weight can make pregnancy and delivery harder on you. And extra pounds may be hard to lose afterward.

Keep watching what you eat. Choose food for the nutrition it provides you and your growing baby.

## How Your Baby Is Growing and Developing

Your baby is continuing to grow and to develop, but now the rapid growth rate slows down a little. As you can see in the illustration on page 191, your baby has a human appearance now.

### ✢ Development of the Heart and Circulatory System

At about the 3rd week of fetal development, two tubes join to form the heart. The heart begins to contract by day 22 of development or about the beginning of the 5th week of gestation. A beating heart is visible as early as 5 to 6 weeks of pregnancy during an ultrasound examination.

The heart tube divides into bulges. These bulges develop into heart chambers, called *ventricles* (left and right) and *atria* (left atrium and right atrium). These divisions occur between weeks 6 and 7. During week 7, tissue separating the left and right atria grows, and an opening between the atria called the *foramen ovale* appears. This opening lets blood pass from one atrium to the other, allowing it to bypass the lungs. At birth, the opening closes.

The ventricles, the lower chambers of the heart (lying below the atria), also develop a partition. The ventricle walls are muscular. The left ventricle pumps blood to the body and brain, and the right ventricle pumps blood to the lungs.

Heart valves develop at the same time as the chambers. These valves fill and empty the heart. Heart sounds and heart murmurs are caused by blood passing through these valves.

Blood from your baby flows to the placenta through the umbilical cord. In the placenta, oxygen and nutrients

**Dad Tip** Offer to run errands. Take her dry cleaning in, and pick it up when it's done. Stop by the bank for her. Take her car to a car wash. Return her library books or rented videos.

are transported from your blood to the fetal blood. Although the circulation of your blood and that of your baby come close, there is no direct connection. These circulation systems are completely separate.

At birth, the baby has to go rapidly from depending entirely on you for oxygen to depending on its own heart and lungs. The foramen ovale closes. Blood goes to the right ventricle, the right atrium and the lungs for oxygenation for the first time. It is truly a miraculous conversion.

At 18 weeks of gestation, ultrasound can detect some abnormalities of the heart. This can be helpful in identifying some problems, such as Down syndrome. A skilled ultrasonographer looks for specific heart defects. If an abnormality is suspected, further ultrasound exams may be ordered to follow a baby's development as pregnancy progresses.

## Changes in You

### ॐ *Does Your Back Ache?*

Nearly every pregnant woman experiences backache at some time in pregnancy. You may have felt it already, or it may come later as you get bigger. Some women have severe back pain following excessive exercise, walking, bending, lifting or standing. It is more common to have mild backache than severe problems. Some women need to take special care getting out of bed or getting up from a sitting position. In severe instances, some women find it difficult to walk.

*Tip for Week 18* During exercise, your oxygen demands increase. Your body is heavier, and your balance may change. You may also tire more easily. Keep these points in mind as you adjust your fitness program.

A change in joint mobility may contribute to the change in your posture and may cause discomfort in the lower back. This is particularly true in the latter part of pregnancy.

The growth of the uterus moves your center of gravity forward, over your legs, which can affect the joints around the pelvis. All your joints are looser. Hormonal increases are potential causes; however,

Your baby continues to grow. By this week, it is about 5 inches (12.5cm) from crown to rump. It looks much more human now.

discomfort may also be an indication of more serious problems, such as pyelonephritis or a kidney stone (see page 196). Check with your doctor if back pain is a chronic problem for you.

What can you do to prevent or lessen your pain? Try some or all of the following tips as early in your pregnancy as possible, and they will pay off as your pregnancy progresses.

- Watch your diet and weight gain.
- Continue exercising within guidelines during pregnancy.
- Get in the habit of lying on your side when you sleep.
- Find time during the day to get off your feet and lie down for 30 minutes on your side.
- If you have other children, take a nap when they take theirs.
- It's OK to take acetaminophen for back pain.
- Use heat on the area that is painful.
- If pain becomes constant or more severe, talk to your doctor about it.

## How Your Actions Affect Your Baby's Development

### ✎ Exercise in the Second Trimester

Everyone has heard stories of women who continued with strenuous exercise or strenuous activities until the day of delivery without problems. Stories are told of Olympic athletes who were pregnant at the time they won medals in the Olympic games. This kind of training and physical stress isn't a good idea for most women during pregnancy.

As your uterus grows and your abdomen gets larger, your sense of balance may be affected. You may feel clumsy. This isn't the time for contact sports, such as basketball, or sports where you might fall easily, injure yourself or be struck in the abdomen.

Pregnant women can participate safely in many sports and exercise activities throughout their pregnancy. This is a different attitude from those held 20, 30 and 40 years ago. Bed rest and decreased activity were common then. Today, we believe exercise and activity can benefit you and your growing baby.

Discuss your particular activities at a prenatal visit. If your pregnancy is high risk or if you have had several miscarriages, it's particularly important to discuss exercise with your doctor *before* starting an activity. Now is not the time to train for any sport or to increase activity. In fact, this may be a good time to decrease the amount or intensity of exercise you are doing. Listen to your body. It will tell you when it's time to slow down.

What about the activities you are already involved in or would like to begin? Below is a discussion of various activities and how they will affect you in your second and third trimester. (See Week 3 for additional information on exercise in pregnancy.)

**Swimming.** Swimming can be good for you when you're pregnant. The support and buoyancy of the water can be relaxing. If you swim, swim throughout pregnancy. If you can't swim and have been involved in water exercises (exercising in the shallow end of a swimming pool), you can continue this throughout your pregnancy as well. This is an exercise you can begin at any time during pregnancy, if you don't overdo it.

**Bicycling.** Now is not the time to learn to ride a bike. If you're comfortable riding and have safe places to ride, you can enjoy this exercise with your partner or family.

Your balance will change as your body changes. This can make getting on and off a bicycle difficult. A fall from a bicycle could injure you or your baby.

A stationary bicycle is good for bad weather and for later in pregnancy. Many doctors suggest you ride a stationary bike in the last 2 to 3 months of pregnancy to avoid the danger of a fall.

**Walking.** Walking is a desirable exercise during pregnancy. It can be a good time for you and your partner to talk. Even when the weather is bad, you can walk in many places, such as an enclosed shopping mall, to get a good workout. Two miles of walking at a good pace is adequate. As pregnancy progresses, you may need to decrease your speed and distance. Walking is an exercise you can begin at any time during pregnancy, if you don't overdo it.

**Jogging.** Some women continue to jog during pregnancy. Jogging may be permitted during pregnancy, but check with your doctor first. If your pregnancy is high risk, jogging may not be a good idea.

Pregnancy is not the time to increase mileage or to train for a race. Wear comfortable clothing and supportive athletic shoes with good cushioning. Allow plenty of time to cool down.

During the course of your pregnancy, you'll probably need to slow down and to decrease the number of miles you run. You may even change to walking. If you notice pain, contractions, bleeding or other symptoms during or after jogging, call your doctor immediately.

**Other Sports Activities.**

- Tennis and golf are safe to continue in the second and third trimesters but may provide little actual exercise.
- Horseback riding is not advisable during pregnancy at any time.
- Avoid water skiing while you're pregnant.
- Bowling is OK, although the amount of exercise you get varies. Be careful in late pregnancy; you could fall or strain your back. As your balance changes, bowling could become more difficult for you.
- Talk to your doctor about snow skiing before you hit the slopes. Again, in the latter part of pregnancy, your balance changes significantly. A fall could be harmful to you and your baby. Most physicians agree that skiing in the second half of pregnancy is not a good idea. Some doctors may allow skiing in early pregnancy, but only if there are no complications with this or a previous pregnancy.
- Riding snowmobiles, jet skis or motorcycles is not advised. Some doctors may allow you to ride if it is not strenuous. However, most believe the risk is too great, especially if you have had problems during this or a previous pregnancy.

## Your Nutrition

Iron is important to you while you're pregnant. You need about 30mg a day to meet the increased needs of pregnancy, due to the increase in your blood volume. During your pregnancy, your baby draws on your iron stores to create its own stores for its first few months of life. This protects baby from iron deficiency if you breastfeed.

Most prenatal vitamins contain enough iron to meet your needs. If you must take iron supplements, take your iron pill with a glass of orange juice or grapefruit juice to increase its absorption. Avoid drinking milk, coffee or tea when you take an iron supplement or eat iron-rich foods. They prevent the body from absorbing the iron it needs.

If you feel tired, have trouble concentrating, suffer from headaches, dizziness or indigestion, or if you get sick easily, you may have an iron deficiency. An easy way to check is to examine the inside of your lower eyelid. If you're getting enough iron, it should be dark pink. Your nail beds should be pink, too.

Only 10 to 15% of the iron you consume is absorbed by the body. Your body stores it efficiently, but you need to eat iron-rich foods on a regular basis to maintain those stores. Foods that are rich in iron include chicken, red meat, organ meats (liver, heart, kidneys), egg yolks, dried fruit, spinach, kale and tofu. Combining a vitamin-C food and an iron-rich food ensures better iron absorption by the body. A spinach salad with orange or grapefruit sections is a good example.

Your prenatal vitamin contains about 60mg of iron. If you eat a well-balanced diet and take your prenatal vitamin every day, you may not need additional iron. Discuss it with your doctor if you are concerned.

## You Should Also Know

### ♔ Bladder Infections

One of the most common problems of pregnancy is frequent urination. Urinary-tract infections (UTIs) may cause you to urinate even more frequently while you're pregnant. A UTI is the most common problem involving your bladder or kidneys during pregnancy. As the uterus grows larger, it sits directly on top of the bladder and on the ureters, the tubes leading from the kidneys to the bladder. This blocks the flow of urine. Other names for urinary-tract infections are *bladder infections* and *cystitis*.

Symptoms of a bladder infection include the feeling of urgency to urinate, frequent urination and painful urination, particularly at the end of urination. A severe urinary-tract infection may cause blood to appear in the urine.

Your doctor may do a urinalysis and urine culture at your first prenatal visit. He or she may check your urine for infection at other times during pregnancy and when bothersome symptoms arise.

You can help avoid infection by not holding your urine. Empty your bladder as soon as you feel the need. Don't wait to go to the bathroom; it could lead to a urinary-tract infection. Drink plenty of fluid; cranberry juice may help you avoid infections. For some women, it helps to empty the bladder after having intercourse.

If you have a urinary-tract infection (UTI) during pregnancy, call your doctor, and take care of it. Research has found that risks of giving birth to a child who is mentally retarded or who will exhibit developmental delays increases when UTIs are left untreated. UTIs during pregnancy might also be a cause of premature labor or a low-birthweight infant.

If you feel uncomfortable taking medication for the problem, understand that there are many safe antibiotics available. If you have a UTI, take the full course of antibiotics prescribed for you. It may be harmful to your baby if you don't treat the problem!

If left untreated, urinary-tract infections can get worse. They can even lead to pyelonephritis, a serious kidney infection (see the discussion below).

**Pyelonephritis.** A more serious problem resulting from a bladder infection is pyelonephritis. This type of infection occurs in 1 to 2% of all pregnant women.

Symptoms include frequent urination, a burning sensation during urination, the feeling you need to urinate and nothing will come out, high fever, chills and back pain. Pyelonephritis may require hospitalization and treatment with intravenous antibiotics.

If you have pyelonephritis or recurrent bladder infections during pregnancy, you may have to take antibiotics throughout pregnancy to prevent reinfection.

**Kidney Stones.** Another problem involving the kidneys and bladder is kidney stones (renal calculi). They occur about once in every 1500 pregnancies. Kidney stones cause severe pain in the back or lower abdomen. They may also be associated with blood in the urine.

A kidney stone during pregnancy can usually be treated with pain medication and by drinking lots of fluids. In this way, the stone may be passed without surgical removal or lithotripsy (an ultrasound procedure).

# Week 19

*Age of Fetus—17 Weeks*

## How Big Is Your Baby?

Crown-to-rump length of the growing fetus is 5¼ to 6 inches (13 to 15cm) by this week. Your baby weighs about 7 ounces (200g). It's incredible to think your baby will increase its weight more than 15 times between now and delivery!

## How Big Are You?

You can feel your uterus about ½ inch (1.3cm) below your umbilicus. The illustration on page 200 gives you a good idea of the relative size of you, your uterus and your developing baby. A side view really shows the changes in you!

Your total weight gain at this point is between 8 and 14 pounds (3.6 and 6.3kg). Of this weight, only about 7 ounces (200g) is your baby! The placenta weighs about 6 ounces (170g); the amniotic fluid weighs another 11 ounces (320g). The uterus weighs 11 ounces (320g). Your breasts have each increased in weight by about 6½ ounces (180g). The rest of the weight you have gained is your increased blood volume and other maternal stores.

## How Your Baby Is Growing and Developing

### ✌ *Your Baby's Nervous System*

The beginning of the baby's nervous system (brain and other structures, such as the spinal cord) is seen as early as week 4 as the neural plate begins to develop. By week 6, the main divisions of the central nervous system are established.

These divisions consist of the forebrain, midbrain, hindbrain and spinal cord. In week 7, the forebrain divides into the two hemispheres that will become the two cerebral hemispheres of the brain.

### ✌ *Hydrocephalus*

Organization and development of the brain continues from this early beginning. Cerebral spinal fluid (CSF), which circulates around the brain and the spinal cord, is made by the choroid plexus. Fluid must be able to flow without restriction. If openings are blocked and flow is restricted for any reason, it can cause *hydrocephalus* (water on the brain).

Hydrocephalus causes enlargement of the head. Occurring in about 1 in 2000 babies, it is responsible for about 12% of all severe birth defects found at birth.

Hydrocephalus is often associated with spina bifida and occurs in about 33% of those cases. It can also be associated with meningomyelocele and omphalocele (hernias of the spine and navel). Between 15 and 45 ounces of fluid (500 to 1500ml) can accumulate, but much more than that has been found. Brain tissue is compressed by all this fluid, which is a major concern.

Ultrasound is the best way to diagnose the problem. Hydrocephalus can usually be seen on ultrasound by 19 weeks of pregnancy. Occasionally it is found by routine exams and by "feeling" or measuring your uterus.

Comparative size of the uterus at 19 weeks of pregnancy (fetal age—17 weeks). The uterus can be felt just under the umbilicus (bellybutton).

In the past, nothing could be done about hydrocephalus until after delivery. Today, intrauterine therapy—treatment while the fetus is still in the uterus—can be performed in some cases.

There are two methods of treating hydrocephalus in utero (inside the uterus). In one method, a needle passes through the mother's abdomen into the area of the baby's brain where fluid is collecting. Some fluid is removed to relieve pressure on the baby's brain. In another method, a small plastic tube is placed into the area where fluid collects in the baby's brain. This tube is left in place to drain fluid continuously.

Hydrocephalus is a high-risk problem. These procedures are highly specialized and should be performed only by someone experienced in the latest techniques. This requires consultation with a perinatologist specializing in high-risk pregnancies.

## Changes in You

### ∼ *Feeling Dizzy*

Feeling dizzy during pregnancy is a fairly common symptom, often caused by hypotension (low blood pressure). It usually doesn't appear until the second trimester but may occur earlier.

There are two common reasons for hypotension during pregnancy. It can be caused by the enlarging uterus putting pressure on your aorta and vena cava. This is called *supine hypotension* and occurs when you lie down. You can alleviate or prevent it by not sleeping or lying on your back.

The second cause of hypotension is rising rapidly from a sitting, kneeling or squatting position. This is called *postural hypotension*. Your blood pressure drops when you rise rapidly as blood leaves your brain because of gravity. This problem is cured by rising slowly.

If you are anemic, you may feel dizzy, faint or tired, or you may fatigue easily. Your blood is checked routinely during pregnancy. Your doctor will tell you if you have anemia. (See Week 22 for more information about anemia.)

Pregnancy also affects your blood-sugar level. High blood sugar (hyperglycemia) or low blood sugar (hypoglycemia) can make you feel dizzy or faint. Many doctors routinely test pregnant women for problems with blood sugar during pregnancy, particularly if they have problems with dizziness or a family history of diabetes. Most women can avoid or improve the problem by eating a balanced diet, not skipping meals and not going a long time without eating. Carry a piece of fruit or several crackers with you for a quick boost in blood sugar when you need it.

### Eat More Meals Every Day!

Researchers have found that pregnant women who eat frequent, small meals during the day may provide better nutrition to their growing babies than women who eat three large meals. Though they are eating the same amount of calories, there is a difference.

Studies have found that keeping the blood level of maternal nutrients constant (by eating frequent, small meals) is better for fetal development than the mother-to-be eating a large meal, then not eating again for quite a while. Three larger meals means that nutrient levels rise and fall during the day, which isn't as beneficial for the growing baby. Eating small meals frequently can also help alleviate or avoid some other problems associated with pregnancy, such as nausea, heartburn and indigestion.

## How Your Actions
## Affect Your Baby's Development

### ᴥ *Warning Signs during Pregnancy*

Many women are nervous because they don't think they would know if something important or serious happened during pregnancy. Most women have few, if any, problems during pregnancy. If you are concerned, read the list below of the most important symptoms to be aware of. Call your doctor if you experience any of the following:

- vaginal bleeding
- severe swelling of the face or fingers
- severe abdominal pain
- loss of fluid from the vagina, usually a gush of fluid, but sometimes a trickle or continuous wetness

- a big change in the baby's movement or a lack of movement
- high fever (more than 101.6F; 38.7C) or chills
- severe vomiting or an inability to keep food or liquid down
- blurring of vision
- painful urination
- a headache that won't go away or a severe headache
- an injury or accident, such as a fall or automobile accident, that causes you concern about the well-being of your baby

One way to get to know your doctor better is to ask his or her opinion about your concerns. Don't be embarrassed to ask questions about anything; your doctor has probably heard it before. And he or she would rather know about problems while they are easier to deal with.

**Referral to a Perinatologist.** If problems warrant it, you may be referred to a perinatologist, an obstetrician who has spent an additional 2 years or more in specialized training. These specialists have experience caring for women with high-risk pregnancies.

You may not have a high-risk pregnancy at the beginning of your pregnancy. However, if problems develop with you (such as premature labor) or your baby (such as spina bifida), you may be referred to a perinatologist for consultation and possible care during your pregnancy. You may be able to return to your regular doctor for your delivery.

If you are seeing a perinatologist, you may have to deliver your baby at a hospital other than the one you had chosen. This is usually because the hospital has specialized facilities or can administer specialized tests to you or your baby.

## Your Nutrition

### ∽ *Herbal Use in Pregnancy*
In the past, have you used herbs and botanicals, in the forms of teas, tinctures, pills or powders, to treat various medical and health problems?

We advise you *not* to treat yourself with an herbal remedy during pregnancy *without checking first with your doctor!*

You may believe an herbal remedy is OK to use, but it could be dangerous during pregnancy. For example, if you are constipated, you may decide to use senna as a laxative. However, senna stimulates uterine muscles and may cause a miscarriage. Some herbs may irritate your bowels and baby's bowels, too. So play it safe—be extremely careful with any substance your doctor has not specifically recommended for you. Always check with him or her first before you take anything!

### ᔡ Pay Attention to Your Calcium Intake

It's very important for you to get enough calcium every day. You need 1200mg each day during pregnancy—50% more than before pregnancy. For information on calcium and some tips on ways to add it to your food plan, see the nutrition discussion in Week 7.

## You Should Also Know

### ᔡ Allergies during Pregnancy

Allergies sometimes get a little worse during pregnancy. If you have allergy medication, don't assume it's safe to take. Some types of allergy medication may not be advised. Many allergy medicines are combinations of several medicines that you should be careful about using during pregnancy. Ask your doctor about your medicine, whether prescription or nonprescription. This advice also applies to nasal sprays.

Medications that are OK to use during pregnancy include antihistamines and decongestants. Decongestants that contain oxymetazoline, such as Afrin, may be recommended. Allergy-blocking nasal sprays that contain cromolyn sodium, such as Nasalcrom, are also safe to use.

**Dad Tip** When you can, take some time off from work or other obligations to spend time with your partner. Together, focus on planning your pregnancy and preparing for the birth of your baby.

Ask your doctor which brands are safest for you to use if your allergy problems interfere with your normal lifestyle.

To help deal with allergies, try to avoid anything that triggers them. For example, if dust bothers you, keep windows closed and avoid outdoor activities in the morning, when the pollen is usually at its worst. Wear a mask when you vacuum. Use a humidifier if you live in a very dry climate. To help deal with the problem, drink plenty of fluid.

*Tip for Week 19* Fish can be a healthful food choice during pregnancy, but don't eat shark, swordfish or tuna (fresh or frozen) more than once a week.

Some fortunate women notice their allergies get better during pregnancy, and symptoms improve. Certain things they had trouble with before pregnancy are no longer a problem.

### ✥ Will You Be a Single Mother?

Many women choose to have a child without a spouse; situations vary from woman to woman. Some women are deeply involved with their partner, the baby's father, but have chosen not to marry. Some women are pregnant without their partner's support. Still other single women have chosen donor (artificial) insemination as a means of getting pregnant.

No matter what the personal situation, many concerns are shared by all of them. This discussion reflects some of the issues they have raised.

In most situations—whether a mother is single, widowed or divorced—a child's overall environment is more important than the presence of a man in the household. Eighty-six percent of single-parent households in the United States are headed by women. Recent studies indicate that if a woman has other supportive adults to depend on, a child can fare well in a home headed by a single woman.

Some people may think your choice is unwise and tell you so. However, it's no one's business but your own. If someone is intent on giving you a hard time, change the subject. Don't discuss your reasons for having a baby with anyone unless you *want* to.

Even if you are "alone," you're not really alone. Seek support from family and friends. Mothers of young children can identify with your experiences—they have had similar ones recently. If you have friends or family members with young children, talk with them. You would probably share your concerns with these people even if you were married. Try not to let your particular situation alter this.

Finding people you can count on for help during your pregnancy and after your baby arrives is important. One woman said she thought about whom she would call at 2am if her baby were crying uncontrollably. When she answered that question, she had the name of someone she believed she could count on in any type of emergency—during and after pregnancy!

It may help to choose someone to be with you when you labor and deliver, and who will be there to help afterward. The only part of labor and delivery that might require special planning because you're single is your plan to get to the hospital when you go into labor. One woman wanted her friend to drive, but couldn't reach her when the time came. Her next option (all part of the plan) was to call a taxi, which got her to the hospital in plenty of time.

**Legal Questions.** Because your situation is unique, it's important to have answers to questions. The following questions have been posed by women who chose to be single mothers. We repeat them here without answers because they are legal questions that should be reviewed with an attorney in your area who specializes in family law. These can help you clarify the kinds of questions you need to consider as a single mother.

- A friend who's had a baby by herself told me I'd better consider the legal ramifications of this situation. What was she talking about?
- I've heard that in some states, if I'm unmarried, I have to get a special birth certificate. Is that true?
- I'm having my baby alone, and I'm concerned about who can make medical decisions for me and my expected baby. Can I do anything about this concern?
- I'm not married, but I am deeply involved with my baby's father. Can my partner make medical decisions for me if I have problems during labor or after the birth?

- If anything happens to me, can my partner make medical decisions for our baby after it is born?
- What are the legal rights of my baby's father if we are not married?
- Do my partner's parents have legal rights in regard to their grandchild (my child)?
- My baby's father and I went our separate ways before I knew I was pregnant. Do I have to tell him about the baby?
- I chose to have donor (artificial) insemination. If anything happens to me during my labor or delivery, who can make medical decisions for me? Who can make decisions for my baby?
- I got pregnant by donor insemination. What do I put on the birth certificate under "father's name"?
- Is there a way I can find out more about my sperm donor's family medical history?
- Will the sperm bank send me notices if medical problems appear in my sperm donor's family?
- As my child grows up, she may need some sort of medical help (such as a donor kidney) from a sibling. Will the sperm bank supply family information?
- I had donor insemination, and I'm concerned about the rights of the baby's father to be part of my child's life in the future. Should I be concerned?
- What type of arrangements must I make for my child in case of my death?
- Someone joked to me that my child could marry its sister or brother some day and wouldn't know it because I had donor insemination. Is this possible?
- Are there any other things I should consider because of my unique situation?

# Week 20

*Age of Fetus—18 Weeks*

## How Big Is Your Baby?

At this point in development, the crown-to-rump length is 5⅔ to 6½ inches (14 to 16cm). Your baby weighs about 9 ounces (260g).

## How Big Are You?

Congratulations—20 weeks marks the midpoint. You're halfway through your pregnancy! Remember, the entire pregnancy is 40 weeks from the beginning of your last period if you go full term.

Your uterus is probably about even with your bellybutton. Your doctor has been watching your growth and the enlargement of your uterus. Growth to this point may have been irregular but usually becomes more regular after the 20th week.

### ❧ Measuring the Growth of Your Uterus

Your uterus is measured often to keep track of your baby's growth. Your doctor may use a measuring tape or his or her fingers and measure by finger breadth.

Your physician needs a point of reference against which to measure your growth. Some doctors measure from your bellybutton. Many measure from the pubic symphysis. The *pubic symphysis* is the place where the pubic bones meet in the middle-lower part of your abdomen. This bony area is just above your urethra (where urine comes out), 6 to 10 inches (15.2 to 25.4cm) below the bellybutton, depending on how tall you are. It may be felt 1 or 2 inches (2.5 to 5cm) below your pubic hairline.

Measurements are made from the pubic symphysis to the top of the uterus. After 20 weeks of pregnancy, you should grow almost ½ inch (1cm) each week. If you are 8 inches (20cm) at 20 weeks, at your next visit (4 weeks later), you should measure about 10 inches (24cm).

If you measure 11¼ inches (28cm) at this point in pregnancy, you may require further evaluation with ultrasound to determine if you are carrying twins or to see if your due date is correct. If you only measure 6 inches (15 to 16cm) at this point, it may be a reason to do further evaluation by ultrasound. Your due date could be wrong, or there may be a concern about intrauterine-growth restriction or some other problem.

Not every doctor measures the same way, and not every woman is the same size. Babies vary in size. If pregnant friends ask, "How much did you measure?" don't worry if their measurements are different. Measurements differ among women and are often different for a woman from one pregnancy to another.

If you see a doctor you don't normally see or if you see a new doctor, you may measure differently. This does not indicate a problem or that someone is measuring incorrectly. It's just that everyone measures a little differently.

*Tip for Week 20* An ultrasound test done at this point in pregnancy may make it possible to determine the sex of the baby, but the baby must cooperate. Sex is recognized by seeing the genitals. Even if the sex looks obvious, ultrasound operators have been known to be mistaken about a baby's sex.

Having the same person measure you on a regular basis can be helpful in following the growth of your baby. Within limits, changing measurements are a sign of fetal well-being and fetal growth. If they appear abnormal, it can be a warning sign. If you're concerned about your size and the growth of your pregnancy, discuss it with your physician.

# How Your Baby Is
# Growing and Developing

### ✎ *Your Baby's Skin*

The skin covering your baby begins growing from two layers. These layers are the *epidermis*, which is on the surface, and the *dermis*, which is the deeper layer. By this point in your pregnancy, the epidermis is arranged in four layers. One of these layers contains epidermal ridges, which are responsible for surface patterns on fingertips, palms and soles. They are genetically determined.

The dermis lies below the epidermis. It forms projections that push upward into the epidermis. Each projection contains a small blood vessel (capillary) or a nerve. This deeper layer also contains large amounts of fat.

When a baby is born, its skin is covered by a white substance that looks like paste. Called *vernix,* it is secreted by the glands in the skin beginning around 20 weeks of pregnancy. Vernix protects your growing baby's skin from amniotic fluid.

Hair appears at around 12 to 14 weeks of pregnancy. It grows from the epidermis; hair ends (hair papillae) push down into the dermis. Hair is first seen on the fetus on the upper lip and eyebrow. It is usually shed around the time of birth and is replaced by thicker hair from new follicles.

### ✎ *Ultrasound Pictures*

The illustration on the opposite page shows an ultrasound exam (and an interpretive illustration of the ultrasound) in a pregnant woman at about 20 weeks gestation. An ultrasound is often easier to understand when it is actually being done. The pictures you see are more like motion pictures.

If you look closely at the illustration, it may make sense to you. Read the labels, and try to visualize the baby inside the uterus. An ultrasound picture is like looking at a slice of an object. The picture you see is 2-dimensional.

**Dad Tip** Around 20 weeks of pregnancy, your partner may have an ultrasound exam. Try to be present for this test. Ask your partner to consider your schedule when making the appointment for her ultrasound.

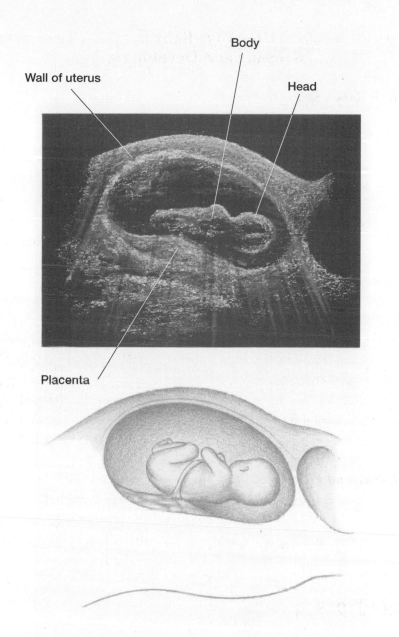

Body

Wall of uterus

Head

Placenta

Ultrasound of a baby at 20 weeks gestation (fetal age—18 weeks). The interpretive illustration may help you see more detail.

Having one of those ultrasound "keep-sakes" done at your local mall may not be a good idea. Casual use of any medical test just for entertainment is never advised. One of our concerns is that your ultrasound may show an abnormality and you may not be told about it. It isn't a good idea to substitute these entertaining tests for regular medical tests your doctor orders.

An ultrasound done at this point in pregnancy is helpful for confirming or helping to establish your due date. If the ultrasound is done very early or very late (first or last 2 months), the accuracy of dating a pregnancy is not as good. If two or more fetuses are present, they can usually be seen. Some fetal problems can also be seen at this time.

### ♂ Percutaneous Umbilical-Cord Blood Sampling

Percutaneous umbilical-cord blood sampling (PUBS), also called *cordocentesis,* is a test done on the fetus while it is still developing inside your uterus. The advantage of the test is that results are available in a few days. The disadvantage is that it carries a slightly higher risk of miscarriage than amniocentesis does.

Guided by ultrasound, a fine needle is inserted through the mother's abdomen into a tiny vein in the umbilical cord. A small sample of the baby's blood is removed for analysis. PUBS detects blood disorders, infections and Rh-incompatibility.

The baby's blood can be checked before birth, and the baby can be given a blood transfusion, if necessary. This procedure can help prevent life-threatening anemia that may develop if the mother is Rh-negative and has antibodies that are destroying her baby's blood. If you are Rh-negative, you should receive RhoGAM after this procedure.

## Changes in You

### ♂ Stretching Abdominal Muscles

Your abdominal muscles are being stretched and pushed apart as your baby grows. Muscles are attached to the lower portion of your ribs and run vertically down to your pelvis. They may separate in the midline. These muscles are called the rectus muscles; when they separate, it is a hernia called a *diastasis recti*.

You will notice the separation most often when you are lying down and you raise your head, tightening your abdominal muscles. It will look like there is a bulge in the middle of your abdomen. You might even feel the edge of the muscle on either side of the bulge. It isn't painful and doesn't harm you or your baby. What you feel in the gap between the muscles is the uterus. You may feel the baby's movement more easily here.

If this is your first baby, you may not notice the separation at all. With each pregnancy, separation is often more noticeable. Exercising can strengthen these muscles, but you may still have the bulge or gap.

Following pregnancy, these muscles tighten and close the gap. The separation won't be as noticeable, but it may still be present. A girdle probably won't help get rid of the bulge or gap.

## How Your Actions Affect Your Baby's Development

### ∾ *Sexual Relations*

Pregnancy can be an important time of growing closer to your partner. As you get larger, sexual intercourse may become difficult because of discomfort for you. With some imagination and with different positions (ones in which you are not on your back and your partner is not directly on top of you), you can continue to enjoy sexual relations during this part of your pregnancy.

If you feel emotional pressure from your partner—either his concern about the safety of intercourse or requests for frequent sexual relations—discuss it openly with him. Don't be afraid to invite your partner to prenatal visits to discuss these things with your doctor.

If you're having problems with contractions, bleeding or complications, you and your partner should talk with your doctor. Together you can decide whether you should continue to have sexual relations during your pregnancy.

## Your Nutrition

Many women use artificial sweeteners to help cut calories. Aspartame and saccharin are the two most common artificial sweeteners added to foods and beverages. Aspartame (sold under the brand names Nutrasweet and Equal) may be the most popular artificial sweetener. It is used in many foods and beverages to help reduce calorie content. Saccharin is also added to many foods and beverages. A fairly new product, Splenda, is also being marketed.

### ✑ Aspartame

Aspartame is a combination of phenylalanine and aspartic acid, two amino acids. There has been controversy as to its safety. We advise you to substitute foods that do not contain the sweetener. At this point, we're unsure about its safety for pregnant women and their developing babies. If you suffer from phenylketonuria, you must follow a low-phenylalanine diet or your baby may be adversely affected. Phenylalanine in aspartame contributes to phenylalanine in the diet.

### ✑ Saccharin

Saccharin is another artificial sweetener used in many foods and beverages. Although it is not used as much today as in the past, it still appears in many foods, beverages and other substances. The Center for Science in the Public Interest reports testing of saccharin does not indicate that it is safe to use during pregnancy. It would probably be better to avoid using this product while you're pregnant.

### ✑ Avoid Aspartame and Saccharin

Don't use these artificial sweeteners or food additives during pregnancy, if you can avoid them. It's probably best to eliminate any substance you don't really need from the foods you eat and the beverages you drink. Do it for the good of your baby.

### ↣ *Splenda*

In 1998, the Food and Drug Administration announced approval of the use of Splenda as a sweetener in a wide variety of food products. At this time, you can buy it in pourable or packet form, and it is also found in a variety of products.

Splenda is a trade name for a low-calorie sweetener called *sucralose,* and it is made from sugar. Sucralose passes through the body without being metabolized—your body does not recognize it as either a sugar or a carbohydrate, which makes it low calorie.

Sucralose is used in salad dressings, baked goods, desserts, dairy products beverages, jams and jellies, coffee and tea, syrups and chewing gum. **Splenda is safe for pregnant and nursing women to use.**

## You Should Also Know

### ↣ *Hearing Your Baby's Heartbeat*

It may be possible to hear your baby's heartbeat with a stethoscope at 20 weeks. Before doctors had doppler equipment that enabled them to hear the heartbeat and ultrasound to see the heart beating, a stethoscope helped the listener hear the baby's heartbeat. This usually occurred after quickening for most women.

The sound you hear through a stethoscope may be different than what you are used to hearing at the doctor's office. The sound isn't loud. If you've never listened through a stethoscope, it may be difficult to hear at first. It does get easier as the baby gets larger and sounds are louder.

If you can't hear your baby's heartbeat with a stethoscope, don't worry. It's not always easy for a doctor who does this on a regular basis!

If you hear a swishing sound (baby's heartbeat), you have to differentiate it from a beating sound (mother's heartbeat). A baby's heart
beats rapidly, usually 120 to 160 beats every minute. Your heartbeat or
pulse rate is slower, in the range of 60 to 80 beats a minute. Ask your
doctor to help you distinguish the sounds.

# Week 21

*Age of Fetus—19 Weeks*

## How Big Is Your Baby?

Your baby is getting larger in this first week of the second half of your pregnancy. It now weighs about 10½ ounces (300g), and its crown-to-rump length is about 7¼ inches (18cm). It is about the size of a large banana.

## How Big Are You?

You can feel your uterus about half an inch (1cm) above your belly-button. At the doctor's office, your uterus measures almost 8½ inches (21cm) from the pubic symphysis. Your weight gain should be between 10 and 15 pounds (4.5 and 6.3kg).

*Tip for Week 21* A good way to add calcium to your diet is to cook rice and oatmeal in skim milk instead of water.

By this week, your waistline is definitely gone. Your friends and relatives—and strangers, too—can tell you're pregnant. It would be hard to hide your condition!

# How Your Baby Is
# Growing and Developing

The rapid growth rate of your baby has slowed. However, the baby continues to grow and to develop. Different organ systems within the baby are maturing.

## ☞ The Fetal Digestive System

The fetal digestive system is functioning in a simple way. By the 11th week of pregnancy, the small intestine begins to contract and relax, which pushes substances through it. The small intestine is capable of passing sugar from inside itself into the baby's body.

By 21 weeks of pregnancy, development of the fetal digestive system enables the fetus to swallow amniotic fluid. After swallowing amniotic fluid, the fetus absorbs much of the water in it and passes unabsorbed matter as far as the large bowel.

## ☞ Fetal Swallowing

As mentioned above, your baby swallows before it is born. Using ultrasound, you can observe the baby swallowing at different stages of pregnancy. We have seen babies swallowing amniotic fluid as early as 21 weeks of pregnancy.

Why does a baby in the womb swallow? Researchers believe swallowing amniotic fluid may help growth and development of the fetal digestive system. It may also condition the digestive system to function after birth.

**Dad Tip** It's not too early to start thinking about baby names. Sometimes couples have very different ideas about names for their child. There are lots of books available to help you. Do you plan to honor a close friend or relative by using their name? Will you use a family name? What problems could arise if you choose a peculiar, difficult-to-say or hard-to-spell name? What do the initials spell out? What nicknames go with the name? Start thinking about it now, even if you decide you won't pick a name until after you meet your baby.

Studies have determined how much fluid a fetus swallows and passes through its digestive system. Evidence indicates babies at full-term may swallow large amounts of amniotic fluid, as much as 17 ounces (500ml) of amniotic fluid in a 24-hour period.

Amniotic fluid swallowed by the baby contributes a small amount to its caloric needs. Researchers believe it may contribute essential nutrients to the developing baby.

### ᔐ *Meconium*

During your pregnancy, you may hear the term *meconium* and wonder what it means. It refers to undigested debris from swallowed amniotic fluid in the fetal digestive system. Meconium is made mostly of mucosal cells from the lining of the baby's gastrointestinal tract. It contains no bacteria, so it is sterile.

It is a greenish-black to light-brown substance that your baby passes from its bowels before delivery, during labor or after birth.

Passage of meconium into the amniotic fluid may be caused by distress in the fetus. Meconium seen during labor may be an indication of fetal distress.

If a baby has had a bowel movement before birth and meconium is present in the amniotic fluid, the fetus may swallow the fluid. If baby inhales meconium into the lungs, it could develop pneumonia or pneumonitis. For this reason, if meconium is seen at delivery, an attempt is made to remove it from the baby's mouth and throat with a small suction tube.

## Changes in You

In addition to your growing uterus, other parts of your body continue to change and to grow. You may notice swelling in your lower legs and feet, particularly at the end of the day. If you're on your feet a lot, you may notice less swelling if you're able to get off your feet and rest for a while during the day.

### ✑ *Blood Clots in the Legs*

A serious complication of pregnancy is a blood clot in the legs or groin. Symptoms of the problem are swelling of the legs accompanied by leg pain and redness or warmth over the affected area in the legs.

This problem has many names, including *venous thrombosis, thromboembolic disease, thrombophlebitis* and *lower deep-vein thrombosis.* The problem is not limited to pregnancy, but pregnancy is a time when it is more likely to occur. This is due to the slowing of blood flow in the legs because of uterine pressure and changes in the blood and its clotting mechanisms.

The most probable cause of blood clots in the legs during pregnancy is decreased blood flow, also called *stasis.* If you have had a previous blood clot—in your legs or any other part of your body—tell your doctor at the beginning of your pregnancy. He or she needs to know this important information.

**Deep-Vein Thrombosis.** Superficial thrombosis and deep-vein thrombosis in the leg are different conditions. A blood clot in the superficial veins of the leg is not as serious. This condition is usually noted in veins close to the surface of the skin that can often be felt on the surface. This type of clot is treated with a mild pain reliever, such as acetaminophen, elevation of the leg, support of the leg with an Ace bandage or support stockings, and occasionally heat. If the condition doesn't improve rapidly, deep-vein thrombosis must be considered.

Deep-vein thrombosis (DVT) is more serious; it requires diagnostic procedures and treatment. Symptoms of deep-vein thrombosis in the lower leg can differ greatly, depending on the location of the clot and how bad it is. The onset of deep-vein thrombosis can be rapid, with severe pain and swelling of the leg and thigh.

If you have had a blood clot in the past for any reason, pregnancy-related or not, see your doctor early in pregnancy. Tell him or her at your first prenatal visit about any previous problems you've had with blood clots.

The greatest danger from deep-vein thrombosis is a pulmonary embolism, in which a piece of the blood clot breaks off and travels from the legs to the lungs. This is a rare problem during pregnancy and is reported in only 1 in every 3000 to 7000 deliveries. Although it is a serious complication in pregnancy, it can often be avoided with early treatment.

**Symptoms to Watch For.** With deep-vein thrombosis (DVT), the leg may occasionally appear pale and cool, but usually a portion of the leg is tender, hot and swollen. Often skin over the affected veins is red. There may even be streaks of red on the skin over veins where blood clots have occurred.

Squeezing the calf or leg may be extremely painful, and it may be equally painful to walk. One way to tell if you have deep-vein thrombosis is to lie down and flex your toes toward your knee. If the back of the leg is tender, it is a positive indication of this problem; this is called *Homan's sign.* (This type of pain may also occur with a strained muscle or a bruise.) Check with your doctor if this occurs.

**Diagnosing the Problem.** Diagnostic studies of DVT may be different for a pregnant woman than for a nonpregnant woman. In the nonpregnant woman, an X-ray may be accompanied by an injection of dye into leg veins to look for blood clots. This test is not usually performed on a pregnant woman because of exposure to radiation and the dye. Ultrasound is used to diagnose this problem in pregnant women. Most major medical centers offer it, but the test is not available everywhere.

**Treating DVT.** Treatment of DVT usually consists of hospitalization and heparin therapy. Heparin (a blood thinner) must be given intravenously; it cannot be taken as a pill. It is safe during pregnancy and is not passed to the fetus. A woman may be required to take extra calcium during pregnancy if she receives heparin. While heparin is being administered, the woman is required to stay in bed. The leg may be elevated and heat applied. Mild pain medicine is prescribed.

Recovery time, including hospitalization, may be 7 to 10 days. After this time, the woman continues taking heparin until delivery. Following pregnancy, she will need to continue taking a blood thinner for up to several weeks, depending on the severity of the clot.

If a woman has a blood clot during one pregnancy, she will likely need heparin during subsequent pregnancies. If so, heparin can be given by an in-dwelling I.V. catheter or by daily injections the woman administers to herself under her doctor's supervision.

Another medication used to treat deep-vein thrombosis is warfarin, an oral medication. Warfarin (Coumadin) is not given during pregnancy because it crosses the placenta and can be harmful to the baby. Warfarin is usually given to the woman after pregnancy to prevent blood clots. It may be prescribed for a few weeks or a few months, depending on the severity of the clot.

## How Your Actions Affect Your Baby's Development

### ↗ Safety of Ultrasound

On the opposite page is an illustration of an ultrasound exam, accompanied by an interpretive illustration. These show a baby inside a uterus; the mother-to-be also has a large cyst in her abdomen.

Many women wonder about the safety of ultrasound exams. Most medical researchers agree ultrasound exams do not pose any risk to you or your baby. Researchers have looked for potential problems many times without finding evidence of any.

Ultrasound is an extremely valuable tool in diagnosing problems and answering some questions during pregnancy. Information that ultrasound testing provides can be reassuring to the doctor and the pregnant woman.

If your doctor has recommended ultrasound for you and you're concerned about it, discuss it with him or her. He or she may have an important reason for doing an ultrasound exam. It could affect the well-being of your developing baby.

Ultrasound may be used to detect problems. In this ultrasound of a baby in-utero, there is a cyst in the mother-to-be's abdomen. The interpretive illustration clarifies the ultrasound image.

## Your Nutrition

Some women experience food cravings during pregnancy. Food cravings have long been considered a nonspecific sign of pregnancy. Craving a particular food can be both good and bad. If the food you crave is nutritious and healthful, eat it in moderation. Don't eat food that isn't good for you. If you crave foods that are high in fat and sugar or loaded with empty calories, be careful. Take a little taste, but don't let yourself go. Try eating another food, such as a piece of fresh fruit or some cheese, instead of indulging in your craving.

### What Foods Do Pregnant Women Crave?

Recent research indicates three common cravings among pregnant women.

- 33% crave chocolate
- 20% crave sweets of some sort
- 19% crave citrus fruits and juices

We don't understand all the reasons a woman might crave a food while she's pregnant. We believe the hormonal and emotional changes that occur in pregnancy contribute to the situation.

On the opposite side of cravings is food aversion. Some foods that you have eaten without problems before pregnancy may now make you sick to your stomach. This is common. Again, we believe the hormones of pregnancy are involved. In this case, hormones affect the gastrointestinal tract, which can affect your reaction to some foods.

## You Should Also Know

### ᧞ Will You Get Varicose Veins?

Varicose veins, also called *varicosities* or *varices,* occur to some degree in most pregnant women. There appears to be an inherited predisposition to varicose veins that can be made more severe by pregnancy, increased age and pressure caused by standing for long periods of time.

Varicose veins are blood vessels that are engorged with blood. They occur primarily in the legs but may also be present in the vulva and rectum. The change in blood flow and pressure from the uterus make varices worse, which causes discomfort.

In most instances, varicose veins become more noticeable and more painful as pregnancy progresses. With increasing weight (especially if you spend a lot of time standing), they may worsen.

Symptoms vary. For some, the main symptom is a blemish or purple-blue spot on the legs with little or no discomfort, except perhaps in the evening. Other women have bulging veins that require elevation at the end of the day.

Following pregnancy, swelling in the veins should go down, but varicose veins probably won't disappear altogether. Various methods, including laser treatment, injection and surgery, can get rid of these veins; the surgery is called *vein stripping*. It would be unusual to operate on varicose veins during pregnancy, although it is a treatment to consider when you are not pregnant.

**Treating Varicose Veins.** Following these measures may help keep veins from swelling as much.

- Wear medical support hose; many types are available. Ask your doctor for a recommendation.
- Wear clothing that doesn't restrict circulation at the knee or the groin.
- Spend as little time on your feet as you can. Lie on your side or elevate your legs when possible. This enables veins to drain more easily.
- Wear flat shoes when you can.
- Don't cross your legs. It cuts off circulation and can make problems worse.
- The type of exercise you choose may compound the problem. High-impact exercise, such as step aerobics or jogging, can cause trauma to the veins. Low-impact exercises, such as biking, prenatal yoga or using an elliptical trainer, may be a better choice.

# Week 22

*Age of Fetus—20 Weeks*

## How Big Is Your Baby?

Your baby now weighs about 12¼ ounces (350g). Crown-to-rump length at this time is about 7⅔ inches (19cm).

## How Big Are You?

Your uterus is now about ¾ inch (2cm) above your bellybutton or almost 9 inches (22cm) from the pubic symphysis. You may feel "comfortably pregnant." Your enlarging abdomen is not too large and doesn't get in your way much. You're still able to bend over and to sit comfortably. Walking shouldn't be an effort. Morning sickness has probably passed, and you're feeling pretty good. It's kind of fun being pregnant now!

*Tip for Week 22* Drink extra fluids (water is best) throughout pregnancy to help your body keep up with the increase in your blood volume. You'll know you're drinking enough fluid when your urine looks almost like clear water.

By the 22nd week of pregnancy (fetal age—20 weeks), your baby's eyelids and eyebrows are well developed. Fingernails have grown and now cover the fingertips.

## How Your Baby Is
## Growing and Developing

Your baby continues to grow; its body is getting larger every day. As you can see by looking at the illustration on the previous page, your baby's eyelids, and even the eyebrows, are developed. Fingernails are also visible.

### ✌ Liver Function

Your baby's organ systems are becoming specialized for their particular functions. Consider the liver. The function of the fetal liver is different from that of an adult. Enzymes (chemicals) are made in an adult liver that are important in various body functions. In the fetus, these enzymes are present but in lower levels than those present after birth.

An important function of the liver is the breakdown and handling of bilirubin. Bilirubin is produced by the breakdown of blood cells. The life span of a fetal red blood cell is shorter than that of an adult. Because of this, a fetus produces more bilirubin than an adult does.

The fetal liver has a limited capacity to convert bilirubin, then remove it from the fetal bloodstream. Bilirubin passes from fetal blood through the placenta to your blood. Your liver helps get rid of fetal bilirubin. If a baby is born prematurely, it may have trouble processing bilirubin because its own liver is too immature to get rid of bilirubin from the bloodstream.

A newborn baby with high bilirubin may exhibit *jaundice.* Jaundice in a newborn is typically triggered by the transition from bilirubin being handled by the mother's system to the baby handling it on its own. The baby's liver can't keep up. Jaundice is more likely to occur in an immature infant when the liver is not ready to take over this function.

A baby with jaundice has a yellow tint to the skin and eyes. Jaundice is usually treated with phototherapy. Phototherapy uses light that penetrates the skin and destroys the bilirubin.

(For detailed information about this and other situations that might occur with your newborn, read our book *Your Baby's First Year Week by Week.*)

## Changes in You

### ✌ *Fetal Fibronectin*

In some cases, normal discomforts of pregnancy, such as lower-abdominal pain, dull backache, pelvic pressure, uterine contractions (with or without pain), cramping and a change in vaginal discharge may be confused with preterm labor. Until now, we have not had a reliable method of determining if a woman was truly at risk of delivering a preterm baby. A test is now available that can help doctors make this determination.

Fetal fibronectin (fFN) is a protein found in the amniotic sac and fetal membranes. However, after 22 weeks of pregnancy, fFN is not normally present until around week 38.

When it is present in the cervical-vaginal secretions of a pregnant woman after 22 weeks (and before week 38), it indicates increased risk for preterm delivery. If it is absent, risk of premature labor is low, and the woman probably won't deliver within the next 2 weeks.

The test is performed like a Pap smear. A swab of vaginal secretions is taken from the top of the vagina, behind the cervix. It is sent to the lab, and results are available within 24 hours.

### ✌ *What Is Anemia?*

Anemia is a common problem during pregnancy. If you suffer from anemia, treatment is important for you and your baby. If you are anemic, you won't feel well during pregnancy. You'll tire easily. You may experience dizziness.

There is a fine balance in your body between the production of blood cells that carry oxygen to the rest of your body and the destruction of these cells. Anemia is the condition in which the number of red blood cells is low. If you are anemic, you have an inadequate number of red blood cells.

During pregnancy, the number of red blood cells in your bloodstream increases. The amount of *plasma* (the liquid part of the blood) also increases but at a higher rate. Your doctor keeps track of these changes in your blood with a *hematocrit* reading. Your hematocrit is a measure of the percentage of the blood that is red blood cells. Your *he-moglobin* level is also tested. Hemoglobin is the protein component of red blood cells. If you are anemic, your hematocrit is lower than 37 and your hemoglobin is under 12.

A hematocrit determination is usually made at the first prenatal visit along with other lab work. It may be repeated once or twice during pregnancy. It is done more often if you are anemic.

There is always some blood loss at delivery. If you're anemic when you go into labor, you are at higher risk of needing a blood transfusion after your baby is born. Follow your doctor's advice about diet and supplementation if you suffer from anemia.

**Iron-Deficiency Anemia.**  The most common type of anemia seen in pregnancy is *iron-deficiency anemia*. During pregnancy, your baby uses some of the iron stores you have in your body. If you have iron-deficiency anemia, your body doesn't have enough iron left to make red blood cells because the baby has used some of your iron for its own blood cells.

Most prenatal vitamins contain iron, but it is also available as a supplement. If you are unable to take a prenatal vitamin, you may be given 300 to 350mg of ferrous sulphate or ferrous gluconate 2 or 3 times a day. Iron is the most important supplement to take. It is required in almost all pregnancies.

Even with supplemental iron, some women develop iron-deficiency anemia during pregnancy. Several factors may make a woman more likely to have this condition in pregnancy, including:

- failure to take iron or failure to take a prenatal vitamin containing iron
- bleeding during pregnancy
- multiple fetuses
- previous surgery on the stomach or part of the small bowel (making it difficult to absorb an adequate amount of iron before pregnancy)
- antacid overuse that causes a decrease in iron absorption
- poor dietary habits

The goal in treating iron-deficiency anemia is to increase the amount of iron you consume. Iron is poorly absorbed through the gastrointestinal tract and must be taken on a daily basis. It can be given as an injection, but it's painful and may stain the skin.

Side effects of taking iron supplements include nausea and vomiting, with stomach upset. If this occurs, you may have to take a lower dose. Taking iron may also cause constipation.

If you cannot take an oral iron supplement, an increase in dietary iron from foods, such as liver or spinach, may help prevent anemia. Ask your doctor for information on what types of foods you should include in your diet.

**Sickle-Cell Anemia.** For women who are dark-skinned and of Mediterranean or African descent, sickle-cell anemia can cause significant problems during pregnancy. Anemia occurs in these cases because the bone marrow, which produces the body's red blood cells, cannot replace red blood cells as quickly as they are destroyed. In sickle-cell anemia, the red blood cells produced are also abnormal, which can cause severe pain because they become blocked in the blood vessels and cannot flow.

You may carry the trait for sickle-cell anemia without having the disease. You could possibly pass the trait or the disease to your baby. Tell your doctor of any family history of the disease.

A blood test easily detects the sickle-cell trait. Sickle-cell anemia can be diagnosed in the fetus with amniocentesis (discussed in Week 16) or chorionic villus sampling (discussed in Week 10).

Women with the sickle-cell trait are more likely to have pyelonephritis (see Week 18) and bacteria in the urine during pregnancy. They are also susceptible to developing sickle-cell anemia during pregnancy.

A woman who has sickle-cell anemia may have repeated episodes of pain (sickle crises) throughout her lifetime. Pain in the abdomen or limbs is caused by the blockage of blood vessels by abnormal red blood cells. Episodes of pain may be severe and may require hospitalization for treatment with fluids and pain medication.

Hydroxyurea has proved effective as a treatment, but its use carries some risks. Because we do not have research data on long-term effects, pregnant women are advised not to use it.

Risks to a pregnant woman with sickle-cell disease are those of painful sickle crisis, infections and even congestive heart failure. Risks to the fetus include a high incidence of miscarriage and stillbirth, estimated to be as high as 50%. Even though the risks are greater, many women with sickle-cell anemia have successful pregnancies.

**Thalassemia.** Another type of anemia encountered less frequently is thalassemia, which occurs most often in Mediterranean populations. It is characterized by underproduction of part of the simple protein that makes up red blood cells, and anemia results. If you have a family history of thalassemia or know you have thalassemia, discuss it with your doctor.

## How Your Actions
## Affect Your Baby's Development

### ∽ *When You Feel "Under the Weather"*
It's possible you could have diarrhea or a cold during pregnancy, as well as other viral infections such as the flu. These problems may raise concerns for you.

* What can I do when I feel ill?
* What medication or treatment is acceptable?
* If I'm sick, should I take my prenatal vitamins?
* If I'm sick and unable to eat my usual diet, what should I do?

If you become sick during pregnancy, don't hesitate to call your doctor's office. Get your doctor's advice about a plan of action. He or she will be able to advise you about what medications you may be able to take to help you feel better. Even if it's only a cold or the flu, your doctor wants to know when you're feeling ill. If any further measures are needed, your doctor will recommend them.

Is there anything you can do to help yourself? Yes, there is. If you have diarrhea or a possible viral infection, increase your fluid intake. Drink a lot of water, juice and other clear fluids, such as broth. You may find a bland diet without solid food helps you feel a little better.

Going off your regular diet for a few days won't be harmful to you or your baby, but you do need to drink plenty of fluids. Solid foods may be difficult for you to handle and can make diarrhea a bigger problem. Milk products may also make diarrhea worse.

**Dad Tip** When you ride together in the car with your partner, ask if you can help her in any way. You may offer to assist her getting in and out of the car. You may propose trading vehicles (if you have more than one), if it's more comfortable for her to drive the other car. Ask if she needs help adjusting her seat belt or the car seat. Try to make riding and driving as easy and accessible as possible for her.

If diarrhea continues beyond 24 hours, call your doctor. Ask which medications you can take for diarrhea during pregnancy.

If you are sick, it's OK to skip your prenatal vitamin for a few days. However, begin taking it again when you are able to keep food down.

Don't take any medication without consulting your doctor first. Usually a viral illness with diarrhea is a short-term problem and won't last more than a few days. You may have to stay home from work or rest in bed until you feel better.

## Your Nutrition

You need to drink water and other fluids during pregnancy—lots of it! Fluid helps your body process nutrients, develop new cells, keep up your blood volume and regulate body temperature. You may feel better during your pregnancy if you drink more water than you normally do.

Studies show that for every 15 calories your body burns, you need about 1 tablespoon of water. If you burn 2000 calories a day, you need to drink about 2 quarts of water! Because your calorie needs increase during pregnancy, so does your need for water. Six to eight glasses a day is a good target. You can meet your goal of at least 2 quarts a day by sipping water and other fluids throughout the day. If you decrease your consumption later in the day, you may save yourself some trips to the bathroom at night.

Some women wonder if they can drink other beverages besides water. Water is the best source of fluid; however, other fluid sources help meet your needs. You can drink milk, vegetable juice, fruit juice and some herbal teas. Eating vegetables and fruits, other milk products, meat and grain products also help you meet your fluid-consumption target. Avoid tea, coffee and cola—they may contain sodium and caffeine, which act as diuretics. They essentially *increase* your water needs.

Some of the common problems women experience during pregnancy may be eased by drinking water. Headaches, uterine cramping and bladder infections may be less of a problem for you when you drink lots of water.

Check your urine to see if you're drinking enough. If it is light yellow to clear, you're getting enough fluid. Dark-yellow urine is a sign to increase your fluid intake. Don't wait till you get thirsty to drink something. By the time you get thirsty, you've already lost at least 1% of your body's fluids.

## You Should Also Know

### ☞ *Stress during Pregnancy*
Feeling stress is common during pregnancy. Your body is changing, you and your partner are facing the prospect of parenthood and you may not be feeling very well. You may feel stress from working or other obligations. Relax, and take it easy! Stress isn't good for anyone, especially a pregnant woman.

There are quite a few things you can do to help relieve stress in your life right now. Try them, and encourage your partner to try them, too, if he's also feeling stressed out.

- Get enough sleep each night. Lack of sleep can make you feel stressed.
- Rest and relax during the day. Read or listen to music during a quiet period.
- Exercise to help you work off stress. Take a walk or visit the gym. Put on an exercise video for pregnant women. Do something active and physical (but not too physical) to relieve stress. Ask your partner to join you.
- Eat nutritiously. Having enough calories available all through the day will help you avoid "lows."
- Do something you enjoy, and do it for you.
- Put on a happy face. Sometimes just changing how you think about something—deciding to be more positive—can have an effect on you. Smiling instead of frowning can help ease stress.
- If smells are important to you, make sure you include them in your life. Burn scented candles, or buy fragrant flowers to help you relax.
- Don't be the "Lone Ranger." Share your concerns with your partner, or find a group of pregnant women you can talk with.

### ↷ *Appendicitis*

Appendicitis can happen at any time, even during pregnancy. Pregnancy can make the diagnosis difficult because some of the symptoms are typical in a normal pregnancy, such as nausea and vomiting. Diagnosis is also difficult because as the uterus grows larger, the appendix moves upward and outward, so pain and tenderness are located in a different place than normal. See the illustration on page 236.

Treatment for appendicitis is immediate surgery. This is major abdominal surgery, with a 3- or 4-inch incision, and it requires a few days

At 34 weeks

At 20 weeks

Before pregnancy

Bellybutton

Location of the appendix at various times during pregnancy.

in the hospital. Laparoscopy, with smaller incisions, is used in some situations, but laparoscopy may be more difficult to perform during pregnancy because of the enlarged uterus.

Serious complications can arise when an infected appendix ruptures. Most physicians believe it's better to operate and remove a "normal" appendix than to risk infection of the abdominal cavity if the infected appendix ruptures. Antibiotics are administered; many antibiotics are safe to use during pregnancy.

# *Week 23*

## *Age of Fetus—21 Weeks*

## How Big Is Your Baby?

By this week, your baby weighs almost 1 pound (455g)! Its crown-to-rump length is 8 inches (20cm). Your baby is about the size of a small doll.

## How Big Are You?

Your uterus extends about 1½ inches (3.75cm) above your bellybutton or about 9¼ inches (23cm) from the pubic symphysis. The changes in your abdomen are progressing slowly, but you definitely have a round appearance now. Your total weight gain should be between 12 and 15 pounds (5.5 and 6.8kg).

## How Your Baby Is Growing and Developing

Baby continues to grow. Its body is getting plumper but skin is still wrinkled; it will gain even more weight. See the illustration on page 239.

By the 23<sup>rd</sup> week of pregnancy (fetal age—21 weeks), your baby's eyelids and eyebrows are well developed.

Lanugo hair on the body occasionally turns darker at this time. The baby's face and body begin to assume more of the appearance of an infant at birth.

### ✣ *Fetal Pancreas Function*

Your baby's pancreas is developing. This organ is important in hormone production, particularly insulin production; insulin is necessary for the body to break down and to use sugar.

When the fetus is exposed to high blood-sugar levels, the fetal pancreas responds by increasing the blood-insulin level. Insulin has been identified in a fetal pancreas as early as 9 weeks of pregnancy. Insulin in fetal blood has been detected as early as 12 weeks of pregnancy.

Insulin levels are generally high in the blood of babies born to diabetic mothers. That is one reason your doctor may monitor you for diabetes.

## Changes in You

At this point, friends may comment on your size. They may say you must be carrying twins because you're so large. Or they may say you're too small for how far along you think you are. If these comments concern you, discuss them with your doctor.

Your doctor will measure you at every visit after this point. He or she is watching for changes in your weight gain and in the size of your uterus. Remember that women and babies are different sizes and grow at different rates. What's important for you is continual change and continual growth.

As your baby gets larger, the placenta gets larger. The amount of amniotic fluid also increases.

### ✣ *Loss of Fluid*

As your pregnancy progresses, your uterus grows larger and gets heavier. In early pregnancy, it lies directly behind the bladder, in front of the rectum and the lower part of the colon, which is part of the bowel.

Later in pregnancy, the uterus sits on top of the bladder. As it increases in size, it can put a great deal of pressure on your bladder. You may notice times when your underwear is wet.

You may be uncertain whether you have lost urine or if you are leaking amniotic fluid. It may be difficult to tell the difference between the two. However, when your membranes rupture, you usually experience a gush of fluid or a continual leaking from the vagina. If you experience this, call your doctor immediately!

### ⤳ *Emotional Changes Continue*

Do you find your mood swings are worse? Are you still crying easily? Do you wonder if you'll ever be in control again?

Don't worry. These emotions are typical at this point in your pregnancy. Most authorities believe they occur from the hormonal changes that continue throughout pregnancy.

There is little you can do about periods of moodiness. If you think your partner or others are suffering from your emotional outbursts, talk about it with them. Explain that these feelings are common in pregnant women. Ask them to be understanding. Then relax, and try not to get upset about it. Feeling emotional is a normal part of being pregnant.

## How Your Actions Affect Your Baby's Development

### ⤳ *Diabetes and Pregnancy*

Once a very serious problem during pregnancy, diabetes continues to be an important complication. Today, however, many diabetic women go through pregnancy safely with proper medical care and good nutrition—and by following their doctor's instructions.

Before insulin was available, it was unusual for a diabetic woman to get pregnant. With the discovery of insulin and the development of various ways to monitor a fetus, it is uncommon to have a severe problem today. Survival rate of babies is good.

Diabetes is a condition defined as a lack of insulin in the bloodstream. Insulin is important for breaking down sugar and transporting it to the cells. If you do not have insulin, you will have high blood sugar and a high sugar content in your urine.

There are two types of diabetes. *Type 1* causes the body to stop making insulin; *Type 2* causes the body to use insulin ineffectively. Research has found that Type 2 diabetes is becoming more common in pregnant women. The result of either type is that too much sugar circulates in the woman's blood.

Diabetes during pregnancy can cause several medical problems, including kidney problems, eye problems and other blood or vascular problems, such as atherosclerosis or myocardial infarction (heart attack). These can be serious for you and your baby.

> *Ðad Ꮯip*  Are you also having pregnancy symptoms? Studies show that as many as 50% of all fathers-to-be experience physical symptoms of pregnancy when their partner is pregnant. *Couvade,* a French term meaning "to hatch," is used to describe the condition in a man. Symptoms for an expectant father may include nausea, weight gain and cravings for certain foods.

**Controlling Diabetes during Pregnancy.** If your diabetes is not controlled during pregnancy, you have a greater chance of giving birth to a large baby. This increases your chances of having a C-section. You also increase your risk of pre-eclampsia. In addition, the baby is at greater risk of hypoglycemia (low blood sugar) and jaundice.

One way to maintain steady blood-sugar levels is never to skip meals and to get enough exercise, according to your finger sticks. You may have to adjust the amount of oral medication you usually take, and insulin may need to be added during pregnancy. If you already take insulin, you may need to adjust your dosage, the timing of your dosage or the amount of insulin you take. You may also have to check your blood-sugar levels 4 to 8 times a day.

Insulin is the safest way to control your diabetes during pregnancy. However, long-lasting insulin should be avoided by pregnant women.

Oral hypoglycemic medications, such as metformin, are not recommended for use during pregnancy.

**Diagnosing Diabetes in Pregnancy.** Pregnancy is well known for its tendency to reveal women who are predisposed to diabetes. Women who have trouble with high blood-sugar levels during pregnancy are more likely to develop diabetes in later life. Symptoms of diabetes include the following:

- more frequent urination
- blurred vision
- weight loss
- dizziness
- increased hunger

It may be necessary to do blood tests to diagnose diabetes during pregnancy. In some areas, this testing is done routinely. If you have diabetes or know members of your family who have diabetes now or have had diabetes in the past, tell your doctor. He or she will decide what course of action is best for you.

**Gestational Diabetes.** Some women develop diabetes only during pregnancy; it is called *gestational diabetes*. Gestational diabetes affects about 10% of all pregnancies. After pregnancy is over, nearly all women who experience this problem return to normal, and the problem disappears. However, if gestational diabetes occurs with one pregnancy, there is almost a 90% chance it will recur in subsequent pregnancies.

We believe gestational diabetes occurs for two reasons. One is the mother's body produces less insulin during pregnancy. The second is the mother's body can't use insulin effectively. Both situations result in high blood-sugar levels.

A woman's weight when she was born may be an indicator of her chances of developing gestational diabetes. One study showed women who were in the *bottom 10th percentile* of weight when they were born were 3 to 4 times more likely to develop gestational diabetes during pregnancy.

If left untreated, gestational diabetes can be serious for you and your baby. You will both be exposed to a high concentration of sugar, which is not healthy for either of you. You might experience *polyhydramnios* (excessive amounts of amniotic fluid). This may cause premature labor because the uterus becomes overdistended.

A woman with gestational diabetes may have a long labor because the baby is quite large. Sometimes a baby cannot fit through the birth canal, and a Cesarean delivery is required.

If your blood-sugar level is high, you may experience more infections during pregnancy. The most common infections include those in the kidneys, the bladder, the cervix and the uterus.

Treatment of gestational diabetes includes regular exercise and increased fluid intake. Diet is essential in handling this problem. Your doctor will probably recommend a six-meal, 2000- to 2500-calorie per day eating plan. You may also be referred to a dietitian.

## Your Nutrition

### ∼ *Your Sodium Intake*
You may need to be careful with your sodium intake during pregnancy. Consuming too much sodium may cause you to retain water, which can cause swelling and bloating. Avoid foods that contain lots of sodium or salt, such as salted nuts, potato chips, pickles, canned foods and processed foods.

*Tip for Week 23* Keep your consumption of sodium to 3 grams (3000mg) or less a day. This may help you reduce fluid retention.

Read food labels. They list the amount of sodium in a serving. Some books list the sodium content of foods without labels, such as fast foods. Check them out. You'll be surprised how many milligrams of sodium a fast-food hamburger contains!

Look at the chart on the opposite page, which lists some common foods and their sodium content. You can see foods that contain sodium

## Sodium Content of Various Foods

| Food | Serving Size | Sodium Content (mg) |
|------|--------------|---------------------|
| American cheese | 1 slice | 322 |
| Asparagus | 14.5-oz. can | 970 |
| Big Mac hamburger | 1 regular | 963 |
| Chicken a la king | 1 cup | 760 |
| Cola | 8 oz. | 16 |
| Cottage cheese | 1 cup | 580 |
| Dill pickle | 1 medium | 928 |
| Flounder | 3 oz. | 201 |
| Gelatin, sweet | 3 oz. | 270 |
| Ham, baked | 3 oz. | 770 |
| Honeydew melon | ½ | 90 |
| Lima beans | 8½ oz. | 1070 |
| Lobster | 1 cup | 305 |
| Oatmeal | 1 cup | 523 |
| Potato chips | 20 regular | 400 |
| Salt | 1 teaspoon | 1938 |

do not always taste salty. Read labels, and check other available information before you eat!

## You Should Also Know

### ◌ *Sugar in Your Urine*

It is common for nondiabetic pregnant women to have a small amount of sugar in their urine. This occurs because of changes in sugar levels and how sugar is handled in the kidneys, which control the amount of sugar in your system. If excess sugar is present, you will lose it in your urine. Sugar in the urine is called *glucosuria*. It is common during pregnancy, particularly in the second and third trimesters.

Many doctors test every pregnant woman for diabetes, usually around the end of the second trimester. Testing is particularly important if you have a family history of diabetes. Blood tests used to diagnose diabetes are a fasting blood-sugar and glucose-tolerance test (GTT).

For a fasting blood-sugar test, you eat your normal meal the evening before the test. In the morning, before eating anything, you go to the lab and have a blood test done. A normal result indicates that diabetes is unlikely. An abnormal result is a high level of sugar in the blood, which needs further study.

Further study involves the glucose-tolerance test. You have to fast after dinner the night before this test. In the morning at the lab, you are given a solution to drink that has a measured amount of sugar in it. It is similar to a bottle of soda pop but doesn't taste as good. After you drink the solution, blood is drawn at predetermined intervals; usually at 30 minutes, 1 hour and 2 hours and sometimes even 3 hours. Drawing the blood at intervals gives an indication of how your body handles sugar.

If you need treatment, your doctor will devise a plan for you.

# Week 24

*Age of Fetus—22 Weeks*

## How Big Is Your Baby?

By this week, your baby weighs about 1¼ pounds (540g). Its crown-to-rump length is about 8½ inches (21cm).

## How Big Are You?

Your uterus is now about 1½ to 2 inches (3.8 to 5.1cm) above the bellybutton. It measures almost 10 inches (24cm) above the pubic symphysis.

## How Your Baby Is Growing and Developing

Your baby is filling out. Its face and body look more like that of an infant at the time of birth. Although it weighs a little over 1 pound at this point, it is still very tiny.

### ⌁ *Role of the Amniotic Sac and Amniotic Fluid*

By about the 12th day after fertilization, there is an early beginning of the amniotic sac. The baby grows and develops in the amniotic fluid inside the amniotic sac. (See the illustration on the opposite page.) Amniotic fluid has several important functions.

- It provides an environment in which the baby can move easily.
- It cushions the fetus against injury.
- Amniotic fluid regulates temperature for the baby.
- It provides a way of assessing the health and maturity of the baby.

Amniotic fluid increases rapidly from an average volume of 1½ ounces (50ml) by 12 weeks of pregnancy to 12 ounces (400ml) at mid-pregnancy. The volume of amniotic fluid continues to increase as your due date approaches until a maximum of about 2 pints (1 liter) of fluid is reached at 36 to 38 weeks gestation.

Composition of amniotic fluid changes during pregnancy. During the first half of pregnancy, amniotic fluid is similar to maternal plasma (the fluid in your blood without blood cells), except it has a much lower protein content. As pregnancy advances, fetal urine makes an increasingly important contribution to the amount of amniotic fluid present. Amniotic fluid also contains old fetal blood cells, lanugo hair and vernix.

*Tip for Week 24* Overeating and eating before going to bed at night are two major causes of heartburn. Eating five or six small, nutritious meals a day and skipping snacks before bedtime may help you feel better.

The fetus swallows amniotic fluid during much of pregnancy. If it can't swallow amniotic fluid, you will develop a condition of excess amniotic fluid, called *hydramnios* or *polyhydramnios*. If the fetus swallows but doesn't urinate (for example, if the baby lacks kidneys), the volume of amniotic fluid surrounding the fetus may be very small. This is called *oligohydramnios*.

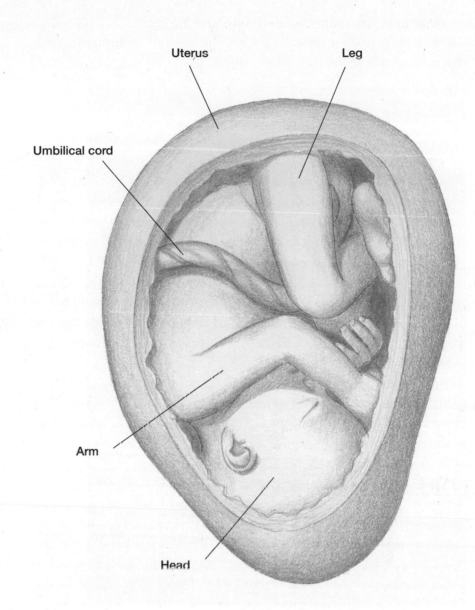

Uterus

Leg

Umbilical cord

Arm

Head

The fetus doesn't appear to have a great deal of room to move in the uterus by the 24th week. As the weeks pass, space gets even tighter.

Amniotic fluid is important. It provides the baby space to move and allows it to grow. If there is an inadequate amount of amniotic fluid, the baby usually shows decreased growth.

## Changes in You

### ↷ Nasal Problems

Some women complain of stuffiness in their nose or frequent nose-bleeds during pregnancy. Some researchers believe these symptoms occur because of changes in circulation due to hormonal changes during pregnancy. This can cause the mucous membranes of your nose and nasal passageways to swell and to bleed more easily.

Some decongestants and nasal sprays have been proved safe for use during pregnancy. Some brands to consider include chlorpheniramine (Chlor-Trimeton) decongestants and oxymetazoline (Afrin, Dristan Long-Lasting) nasal sprays. Before you begin using any product, discuss it with your doctor.

It may also help to use a humidifier, particularly during the winter months when heating may dry out the air. Some women get relief from increasing their fluid intake and/or using a gentle lubricant in their nose, such as petroleum jelly.

### ↷ Depression during Pregnancy

Many people have heard about postpartum depression (feeling blue or being depressed after baby's birth). There has been a great deal of information on the subject in the media in the last few years. However, you probably haven't heard much about depression *during* pregnancy, but it does occur. Studies show that up to 25% of all moms-to-be experience some degree of depression, and nearly 10% will experience a major depression.

When you are pregnant, your body goes through many changes. It may be hard to distinguish between some of the normal pregnancy changes and signs of depression. Many symptoms of depression are similar to those of pregnancy, including fatigue and sleeplessness. The difference is how intense the symptoms are and how long they last. Some common symptoms of depression include:

- overpowering sadness that lasts for days, without an obvious cause
- difficulty sleeping, or waking up very early
- wanting to sleep all the time or great fatigue (this can be normal early in pregnancy but usually gets better after a few weeks)
- no appetite (as distinguished from nausea and vomiting)
- lack of concentration
- thoughts of harming yourself

If you have these symptoms and they don't get better in a few weeks or every day seems to be bad, talk to your doctor. There are medications that can help, such as antidepressants; some are safe to use during pregnancy. If your depression is severe, medication may be necessary for your good health and the good health of your baby. In addition, counseling may be recommended.

Other suggestions for dealing with depression include getting enough exercise and being sure you get enough B vitamins, folic acid and omega-3 fatty acids (see the discussion of fish in Week 26). Additional therapies include massage and reflexology.

Another option for treating this type of depression is light therapy, similar to the type of treatment given to those who suffer from "seasonal affective disorder." When a person is depressed, exposure to bright-white fluorescent light for 60 minutes a day, up to 5 times a week, has proved beneficial. A recent study showed that moods improved in about 50% of those who underwent the treatment. We believe that bright light influences your biorhythms and helps release certain hormones that help deal with depression.

If you believe you are depressed, bring it up at a prenatal visit. There are steps you and your doctor can take to help you feel better again. It's important to do it for yourself and your baby!

## How Your Actions Affect Your Baby's Development

### ∾ What Your Baby Can Hear

Can a growing baby hear sounds while it's inside the uterus? From various research studies, we know that sounds can penetrate amniotic fluid and reach your baby's developing ears.

If you work in a noisy place, you may want to request a quieter area during your pregnancy. From data gathered in some studies, it is believed that chronic loud noise and short, intense bursts of sound may cause hearing damage to the fetus before and after birth.

It's OK to expose your growing baby to loud noises, such as a concert, every once in a while. But if you are repeatedly exposed to noise that is so loud it forces you to shout, there may be potential danger to your baby.

## Your Nutrition

Many pregnant women are concerned about eating out. Some want to know if they can eat certain types of food, such as Mexican, Vietnamese, Thai or Greek food. They're concerned that spicy or rich foods could be harmful to the baby. It's OK to eat out, but you might find certain foods don't agree with you.

The best types of food to eat at restaurants are those you tolerate well at home. Chicken, fish, fresh vegetables and salads are usually good choices. Restaurants that feature spicy foods or unusual cuisine may cause you stomach or intestinal distress. You may even notice an increase in weight from water retention after eating at a restaurant.

During pregnancy, avoid restaurants that serve highly

**Dad Tip**   Now is a good time to find out about prenatal classes in your area. Find out how many classes there are, when and where to register and the registration cost. You may be able to take classes at the hospital or birthing center where you plan to deliver. Try to *complete* the classes at least 1 month *before* your baby is due.

salted food, food high in sodium or food loaded with calories and fat, such as gravies, fried food, junk food and rich desserts. It may be difficult to control your calorie intake at specialty restaurants.

Another challenge of eating out is maintaining a healthy diet if you work outside the home. It may be necessary to go to business lunches or to travel for your company. Be selective. If you can choose off the menu, look for healthy or low-fat choices. You may ask about preparation—maybe a dish can be steamed instead of fried. On a business trip, take along some of your own food. Choose healthy, nonperishable foods, such as fruits and vegetables, that don't need refrigeration.

## You Should Also Know

### ✎ *How Pregnancy Affects You Sexually*

Pregnancy and sex. Are you interested? Is it just too much to think about right now? Has your sexual desire increased? Is sex the last thing on your mind?

Generally, women experience one of two sex-drive patterns during pregnancy. One is a lessening of desire in the first and third trimesters, with an increase in the second trimester. The second is a gradual decrease in desire for sex as pregnancy progresses.

During the first trimester, you may experience fatigue and nausea. During the third trimester, your weight gain, enlarging abdomen, tender breasts and other problems may make you desire sex less. This is normal. Tell your partner how you feel, and try to work out a solution that is satisfactory to you both.

Pregnancy actually enhances the sex drive for some women. In some cases, a woman may experience orgasms or multiple orgasms for the first time during pregnancy. This is due to heightened hormonal activity and increased blood flow to the pelvic area.

Some women feel less attractive during pregnancy because of their size and the changes in their bodies. Discuss your feelings with your partner. Tenderness and understanding can help you both.

You may find new positions for lovemaking are necessary as pregnancy progresses. Your abdomen may make some positions more uncomfortable than others. In addition, we advise you not to lie flat on your back after 16 weeks until the baby's birth because the weight of the uterus restricts circulation. You might try lying on your side or use a position that puts you on top.

**When to Avoid Sexual Activity.** Some situations should alert you to abstain from sexual activity. If you have a history of early labor, your doctor may warn against intercourse and orgasm; orgasm causes mild uterine contractions. Chemicals in semen may also stimulate contractions, so it may not be advisable for a woman's partner to ejaculate inside her.

If you have a history of miscarriage, your doctor may caution you against sex and orgasm. However, no data actually links sex and miscarriage. Avoid sexual activity if you have placenta previa or a low-lying placenta, an incompetent cervix, premature labor, ruptured bag of waters, pain with intercourse, unexplained vaginal bleeding or discharge, either partner has an unhealed herpes lesion or you believe labor has begun.

**Sexual Practices to Avoid.** Some sexual practices should be avoided when you're pregnant. Don't insert any object into the vagina that could cause injury or infection. Blowing air into the vagina is dangerous because it can force a potentially fatal air bubble into a woman's bloodstream. (This can occur whether or not you are pregnant.) Nipple stimulation releases oxytocin, which causes uterine contractions; you might want to discuss this practice with your doctor.

### ✎ An Incompetent Cervix

An incompetent cervix refers to the painless premature dilatation of the cervix, which usually results in delivery of a premature baby. It can be an important problem during pregnancy.

Dilatation (stretching of the cervix) goes unnoticed by the woman until the baby is delivering; it often occurs without warning. Diagnosis is usually made after one or more deliveries of a premature infant without any pain before delivery.

The cause of cervical incompetence is usually unknown. Some medical researchers believe it occurs because of previous injury or surgery to the cervix, such as dilatation and curettage (D&C) for an abortion or a miscarriage.

Usually the cervix doesn't dilate in this way before the 16th week of pregnancy. Before this time, the products of conception are not heavy enough to cause the cervix to dilate and to thin out.

A pregnancy that is lost from an incompetent cervix is completely different from a miscarriage. A miscarriage during the first trimester is common. Incompetent cervix is a relatively rare complication in pregnancy.

Treatment for an incompetent cervix is usually surgical. The weak cervix is reinforced with a suture that sews the cervix shut, called a *McDonald cerclage*.

If this is your first pregnancy, there is no way you can know whether you have an incompetent cervix. If you have had problems in the past or have had premature deliveries and have been told you might have an incompetent cervix, share this important information with your doctor.

# Week 25

*Age of Fetus—23 Weeks*

## How Big Is Your Baby?

Your baby now weighs about 1½ pounds (700g), and crown-to-rump length is about 8¾ inches (22cm). Remember, these are average lengths and weights, and vary from one baby to another and from one pregnancy to another.

## How Big Are You?

Look at the illustration on the opposite page. By this week of pregnancy, your uterus has grown quite a bit. When you look at a side view, you're obviously getting bigger.

The measurement from the pubic symphysis to the top of your uterus is about 10 inches (25cm). If you saw your doctor when you were 20 or 21 weeks pregnant, you have probably grown about 1½ inches (4cm). At this point, your uterus is about the size of a soccer ball.

The top of the uterus is about halfway between your bellybutton and the lower part of your sternum. (The sternum is the bone between your breasts where the ribs come together.)

Comparative size of the uterus at 25 weeks of pregnancy (fetal age—
23 weeks). The uterus can be felt about 2 inches (5cm) above your
umbilicus (bellybutton).

# How Your Baby Is
# Growing and Developing

### ᔆ *Survival of a Premature Baby*

It may be hard to believe, but if your baby were delivered now, it would have a chance of surviving. Some of the greatest advances in medicine have been in the care of the premature baby. No one wants a baby to deliver this early, but with new treatment methods, such as ventilators, monitors and medication, a baby does have a chance of surviving.

The baby weighs less than 2 pounds and is extremely small. Survival is difficult for an infant delivered this early. The baby would probably spend several months in the hospital, with risks of infection and other possible complications. Also see the discussion in Week 29.

### ᔆ *Is It a Boy? Is It a Girl?*

One of the most common questions parents-to-be ask is, "What is the sex of our baby?" Amniocentesis can determine the sex of the baby by chromosome study. Ultrasound examination can also be used to reveal the sex of the baby but may be inaccurate. Don't get your heart set on a particular sex if ultrasound is used. For many people, not knowing is part of the fun of having a baby.

Some people believe a baby's heartbeat rate can indicate its sex. A normal heart rate for a baby ranges from 120 to 160 beats a minute. Some believe a fast heartbeat indicates a girl, and a slow heartbeat indicates a boy. Unfortunately, there is no scientific proof of this. Don't pressure your doctor to guess based on this method because it is *only* a guess.

A more reliable source might be a mother, mother-in-law or someone who can look at you and tell by how you're carrying the baby if it is a boy or girl. Although we make this statement with our tongues placed firmly in our cheeks, many people believe it's true. Some people claim they're never wrong about guessing or predicting the sex of a baby before birth. Again, there is no scientific basis for this method.

Your doctor is more concerned about your health and well-being, and that of your baby. He or she will concentrate on making sure you and your baby, whether it's a boy or girl, are progressing through pregnancy safely and that you both get through pregnancy, labor and delivery in good health.

## Changes in You

### ✣ *Itching*

Itching (*pruritus gravidarum*) is a common symptom during pregnancy. There are no bumps or lesions on the skin; it just itches. Nearly 20% of all pregnant women suffer from itching, often in the last weeks of pregnancy, but it can occur at any time. It may occur with each pregnancy and may also appear when you use oral contraceptives. The condition doesn't present any risk to you or your baby.

As your uterus has grown and filled your pelvis, your abdominal skin and muscles have stretched. Itchiness is a natural consequence. Lotions are OK to use to help reduce itching. Try not to scratch and irritate your skin—that can make it worse! You might want to ask your doctor about taking antihistamines or using cooling lotions containing menthol or camphor. Often no treatment is needed.

> ### *Tip for Week 25*
> Pregnancy can be a time of communication and personal growth with your partner. Listen when he talks. Let him know he is an important source of emotional support for you.

### ✣ *Stress Can Affect You*

Stress in your life can have an impact on your pregnancy. Research is showing an increasing connection between stress experienced by the mother-to-be and pregnancy problems, such as pre-eclampsia, miscarriage and premature labor.

If you have major stress in your life right now—you've lost your job or moved, or someone close to you has died—be sure to take good care of yourself. Eat well, get enough rest and try to de-stress. Talking about it can help—ask your doctor to recommend a support group.

## How Your Actions
## Affect Your Baby's Development

### ᔕ Falling and Injuries from Falls

A fall is the most frequent cause of minor injury during pregnancy. Fortunately, a fall is usually without serious injury to the baby or mother. The uterus is well protected in the abdomen inside the pelvis. The baby is protected against injury by the cushion of amniotic fluid surrounding it. Your uterus and abdominal wall also offer some protection.

**If You Fall.** If you fall, contact your doctor; he or she may want to examine you. You may feel reassured if you are monitored and your baby's heartbeat is checked. The baby's movement after a fall can be reassuring.

Minor injuries to the abdomen are treated in the usual fashion, as though you were not pregnant. However, avoid X-rays if possible.

Ultrasound evaluation may be important after a fall. This is judged on an individual basis, depending on the severity of your symptoms and your injury.

**Take Care to Avoid Falls.** Remember your balance and mobility change as you grow larger during pregnancy. Be careful during the winter when parking lots and sidewalks may be wet or icy. Many pregnant women also fall on stairs; always use the handrail. Walk in well-lit areas, and try to stay on sidewalks.

Slow down a little as you get larger; you won't be able to get around as quickly as you normally do. With the change in your balance, plus any dizziness you may experience, it's important to be vigilant to try to avoid falling.

**Signs to Watch for after a Fall.** Some signs can alert you to a problem after a fall:

- bleeding
- a gush of fluid from the vagina, indicating rupture of membranes
- severe abdominal pain

Placental abruption (discussed in Week 33) is one of the most serious events that can occur because of a fall or injury. With placental abruption, the placenta prematurely separates from the uterus. Another significant injury is a broken bone or an injury that immobilizes you. (See the discussion below.)

**Treating Broken Bones.** Sometimes a fall or accident causes a broken bone, which may require X-rays and surgery. Treatment cannot be delayed until after pregnancy; the problem must be dealt with immediately. If you find yourself in such a situation, insist your OB/GYN be contacted before any test is done or treatment is started.

If X-rays are required, your pelvis and abdomen must be shielded. If they cannot be shielded, the need for the X-ray must be weighed against the risks it poses to the baby.

Anesthesia or pain medication may be necessary with a simple break that requires setting or pinning. It is best for you and the baby to avoid general anesthesia if possible. You may need pain medication, but keep its use to a minimum.

If general anesthesia is required to repair a break, the baby should be monitored closely. You may not have a lot of choice in the matter. Your surgeon and OB/GYN will work together to provide the best care for you and your baby.

## Your Nutrition

Pregnancy increases your need for vitamins and minerals. It's best if you can meet most of these needs through the foods you eat. However, being realistic, we know that's difficult for many women. That's one reason your doctor prescribes a prenatal vitamin for you—to help you meet your nutritional needs.

Some women do need extra help during pregnancy—supplements are often prescribed for them. These pregnant women include teenagers (whose bodies are still growing), severely underweight women, women who ate a poor diet before conception and women who have

## Some Alternative Food Choices

As you move through your pregnancy, you may find adding nutritious foods to your eating plan is getting harder. You may be bored with the foods you've been eating. The points below may help make it easier to choose different healthy foods.

- Complex carbohydrates that are high in fiber provide your body with a constant source of energy and help you feel full longer. Try whole-wheat bagels, tortillas or risotto.
- Green leafy veggies, such as spinach and broccoli, contain different nutrients than orange vegetables, such as yams or carrots. Try to have a combination of these every day. One great dish that may satisfy your needs and taste great at the same time is a "Squash Bake." In a non-stick frying pan, heat a little water, then add cut up zucchini, tomatoes, yellow squash and onions. Cover and cook for 30 to 45 minutes.
- Foods high in nutrients, such as fruits and vegetables, provide a lot of vitamins and minerals but are not usually high in calories. For example, kiwi fruit has more vitamins C and E per serving than any other fruit. It's also a natural laxative.
- When choosing lettuce, darker is better. Romaine and spinach have a lot of vitamin A and folic acid. Iceberg lettuce has the most fiber and is a good source of potassium. Arugula and leaf lettuce add texture and vitamins A and C.
- To help control a sweet tooth, limit yourself to 100 calories of candy a day–a handful of jelly beans, four Hershey's Kisses or half a regular candy bar. Read labels!
- Looking for some different ways to get the nutrients you need? For a vegetable serving, try ½ cup spaghetti sauce. For a serving from the bread and cereal group, 3 cups popped popcorn meet your needs. And when you're looking for protein, choose from ¼ cup egg substitute, 2 tablespoons of any kind of nut butter or 4 ounces textured vegetable protein.

previously given birth to multiples. Women who smoke or drink heavily need supplements, as do some who have a chronic medical condition, those who take certain medications and those who have problems digesting cow's milk, wheat and other essential foods. In some cases, vegetarians may need supplements.

Your doctor will discuss the situation with you. If you need more than a prenatal vitamin, he or she will advise you.

Caution: Never take *any* supplements without your doctor's OK! (See also the Nutrition discussion in Week 27.)

## You Should Also Know

### ~ *Thyroid Disease*

Thyroid problems and thyroid disease can affect your pregnancy. Thyroid hormone is made in the thyroid gland; this hormone affects your entire body and is important in your metabolism.

Thyroid-hormone levels may be high or low. High levels of thyroid cause a condition called *hyperthyroidism;* low levels cause *hypothyroidism.* Women who have a history of miscarriage or premature delivery or who have problems around the time of delivery may have problems with their thyroid-hormone levels.

**Symptoms You May Notice.** Symptoms of thyroid disease may be hidden by pregnancy. Or you may notice changes during pregnancy that cause you and your doctor to suspect the thyroid is not functioning properly. These changes could include an enlarged thyroid, changes in your pulse, redness of the palms and warm, moist palms. Because thyroid-hormone levels can change during pregnancy (*because* of pregnancy), your doctor must be careful interpreting lab results about this hormone while you're pregnant.

> **Dad Tip** Offer to do the shopping. This may be an unsettling prospect for some men, but cell phones have made men better shoppers. Even if you don't shop solo, go with your partner to lift and to carry her purchases.

**Thyroid Test.** The thyroid is tested primarily by blood tests (a thyroid panel), which measure the amount of thyroid hormone produced. The tests also measure levels of another hormone, thyroid-stimulating hormone (TSH), made at the base of the brain. An additional test, an X-ray study of the thyroid (radioactive iodine scan), should not be done during pregnancy.

**Treatment of Thyroid Disease.** If you have hypothyroidism, thyroid replacement (thyroxin) is prescribed. It is believed to be safe during pregnancy. Your doctor may check the level during pregnancy with a blood test to make sure you are receiving enough of the hormone.

If you have hyperthyroidism, the medication propylthiouracil is used for treatment. It does pass through the placenta to the baby. Your doctor will prescribe the lowest possible amount to reduce risk to your baby. Blood testing during pregnancy is necessary to monitor the amount of medication needed. Iodide is another medication used for hyperthyroidism. Avoid iodide during pregnancy because of harmful effects to a developing baby.

After delivery, it's important to test the baby and to watch for signs of thyroid problems related to the medications prescribed during pregnancy. If you have a past history of problems with your thyroid, if you are now taking medication or if you have taken medication in the past for your thyroid, tell your doctor. Discuss treatment during pregnancy.

## Are You Concerned about Anthrax?

Recently in the press, concern has been expressed about exposure to anthrax. Are you concerned about the correct treatment for a pregnant woman? Research indicates pregnant and breastfeeding women should be treated *only* if there is "a confirmed environmental contamination or if they are exposed to a high-risk source, as determined by the local Department of Health." Initial treatment is with ciprofloxacin (Cipro) antibiotics, which are safe to use during pregnancy.

# Week 26

*Age of Fetus—24 Weeks*

## How Big Is Your Baby?

Your baby now weighs almost 2 pounds (.91kg). By this week, its crown-to-rump length is around 9¼ inches (23cm). See the illustration on page 267. Your baby is beginning to put on weight.

## How Big Are You?

The measurement of your uterus is about 2½ inches (6cm) above your bellybutton or nearly 10½ inches (26cm) from your pubic symphysis. During this second half of pregnancy, you will grow nearly ½ inch (1cm) each week. If you have been following a nutritious, balanced meal plan, your total weight gain is probably between 16 and 22 pounds (7.2 to 9.9kg).

*Tip for Week 26* Lying on your side (your left side is best) when you rest provides the best circulation to your baby. You may not experience as much swelling if you rest on your left side during the day.

## How Your Baby Is
## Growing and Developing

By now you have heard your baby's heartbeat at several visits. Listening to your developing baby's heartbeat is reassuring.

The fetus now has distinct sleeping and waking cycles. You may find a pattern; at certain times of the day your baby is very active, while at other times he or she is asleep. In addition, all five senses are now fully developed.

### ❧ Heart Arrhythmia

When listening to your baby's heartbeat during pregnancy, you may be startled to hear a skipped beat. An irregular heartbeat is called an *arrhythmia*. This is best described by regular pulsing or pounding with an occasional skipped or missed heartbeat. Arrhythmias in a fetus are not unusual.

There are many causes of fetal arrhythmias. An arrhythmia may occur as the heart grows and develops. As the heart matures, the arrhythmia often disappears. It may occur in the fetus of a pregnant woman who has lupus.

If an arrhythmia is discovered before labor and delivery, you may require fetal heart-rate monitoring during labor. When an arrhythmia is detected during labor, it may be desirable to have a pediatrician present at the time of delivery. He or she will make sure the baby is all right or is treated right away if a problem exists.

## Changes in You

You are getting bigger as your uterus, placenta and baby grow larger. Discomforts such as back pain, pressure in your pelvis, leg cramps and headaches may occur more frequently.

Time is passing quickly. You are approaching the end of the second trimester. Two-thirds of the pregnancy is behind you; it won't be long until your baby is born.

By this week, your baby weighs about 2 pounds (910g). It is now putting on some weight and filling out.

## How Your Actions
## Affect Your Baby's Development

### ᔗ *How to Have a Successful Labor and Delivery*

It's not too early to start thinking about your labor and delivery. One way to have a successful labor and delivery is to understand what elements contribute to that success. Below are some things you may want to consider as you progress through your pregnancy.

Become informed about pregnancy and the birth experience. Knowledge is power. When you understand what can and will occur during your pregnancy, you may be able to relax more. Read our other pregnancy books, discuss questions and concerns with your physician and share information and your knowledge with your partner.

The relationships you have with your physician and other members of your healthcare team are very important. Be a good patient by following medical suggestions, watching your weight, eating healthfully, taking your prenatal vitamins and attending all your prenatal appointments and tests. Expect your medical team to work hard for you. Each of you should support the other.

Being able to help make decisions that affect your medical care, including birth positions, pain-relief methods, feeding baby and your partner's level of participation in labor and delivery, helps you feel more in control during labor and delivery. Discuss questions and various situations with your physician at prenatal appointments.

### ᔗ *Will Working at a Computer Terminal Hurt Your Baby?*

Many women are concerned about working in front of a computer screen. Currently nothing suggests that working at a computer terminal is likely to harm your unborn baby.

If you work at a computer, consider the way you sit and how long you sit. (This is true for any job where you sit most of the time.) Sit in a chair that offers good support for your back and legs. Don't slouch or cross your legs when sitting. Rest your feet on a low stool or box to relieve back strain. Be sure to get up and walk around at least once every 15 minutes—you need to keep good circulation in your legs.

### ᔗ *Home Uterine Monitoring*

Home uterine monitoring is used to identify women with premature labor. Conditions associated with premature delivery include a previous preterm delivery, infections, premature rupture of membranes, pregnancy-induced hypertension and multiple fetuses.

Home uterine monitoring combines recording uterine contractions with daily telephone contact with the doctor. A recording of contractions is transmitted from the woman's home by telephone to a center where contractions can be evaluated. Thanks to personal computers, your doctor may be able to view the recordings at his or her office or home.

Cost for home monitoring varies but runs between $80 and $100 a day; some insurance companies cover it. The cost of home monitoring can often be justified if a premature delivery is prevented—it saves thousands of dollars in the care of a premature baby (sometimes more than $100,000).

Not everyone agrees that home monitoring is beneficial or cost-effective. It may be difficult to identify all the women who need this type of monitoring. The need for home uterine monitoring should be considered on an individual basis. Discuss this option with your physician if you have experienced preterm labor in the past or have other risk factors for premature birth.

## Your Nutrition

### ᔗ *Eating Fish during Your Pregnancy*

Eating fish is healthful; it is particularly good for you during pregnancy. Women who eat a variety of fish during pregnancy have longer pregnancies and give birth to babies with higher birth weights, according to some studies. This is important because the longer a baby stays in the uterus, the better its chances are of being strong and healthy at delivery.

Recent studies have shown that women who eat fish during pregnancy may have fewer problems with premature labor. This benefit may be from the omega-3 fatty acids contained in fish that cause a

**Dad Tip** About now, your partner may not feel very attractive. Take her on a date—go to dinner and a movie! Tell her she's beautiful. Take a full-view picture of her as a remembrance of how lovely she is now.

hormonal response to help protect you from premature labor. Omega-3 fatty acids may also help prevent pregnancy-induced hypertension and pre-eclampsia.

Many fish are safe to eat, and you should include them in your diet. Most fish is low in fat and high in vitamin B, iron, zinc, selenium and copper. Many fish choices are excellent, healthful additions to your diet, and you can eat them as often as you like. See the chart on the opposite page for a list of good choices.

**Omega-3 Fatty Acids.** Anchovies, herring, mullet, mackerel (not King mackerel), salmon, sardines and trout are some fish with a lot of omega-3 fatty acids. If you're a vegetarian or you don't like fish, add canola oil, flaxseed, soybeans, walnuts and wheat germ to your food plan because these foods contain linolenic oil, which is a type of omega-3 fatty acid.

Some researchers believe eating fatty fish or ingesting omega-3 fatty acids in another form (such as fish-oil capsules) may also enhance your baby's intellectual development. Studies have shown that fish oil is important to fetal brain development. One study of pregnant women demonstrated that when a pregnant woman eats fish oil, it reaches the brain of the developing fetus.

It's important to include omega-3 fatty acids in your eating plan. However, studies have found it's best not to exceed 2.4g of omega-3 fatty acids a day.

**Methyl-mercury Poisoning.** Some fish are contaminated with a dangerous substance as the result of man-made pollution. People who eat these fish are at risk of methyl-mercury poisoning. Mercury is a naturally occurring substance as well as a pollution by-product. Mercury becomes a problem when it is released into the air as a pollutant. It settles into the oceans and from there winds up in some types of fish.

The FDA has determined that a certain level of methyl mercury in fish is dangerous for humans. We know methyl mercury can pass from mother to fetus across the placenta. Research has shown that 60,000 children are born each year who are at risk of developing neurological problems linked to the consumption of seafood by their mothers during pregnancy. Because of rapid brain development, a fetus may be more vulnerable to methyl-mercury poisoning.

Studies indicate that pregnant women and those trying to conceive should be cautious—some kinds of fish should not be eaten more than once a month. These fish include shark, swordfish and tuna (fresh or frozen). If you're nursing, limit your consumption of these fish to once a week. Canned tuna is a little safer but don't eat more than one 6-ounce can a week.

Some freshwater fish may also be risky to eat, such as walleye and pike. To be on the safe side, consult local or state authorities for any advisories on eating freshwater fish.

### *Good Fish and Shellfish Choices*

Below is a list of fish you can eat as often as you like during pregnancy.

| | |
|---|---|
| bass | marlin |
| catfish | ocean perch |
| cod | orange roughy |
| croaker | Pacific halibut |
| flounder | pollack |
| freshwater perch | red snapper |
| haddock | salmon |
| herring | scrod |
| mackerel | sole |

You may eat the following shellfish as often as you like if you thoroughly cook them.

| | |
|---|---|
| clams | oysters |
| crab | scallops |
| lobster | shrimp |

**Remember: Don't exceed a total of 12 ounces of fish a week!**

**Some Additional Cautions about Fish.** Other environmental pollutants can appear in fish. Dioxin and PCBs (polychlorinated biphenyls) are found in some fish, such as bluefish or lake trout; avoid them.

Parasites, bacteria, viruses and toxins can also contaminate fish. Eating infected fish can make you sick, sometimes severely so. Sushi and ceviche are fish dishes that could contain viruses or parasites. Raw shellfish, if contaminated, could cause hepatitis-A, cholera or gastroenteritis. Avoid *all* raw fish during pregnancy! Other fish to avoid during pregnancy include some found in warm tropical waters, especially Florida, the Caribbean and Hawaii. Avoid the following "local" fish from those areas: amberjack, barracuda, bluefish, grouper, mahimahi, snapper and fresh tuna.

We advise pregnant women not to eat sushi; however there are a couple of "sushi" dishes that are OK to eat. Sushi made with *cooked* eel and rolls with *steamed* crab and veggies are acceptable.

If you are unsure about whether you should eat a particular fish or if you would like further information, call the Food and Drug Administration on its toll-free telephone hotline at 800-332-4010.

## You Should Also Know

### ∿ Retin-A

Retin-A (tretinoin), not to be confused with Accutane (isotretinoin), is a cream or lotion used to treat acne and to help get rid of fine wrinkles on the face. **If you are pregnant and using Retin-A, stop using it immediately!**

We don't have enough data to know if it's safe to use during pregnancy. We do know any type of medication you use—whether taken internally, inhaled, injected or used topically (spread on the skin)—gets into your bloodstream. Any substance in your bloodstream can be passed to your baby.

Some medications a mother-to-be uses become concentrated in the baby. Your body can handle it, but your baby's body may not be able to. If some substances build up in the baby, they can have significant effects on its development. In the future, we may know more about its effects on a growing baby. At this time, it's best to avoid using Retin-A for the sake of your baby.

### ∿ Steroid Creams and Ointments

Skin conditions may arise during pregnancy that require treatment with creams or ointments. This treatment could include steroid preparations. Before you use anything of this type, consult with your doctor.

## ᴖ *Seizures*

A history of seizures—before pregnancy, during a previous pregnancy or during this pregnancy—is information you must share with your doctor. Another term for seizure is *convulsion*.

Seizures can and usually do occur without warning. A seizure indicates an abnormal condition related to the nervous system, particularly the brain. During a seizure, a person often loses body control. The serious nature of this problem during pregnancy is compounded because of concern about the baby's safety.

If you have never had a problem with seizures, know that a short episode of dizziness or lightheadedness is *not* usually a seizure. Seizures are usually diagnosed by someone observing the seizure and noting the symptoms previously mentioned. An electroencephalogram (EEG) may be needed to diagnose a seizure.

**Medications to Control Seizures.** If you take medication for seizure control or prevention, share this important information with your doctor at the beginning of pregnancy. Medication can be taken during pregnancy to control seizures, but some medications are safer than others.

For example, Dilantin can cause birth defects in a baby, which include facial problems, microcephaly (a small head) and developmental delay. Other medications are used during pregnancy for seizure prevention. One of the more common is phenobarbital, but there is some concern about the safety of this medication.

Seizures during pregnancy or at any other time require serious discussion with your doctor and increased monitoring during pregnancy. If you have questions or concerns about a history of possible seizures, talk to your doctor about them.

# Week 27

*Age of Fetus—25 Weeks*

## How Big Is Your Baby?

This week marks the beginning of the 3rd trimester. In addition to weight and crown-to-rump length, we're adding total length of your baby's body from head to toe. This will give you an even better idea of how big your baby is during this last part of your pregnancy.

Your baby now weighs a little more than 2 pounds (1kg), and crown-to-rump length is about 9⅔ inches (24cm) by this week. Total length is about 15¼ inches (34cm). See the illustration on page 276.

*Tip for Week 27* Childbirth-education classes are not just for couples. Classes are often offered for single mothers or for pregnant women whose partners cannot come to classes. Ask your physician about classes for you.

## How Big Are You?

Your uterus is about 2¾ inches (7cm) above your bellybutton. If measured from the pubic symphysis, it is more than 10½ inches (27cm) from the pubic symphysis to the top of the uterus.

# How Your Baby Is Growing and Developing

## ⌁ *Eye Development*

Eyes first appear around day 22 of development in the embryo (about 5 weeks gestation). In the beginning, they look like a pair of shallow grooves on each side of the developing brain. These grooves continue to develop and eventually turn into pockets called *optical vesicles*. The lens of each eye develops from the ectoderm. (We discuss ectoderm in Week 4.)

Early in development, eyes are on the side of the head. They move toward the middle of the face between 7 and 10 weeks of gestation.

At about 8 weeks gestation, blood vessels form that lead to the eye. During the 9th week of gestation, the pupil forms, which is the round opening in the eye. At that time, the nerve connection from the eyes to the brain begins to form, called the *optic nerve*.

Eyelids that cover the eyes are fused (connected together) at around 11 to 12 weeks. They remain fused until about 27 to 28 weeks of pregnancy, when they open.

The retina, at the back of the eye, is light-sensitive. It is the part of the eye where light images come into focus. It develops its normal layers by about 27 weeks of pregnancy. These layers receive light and light information, and transmit it to the brain for interpretation— what we know as "sight."

**Congenital Cataracts.** A congenital cataract is an eye problem that may be present at birth. Most people believe cataracts occur only in old age, but that's a misconception. They can appear in a newborn baby!

Instead of being transparent or clear, the lens that focuses light onto the back of the eye is opaque or cloudy. This problem is usually caused by a genetic predisposition (it is inherited). However, it has been found in children born to mothers who had German measles (rubella) around the 6th or 7th week of pregnancy.

Around this time, your baby's eyelids open. Your baby begins opening and closing its eyes while still inside your uterus.

**Microphthalmia.** Another congenital eye problem is microphthalmia, in which the overall size of the eye is too small. The eyeball may be only two-thirds its normal size. This abnormality often occurs with other abnormalities of the eyes. It frequently results from maternal infections, such as cytomegalovirus (CMV) or toxoplasmosis, while the baby is developing inside the uterus.

## Changes in You

### ↣ *Feeling Baby Move*
Feeling your baby move (quickening) is one of the more precious parts of pregnancy. This action can be the beginning of your bonding with your baby. Many women feel they begin to relate to the baby and its personality before delivery by feeling the baby's movements. This movement is usually reassuring and a sensation most pregnant women enjoy. Your partner can experience and enjoy the baby's movements by feeling your abdomen when the baby is active.

↣ **Your Baby's Movements.** Movement of your baby can vary in intensity. It can range from a faint flutter, sometimes described as a feeling of a butterfly or a gas bubble in early pregnancy, to brisk motions or even painful kicks and pressure as your baby gets larger.

Women often ask how often a baby should move. They want to know if they should be concerned if the baby moves too much or doesn't move enough. These are hard questions to answer because your sensation is different from that of another woman. The movement of each baby you carry may be different. It is usually more reassuring to have a baby move frequently. But it isn't unusual for a baby to have quiet times when there is not as much activity.

If you've been on the go, you may not have noticed the baby move because you've been active and busy. It may help to lie on your side to notice if the baby is moving or still. Many women report their baby is much more active at night, keeping them awake and making it hard to sleep.

If your baby is quiet and not as active as what seems normal or what you expected, discuss it with your doctor. You can always go to the doctor's office to hear the baby's heartbeat if the baby hasn't been moving in its usual pattern. In most instances, there is nothing to worry about.

**Kick Count.** Toward the end of pregnancy, you may be asked to record how often you feel the baby move. This test is done at home and is called a *kick count*. It provides reassurance about fetal well-being; this information is similar to that learned by a nonstress test. See the discussion in Week 41.

Your doctor may use one of two common methods. The first is to count how many times the baby moves in an hour. The other is to note how long it takes for baby to move 10 times. Usually you can choose when you want to do the test. After eating a meal is a good time because baby is often more active then. This test is usually done at home.

**Pain Under Your Ribs When Baby Moves.** Some women complain of pain under their ribs and in their lower abdomen when their baby moves. This type of pain isn't an unusual problem, but it may cause enough discomfort to concern you. The baby's movement has increased to a point where you will probably feel it every day, and movements are getting stronger and harder. At the same time, your uterus is getting larger and putting more pressure on all your organs. Your growing, expanding uterus presses on the small bowel, bladder and rectum.

If the pressure really is pain, don't ignore it. You need to discuss it with your doctor. In most cases, it isn't a serious problem.

### ❧ *Discovering a Breast Lump*

Discovering a breast lump is important, during pregnancy or any other time. It's important for you to learn at an early age how to do a breast exam on yourself and to perform this on a regular basis (usually after every menstrual period). Nine out of 10 breast lumps are found by women examining themselves.

Your doctor will probably perform breast exams at regular intervals, usually when you have your annual Pap smear. If you have an exam every year and are lump-free, it helps assure you no lumps are present before you begin pregnancy.

Finding a breast lump may be delayed during pregnancy because of changes in your breasts. It may be more difficult to feel a lump. Enlargement of the breasts during pregnancy and nursing tends to hide lumps or masses in the tissue of the breast.

Examine your breasts during pregnancy as you do when you are not pregnant. Do it every 4 or 5 weeks—the first day of every month is a good time to do it.

**Tests for Breast Lumps.** The routine test for breast lumps is examination by yourself or your doctor. Other tests include X-ray examination, called a *mammogram*, and ultrasound examination of the breast.

If a lump is found, it may be necessary to have a mammogram or an ultrasound exam performed on the breast. Because a mammogram utilizes X-rays, your pregnancy must be protected during the procedure, usually by shielding your abdomen with a lead apron.

It has not been shown that pregnancy accelerates the course or growth of a breast lump. But we do know it is sometimes more difficult to find a breast lump because of breast changes during pregnancy.

**Treatment during Pregnancy.** Often a lump in the breast can be drained or aspirated. Fluid removed from the cyst is sent to the lab for evaluation to ensure there are no abnormal cells. If a lump or cyst cannot be drained by a needle, a biopsy of the cyst or lump may be necessary. If fluid is clear, it's a good sign. Bloody fluid is of more concern and must be studied under a microscope in the laboratory.

If examination of a lump indicates breast cancer, treatment may begin during pregnancy. Treatment complications during pregnancy include risks to the fetus related to chemotherapy, radiation or medication, such as anesthesia or pain medicine for a biopsy. If a lump is cancerous, the need for radiation therapy and chemotherapy must be considered, along with the needs of the pregnancy.

# How Your Actions
# Affect Your Baby's Development

### ☙ *Prenatal Classes*

When should you think about signing up for prenatal classes? Even though it's just the beginning of the third trimester, now's the time to register for these classes. It's a good idea to get signed up for classes so you can finish them before you get to the end of your pregnancy. By doing this, you'll have time to practice what you learn. You won't be just beginning your classes when you deliver!

**Should You and Your Partner Take Prenatal Classes?**    During pregnancy, you have probably been learning what's going to happen at delivery by talking with your doctor and by asking questions. You have also learned what lies ahead from reading materials given to you at prenatal visits, from our other books, such as *Your Pregnancy Questions and Answers*, *Your Pregnancy after 35*, *Your Pregnancy for the Father-to-Be* or *Your Pregnancy—Every Woman's Guide* or from other sources. Childbirth classes offer yet another way to learn about this important part of pregnancy. They help you prepare for labor and delivery.

By meeting in class on a regular basis, usually once a week for 4 to 6 weeks, you can learn about many things that concern you. Classes often cover a wide range of subjects, including the following areas.

- What are the different childbirth methods?
- What is "natural childbirth"?
- What is a Cesarean delivery?
- What pain-relief methods are available?
- What you need to know (and practice) for the childbirth method you choose.
- Will you need an episiotomy?
- Will you need an enema?
- When is a fetal monitor necessary?
- What's going to happen when you reach the hospital?
- Is an epidural or some other type of anesthesia right for you?

These are important questions. Discuss them with your doctor, if they are not answered in your childbirth-education classes.

**Who Goes to Prenatal Classes?** Classes are usually held for small groups of pregnant women and their partners or labor coaches. This is an excellent way to learn. You can interact with other couples and ask questions. You'll discover other women are concerned about many of the same things you are, such as labor and pain management. It's good to know you aren't the only one thinking about what lies ahead.

Prenatal classes are not only for first-time pregnant women. If you have a new partner, if it has been a few years since you've had a baby, if you have questions or if you would like a review of what lies ahead, a prenatal class can help you.

These classes may help reduce any worry or concern you and your partner feel about labor and delivery. And they'll help you enjoy the birth of your baby even more.

**Where Do You Take Classes?** Childbirth classes are offered in various settings. Most hospitals that deliver babies offer prenatal classes, often taught by the labor-and-delivery nurses or by a midwife. Other types of classes have different degrees of involvement.

This means the time commitment or depth of the subject covered is different for each of the various classes that may be available. Ask at the doctor's office about classes they recommend. They can help you decide which type of class would be best for you.

**What Will You Learn?** Classes are intended to inform you and your partner or labor coach about pregnancy, what happens at the hospital and what happens during labor and delivery. Some couples find classes are a good opportunity to get a partner more involved and to help make him feel more comfortable with the pregnancy. This may give him the opportunity to take a more active part at the time of labor and delivery, as well as during the rest of the pregnancy. See also the discussion in Week 31 of different childbirth methods.

**Can You Take Prenatal Classes if You Have Problems?** If you have problems getting to a prenatal class because of cost or time or because you're on bed rest, it may be possible to take classes at home. Some instructors will come to your home for private sessions with you and your partner. Or you might use some videos. *Great Expectations: Laugh and Learn About Childbirth* is a two-videotape set that may provide you with a lot of the information you would learn in a class. The set is available for $65, including shipping and handling; call 877-715-2844 or visit www.laughandlearn.com for further information.

### ✧ Infant-Restraint Seats

It isn't too early to think about infant- and child-restraint systems. Some people believe they can hold their baby safely in an accident. Others say their child won't sit still in a restraint.

In an accident, an unrestrained child becomes a missile. The force of a crash can literally pull a child out of an adult's arms! One study showed *more than 30 deaths a year* occur to unrestrained infants going home from the hospital after birth. In nearly all cases, if the baby had been in an approved infant-restraint system, he or she would have survived the accident.

> **Dad Tip**  Offer to do chores that may be more difficult for your partner now. Cleaning the bathtub or the toilet can be a big help. You can add to her safety by putting away anything that belongs in a high or difficult-to-reach location.

Start early to teach your child safety. If you always place your child in a restraint system in the car, it will become a natural thing to do. You can increase your child's acceptance of a restraint if you wear seat belts, too!

All states now have infant-restraint laws. Call your local police department or hospital for further information.

Many hospitals require you to take your baby home from the hospital in an approved infant-restraint system. If you want additional information, a pediatrician or the American Academy of Pediatrics can provide a list of safe child- and infant-restraint systems. Consumer magazines rate them quite frequently. Check your local library.

## Your Nutrition

Some important vitamins you may need during pregnancy include vitamin A, vitamin B and vitamin E. Let's examine each vitamin and how it helps you during pregnancy.

**Vitamin A**—This vitamin is essential to human reproduction. Fortunately, deficiency in North America is not common. What is of more concern today is the *excessive use* of the vitamin before conception and in early pregnancy. (This discussion concerns only the retinol forms of vitamin A, usually derived from fish oils. The beta-carotene form, of plant origin, is believed to be safe.)

The RDA (recommended dietary allowance) is 2700IU (international units) for a woman of childbearing age. The maximum dosage is 5000IU. Pregnancy does not change these requirements. You probably get vitamin A from the foods you eat, so supplementation during pregnancy is not recommended. Read food labels to check your vitamin-A intake.

**Vitamin B**—B vitamins important to you in pregnancy include $B_6$, $B_9$ (folic acid) and $B_{12}$. They influence the development of your baby's nerves and the formation of blood cells. If you don't take in enough $B_{12}$ during pregnancy, you could develop anemia. Good food sources of B vitamins include milk, eggs, tempeh, miso, bananas, potatoes, collard greens, avocados and brown rice.

**Vitamin E**—This is an important vitamin during pregnancy because it helps metabolize fats and helps build muscles and red-blood cells. You can usually get enough vitamin E if you eat meat. Vegetarians and pregnant women who can't eat meat may have a harder time getting enough vitamin E. Foods rich in the vitamin include olive oil, wheat germ, spinach and dried fruit. You may want to check with your doctor or read the label on your prenatal vitamin to see if it supplies 100% of the RDA.

Be cautious with *every* substance you take during pregnancy. If you have questions, discuss them with your doctor.

## You Should Also Know

### ⌒ *Systemic Lupus Erythematosus (SLE)*

Some women have conditions before pregnancy that require them to take medication for the rest of their lives. They are often concerned about the effects medication may have on their developing babies. One such condition is *systemic lupus erythematosus* (SLE).

Many young women have lupus and take steroids to control the problem. They want to know if medication they take can harm their baby. Should they continue to take steroids during pregnancy?

Lupus is an autoimmune disorder of unknown cause that occurs most often in young or middle-aged women. (Women have lupus much more frequently than men—about nine women to every man.) Those who have lupus have a large number of antibodies in their bloodstream. These antibodies are directed toward the woman's own tissues, which causes problems.

The diagnosis of SLE is made through blood tests, which look for the suspect antibodies. Blood tests done for lupus are a lupus antibody test and an antinuclear antibody test.

Antibodies can be directed to various organs in the body and may actually damage an organ. Affected organs include joints, skin, kidneys, muscles, lungs, the brain and the central nervous system. The most common symptom of lupus is joint pain, which is often mistaken for arthritis. Other symptoms include lesions, rashes or sores on the skin, fever and hypertension.

We don't have a cure for lupus. Systemic lupus erythematosus is generally unaffected by pregnancy. However, miscarriage, premature delivery and complications around the time of delivery are slightly increased in a woman with lupus. If kidneys were involved and there was kidney damage during flareups, you must be on the lookout for kidney problems during pregnancy.

Steroids, short for corticosteroids, are generally prescribed to treat lupus. The primary medication used is prednisone. It is usually prescribed on a daily basis. It may be unnecessary to take prednisone every day, unless complications from lupus occur during pregnancy.

### ✂ *Exercise Software*

Do you need to be reminded to exercise during the day? Now there's software you can load onto your computer to help you keep in shape. The program, StretchWare, is available from Shelter Publications and can lead you through many different routines. You can work your hands, shoulders, lower back, legs or neck—each routine is fast and easy.

# Week 28

*Age of Fetus—26 Weeks*

## How Big Is Your Baby?

Your baby weighs nearly 2½ pounds (1.1kg). Crown-to-rump length is close to 10 inches (25cm). Total length is 15¾ inches (35cm).

## How Big Are You?

Your uterus is now well above your umbilicus. Sometimes this growth seems gradual. At other times, it may seem as though changes happen rapidly, as if overnight.

Your uterus is about 3¾ inches (8cm) above your bellybutton. If you measure from the pubic symphysis, it is about 11 inches (28cm) to the top of the uterus. Your weight gain by this time should be between 17 and 24 pounds (7.7 and 10.8kg).

*Tip for Week 28* Even though delivery is several weeks away, it is not too early to begin making plans for the trip to the hospital. This includes knowing how to reach your partner (keep all of his phone numbers with you). Also consider what you will do if he isn't near enough to take you. Who are potential drivers? How do you get hold of them? Make plans now!

# How Your Baby Is Growing and Developing

Until this time, the surface of the baby's developing brain has appeared smooth. At around 28 weeks of pregnancy, the brain forms characteristic grooves and indentations on the surface. The amount of brain tissue also increases.

Your baby's eyebrows and eyelashes may be present. Hair on the baby's head is growing longer. The baby's body is becoming plumper and rounder. It's beginning to fill out a little because of increased fat underneath the skin. Before this time, the baby had a thin appearance.

Your baby now weighs almost 2½ pounds (1.1kg). This is an amazing growth compared to just 11 weeks ago, when it weighed only about 3½ ounces (100g) at 17 weeks of pregnancy. Your baby has increased its weight more than 10 times in 11 weeks! In the last 4 weeks, from the 24th week of your pregnancy to this week, its weight has doubled. Your baby is growing rapidly!

## Changes in You

### ↣ *The Placenta*

The placenta plays a critical role in the growth, development and survival of the baby. The illustration on page 288 shows the fetus attached to the umbilical cord, which attaches to the placenta.

Two important cell layers, the amnion and the chorion, are involved in the development of the placenta and the amniotic sac. Development and function of the cell layers is complicated, and their description is beyond the scope of this book. However, the amnion is the layer around the amniotic fluid in which the fetus floats.

The placenta begins to form with trophoblastic cells. These cells grow through the walls of maternal blood vessels and establish contact with your bloodstream without your blood and fetal blood mixing. (Fetal circulation is separate from your circulation.) These cells grow into the blood vessels without making a vascular connection (or open-

Placenta

Umbilical cord

The placenta, shown here with the fetus, carries oxygen and nutrients to the growing baby. It is an important part of pregnancy.

ing) between the blood vessels. But fetal blood flow in the placenta is close to your blood flow in the placenta.

We have closely followed your baby's weight gain in this book. The placenta is also growing at a rapid rate. At 10 weeks gestation, the placenta weighed about ¾ ounce (20g). Ten weeks later, at 20 weeks gestation, it weighs almost 6 ounces (170g). In another 10 weeks, the placenta will have increased to 15 ounces (430g). At full term, 40 weeks, it can weigh almost 1½ pounds (650g)!

Fetal blood vessels and the developing placenta begin connecting as early as the 2nd or 3rd week of development. Around the 3rd week of gestation, projections (villi) at the base of the placenta become firmly attached to the underlying layer of the uterus.

Villi are important during pregnancy. The space around the villi (intervillus space) becomes honeycombed with maternal blood vessels. The villi absorb nutrients and oxygen from the maternal blood; these are transported to the growing baby through the umbilical vein in the umbilical cord. Waste products from the baby are brought through the umbilical arteries to the intervillus space and are transferred to the maternal bloodstream. In this way, the baby gets rid of waste products.

**What Does the Placenta Do?** The placenta is involved in moving oxygen and carbon dioxide to and from the baby. It is also involved in nutrition and the excretion of waste products from the baby.

In addition to these functions, the placenta has an important hormonal role. It produces human chorionic gonadotropin (HCG) (discussed in Week 5). This hormone is found in your bloodstream in measurable amounts within 10 days after fertilization. Pregnancy tests check HCG levels to determine if a woman is pregnant. The placenta also begins making the hormones estrogen and progesterone by the 7th or 8th week of pregnancy.

**What Does the Placenta Look Like?** At full term, a normal placenta is flat, has a cakelike appearance and is round or oval. It is about 6 to 8 inches (15 to 20cm) in diameter and ¾ and 1¼ inches (2 to 3cm) thick at its thickest part. It weighs between 17½ and 24 ounces (500 to 650g) on average.

Placentas vary widely in size and shape. A placenta that is too large (placentamegaly) can be found when a woman is infected with syphilis or when a baby has erythroblastosis (Rh-sensitization of the baby). Sometimes it occurs without any obvious explanation. A small placenta may be found in normal pregnancies but may also be found with intrauterine-growth restriction.

The part of the placenta that attaches to the wall of the uterus has a beefy or spongy appearance. The fetal side of the placenta, the side closest to the baby inside the amniotic sac, is smooth. It is covered with amniotic and chorionic membranes.

The placenta is a red or reddish-brown color. Around the time of birth, the placenta may have white patches on it, which are calcium deposits.

In multiple pregnancies, there may be more than one placenta, or there may be one placenta with more than one umbilical cord coming from it. Usually with twins, there are two amniotic sacs, with two umbilical cords running to the fetuses from one placenta.

The umbilical cord, which is the attachment from the placenta to the baby, contains two umbilical arteries and one umbilical vein, which carry blood to and from the baby. The cord is about 22 inches (55cm) long and is usually white.

A few women experience problems involving the placenta during pregnancy. These include placental abruption (see Week 33) and placenta previa (see Week 35). After delivery, a retained placenta is sometimes a problem (see Week 38).

## How Your Actions
## Affect Your Baby's Development

### ᕬ *Dealing with Maternal Asthma*
Asthma is a respiratory illness characterized by an increased responsiveness or sensitivity to stimulation of the trachea and the bronchi, both important to breathing. Problems with asthma are manifested by difficulty breathing, shortness of breath, coughing and wheezing. (Wheezing is a noise like a whistling or a hissing made as air moves through narrowed airways.)

Asthma comes and goes, with acute worsening of symptoms interspersed with symptom-free periods. It affects about 2% of the population in the United States and Canada. It is equally common in other countries.

It may occur at any age, but about 50% of all asthma cases occur before age 10. Another 33% of the cases occur by age 40. Pregnancy does not seem to cause any consistent, predictable problem with asthma. Some pregnant women appear to get better during pregnancy, while others remain about the same. A few get worse.

**Asthma in Pregnancy.** Uncontrolled asthma can be serious during pregnancy. It can contribute to high blood pressure in the mother and to premature birth, low-birthweight babies or smaller babies. Medications currently in use to treat asthma appear to be safe. Research has shown that inhalers have less of an effect on baby because less medication enters the mother's bloodstream.

> **Ðad Tip** Your partner has been feeling the baby move for 2 or 3 months. Around this time, you may be able to feel it, too! Gently place your hand on her abdomen, and leave it there for a while. Your partner can tell you when the baby is moving.

### ๛ *Treating Asthma Attacks*
Most pregnant women with asthma can have a safe pregnancy, labor and delivery. If a woman has severe asthma attacks when she isn't pregnant, she may also have severe attacks during pregnancy.

During pregnancy, your oxygen consumption increases by about 25%. That's why asthma treatment is so important during pregnancy—so baby can get the oxygen it needs to grow and to develop. The treatment plan used before pregnancy will probably continue to be helpful. This includes medications prescribed for asthma before or during pregnancy.

Asthma medication, such as terbutaline, and steroids, such as hydrocortisone or methylprednisolone, can be used during pregnancy. Aminophylline or theophyline may also be used. Also safe to use while you're pregnant are metaproterenol (Alupent) and albuterol (Ventolin).

If your asthma is severe, your physician may prescribe an anti-inflammatory nasal spray, such as cromolyn sodium (Nasalcrom) or an inhaled steroid, such as beclomethasone (Vanceril). Discuss the situation at one of your early prenatal visits.

## Your Nutrition

You may be wondering what kinds of foods to eat and what to delete from your diet during this stage of your pregnancy. Look at the chart below; it offers you some guidance.

### What Kinds of Foods Do I Eat?

| Foods to Eat | Servings per Day |
|---|---|
| Dark-green or dark-yellow fruits and vegetables | 1 |
| Fruits and vegetables with vitamin C (tomatoes, citrus) | 2 |
| Other fruits and vegetables | 2 |
| Whole-grain breads and cereals | 4 |
| Dairy products, including milk | 4 |
| Protein sources (meat, poultry, eggs, fish) | 2 |
| Dried beans and peas, seeds and nuts | 2 |

| Foods to Eat in Moderation | | Foods to Avoid |
|---|---|---|
| Caffeine | 200mg | Anything containing alcohol |
| Fat | limited amounts | Food additives, when possible |
| Sugar | limited amounts | |

## You Should Also Know

### ✌ Additional Testing and Procedures

Twenty-eight weeks of gestation is a time when many doctors initiate or repeat certain blood tests or procedures. Glucose-tolerance testing for diabetes may also be done at this time.

If you are Rh-negative, you will probably receive an injection of RhoGAM at this point in your pregnancy. This injection keeps you from becoming sensitized if your baby's blood mixes with yours. RhoGAM protects against sensitization until the time of delivery.

### ✎ *How Is the Baby Lying?*

It is common at this point in pregnancy to ask your doctor how the baby is lying. Is the baby head first? Is it bottom first (breech)? Is the baby lying sideways?

It's difficult—usually impossible—at this point in pregnancy to tell just by feeling your abdomen how the baby is lying and if it is coming bottom first, feet first or head first. The baby changes position throughout pregnancy.

It doesn't hurt to try to feel the abdomen to see where the head or other parts are located. In another 3 to 4 weeks, the baby's head will be harder; it will be easier at that time for your doctor to determine how the baby is lying (called *presentation of the fetus*).

## Is Home Birth Safe?

In the recent past, there has been a growing interest in giving birth at home, in part because some women feel giving birth at home is "more natural." Another factor in this decision may be the high cost of labor and delivery, especially if you don't have full insurance coverage. Indeed, you may have heard from friends or acquaintances that they had a home birth and everything went fine. But is it really safe?

By any doctor's standards, the answer is a resounding "No!" Research has shown that giving birth at home is an extremely risky undertaking. One study showed twice as many infant deaths and various serious, dangerous complications when babies are delivered at home. There were also dangers to the mom—first-time pregnant women who delivered at home had nearly triple the risk of complications following the birth. In addition, the chance of serious problems increased when the woman suffered from gestational diabetes or high blood pressure or when she carried more than one baby.

The American College of Obstetricians and Gynecologists has firmly stated that home birthing is hazardous to a woman and her baby. We must concur. Although we cannot recommend a home birth, you may be interested in a more natural setting for giving birth to your baby. Discuss it with your doctor. He or she may be able to recommend some actions that can be taken to provide a more natural birthing experience while allowing you to deliver in the safety of a hospital or properly equipped birthing center.

# Week 29

## Age of Fetus—27 Weeks

## How Big Is Your Baby?

By this time, your baby weighs about 2¾ pounds (1.25kg). Crown-to-rump length is almost 10½ inches (26cm). Total fetal length is 16¾ inches (37cm).

## How Big Are You?

Measuring from your bellybutton, your uterus is about 3½ to 4 inches (7.6 to 10.2cm) above it. Your uterus is about 11½ inches (29cm) above the pubic symphysis. If you saw your doctor 4 weeks ago, around the 25th week of pregnancy, you probably measured about 10 inches (25cm) at that time. You've grown about 1½ inches (4cm) in 4 weeks. Your total weight gain by this week should be between 19 and 25 pounds (8.55 and 11.25kg).

*Tip for Week 29* If your doctor advises bed rest, follow his or her instructions. It may be difficult for you to stop your activities and sit idly by when you have lots of things to do, but remember, it's for the good health of you and your baby!

# How Your Baby Is
# Growing and Developing

## ↷ *Fetal Growth*

Week by week, we've noted the change in your baby's size as pregnancy progresses. We use average weights to give you an idea of about how large your baby is at a particular time. However, these are only averages; babies vary greatly in size and weight.

Because growth is rapid during pregnancy, infants born prematurely may be tiny. Even a few weeks less time in the uterus can have a dramatic effect on the size of your baby. The baby continues to grow after 36 weeks of gestation but at a slower rate.

A couple of interesting factors about birthweight have been identified.

**Dad Tip** After the baby is born, you may want to take time off to help out at home and to be part of your baby's early development. The Family and Medical Leave Act of 1993 was passed to help people take time off to care for family members. Ask your employer or supervisor now if it applies to you. If it does, and you plan to take time off, begin making arrangements in the next few weeks.

- Boys weigh more than girls.
- Birthweight of an infant increases with the increasing number of pregnancies you have or the number of babies you deliver.

These are general statements and don't apply to everyone, but they appear to apply in many cases. The average baby's birthweight at full term is 7 to 7½ pounds (3.28kg to 3.4kg).

**How Mature Is Your Baby?** A baby born between the 38th and 42nd weeks of pregnancy is a *term baby* or *full-term infant*. Before the 38th week, the term *preterm* can be applied to the baby. After 42 weeks of pregnancy, your baby is overdue and the term *postdate* is used.

When a baby is born before the end of pregnancy, many people use the terms *premature* and *preterm* interchangeably. There is a difference.

An infant that is 32 weeks gestational age but has mature pulmonary or lung function at the time of birth is more appropriately called a "preterm infant" than a premature infant. "Premature" best describes an infant that has immature lungs at the time of birth.

### ∾ Premature Babies

Premature birth increases the risk of problems in the baby. It also increases the risk of fetal death. Babies born prematurely usually weigh less than 5½ pounds (2.5kg).

The illustration on page 301 shows a premature baby with several leads attached to its body to monitor its heart rate. Many other attachments are used, such as I.V.s, tubes and masks that provide oxygen.

In 1950, the neonatal death rate was about 20 per 1000 live births. Today, the rate is less than 10 per 1000 live births. Nearly twice the number of preterm infants survive today than 50 years ago.

The decreasing death rate applies primarily to infants delivered during the 3rd trimester (27 weeks or more of gestation) who weigh at least 2¾ pounds (1kg) and are without birth defects. When gestational age and birthweight are below these levels, the death rate increases.

Better methods of caring for premature babies have contributed to higher survival statistics. Today, infants born as early as 25 weeks of pregnancy may survive. However, the long-term survival and quality of life for these babies remains to be seen as they grow older.

What is the survival rate for premature babies? Recent information indicates for infants who weighed about 1 pound (500g) to 1½ pounds (700g), the survival rate is about 43%. For babies weighing between 1½ pounds and 2¾ pounds (1kg), the survival rate is about 72%. These rates vary from hospital to hospital.

The average hospital stay for premature babies ranges from 125 days for infants weighing between 1⅓ and 1½ pounds (600 and 700g) to 76 days for babies in the 2- to 2¾-pound (900g to 1kg) birthweight range.

Any discussion of survival rates must include the frequency rate of disabilities these premature babies suffer. In the lower-birthweight range, many babies who survived had disabilities. Higher-weight babies also had disabilities, but statistics for this group were much lower.

It's usually best for the baby to remain in the uterus as long as possible, so it can grow and develop fully. Occasionally it is best for the baby to be delivered early, such as when the fetus is not receiving adequate nutrition.

**Causes of Premature Labor and Premature Birth.** In most cases, the causes of premature labor and premature birth are unknown. Causes we do understand include a uterus with an abnormal shape, multiple fetuses, polyhydramnios or hydramnios, placental abruption or placenta previa, premature rupture of membranes, an incompetent cervix, abnormalities of the fetus, fetal death, a retained IUD, serious maternal illness or incorrect estimate of gestational age.

Finding the cause of premature labor and delivery may be difficult. An attempt is always made to determine what causes preterm labor before active labor begins. In this way, treatment may be more effective.

**Tests Your Doctor May Do.** One test, called *SalEst,* can help determine if a woman might go into labor too early. The test measures levels of the hormone estriol in a pregnant woman's saliva. Research has shown that there is often a surge in this chemical several weeks before early labor. A positive result means a woman has a 7 times greater chance of delivering her baby before the 37th week of pregnancy. Another test is fetal fibronectin (fFN); see Week 22.

Some difficult questions that must be answered when premature labor begins include those below.

- Is it better for the infant to be inside the uterus or to be delivered?
- Are the dates of the pregnancy correct?
- Is this really labor?

## Changes in You

### ↷ *Treatment of Premature Labor*
Can anything be done about premature labor? Yes. We now treat premature labor in several different ways.

The treatment most often used for premature labor is bed rest. A woman is advised to stay in bed and lie on her side. (Either side is OK.) Not everyone agrees on this treatment, but bed rest is often successful in stopping contractions and premature labor. If this happens to you and you are advised to rest in bed, it may mean you can't go to work or to continue many activities. It's worth it to agree to bed rest if you can avoid premature delivery of your baby.

If you are confined to bed during your pregnancy, take it easy getting back into the swing of things after baby is born. Lying down for quite a while may result in loss of muscle tone, which can lead to you being out of shape. It can take some time to return to your normal level of activity. Take it easy, and don't rush into any physical activities until you feel up to them. Ease into your post-bed rest life slowly!

**Medications to Help Stop Premature Labor.**  Beta-adrenergic agents, also called *tocolytic agents,* may be used to suppress labor. Beta-adrenergics are muscle relaxants. They relax the uterus and decrease contractions. (The uterus is mainly muscle, which pushes the baby out through the cervix during labor.) At this time, only ritodrine (Yutopar) is approved by the FDA to treat premature labor.

Ritodrine is given in three different forms—intravenously, as an intramuscular injection and as a pill. It is usually initially given intravenously and may require a hospital stay of a couple of days or more. Maternal side effects of ritodrine include rapid heartbeat, hypotension, the feeling of apprehension or fear, chest tightness or chest pain, changes in the heart's electrical activity, fluid in the lungs, maternal metabolic problems, including increased blood sugar, low blood potassium and even acidosis of the blood (similar to a diabetic reaction), headaches, vomiting, shaking, fever and/or hallucinations.

When premature contractions stop, you can be switched to oral medications, which you take every 2 to 4 hours. Ritodrine is approved for use in pregnancies over 20 weeks and under 36 weeks gestation. In some cases, the medication is used without giving an I.V. first. This is

## *Bed-Rest Boredom Relievers*

You may be advised to rest in bed if you experience any number of pregnancy complications. Lying in bed takes the pressure of the baby's weight off your cervix, which can help if you experience premature labor. Resting on your side maximizes the blood flow to your uterus, which brings more oxygen and nutrients to baby.

Bed rest can mean anything from staying in bed part of the day to staying in bed 24/7. It can be pretty boring being confined to bed. Below are some suggestions to help beat bed-rest boredom.

- Spend the day in a room other than your bedroom. Use the living-room or family-room sofa for daytime activities.
- Use foam mattress pads and extra pillows for comfort.
- Keep a telephone close at hand.
- Keep reading material, the television remote control, a radio and other essentials nearby.
- Establish a daily routine. When you get up, change into daytime clothes. Shower or bathe every day. Comb your hair, and put on lipstick. Nap if you need it. Go to bed when you normally do.
- Keep food and drinks close at hand. Use a cooler to keep food and drinks cold. Use an insulated container for hot soup or coffee.
- Start a journal. Our book, *Your Pregnancy Journal Week by Week*, is easy to use and lets you record your thoughts and feelings to share with your partner now and your child later.
- Do some crafts that aren't messy, such as cross stitch, knitting, crocheting, drawing or hand sewing. Make something for baby!
- Use the time to read and to prepare for baby's arrival.
- Spend some time planning baby's room (someone else will have to carry through on it), deciding what you'll need for a layette and making a list of all the necessary items you'll need after baby comes home.
- Sort! Use the time to sort through recipes, to put pictures in albums, go through your coupons or make a scrapbook of information for after baby's arrival.
- Call your favorite local charity or political organization, and volunteer to make phone calls, stuff envelopes or write letters.
- For support, contact other women who have been on bed rest. A national support group helps women with high-risk pregnancies. They can provide you with information and put you in touch with other women who have had the same experience. Contact *Sidelines* at 714-497-2265.

done most often in women with a history of premature labor or for a woman with multiple pregnancies.

Similar problems as those described above probably occur in the baby. Low blood-sugar levels have been seen in babies after birth in some mothers who took ritodrine before delivery. Rapid heartbeat is also commonly seen in these babies.

A study was recently conducted to investigate ways to help stop premature labor. Researchers found that use of a hormone in some women may reduce their risk of giving birth to a premature baby. The hormone is called *progesterone (17 alpha-hydroxyprogesterone caproate)*.

In the study, women who had had problems with premature labor in previous pregnancies were given a weekly injection of progesterone. This course of treatment substantially reduced the rate of premature deliveries. More studies are needed, but there is hope that this treatment will lead to a decrease in premature birth, which can be a very serious problem.

Terbutaline may also be used as a muscle relaxant to halt premature labor. Although it has been shown to be an effective medication, it has not been approved for this use by the FDA. Side effects of terbutaline are similar to those of ritodrine.

Magnesium sulfate is used to treat pre-eclampsia (see Week 31 for information on pre-eclampsia). We have known for quite a while that magnesium sulfate may also help stop labor. This medication is most often given through an I.V. and requires hospitalization. However, it is occasionally given as an oral preparation, without hospitalization. You must be monitored frequently if you take magnesium sulfate.

Sedatives or narcotics may also be used in early attempts to stop labor. This may consist of an injection of morphine or meperidine (Demerol). This is not a long-term solution but may be effective in initially stopping labor.

**Benefits of Stopping Premature Labor.** Benefits of stopping premature labor include reducing the risks of fetal problems and problems related to premature delivery. If you experience premature labor, you may need to see your doctor frequently. Your doctor will probably

Premature baby (born at 29 weeks of pregnancy) shown with fetal monitors attached to it. Note size of adult hand in comparison.

monitor your pregnancy with ultrasound or nonstress tests. (See the discussion of the nonstress test in Week 41.)

## How Your Actions
## Affect Your Baby's Development

Most of our discussion this week has been devoted to the premature infant and treatment of premature labor. If you are diagnosed as having premature labor and your doctor prescribes bed rest and medications to stop it, follow his or her advice!

If you're concerned about your doctor's instructions, discuss them. If you're told not to work or advised to reduce your activities and you ignore the advice, you're taking chances with your well-being and your unborn baby's. It isn't worth taking risks. Don't be afraid to ask for another opinion or the opinion of a perinatologist if you experience premature labor.

## Your Nutrition

We hope you have been listening to your body during your pregnancy. You rest when you're tired. You go to the bathroom when you first feel the urge. You pay attention to any new discomforts. You may also listen to your body when it comes to food and drink. When you feel hungry or thirsty, you eat or drink something. Eating smaller, more frequent meals provides a constant supply of nutrients to your growing baby.

Keep nourishing snacks near at hand. Raisins, dried fruit and nuts are good choices when you're on the go. Know what time of day or night hunger strikes you the hardest. Be prepared.

Be different, if you want to be. Eat spaghetti for breakfast and cereal for lunch, if that's what appeals to you. Don't force yourself to eat something that turns you off or makes you sick. There's always an alternative. As long as you eat nourishing food and pay attention to the types of foods you eat, you are helping yourself and your growing baby.

## You Should Also Know

### ↷ *Group-B Streptococcus Infection*

Group-B streptococcus *(GBS)* infection rarely causes problems in adults but can cause life-threatening infections in newborns. GBS is often transmitted from person to person by sexual contact.

In women, GBS is most often found in the vagina or rectum. It is possible to have GBS in your system and not be sick or have any symptoms.

The Centers for Disease Control, the American College of Obstetricians and Gynecologists and the American Academy of Pediatrics have developed recommendations aimed at preventing this infection in newborns. One recommendation is that all women who have risk factors be treated for GBS. Risk factors include the following:

- a previous infant with GBS infection
- preterm labor
- ruptured membranes for more than 18 hours
- a temperature of 100.4F (38C) immediately before or during childbirth

The second recommendation is that a GBS culture be taken from the rectal and vaginal areas of all pregnant women at 35 to 37 weeks gestation. Antibiotics, such as penicillin or ampicillin, are given during labor to women with a positive culture.

# Week 30

*Age of Fetus—28 Weeks*

## How Big Is Your Baby?

At this point in your pregnancy, your baby weighs about 3 pounds (1.35kg). Its crown-to-rump length is a little over 10¾ inches (27cm), and total length is 17 inches (38cm).

## How Big Are You?

Measuring from your bellybutton, your uterus is about 4 inches (10cm) above it. From the pubic symphysis, the top of your uterus measures about 12 inches (30cm).

It may be hard to believe you still have 10 weeks to go! You may feel like you're running out of room as your uterus grows up under your ribs. However, your fetus, placenta and uterus, along with the amniotic fluid, will continue to get larger.

The average total healthy weight gain during pregnancy is 25 to 35 pounds (11.4 to 15.9kg). About half of this weight is concentrated in the growth of the uterus, the baby and the placenta, and in the volume of amniotic fluid. This growth is mostly in the front of your abdomen and in your pelvis, where it is noticeable to you. You may experience increasing discomfort in your pelvis and abdomen as pregnancy progresses. At this point, you should be gaining about a pound a week.

## How Your Baby Is Growing and Developing

### ☞ Umbilical-Cord Knots
The illustration this week, page 306, shows a fetus and its umbilical cord. Can you see the knot in the cord? You may wonder how a knot like this can occur. We do not believe the cord grows in a knot.

A baby is usually quite active during pregnancy. We believe these knots occur as the baby moves around in early pregnancy. A loop forms in the umbilical cord; the baby moves through the loop, and a knot results. Your actions do not cause or prevent this kind of complication, which can be serious. A knot in the umbilical cord does not occur often.

*Dad Tip* Now is the time to think about changing your work schedule so you can be around home more during the last part of the pregnancy and after baby is born. Nearly all parents wish they were able to spend more time at home. If you travel a great deal, you may need to alter your schedule so you can be home toward the end of the pregnancy. Babies come on their own schedule. If you want to be present for the delivery, plan ahead!

## Changes in You

### ☞ Rupture of Membranes
The membranes around the baby that contain the amniotic fluid are called the *bag of waters*. They usually do not break until just before labor begins, when labor begins or during labor. But that isn't always the case; sometimes they break earlier in pregnancy.

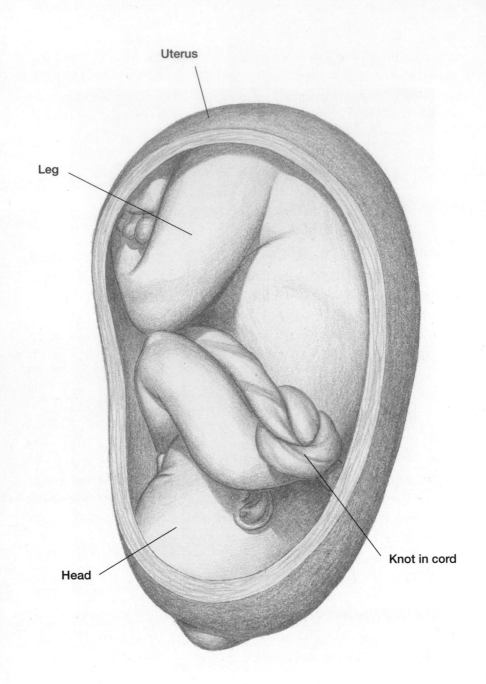

Uterus

Leg

Knot in cord

Head

This fetus has a knot in its umbilical cord.

After your water breaks, you need to take certain precautions. The membranes of pregnancy help protect your baby from infection. When your water breaks and you leak fluid, your risk of infection increases. An infection could be harmful to your baby. Call your doctor immediately when your water breaks.

## How Your Actions Affect Your Baby's Development

### ﹌ *Bathing during Pregnancy*

Many women wonder if bathing in the latter part of pregnancy will in some way harm their baby. Most doctors believe it's safe to bathe throughout pregnancy. They may caution you to be careful as you get in or out of the bathtub. And be sure bath water is not too hot. Most will not tell you to avoid bathing while you're pregnant. How-ever, if you think your water has broken, avoid a tub bath.

*Tip for Week 30*  Good posture can help relieve lower-back stress and eliminate some backache discomfort. Maintaining good posture may take some effort, but it's worth it if it relieves your pain.

Women also want to know how they'll know if their water breaks while they are in the tub or shower. When your water breaks, you'll usually notice a gush of water followed by slow leakage. If your water breaks while you're bathing, you may not notice the initial gush of fluid. However, you'll probably notice the leakage of fluid, which can last for quite a while.

### ﹌ *Choosing Where to Give Birth*

It's probably time to start considering where you want to give birth. In some situations, you may not have a choice. Or in your area, you may have several choices.

Whatever birthing setup you choose, the most important considerations are the health of your baby and the welfare of you both. When you decide where to have your baby, be sure you have answered the following questions, if you can.

- What facilities and staff do you have available?
- What is the availability of anesthesia? Is an anesthesiologist available 24 hours a day?
- How long does it take them to respond and to perform a Cesarean delivery, if necessary? (This should be 30 minutes or less.)
- Is a pediatrician available 24 hours a day for an emergency or problems?
- Is the nursery staffed at all times?
- In the event of an emergency or a premature baby that needs to be transported to a high-risk nursery, how is it done? By ambulance? By helicopter? How close is the nearest high-risk nursery, if not at this hospital?

These may seem like a lot of questions to ask, but the answers can help put your mind at ease. When it's your baby and your health, it's nice to know emergency measures can be employed in an efficient, timely manner when necessary.

**LDRP.** With LDRP (labor, delivery, recovery and postpartum), the room you are admitted to at the beginning of your labor is the room you labor in, deliver in, recover in and remain in for your entire hospital stay. This isn't available everywhere, but these facilities are becoming more popular.

The concept of LDRP has evolved because many women don't want to be moved from the labor area to recovery to another part of the hospital after recovery. The nursery is usually close to labor and delivery and the recovery area. This enables you to see your baby as often as you like and to have your baby in your room for longer periods.

**Labor-and-Delivery Suite.** In many places, you will labor in a labor room, then be moved to a delivery room at the time of birth. Following this, you may go to a postpartum floor, which is an area in the hospital where you will spend the remainder of your hospital stay.

Most hospitals allow you to have your baby in your room as much as you want. This is called *rooming in* or *boarding in*. Some hospitals also have a cot, couch or chair that makes into a bed in your room so your partner can stay with you after delivery. Check the availability of various facilities in the hospitals in your area.

**Birthing Room.** Another option is the birthing room; this generally refers to delivering your baby in the same room you labor in. You don't have to be moved from the room you're laboring in to another place to have the baby. Even if you use a birthing room, you may have to move to another area of the hospital for recovery and the remainder of your stay.

## Your Nutrition

Some women ask if herbal teas are safe to drink during pregnancy. They have heard that some herbal teas can be beneficial to a pregnant woman. Many herbal teas are safe to use; some are not. Herbal teas you can use safely include chamomile, dandelion, ginger root, nettle leaf, peppermint and red raspberry.

You should *not* use some herbal teas while you're pregnant. Studies indicate herbal teas to avoid include blue cohosh, black cohosh, penny-royal leaf, yarrow, goldenseal, feverfew, psyllium seed, mugwort, comfrey, coltsfoot, juniper, rue, tansy, cottonroot bark, large amounts of sage, senna, cascara sagrada, buckthorn, fern, slippery elm and squaw vine.

### Benefits of Drinking Some Herbal Teas

| | |
|---|---|
| **chamomile** | aids digestion |
| **dandelion** | helps with swelling and can soothe an upset stomach |
| **ginger root** | helps with nausea and nasal congestion |
| **nettle leaf** | rich in iron, calcium and other vitamins and minerals |
| **peppermint** | relieves gas pains and calms the stomach |
| **red raspberry** | helps with nausea and stabilizes hormones |

## You Should Also Know

### ᴈ Child-Care Decisions

You may think this is an odd place to put a discussion of child care for a baby that won't even be born for another 10 weeks, but it's important to start thinking about this now if you plan to return to work. Quality care is in high demand and short supply! Experts advise you to begin looking for a child-care situation *at least 6 months* before you need it. For some women, that may be the end of the second trimester!

If you find a situation you like, sign up as soon as possible; there may be a waiting list. If you find something more suitable later, you can always change your mind.

Deciding what type of child care is best for your baby can be a challenging task. You and your partner must make many decisions in selecting the type of care you want for baby. The best way to do that is to know your options before you begin.

Before you can determine which care situation is the best for your family, you must examine your needs and the needs of your child. Your options for child care include:

- in-your-home care by a family member or by a nonrelative
- care in a caregiver's home
- a child-care center

**In-home Care.** You may choose in-home care, either by a relative or nonrelative. It's fairly easy when someone comes to your home to take care of your child. You don't have to get baby ready before you go in the morning, and you never have to take your child out in bad weather. It also takes less time in the morning and evening if you don't have to drop off or to pick up baby.

When the caregiver is a nonrelative, it can be very expensive to have someone come to your home. You are also hiring someone you do not know to come into your home and tend your child. You must be diligent in asking for references and checking them out thoroughly.

**Care in a Caregiver's Home.** You may decide to take your child to someone else's home. A homelike setting may make a child feel more comfortable. However, homes are not regulated in every state, so you must check out each situation very carefully. Call your state Department of Economic Security; ask them to help you find out more information.

**Child-Care Centers.** A child-care center is an environment in which many children are cared for in a larger setting. Centers vary widely in the facilities and activities they provide, the amount of attention they give each child, group sizes and child-care philosophy.

Some child-care centers do not accept infants. Babies have special needs; be sure the place you choose for your infant can meet those needs.

**The Cost of Child Care.** It can cost you a lot to provide child care for your baby. We're not talking about a situation that is out of the ordinary—we're talking about a regular care situation in your home, someone else's home or in a day-care center.

Whether a person comes to your home or you take baby to theirs, you will probably have to pay federal, state and local taxes for your care provider, including Social Security and Medicare taxes. Contact the Internal Revenue Service and your state's Department of Economic Security for further information. If the person works in your home, you may also need to pay Workers' Compensation and unemployment insurance taxes. Be sure you have homeowner's or renter's insurance to cover them while they are at your home.

Be prepared in advance; child-care costs can be pretty high in many areas of the country.

### ᕦ *Cancer and Pregnancy*
Pregnancy is a happy time for most women, filled with anticipation and excitement. Occasionally, however, serious problems can occur. Cancer in pregnancy is one serious complication that occurs rarely.

This discussion is included not to scare you but to provide you with information. It is not a pleasant subject to discuss, especially at this time. However, every woman should have this information available. Its inclusion in this book is twofold:

- to increase your awareness of a serious problem
- to provide you with a resource to help you formulate questions for a dialogue with your doctor if you wish to discuss it

**Cancer before Pregnancy.** If you are now pregnant and you have had cancer in the past, tell your doctor as soon as you discover you are pregnant. He or she may need to make decisions about individualized care for you during pregnancy.

**Cancer in Pregnancy.** The occurrence of cancer at any time is stressful. When cancer occurs during pregnancy, it is even more stressful. The doctor must consider how to treat the cancer, but he or she is also concerned about the developing baby.

The way in which these issues are handled depends on when cancer is discovered. A woman's concerns may include the following.

- Will the pregnancy have to be terminated so the cancer can be treated?
- Will treatment or medications used harm the baby?
- Will the malignancy affect the baby or be passed to the baby?
- Should therapy be delayed until after delivery or after termination of the pregnancy?

Fortunately, many cancers in women occur after the reproductive years, which lowers the likelihood of cancer during pregnancy. Cancer during pregnancy is a rare occurrence and must be treated on an individual basis.

Some cancers found during pregnancy include breast tumors, leukemia and lymphomas, melanomas, gynecologic cancers (cancer of the female organs, such as the cervix, uterus and ovaries) and bone tumors.

Tremendous changes affect your body during pregnancy. Researchers suggest ways these changes can affect the possible discovery of cancer during pregnancy.

• Some believe cancers influenced by the increased hormone levels during pregnancy may increase in frequency during pregnancy.
• Increased blood flow, with accompanying changes in the lymphatic system, may contribute to the transfer of cancer to other parts of the body.
• Anatomical and physiological changes of pregnancy (growth of the abdomen and changes in the breasts) can make it difficult to find or to diagnose an early cancer.

These three beliefs about cancer during pregnancy appear to have some validity but vary widely depending on the cancer and the organ involved.

**Breast Cancer.** Breast cancer is rare in women younger than 35. Fortunately, it is an uncommon complication of pregnancy.

During pregnancy, it may be harder to find breast cancer because of changes in the breasts, such as tenderness, increased size and even lumpiness. Of all women who have breast cancer, about 2% are pregnant at the time of diagnosis. Most evidence indicates pregnancy does not increase the rate of growth or spread of a breast cancer.

Treatment of breast cancer during pregnancy varies and must be individualized. It may require surgery, chemotherapy or radiation; a combination of all these treatments may be used.

A form of breast cancer you should be aware of is *inflammatory breast cancer (IBC)*. Although it is very rare, it can occur during and after pregnancy and may be mistaken for mastitis, which is inflammation of the breast. Symptoms of inflammatory breast cancer include swelling or pain in the breast, redness, nipple discharge or swollen lymph nodes above the collarbone or under the arm. You may feel a lump, although one is not always present.

If you experience any of these symptoms, *do not panic!* Nearly all of the time it will be a breast infection related to breastfeeding. However, if you are concerned, contact your physician. A biopsy is used to diagnose the disease. To learn more about IBC, visit www.ibcsupport.org.

**Cervical Cancers and Pelvic Cancers.** Cervical cancer is believed to occur about once in every 10,000 pregnancies. However, about 1% of the women who have cancer of the cervix are pregnant when it is diagnosed. Cancer of the cervix is curable, particularly if it is found and treated in its early stages.

Malignancies of the vulva, the tissue surrounding the opening to the vagina, have also been reported during pregnancy. It is a rare complication; only a few cases have occurred.

**Other Cancers in Pregnancy.** *Hodgkin's disease* (a form of cancer) commonly affects young people. It is now being controlled for long periods with radiation and chemotherapy. The disease occurs in about 1 of every 6000 pregnancies. Pregnancy does not appear to have a negative effect on the course of Hodgkin's disease.

Pregnant women who have *leukemia* have demonstrated an increased chance of premature labor. They may also experience an increase in bleeding after pregnancy. Leukemia is usually treated with chemotherapy or radiation therapy.

*Melanoma* may occur during pregnancy. A melanoma is a cancer derived from skin cells that produce *melanin* (pigment). A malignant melanoma can spread through the body. Pregnancy may cause symptoms or problems to worsen. A melanoma can spread to the placenta and to the baby.

*Bone tumors* are rare during pregnancy. However, two types of benign (noncancerous) bone tumors can affect pregnancy and delivery. These tumors, *endochondromas* and *benign exostosis*, can involve the pelvis; tumors may interfere with labor. The possibility of having a Cesarean delivery is more likely with these tumors.

# Week 31

*Age of Fetus—29 Weeks*

## How Big Is Your Baby?

Your baby continues to grow. It weighs about 3½ pounds (1.6kg), and crown-to-rump length is 11¾ inches (28cm). Its total length is nearly 18 inches (40cm).

## How Big Are You?

Measuring from the pubic symphysis, it is now a little more than 12 inches (31cm) to the top of the uterus. From your bellybutton, it is almost 4½ inches (11cm).

**Dad Tip** Now's the time to begin discussing baby equipment, such as cribs, car seats and layette items, with your partner. You'll need to make some of these purchases before baby's birth. Most hospitals or birthing centers won't let you take baby home without a car seat.

At 12 weeks gestation, the uterus was just filling your pelvis. As you can see in the illustration on page 318, by this week the uterus fills a large part of your abdomen.

Your total pregnancy weight gain by this time should be between 21 and 27 pounds (9.45 and 12.15kg).

# How Your Baby Is
# Growing and Developing

### ✎ *Intrauterine-Growth Restriction (IUGR)*

*Intrauterine-growth restriction* (IUGR) indicates a newborn infant is small for its gestational age. By definition, its birthweight is below the 10th percentile (in the lowest 10%) for the baby's gestational age. This means 9 out of 10 babies of normal growth are larger.

When gestational age is appropriate—meaning dates are correct and the pregnancy is as far along as expected—and weight falls below the 10th percentile, there is reason for concern. Growth-restricted infants have a higher rate of death and injury than infants in the normal-weight range.

**Diagnosing and Treating IUGR.** Diagnosing IUGR can be difficult. One reason your doctor measures you at each visit is to see how your uterus and baby are growing. A problem is usually found by measuring the uterus over a period of time and finding no change. If you measured 10¾ inches (27cm) at 27 weeks gestation and at 31 weeks you measure only 11 inches (28cm), your doctor might become concerned about IUGR and tests may be ordered.

Diagnosis of this type of problem is one important reason to keep all your prenatal appointments. You may not like being weighed at every appointment, but it helps your doctor see that your pregnancy is growing and the baby is getting bigger.

Intrauterine-growth restriction can be diagnosed or confirmed by ultrasound. Ultrasound may also be used to assure that the baby is healthy and no malformations exist that must be taken care of at birth.

When IUGR is diagnosed, avoid doing anything that could make it worse. Stop smoking. Improve your nutrition. Stop using drugs and alcohol.

Bed rest is another treatment. Resting on your side enables the baby to receive the best blood flow, and better blood flow is the best chance it has to improve growth. If maternal disease causes IUGR, treatment involves improving the mother's general health.

An infant with intrauterine-growth restriction is at risk of dying before delivery. Avoiding this may involve delivering the baby before it is full term. Infants with IUGR may not tolerate labor well; a C-section is more likely because of fetal distress. The baby may be safer outside the uterus than inside of it, in some cases.

**Causes of IUGR.** What causes intrauterine-growth restriction? Below are some conditions that increase the chance of intrauterine-growth restriction or a small fetus.

Smoking and other tobacco use can inhibit a baby's growth. The more cigarettes smoked, the greater the impairment and the smaller the baby.

A woman of average size or smaller who doesn't gain enough weight may have a growth-restricted baby. This is one of the reasons that good nutrition and a healthful diet are so important during pregnancy. Do not attempt to restrict normal weight gain during pregnancy. Research indicates that when calories are restricted to under 1500 a day for an extended time, IUGR may result.

Pre-eclampsia and high blood pressure (hypertension) can have a marked effect on fetal growth. Cytomegalovirus, rubella and other infections may also restrict fetal growth.

Maternal anemia may be a cause of intrauterine-growth restriction. (Anemia is discussed in Week 22.) Abnormalities may cause inhibited growth because the baby receives less nutrition during pregnancy. A woman who has delivered a growth-restricted infant may be more likely to do so again in subsequent pregnancies.

Women who live at high altitudes are more likely to have babies who weigh less than those born to women who live at lower altitudes. Alcoholism and drug use, kidney disease and carrying more than one baby may also be causes of a smaller-than-normal baby.

Other reasons for a small baby, unrelated to IUGR, include the fact that a woman who is small might have a small baby. In addition, prolonged pregnancy can lead to an undernourished, smaller baby. A malformed or abnormal fetus may also be smaller, especially when chromosomal abnormalities are present.

Comparative size of the uterus at 31 weeks of pregnancy (fetal age—29 weeks). The uterus can be felt about 4½ inches (11cm) above the bellybutton.

## Changes in You

### ✑ *Swelling in Your Legs and Feet during Pregnancy*

You may notice, especially as you near the end of pregnancy, that if you take your shoes off and leave them off for a while, you may not be able to put them back on. This problem is related to swelling.

You may also notice that wearing nylon stockings that are tight at the knee (or tight socks) leaves an indentation in your legs. It may look like you still have clothing on. Avoid tight, restrictive clothing if you experience swelling.

Your body produces as much as 50% more blood and body fluids during pregnancy to meet baby's needs. Some of this extra fluid leaks into your body tissues. When your enlarging uterus pushes on pelvic veins, blood flow in the lower part of your body is partially blocked. This pushes fluid into your legs and feet, causing swelling.

The way you sit can also affect circulation of these body fluids. Crossing your legs, either at the knee or at the ankle, restricts blood flow to your legs. To improve circulation, don't cross your legs.

### *Carpal Tunnel Syndrome During Pregnancy*

Carpal tunnel syndrome is characterized by pain in the hand and wrist, which can extend into the forearm and shoulder. The cause of the pain is compression of the median nerve in the wrist. Symptoms can be numbness, tingling or burning of the inner half of one or both hands. At the same time, the fingers feel numb and useless. More than half of the time, both hands are involved.

The problem may occur during pregnancy, due to water retention and swelling in the wrist and arm area. Up to 25% of all women experience mild symptoms during pregnancy, but no treatment is necessary. The full syndrome, in which treatment may be needed, is less frequent; it occurs in only 1 to 2% of all pregnant women.

Treatment depends on symptoms. Carpal tunnel syndrome may be treated with surgery; however, this is rarely performed during pregnancy. In pregnant women, splints are often used during sleep and rest, in an attempt to keep the wrist straight. Most often, symptoms disappear after delivery.

Occurrence of carpal tunnel syndrome during pregnancy does *not* mean you will suffer from this problem after baby's birth. In rare instances, symptoms may recur long after pregnancy. In these cases, surgery may be necessary.

# How Your Actions
# Affect Your Baby's Development

### ∼ *Sleeping Positions*

We've already described the importance of resting on a regular basis and lying on your side when you sleep. (See Week 15.) Now is when it will pay off. You may notice you begin to retain water if you don't lie on your side when sleeping or resting. Lying on your side could help you feel better quickly.

### ∼ *Visiting Your Doctor*

It's important to keep all prenatal appointments with your doctor. It may seem to you that not much happens at these visits, especially when everything is normal and going well. But the information your doctor collects tells him or her a lot about your condition and your baby's.

Your doctor is watching for signs that indicate you might have a problem, such as changes in your blood pressure, changes in your weight or the inadequate growth of the baby. If these problems are not discovered early, they may have serious consequences for you and your baby.

### ∼ *Childbirth Methods*

It's time to start thinking about how you want to deliver your baby. You may think it's too early to do this, but now is the time to start thinking about it. Why? Because many of the methods that are commonly practiced need a lot of time to prepare you and your partner or labor coach to use them.

If you decide you want a particular method, such as Lamaze, you will probably have to sign up fairly early to get a place in a class. In addition, you and your labor coach will want the time to practice what you learn so you will be able to use it during labor and delivery.

**What Is Natural Childbirth?** Some women decide before the birth of their baby that they are going to labor and deliver with *natural childbirth*. What does this mean? The description or definition of natural childbirth varies from one couple to another.

Many people equate natural childbirth with a drug-free labor and delivery. Others equate natural childbirth with the use of mild pain medications or local pain medications, such as numbing medications in the area of the vagina for delivery or for an episiotomy and repair of episiotomy. Most agree that natural childbirth is birth with as few artificial procedures as possible. A woman who chooses natural childbirth usually needs some advance instruction to prepare for it.

**The Three Major Childbirth Philosophies.** There are three major philosophies of natural childbirth—Lamaze, Bradley and Grantly Dick-Read.

- *Lamaze* is the oldest technique of childbirth preparation. It conditions mothers, through training, to replace unproductive laboring efforts with fruitful ones and emphasizes relaxation and breathing as ways to relax during labor and delivery.
- *Bradley* classes teach the Bradley method of relaxation and inward focus; many types of relaxation are used. Strong emphasis is put on relaxation and deep abdominal breathing to make labor more comfortable. Classes begin when pregnancy is confirmed and continue until after the birth.
- *Grantly Dick-Read* is a method that attempts to break the fear-tension-pain cycle of labor and delivery. These classes were the first to include fathers in the birth experience.

**Should You Consider Natural Childbirth?** Natural childbirth isn't for every woman. If you arrive at the hospital dilated 1cm, with strong contractions and in pain, natural childbirth may be hard for you. In this situation, an epidural might be appropriate.

On the other hand, if you arrive at the hospital dilated 4 or 5cm and contractions are OK, natural childbirth might be a reasonable choice. It's impossible to know what will happen ahead of time, but it helps to be aware of, and ready for, everything.

It's important to keep an open mind during the unpredictable process of labor and delivery. Don't feel guilty or disappointed if you can't do all the things you planned before labor. You may need an epidural. Or the birth may not be accomplished without an episiotomy. Don't let anyone make you feel guilty or make you feel as though you've accomplished less if you end up needing a C-section, an epidural or an episiotomy.

Beware of instructors in childbirth-education classes who tell you labor is free of pain, no one really needs a C-section, I.V.s are unnecessary or an episiotomy is foolish. This can create unrealistic expectations for you. If you do need any of the above procedures, you may feel as though you failed during your labor.

The goal in labor and delivery is a healthy baby and a healthy mom. If this means you end up with a C-section, you haven't failed. Be grateful a Cesarean delivery can be performed safely. Babies that would not have survived birth in the past can now be delivered safely. This is a wonderful accomplishment!

## Your Nutrition

Pregnancy precautions can often be applied to everyday life, such as avoiding *salmonella* poisoning. Salmonella bacteria can cause a range of problems, from mild gastric discomfort to severe, sometimes fatal, food poisoning. Any of these could be serious for you.

Salmonella bacteria has many sources—there are over 1400 different strains! They are found in raw eggs and raw poultry. The bacteria is destroyed when a food is cooked, but it's wise to take additional precautions. Keep in mind the following measures to ensure your safety.

- When preparing poultry or products made with raw eggs, clean your counters, utensils, dishes and pans with hot water and soap or a disinfecting agent when you are finished.
- Cook poultry thoroughly.
- Don't eat products made with raw eggs, such as Caesar salad, hollandaise sauce, homemade eggnog, homemade ice cream and

so on. Don't taste cake batter, cookie dough or anything else that contains raw eggs before it is cooked.

• When you eat eggs, be sure they are cooked thoroughly. Boil eggs for at least 7 minutes. Poach eggs for 5 minutes. Fry them on each side for 3 minutes. Don't eat eggs that are cooked "sunny-side up."

## You Should Also Know

### ✑ *Pregnancy-Induced Hypertension*

Pregnancy-induced hypertension (high blood pressure) occurs only during pregnancy. With hypertension of pregnancy, the systolic pressure (the first number) increases to higher than 140ml of mercury or a rise of 30ml of mercury over your beginning blood pressure. A diastolic reading (the second number) of over 90 or a rise of 15ml of mercury also indicates a problem. An example is a woman whose blood pressure at the beginning of pregnancy is 100/60. Later in pregnancy, it is 130/90. This indicates she may be developing high blood pressure or pre-eclampsia.

Your doctor will be able to determine if your blood pressure is rising to a serious level by checking it at every prenatal appointment. That's one of the reasons it is so important to keep all of your prenatal appointments.

### ✑ *What Is Pre-eclampsia?*

*Pre-eclampsia* describes a variety of symptoms that occur only during pregnancy or shortly after delivery. Pre-eclampsia problems are characterized by a collection of symptoms:

• swelling (edema)
• protein in the urine (proteinuria)
• high blood pressure (hypertension)
• a change in reflexes (hyperreflexia)

Other nonspecific, important symptoms of pre-eclampsia include pain under the ribs on the right side, headache, seeing spots or other changes in vision. These are all warning signs. Report them to your doctor immediately, particularly if you've had blood-pressure problems during pregnancy!

*Tip for Week 31* Wearing rings and watches can cause circulation problems. Sometimes a ring becomes so tight on a pregnant woman's finger that the ring must be cut off by a jeweler. You might not want to wear rings if swelling occurs. Some pregnant women purchase inexpensive rings in larger sizes to wear during pregnancy. Or you could put your rings on a pretty chain, and wear them around your neck or on a bracelet.

Pre-eclampsia can progress to *eclampsia*. Eclampsia refers to seizures or convulsions in a woman with pre-eclampsia. Seizures are not caused by a previous history of epilepsy or a seizure disorder.

Most pregnant women have some swelling during pregnancy; swelling in the legs does not mean you have pre-eclampsia. It is also possible to have hypertension during pregnancy without having pre-eclampsia.

**What Causes Pre-eclampsia?** No one knows what causes pre-eclampsia or eclampsia. It occurs most often during a woman's first pregnancy. Women over 35 years old who are having their first baby are more likely to develop high blood pressure and pre-eclampsia. (See Week 16 for more information on pregnancy after 35.)

Some researchers believe that working women are more likely to develop pre-eclampsia than women who do not work. They attribute this increase to *job stress;* if you are in a stressful job situation, discuss it with your physician.

**Treating Pre-eclampsia.** The goal in treating pre-eclampsia is to avoid eclampsia (seizures). That means keeping a close watch on you throughout pregnancy and checking your blood pressure and weight at every prenatal visit.

Weight gain can be a sign of pre-eclampsia or worsening pre-eclampsia. Pre-eclampsia affects weight gain because it increases water retention. If you notice any symptoms, call your doctor's office.

Treatment of pre-eclampsia begins with bed rest at home. You may not be able to work or to spend much time on your feet. Bed rest allows for the most efficient functioning of your kidneys and the greatest blood flow to the uterus. You might want to read the section on *Bed-Rest Boredom Relievers* in Week 29 if you are advised to rest in bed.

Lie on your side, not on your back. Drink lots of water. Avoid salt, salty foods and foods that contain sodium, which make you retain fluid. Diuretics, which were used in the past, are not prescribed to treat pre-eclampsia today and are not recommended.

If you can't rest at home in bed or if symptoms do not improve, your doctor may have to admit you to the hospital or deliver your baby. A baby is delivered for the baby's well-being and to avoid seizures in you.

During labor, pre-eclampsia may be treated with magnesium sulfate. It is given by I.V. to prevent seizures during and after delivery. High blood pressure may be treated with antihypertensive medication.

If you think you've had a seizure, call your doctor immediately! Diagnosis may be difficult. If possible, someone who observed the possible seizure should describe it to your doctor. Eclampsia is treated with medications similar to those prescribed for seizure disorders (see Week 26).

# Week 32

*Age of Fetus—30 Weeks*

## How Big Is Your Baby?

By this week, your baby weighs almost 4 pounds (1.8kg). Crown-to-rump length is over 11½ inches (29cm), and total length is nearly 19 inches (42cm).

## How Big Are You?

Measurement to the top of the uterus from the pubic symphysis is about 12¾ inches (32cm). Measuring from your bellybutton to the top of the uterus now measures almost 5 inches (12cm).

## How Your Baby Is Growing and Developing

### Twins? Triplets? More?

When talking about pregnancies of more than one baby, in most cases we refer to twins. The chance of a twin pregnancy is more likely than pregnancy with triplets, quadruplets or quintuplets (or even more!).

You and your partner may be in shock if you learn you have more than one baby on the way. It's a normal reaction. Eventually the joy of expecting more than one baby may help offset the apprehension and responsibility you may feel. If you are expecting two or more babies, you will visit your doctor more often. You will need to plan carefully for delivery and for the care of the babies after you go home. Read the following pages for information on the many different issues surrounding multiples.

**Identical Twins and Fraternal Twins.**  Twin fetuses usually result (over 65% of the time) from the fertilization of two separate eggs. These are called *dizygotic twins* or *fraternal twins*. With fraternal twins, you can have a boy and a girl.

About 33% of the time, twins come from a single egg that divides into two similar structures. Each has the potential of developing into a separate individual. These are known as *monozygotic twins* or *identical twins*. Identical twins are not always identical. It is possible for fraternal twins to appear more alike than identical twins!

Either or both processes may be involved when more than two fetuses are formed. For example, quadruplets may result from fertilization of one, two, three or four eggs.

Division of the fertilized egg occurs between the first few days and about day 8. In this book, we refer to it as the 3rd week of pregnancy. If division of the egg occurs after 8 days, the result can be twins that are connected, called *conjoined twins*. (Conjoined twins used to be called *Siamese twins*.) These babies may share important internal organs, such as the heart, lungs or liver. Fortunately this is a rare occurrence.

**Frequency of Multiple Births.**  The frequency of twins depends on the type of twins. Identical twins occur about once in every 250 births around the world. This type of twin formation appears to be uninfluenced by age, race, heredity, number of pregnancies or medications taken for infertility (fertility drugs). The incidence of fraternal twins,

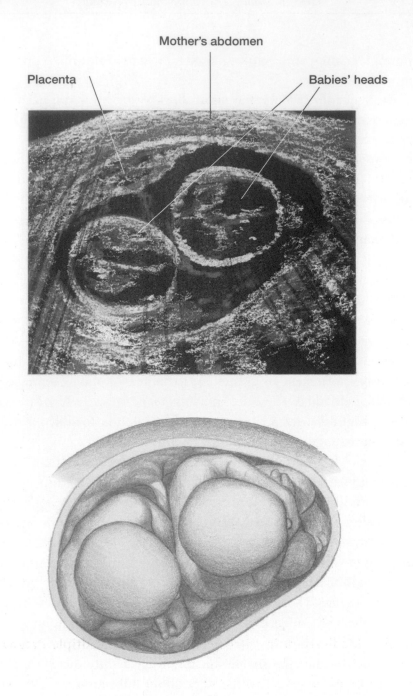

Mother's abdomen

Placenta

Babies' heads

Ultrasound of twins shows two babies in the uterus. If you look closely, you can see the two heads. The interpretive illustration shows how the babies are lying.

however, is influenced by race, heredity, maternal age, the number of previous pregnancies and the use of fertility drugs.

The frequency of multiple fetuses varies significantly among different races. Twins occur in 1 out of every 100 pregnancies in white women compared to 1 out of every 79 pregnancies in black women. Certain areas of Africa have an incredibly high frequency of twins. In some places, twins occur once in every 20 births! Hispanic women also have a higher number of twin births than white women. The occurrence of twins among Asians is less common—about 1 in every 150 births.

Heredity also plays a part in the occurrence of twins. In one study of fraternal twins, the chance of a female twin giving birth to a set of twins herself was about 1 in 58 births.

The occurrence of twins is probably more common than we know. Early ultrasound exams often reveal two sacs or two pregnancies. Later ultrasounds of the same woman may show that one sac (or one pregnancy) has disappeared, while the other pregnancy continues to grow and to develop normally. Some researchers believe these ultrasound results should not be disclosed in the first 8 to 10 weeks of pregnancy. Parents who are informed of twins at this point may be distraught to learn later that one of the babies will not be born.

Triplets occur once in every 8,000 deliveries. Many doctors never deliver or participate in the delivery of triplets in their medical careers. (Dr. Curtis has been fortunate to deliver two sets of triplets.)

Some families are more blessed than others. In one case we know of personally, a woman had three single births. Her 4th pregnancy was twins, and her 5th pregnancy (a year later) was triplets! She and her husband decided on another pregnancy—they were surprised (and probably relieved) when the 6th pregnancy resulted in only one baby.

**Fertility Medication, In Vitro Fertilization and Multiple Pregnancies.** We have known for a long time that fertility drugs increase the chance of multiple pregnancies. Several different medications are used to treat infertility. Each one affects, to a different degree, a woman's chances of conceiving more than one fetus. One of the more common medications is clomiphene (Clomid). It increases the chance of multiple fetuses somewhat less than other medications. But an increased chance is still there.

Twins are more common in pregnancies that result from the use of fertility drugs or with the implantation of more than one embryo with in-vitro fertilization. The percentage of male fetuses decreases as the number of fetuses per pregnancy increases. This means more females are born in these multiple pregnancies.

**Discovering You're Carrying More than One Baby.** Diagnosis of twins was more difficult before ultrasound was available. The illustration on page 328 shows an ultrasound of twins. You can see parts of both fetuses.

It is uncommon to discover twin pregnancies just by hearing two heartbeats. Many people believe when only one heartbeat is heard, there could be no possibility of twins. This may not be the case. Two rapid heartbeats may have a similar or almost identical rate. That could make it difficult to determine that there are two babies.

Measuring and examining your abdomen during pregnancy is important. Usually a twin pregnancy is noted during the second trimester because you are too big and growth seems too fast for a single pregnancy.

Ultrasound examination is the best way to tell if you are carrying more than one baby. Diagnosis can also be made by X-ray after 16 to 18 weeks of pregnancy, when fetal skeletons are visible. However, this method is used infrequently today.

**Do Multiple Pregnancies Have More Problems?** With a multiple pregnancy, the possibility of problems goes up. Possible problems include the following:

- increased risk of miscarriage
- fetal death or mortality
- fetal malformations
- low birthweight or growth restriction
- pre-eclampsia

- problems with the placenta, including placental abruption and placenta previa
- maternal anemia
- maternal bleeding or hemorrhage
- problems with the umbilical cord, including entwinement or tangling of the babies' umbilical cords
- hydramnios or polyhydramnios
- labor complicated by abnormal fetal presentation, such as breech or transverse lie
- premature labor

One of the biggest problems with multiple pregnancies is premature delivery. As the number of fetuses increases, the length of gestation and the birthweight of each baby decreases, although this is not true in every case.

The average length of pregnancy for twins is about 37 weeks. For triplets it is about 35 weeks. For every week the babies remain in the uterus, their birthweights increase, along with the maturity of organs and systems.

Major malformations in multiple pregnancies are more common than they are in single pregnancies. The incidence of minor malformation is twice as high as it is in a single pregnancy. Malformations are more common among identical twins than fraternal twins.

One of the main goals in dealing with multiple fetuses is to continue the pregnancy as long as possible to avoid premature delivery. This may best be accomplished by bed rest. You may not be able to carry on with regular activities during your entire pregnancy. If your doctor recommends bed rest, follow his or her advice.

Weight gain is important with a multiple pregnancy. You will gain more than the normal 25 to 35 pounds, depending on the number of fetuses you are carrying. Supplementation with iron is essential.

Some researchers believe use of a *tocolytic agent* (medication to stop labor), such as ritodrine, is critical in preventing premature delivery. (See Week 29.) These agents are used to relax the uterus to keep you from going into premature labor.

Follow your doctor's instruction closely. Every day and every week you're able to keep the babies inside you are days or weeks you won't have to visit them in an intensive-care nursery while they grow, develop and finish maturing.

**Delivering More Than One Baby.** How multiple fetuses are delivered often depends on how the babies are lying in your uterus. Possible complications of labor and delivery, in addition to prematurity, include the following:

- abnormal presentations (breech or transverse)
- prolapse of the umbilical cord (the umbilical cord comes out ahead of the babies)
- placental abruption
- fetal distress
- bleeding after delivery

Because there is higher risk during labor and delivery, precautions are taken before delivery and during labor. These include the need for an I.V., the presence of an anesthesiologist and the availability and possible presence of pediatricians or other medical personnel to take care of the babies.

With twins, all possible combinations of fetal positions can occur. Both babies may come head first (vertex). They may come *breech*, meaning bottom or feet first. They may come sideways or *oblique*, meaning at an angle that is neither breech nor vertex. Or they may come in any combination of the above. (See the discussion of birth presentation in Week 38.)

When both twins are head first, a vaginal delivery may be attempted and may be accomplished safely. It may be possible for one baby to deliver vaginally. The second one could require a C-section if it turns, the cord comes out ahead of the baby or the baby is distressed following delivery of the first fetus. Some doctors believe delivery of two or more babies requires a C-section.

After delivery of two or more babies, doctors pay close attention to maternal bleeding because of the rapid change in the size of the uterus.

It is greatly overdistended with more than one baby. Medication, usually oxytocin (Pitocin), is given by I.V. to contract the uterus to stop bleeding so the mother doesn't lose too much blood. A heavy blood loss could produce anemia and make a blood transfusion or long-term treatment with iron supplementation necessary.

## Changes in You

Until this week, your visits to the doctor have probably been on a monthly basis, unless you've had complications or problems. At week 32, most doctors begin seeing a pregnant woman every 2 weeks. This will continue until you reach your last month of pregnancy; at that time, you'll probably switch to weekly visits.

By this time, you probably know your doctor fairly well and feel comfortable talking about your concerns. Now is a good time to ask questions and to discuss concerns about labor and delivery. If there are complications or problems later in pregnancy or at delivery, you'll be able to communicate better with your doctor and know what is going on. You'll feel comfortable with the care you're receiving.

*Dad Tip* Together with your partner, make a list of important telephone numbers and keep it with you. Include numbers of your work, your partner's work, the hospital, the doctor's office, a back-up driver, baby-sitter or others. You may also want to make a list of numbers of people you want to call after the delivery of your baby. Take this list to the hospital with you.

Your doctor may plan on talking to you about many things in the weeks to come, but you can't always assume this. You may be taking prenatal classes and hearing different things about labor and delivery, such as stories about enemas, I.V.s and complications. Don't be afraid to ask any questions you have. Most doctors and nurses are receptive to your queries. They want you to discuss things you're concerned about instead of worrying about them unnecessarily.

## How Your Actions
## Affect Your Baby's Development

### ↷ Keep Taking Your Prenatal Vitamins

The vitamins and iron in prenatal vitamins are still essential to your well-being and the well-being of your baby or babies. If you're anemic at the time of delivery, a low blood count could have a negative effect on both or all of you. Your chance of needing a blood transfusion could be higher. Keep taking your prenatal vitamins every day!

## Your Nutrition

If you're expecting more than one baby, your nutrition and weight gain are extremely important during pregnancy. Food is your best source of nutrients and calories, but it's also important for you to take your prenatal vitamin every day. If you don't gain weight early in pregnancy, you have a greater chance of developing pre-eclampsia. Your babies may be tiny, too.

*Tip for Week 32*  Your requirements for calories, protein, vitamins and minerals increase if you carry more than one baby. You'll need to eat about 300 calories a day more *per baby* than for a normal pregnancy. For ideas on how to add those 300 calories, see Week 15.

If you're expecting twins, target weight gain (for a normal-weight woman) is about 45 pounds. Don't be alarmed when your doctor discusses the amount of weight he or she wants you to gain. Studies show that if a woman gains the targeted amount of weight with a multiple pregnancy, her babies are often healthier.

How can you gain the amount of weight you need to gain? Just adding extra calories won't benefit you or your developing babies. Junk food, full of empty calories, doesn't add much. Get your calories from specific sources. For example, it's important to eat an extra serving of a dairy product and an extra serving of a protein each day. These two servings provide you with the extra calcium, protein and iron you require to meet the needs of your growing babies. Discuss the situation with your doctor; he or she may suggest you see a nutritionist.

## You Should Also Know

### ∿ *Postpartum Bleeding and Hemorrhage*

It is normal to lose blood during labor and delivery. However, a heavy postpartum hemorrhage is different and significant. Postpartum hemorrhage is a loss of blood in excess of 17 ounces (500ml) in the first 24 hours after your baby's birth.

There can be many reasons for postpartum hemorrhage. The most common causes include a uterus that will not contract and lacerations or tearing of the vagina or cervix during the birth process.

Other causes include trauma to the genital tract, such as a large or bleeding episiotomy, or a rupture, hole or tear in the uterus. Blood loss may be related to the failure of blood vessels to compress to stop bleeding inside the uterus (where the placenta was attached). This may occur if the uterus fails to contract because of rapid labor, a long labor, several previous deliveries, a uterine infection, an overdistended uterus (with multiple fetuses) or with certain agents used for general anesthesia.

Heavy bleeding may also result from retained placental tissue. In this situation, most of the placenta delivers, but part of it remains inside the uterus. Retained placental tissue may cause bleeding immediately, or bleeding may occur weeks or even months later.

Problems with blood clotting can cause hemorrhaging. This may be related to pregnancy, or it may be a congenital medical problem. Bleeding following delivery requires constant attention from your doctor and the nurses caring for you.

# Week 33

*Age of Fetus—31 Weeks*

## How Big Is Your Baby?

Your baby weighs about 4½ pounds (2kg) by this week. Its crown-to-rump length is about 12 inches (30cm), and total length is nearly 19½ inches (43cm).

## How Big Are You?

Measuring from the pubic symphysis, it is now about 13¼ inches (33cm) to the top of the uterus. Measurement from your bellybutton to the top of your uterus is about 5¼ inches (13cm). Your total weight gain should be between 22 and 28 pounds (9.9 and 12.6kg).

## How Your Baby Is Growing and Developing

### Placental Abruption
The illustration on the opposite page shows placental abruption, which is premature separation of the placenta from the wall of the uterus.

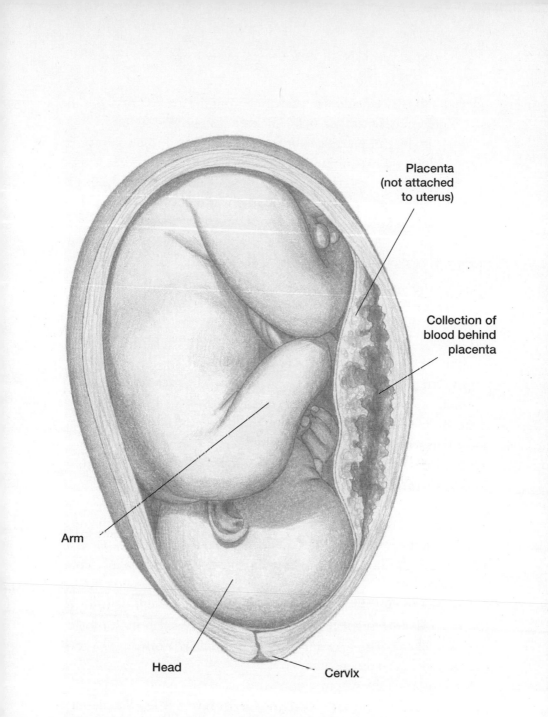

Placenta
(not attached
to uterus)

Collection of
blood behind
placenta

Arm

Head

Cervix

This illustration of placental abruption shows that the placenta has
separated from the wall of the uterus.

Normally, the placenta does not separate from the uterus until after the baby is delivered. Separation before delivery can be very serious.

The frequency of placental abruption is estimated to be about 1 in every 80 deliveries. We do not have a more exact statistic because time of separation varies, altering the risk to the fetus. If the placenta separates at the time of delivery and the infant is delivered without incident, it is not as significant as a placenta separating during pregnancy.

The cause of placental abruption is unknown. Certain conditions may increase its chance of occurrence, including:

- physical injury to the mother, as from a car accident or a bad fall
- a short umbilical cord
- sudden change in the size of the uterus (from rupture of membranes)
- hypertension
- dietary deficiency
- a uterine abnormality, such as a band of tissue or a scar in the uterus where the placenta cannot attach properly
- previous surgery on the uterus (removal of fibroids) or D&C for abortion or miscarriage

Studies indicate that folic-acid deficiency can play a role in causing placental abruption. Others suggest maternal smoking and alcohol consumption may make a woman more likely to have placental abruption.

A woman who has had placental abruption in the past is at increased risk of having it recur. Rate of recurrence has been estimated to be as high as 10%. This can make a pregnancy following placental abruption a high-risk pregnancy.

Separation of the placenta may involve partial or total separation from the uterine wall. The situation is most severe when the placenta totally separates from the uterine wall. The fetus relies entirely on circulation from the placenta. With separation, it cannot receive blood from the umbilical cord, which is attached to the placenta.

**Symptoms of Placental Abruption.**  Symptoms of placental abruption can vary a great deal. There may be heavy bleeding from the vagina, or you may experience no bleeding at all. The illustration on page 337 shows bleeding behind the placenta with complete separation.

Ultrasound may be helpful in diagnosing this problem, although it does not always provide an exact diagnosis. This is particularly true if the placenta is located on the back surface of the uterus where it cannot be seen easily with ultrasound examination.

Other symptoms can include lower-back pain, tenderness of the uterus or abdomen, and contractions or tightening of the uterus. Of the various symptoms associated with placental abruption, the following are the most common.

- Vaginal bleeding occurs in about 75% of all cases.
- Tenderness of the uterus occurs about 60% of the time.
- Fetal distress or problems with the fetal heart rate occur about 60% of the time.
- Tightening or contraction of the uterus occurs about 34% of the time.
- Premature labor occurs in about 20% of the cases.

Serious problems, such as shock, may occur with separation of the placenta. Shock occurs because of the rapid loss of large quantities of blood. Intravascular coagulation, in which a large blood clot develops, can also be a problem. Factors that clot the blood may be used up, which can make bleeding a problem.

**Can Placental Abruption Be Treated?**  Treatment of placental abruption varies, based on the ability to diagnose the problem and the status of the mother and baby. With heavy bleeding, delivery of the baby may be necessary.

When bleeding is not heavy, the problem may be treated with a more conservative approach. This depends on whether the fetus is in distress and if it appears to be in immediate danger.

Placental abruption is one of the most serious problems related to the second and third trimesters of pregnancy. If you have any symptoms, call your doctor immediately!

## Changes in You

### ᕲ *How Will You Know Your Membranes Have Ruptured?*

How will you know when your water breaks? It isn't usually just one gush of water, with no further leakage. There is often a gush of amniotic fluid, usually followed by a leaking of small amounts of fluid. Women describe it as a constant wetness or water running down their leg when they stand. *Continuous* leakage of water is a good clue that your water has broken.

Amniotic fluid is usually clear and watery. Occasionally it may have a bloody appearance, or it may be yellow or green.

It isn't uncommon to have an increase in vaginal discharge or to lose urine in small amounts as your baby puts pressure on your bladder. But there are ways for your doctor to tell if your water has broken. Two tests can be done on the amniotic fluid.

One is a *nitrazine test*. When amniotic fluid is placed on a small strip of paper, it changes the color of the paper. This test is based on the acidity or pH of the amniotic fluid. However, blood can also change the color of nitrazine paper, even if your water hasn't broken.

Another test that may be done is a *ferning test*. Amniotic fluid or fluid from the back of the vagina is taken with a swab and placed on a slide for examination under a microscope. Dried amniotic fluid has the appearance of a fern or branches of a pine tree. Ferning is often more helpful in diagnosing ruptured membranes than looking at color changes on nitrazine paper.

**What Do You Do When Your Water Breaks?**  Your membranes may rupture at any point in pregnancy. Don't assume it will happen only around the time of labor.

If you think your water has broken, notify your doctor. Avoid sexual intercourse at this time. Intercourse increases the possibility of introducing an infection into your uterus and thus to your baby.

## How Your Actions Affect Your Baby's Development

### ✎ *Weight Gain Continues*

You are continuing to gain weight as your pregnancy progresses. You may be gaining weight faster than at any other time during pregnancy. However, *you* are not putting on most of this weight—the baby is! Your baby is going through a period of increased growth and may be gaining as much as 8 ounces (½ pound; 224g) or more every week!

Continue to eat the right foods for you. Heartburn may be more of a problem now because your growing baby may not allow your stomach much room. You may find eating several small meals a day, rather than three large meals, makes you feel more comfortable.

## Your Nutrition

You know the importance of eating a well-balanced diet during pregnancy. Eating fresh fruit and vegetables, dairy products, whole-grain products and protein all contribute to the healthy development of your baby. You may be concerned about what foods to avoid. Some foods may be OK to eat when you're not pregnant but should be avoided now.

When possible, avoid food additives. We aren't certain how they can affect a developing baby, but if you can avoid them, do so. Be careful about pesticides, too. Thoroughly wash and wipe dry all fruits and

*Tip for Week 33* Don't stop eating or start skipping meals as your weight increases. Both you and your baby need all the calories and nutrition you receive from a healthy diet.

vegetables before you eat or prepare them, even if you don't normally eat the peel. Contaminants could get on your hands if you don't wash them. Peel a fruit or vegetable *after* you wash it, if that's the way you normally eat it. It helps to remove even more of the fruit that might be contaminated.

Avoid fish that might be contaminated with PCBs. (See Week 26 for further information.) Buy fish only from a reputable market, or eat those caught only in areas free from contamination. Be vigilant about the foods you consume to protect your growing baby.

## You Should Also Know

### ✎ *Will Your Doctor Perform an Episiotomy?*

An *episiotomy* is an incision made from the vagina toward the rectum during delivery to avoid undue tearing of the area as the baby's head passes through the birth canal. It may be a cut directly in the midline toward the rectum, or it may be a cut to the side. After the baby is delivered, layers are closed separately with absorbable sutures that do not require removal after they heal.

There is little you can do if you need an episiotomy. Some people practice, teach and believe in stretching the birth canal during labor and at the time of delivery to try to avoid an episiotomy. It may work for some, but it doesn't work for every woman. Others suggest an episiotomy to avoid stretching the vagina, bladder and rectum. Stretching the vagina can result in loss of control of your urine or bowels and can change sensations experienced during sexual intercourse.

**Dad Tip** Is your home safe for your new baby? Things to consider when thinking about safety include pets, furniture, secondhand smoke, window coverings or anything else in your home that could pose a danger to your little one. Start now to check for problems so you'll have time to take care of them before baby's birth.

The reason for an episiotomy usually becomes clear at delivery when the baby's head is in the vagina. An episiotomy is a controlled, straight, clean cut. That's better than a tear or rip that could go in many directions, including tearing or ripping into the bladder, large blood vessels or rectum. An episiotomy also heals better than a ragged tear.

Ask your doctor if he or she thinks you may need an episiotomy. Discuss why an episiotomy is necessary. Find out whether it might be a cut in the middle or to the side of the vagina. You might also ask if there is anything you can do to prepare for the possibility of an episiotomy, such as having an enema or stretching the vagina. If a vacuum extractor or forceps are used for delivery, an episiotomy may be done before the device is placed on the baby's head.

Description of an episiotomy also includes a description of the depth of the incision.

- A *first-degree* episiotomy cuts only the skin.
- A *second-degree* episiotomy cuts the skin and underlying tissue.
- A *third-degree* episiotomy cuts the skin, underlying tissue and rectal sphincter, which is the muscle that goes around the anus.
- A *fourth-degree* episiotomy goes through the three layers and through the rectal mucosa.

The most painful part of the entire birth experience might be an episiotomy. It may continue to cause some discomfort as it heals. Don't be afraid to ask for medication to ease any pain. There are many medications that are safe to take, even if you breastfeed your baby, including acetaminophen. Acetaminophen with codeine or other medications may also be prescribed for pain.

# Week 34

## Age of Fetus—32 Weeks

## How Big Is Your Baby?

Your baby weighs almost 5 pounds (2.28kg) by this week. Its crown-to-rump length is about 12¾ inches (32cm). Total length is 19¾ inches (44cm).

## How Big Are You?

Measuring up from your bellybutton, it's about 5½ inches (14cm) to the top of your uterus. From the pubic symphysis, you will measure about 13½ inches (34cm).

It's not important that your measurements match any of your friends' at similar points in their pregnancies. What's important is that you're growing appropriately and that your uterus grows and gets larger at an appropriate rate. These are the signs of normal growth of your baby inside your uterus.

*Tip for Week 34*  A strip of paper, tape or a bandage can help cover a bellybutton that is sensitive or unsightly (poking through your clothing).

# How Your Baby Is Growing and Developing

### ∽ *Testing Your Baby before Birth*

An ideal test done before delivery would determine if the fetus is healthy. It would be able to detect major fetal malformations or fetal stress, which could indicate an impending problem.

Ultrasound accomplishes some of these goals by enabling doctors to observe the baby inside the uterus, as well as to evaluate the brain, heart and other organs of the fetal body. Along with ultrasound examinations, fetal monitoring in the form of a nonstress test and a contraction stress test can indicate fetal well-being or problems. (See Week 41 for discussions of the nonstress test and the contraction stress test.)

## Changes in You

### ∽ *Will Your Baby Drop?*

A few weeks before labor begins or at the beginning of labor, you may notice a change in your abdomen. When examined by your doctor, measurement from your bellybutton or the pubic symphysis to the top of the uterus may be smaller than what you noticed on a previous visit. This phenomenon occurs as the head of the baby enters the birth canal. This change is often called *lightening*.

Don't be concerned if you don't notice lightening or a drop of the fetus. This doesn't occur with every woman or with every pregnancy. It's also common for your baby to drop just before labor begins or during labor.

With lightening, you may experience benefits and problems. One benefit may be more room in your upper abdomen. This gives you more room to breathe because there's more room for your lungs to expand. However, with the descent of the baby, you may notice more pressure in your pelvis, bladder and rectum, which can make you more uncomfortable.

In some instances, your doctor may examine you and tell you your baby is "not in the pelvis" or "is high up." He or she is saying the baby has not yet descended into the birth canal. However, this situation can change quickly.

If your doctor says your baby is "floating" or "ballotable," it means part of the baby is felt high in the birth canal. But the baby is not engaged (fixed) in the birth canal at this point. The baby may even move away from your doctor's fingers when you are examined.

### ✧ Uncomfortable Feelings You May Experience

At this point in their pregnancies, some women have the uncomfortable feeling the baby is going to "fall out." This feeling is related to pressure the baby exerts because it has moved lower in the birth canal. Some women describe the feeling as an increase in pressure.

If you're concerned or worried about it, consult your doctor. It may be a reason to perform a pelvic exam to see how low the baby's head is. In almost all cases, the baby will not be coming out. But because it is at a lower position than what you're used to, the baby will exert more pressure than you have noticed during recent weeks.

Another feeling associated with increased pressure may occur around this week. Some pregnant women have described it as a "pins-and-needles" sensation. The feeling is tingling, pressure or numbness in the pelvis or pelvic region from the pressure of the baby. It is a common symptom and shouldn't concern you.

These feelings may not be relieved until delivery occurs. You can lie on your side to help decrease pressure in your pelvis and on the nerves, vessels and arteries in the pelvic area. If the problem is severe, talk to your doctor about it.

### ✧ Braxton-Hicks Contractions and False Labor

Ask your doctor what the signs of labor contractions are; they are usually regular. They increase in duration and strength over time. You'll notice a regular rhythm to real labor contractions. You'll want to time them so you know how frequently they occur and how long they last. When you go to the hospital depends in part on your contractions.

*Braxton-Hicks contractions* are painless, nonrhythmical contractions you may be able to feel when you place your hand on your abdomen.

Comparative size of the uterus at 34 weeks of pregnancy (fetal age—
32 weeks). The uterus can be felt about 5¾ inches (14cm) above your
bellybutton.

These contractions often begin early in pregnancy and are felt at irregular intervals. They may increase in number and strength when the uterus is massaged. Like false labor, they are not positive signs of true labor.

False labor often occurs before true labor begins. False-labor contractions can be painful and may appear to be real labor to you. See the box below.

In most instances, false-labor contractions are irregular. They are usually of short duration (less than 45 seconds). The discomfort of the contraction may occur in various parts of your body, such as the groin, lower abdomen or back. With true labor, uterine contractions produce pain that starts at the top of the uterus and radiates over the entire uterus, through the lower back into the pelvis.

False labor is usually seen in late pregnancy. It seems to occur more often in women who have been pregnant before and delivered more babies. It usually stops as quickly as it begins. There doesn't appear to be any danger to your baby.

## True Labor or False Labor?

| Considerations | True Labor | False Labor |
|---|---|---|
| Contractions | Regular | Irregular |
| Time between contractions | Come closer together | Do not get closer together |
| Contraction intensity | Increases | Doesn't change |
| Location of contractions | Entire abdomen | Various locations or back |
| Effect of anesthetic or pain relievers | Will not stop labor | Sedation may stop or alter frequency of contractions |
| Cervical change | Progressive cervical change (effacement and dilatation) | No cervical change |

## How Your Actions
## Affect Your Baby's Development

The end of your pregnancy begins with labor. Some women are concerned (or hope!) that their actions can cause labor to begin. The old wives' tales about going for a ride over a bumpy road or taking a long walk to start labor aren't true.

We do know intercourse and stimulation of the nipples may cause labor to start in some cases, but this isn't true for every woman. Going about your daily activities (unless your doctor has advised bed rest) will not cause labor to start before your baby is ready to be born. In the following weekly discussions, we continue to discuss what labor involves and the many issues surrounding this climactic event.

## Your Nutrition

### ᕗ *Cholesterol Check*
It's a waste of time and effort to have your cholesterol level checked during pregnancy. The level of cholesterol in your blood rises during pregnancy due to hormonal changes. Wait until after you have your baby or stop breastfeeding to check your cholesterol.

### ᕗ *A Vitamin-Rich Snack*
When you're looking for something to snack on, you might not think of a baked potato, but it's an excellent snack! You get protein, fiber, calcium, iron, B vitamins and vitamin C when you eat a potato. Bake up a few, and store them in the refrigerator. Heat one up when you're hungry. Broccoli is another food filled with vitamins. Add it to your baked potato, and top both with some plain yogurt, cottage cheese or nonfat sour cream for a delicious treat!

*Dad Tip* Preregister at the hospital to save you time and inconvenience when you finally get there for baby's birth. Ask your partner to inquire at the doctor's office, or ask about preregistering in your prenatal classes. If your doctor or prenatal instructor doesn't know, call the hospital and ask.

## You Should Also Know

### ✍ What Is a "Bloody Show"?

Often following a vaginal examination or with the beginning of early labor and early contractions, you may bleed a small amount. This is called a *bloody show;* it can occur as the cervix stretches and dilates. You should not lose a lot of blood. If it causes you concern or appears to be a large amount of blood, call your doctor immediately.

Along with a bloody show, you may pass a mucus plug at the beginning of labor. This is different from your bag of waters breaking (ruptured membranes). Passing this mucus plug doesn't necessarily mean you'll have your baby soon or even that you'll go into labor in the next few hours. It poses no danger to you or your baby.

### ✍ Timing Contractions

Most women are instructed in prenatal classes or by their doctor about how to time contractions during labor. To time how long a contraction lasts, begin timing when the contraction starts and end timing when the contraction lets up and goes away.

It's also important to know how often contractions occur. There is much confusion about this. You can choose from two methods. Ask your doctor which method he or she prefers.

- Note the time period from when a contraction starts to the time the next contraction starts. This is the most commonly used method and the most reliable.
- Note the time period from when a contraction ends to the time the next contraction starts.

It's helpful for you and your partner or labor coach to time your contractions before calling your doctor or the hospital. Your doctor will probably want to know how often contractions occur and how long each contraction lasts. With this information, your doctor can decide when you should go to the hospital.

# Week 35

*Age of Fetus—33 Weeks*

## How Big Is Your Baby?

Your baby now weighs over 5½ pounds (2.5kg). Crown-to-rump length by this week of pregnancy is about 13¼ inches (33cm). Its total length is 20¼ inches (45cm).

## How Big Are You?

Measuring from your bellybutton, it is now about 6 inches (15cm) to the top of your uterus. Measuring from the pubic symphysis, the distance is about 14 inches (35cm). By this week, your total weight gain should be between 24 and 29 pounds (10.8 and 13kg).

**Dad Tip** At a prenatal visit, ask the doctor about your part in the delivery. There may be some things you'd like to do, such as cutting the cord or videotaping your baby's birth. It's easier to talk about these things ahead of time. Not every new father wants an active role in the delivery. That's OK, too.

## How Your Baby Is Growing and Developing?

### ✣ *How Much Does Your Baby Weigh?*

You have probably asked your doctor several times how big your baby is or how much your baby will weigh when it's born. Next to asking about the sex of a baby, this is the most frequently asked question.

You're getting larger. Your increasing size is due to the growth of baby and placenta as well as the increased amount of amniotic fluid. All these factors make estimating fetal weight more difficult.

**Using Ultrasound to Estimate Fetal Weight.** Ultrasound can be used to estimate fetal weight, but errors in weight estimates can and do occur. The accuracy of predicting fetal weight using ultrasound has improved. Making an accurate estimate can be valuable.

Several measurements are used in a formula or computer program to estimate a baby's weight. These include diameter of the baby's head, circumference of the baby's head, circumference of the baby's abdomen, length of the femur of the baby's leg and, in some instances, other fetal measurements.

Many feel that ultrasound is the method of choice to estimate fetal weight. But even with ultrasound, estimates may vary as much as half a pound or more (225g) in either direction.

**Will Your Baby Fit through the Birth Canal?** Even with a fetal-weight estimate, whether by your doctor or by ultrasound, we can't tell if the baby is too big for you or whether you'll need a C-section. Usually, it's necessary for you to labor to be able to see how the baby fits into your pelvis and if there is room for it to pass through the birth canal.

In some women who appear to be average or better-than-average size, a 6- or 6½-pound (2.7- to 2.9-kg) baby won't fit through the pelvis. Experience has also shown that women who may appear petite are sometimes able to deliver 7½-pound (3.4-kg) or larger babies without

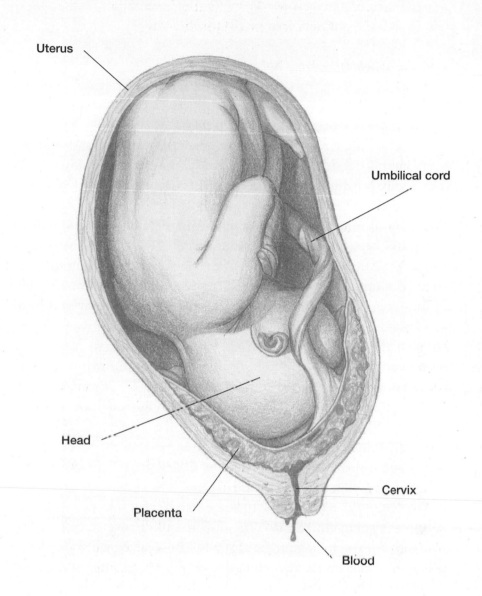

Uterus

Umbilical cord

Head

Cervix

Placenta

Blood

In this illustration of placenta previa, note how the placenta completely covers the cervical opening to the uterus. (See page 356 for more information.)

much difficulty. The best test or method of evaluating whether your baby will deliver through your pelvis is labor.

## Changes in You

### ↝ *Emotional Changes in Late Pregnancy*

As you come closer to delivery, you and your partner may become more anxious about the events to come. You may even have more mood swings, which seem to occur for no reason. You may become more irritable, which can place a significant strain on your relationship. You may be concerned about insignificant or unimportant things. Your concern about the health and well-being of the baby may also increase during the last weeks of your pregnancy. This can include concern about how well you will tolerate labor and how you will get through delivery. You may be concerned about whether you'll be a good mother or be able to raise a baby properly.

While these emotions rage inside you, you'll notice you're getting bigger and aren't able to do things you used to do. You may feel more uncomfortable, and you may not be sleeping well. These things can all work together to make your emotions swing wildly from highs to lows.

**How Can You Deal with These Changes?** Emotional changes are normal; don't feel as though you're alone. Other pregnant women and their partners have the same concerns.

Talk with your partner about your concerns. Tell him how you feel and what's going on. You may be surprised to discover the concerns your partner has about you, the baby and his role during labor and delivery. By talking about these things, your partner may find it easier to understand what you're experiencing, including mood swings and crying spells.

Discuss emotional problems with your doctor. He or she may be able to reassure you that what you're going through is normal. Take advantage of prenatal classes and information available about pregnancy and delivery.

Emotional changes often occur, so be ready for them. Ask your partner, the nurse in the doctor's office and your doctor to help you understand what is normal and what can be done about mood swings.

## How Your Actions Affect Your Baby's Development

### ✨ Preparing for Baby's Birth

At this point, you may be feeling a little nervous about the birth. You might be afraid you won't know when it's time to call the doctor or go to the hospital. Don't hesitate to talk to your doctor about it at one of your visits. He or she will tell you what signs to watch for. In prenatal classes, you should also learn to recognize the signs of labor and when you should call your doctor or go to the hospital.

Your bag of waters may rupture before you go into labor. In most cases, you'll notice this as a gush of water followed by a steady leaking. (See Week 33.)

During the last few weeks of pregnancy, have your suitcase packed and ready to go. See the list in Week 36 for some helpful suggestions, so you'll have the things you want when you get to the hospital.

If you can, tour the hospital facilities a few weeks ahead of your scheduled due date. Find out where to go and what to do when you get there.

Talk with your partner about the best ways to reach him if you think you are in labor. If either of you has a cell phone, it's probably the easiest way to stay in touch. You might have him check with you periodically. It's also common for a partner to wear a pager if he is often away from a phone, especially during the last few weeks of pregnancy.

Ask your doctor what you should do if you think you're in labor. Is it best to call the office? Should you go directly to the hospital? Should you call the answering service? By knowing what to do, and when, you'll be able to relax a little and not worry about the beginning of labor and delivery.

Preregistering at the Hospital. Your doctor has recorded various things that have occurred during your pregnancy. A copy of this record is usually kept in the labor-and-delivery area.

It may be helpful and save you time if you register at the hospital a few weeks before your due date. You will be able to do this with forms you get at your doctor's office or by getting forms from the hospital. It's wise to do this before you go to the hospital in labor because by then you may be in a hurry or concerned with other things.

You should know certain facts that may not be included in your chart:

- your blood type and Rh-factor
- when your last period was and what your due date is
- details of any past pregnancies, including complications
- your doctor's name
- your pediatrician's name

## Your Nutrition

Your body continues to need lots of vitamins and minerals for your developing baby. And you'll need even more of them if you choose to breastfeed! On the opposite page is a chart showing your daily vitamin and mineral requirements during pregnancy and breastfeeding. It's important to realize how necessary your continued good nutrition is for you and your baby.

## You Should Also Know

### ∽ What Is Placenta Previa?

With *placenta previa*, the placenta lies close to the cervix or covers the cervix. This problem is not common; it happens about once in every 170 pregnancies. The illustration on page 353 shows placenta previa.

Placenta previa is serious because of the chance of heavy bleeding. Bleeding may occur during pregnancy or during labor.

## Nutrient Requirements during Pregnancy and Breastfeeding

| Vitamins & Minerals | During Pregnancy | During Breastfeeding |
|---|---|---|
| A | 800mcg | 1300mcg |
| B₁ (thiamine) | 1.5mg | 1.6mg |
| B₂ (riboflavin) | 1.6mg | 1.8mg |
| B₃ (niacin) | 17mg | 20mg |
| B₆ | 2.2mg | 2.2mg |
| B₁₂ | 2.2mcg | 2.6mcg |
| C | 70mg | 95mg |
| Calcium | 1200mg | 1200mg |
| D | 10mcg | 10mcg |
| E | 10mg | 12mg |
| Folic acid (B₉) | 400mcg | 280mcg |
| Iron | 30mg | 15mg |
| Magnesium | 320mg | 355mg |
| Phosphorous | 1200mg | 1200mg |
| Zinc | 15mg | 19mg |

The cause of placenta previa is not completely understood. Risk factors for an increased chance of placenta previa include previous Cesarean delivery, many previous pregnancies and increased maternal age.

Symptoms of Placenta Previa. The most characteristic symptom of placenta previa is painless bleeding without any contractions of the uterus. This doesn't usually occur until close to the end of your second trimester or later when the cervix thins out, stretches and tears the placenta loose.

Bleeding with placenta previa may occur without warning and may be extremely heavy. It occurs when the cervix begins to dilate with early labor, and blood escapes.

Placenta previa should be suspected when a woman experiences vaginal bleeding during the latter half of pregnancy. The problem cannot be diagnosed with a physical exam because a pelvic examination may cause heavier bleeding. Doctors use ultrasound to identify placenta previa. Ultrasound is particularly accurate in the second half of pregnancy because the uterus and placenta get bigger, and things are easier to see.

Your doctor may advise you not to have a pelvic exam if you have placenta previa. This is important to remember if you see another doctor or when you go to the hospital.

The baby is more likely to be in a breech position with placenta previa. For this reason, and to control bleeding, a Cesarean delivery is usually performed. Cesarean delivery with placenta previa offers the advantage of delivering the baby, then removing the placenta so the uterus can contract. Bleeding can be kept to a minimum.

*Tip for Week 35*   Maternity bras are designed to provide extra support to your growing breasts. You may feel more comfortable wearing one during the day and at night while you sleep.

# Week 36

*Age of Fetus—34 Weeks*

## How Big Is Your Baby?

By this week, your baby weighs about 6 pounds (2.75kg). Its crown-to-rump length is over 13½ inches (34cm), and total length is 20¾ inches (46cm).

## How Big Are You?

Measuring from the pubic symphysis, it's about 14½ inches (36cm) to the top of your uterus. If you measure from your bellybutton, it's more than 5½ inches (14cm) to the top of your uterus.

You may feel as though you've run out of room! Your uterus has grown bigger in the past few weeks as the baby has grown inside of it. Now your uterus is probably up under your ribs.

*Tip for Week 36* Now is the time to find a pediatrician for your baby. Ask for referrals; your pregnancy doctor might be able to give you one. Or ask family, friends or people in your childbirth-education classes for names of doctors they like.

# How Your Baby Is
# Growing and Developing

### ༀ *Maturity of Your Baby's Lungs and Respiratory System*

An important part of your baby's development is maturation of the lungs and respiratory system. When a baby is born prematurely, a common problem is development of *respiratory-distress syndrome* in the newborn. This problem is also called *hyaline membrane disease*. In this situation, lungs are not completely mature, and the baby can't breathe on its own without help. Oxygen is necessary. The baby may require a machine, such as a ventilator, to breathe for it.

In the early 1970s, scientists developed two methods for evaluating fetal-lung maturity. An amniocentesis test must be done for both tests. The first method, the *L/S ratio*, enables doctors to determine in advance if a baby can breathe on its own after delivery.

The L/S-ratio test doesn't usually indicate a baby's lungs are mature until at least 34 weeks of pregnancy. At that time, the relationship between two factors in the amniotic fluid changes. Levels of lecithin go up, while levels of sphingomyelin stay the same. The ratio between these two levels indicates if a baby's lungs are mature.

The *phosphatidyl glycerol (PG)* test is another way doctors can evaluate the maturity of the baby's lungs. This test is either positive or negative. If phosphatidyl glycerol is present in the amniotic fluid (positive result), the infant will probably not suffer respiratory distress upon delivery.

Specific cells in the lungs produce chemicals that are essential for respiration immediately after birth. An important part of a newborn baby's breathing is determined by the chemical *surfactant*. A baby born prematurely may not have surfactant in its lungs. Surfactant can be introduced directly into the lungs of the newborn to prevent respiratory-distress syndrome. The chemical is available for immediate use by the baby. Many premature babies who receive surfactant do not have to be put on respirators—they can breathe on their own!

## Changes in You

You have only 4 to 5 weeks to go until your due date. It's easy to get anxious for your baby to be delivered. However, don't ask your doctor to induce labor at this point.

You may have gained 25 to 30 pounds (11.25 to 13.5kg), and you still have a month to go. It isn't unusual for your weight to stay the same at each of your weekly visits after this point.

The maximum amount of amniotic fluid surrounds the baby now. In the weeks to come, the baby continues to grow. However, some amniotic fluid is reabsorbed by your body, which decreases the amount of fluid around the baby and decreases the amount of room in which the baby has to move. You may notice a difference in sensation of fetal movements. For some women, it feels as if the baby is not moving as much as it had been.

### ✐ *What Is Labor?*

It is important to understand a little about the labor process. Then you'll be more informed when labor occurs, and you'll know what to do when it begins. What causes labor? Why does it happen?

Unfortunately, we don't have good answers to these questions. The factors that cause labor to begin are still unknown. There are many theories as to why labor happens when it does. One theory is that hormones made by the mother and fetus together trigger labor. Or it could be that the fetus produces some hormone that causes the uterus to contract.

Labor is defined as the dilatation (stretching and thinning) of your cervix. This occurs because the uterus, which is a muscle, contracts (tightens) and relaxes to squeeze out its contents (the baby). As the baby is pushed out, the cervix stretches.

At various times, you may feel tightening, contractions or cramps, but it isn't actually labor until there is a *change in the cervix*. As you can see from the discussion that begins on the next page, there are many aspects to labor. You'll go through them all as you deliver your baby.

**Three Stages of Labor.**  There are three distinct stages of labor.

**Stage one**—The first stage of labor begins with uterine contractions of great enough intensity, duration and frequency to cause thinning (effacement) and opening (dilatation) of the cervix. The first stage of labor ends when the cervix is fully dilated (usually 10cm) and sufficiently open to allow the baby's head to come through it.

**Stage two**—The second stage of labor begins when the cervix is completely dilated at 10cm. This stage ends with the delivery of the baby.

**Stage three**—The third stage of labor begins after delivery of the baby. It ends with delivery of the placenta and the membranes that have surrounded the fetus.

Some doctors have even described a 4th stage of labor, referring to a time period after delivery of the placenta during which the uterus contracts. Contraction of the uterus is important in controlling bleeding that can occur after delivery of the baby and the placenta.

**How Long Will Labor Last?**  The length of the first and second stages of labor, from the beginning of cervical dilatation to delivery of the baby, can last 14 to 15 hours or more in a first pregnancy. Women have had faster labors than this, but don't count on it.

A woman who has already had one or two children will probably have a shorter labor, but don't count on that either! The average time for labor is usually decreased by a few hours for a second or third delivery.

Everyone's heard of women who barely make it to the hospital or had a 1-hour labor. For every one of those patients, there are many women who have labored 18, 20, 24 hours or longer.

It's almost impossible to predict the amount of time that will be required for labor. You may ask your doctor about it, but his or her answer is only a guess.

*Dad Tip*  Pack for yourself, too! Some essential items you might need include magazines, phone numbers, a change of clothes and something to sleep in, a camera, film, new battery, snacks, a telephone calling card or lots of change, insurance information, a comfortable pillow and extra cash.

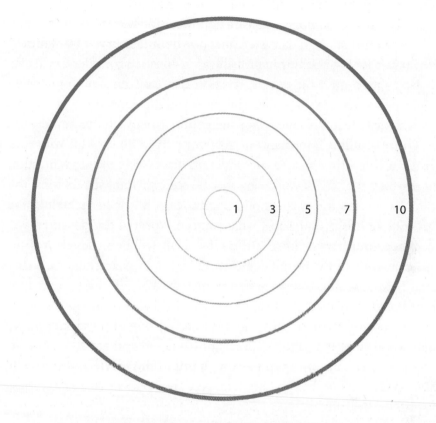

Cervical dilatation in centimeters (shown actual size).

## How Your Actions
## Affect Your Baby's Development

### ✑ *Choosing Your Baby's Doctor*

At this point in your pregnancy, it's time to choose a doctor for your baby. You might choose a pediatrician—a doctor who specializes in treating children. Or you might choose a family practitioner. If the doctor you are seeing during pregnancy is a family practitioner, and you want him or her to care for your baby, you probably don't need to consider this at all.

It's good to meet the doctor who will care for baby before the birth. Many pediatricians welcome it. This gives you the opportunity to discuss matters that are important to you and your partner with this new doctor.

The first visit is important, so ask your partner to go with you. Your visit is an ideal time for the two of you to discuss any concerns or questions about the care of your baby and to receive helpful suggestions. You can also discuss the doctor's philosophy, learn his or her schedule and "on-call" coverage, and clarify what you can expect of this physician.

When your baby is born, the pediatrician will be notified so he or she can come to the hospital and check the baby. Selecting a pediatrician before the birth ensures that your baby will see the same doctor for follow-up visits at the hospital and at the doctor's office.

If you belong to an HMO, and there are a group of physicians in pediatrics, arrange a meeting with one physician. If you have a conflict or don't see eye to eye with this person on important matters, you may be able to choose another pediatrician. Ask your patient advocate for information and advice.

**Questions to Ask a Pediatrician.** The questions below may help you create a useful dialogue with your pediatrician. You will probably have other questions, too.

- What are your qualifications and training?
- Are you board certified? If not, will you be soon?
- What hospital(s) are you affiliated with?
- Do you have privileges at the hospital where I will deliver?

- Will you do the newborn exam?
- If I have a boy, will you perform the circumcision (if we want to have it done)?
- What is your availability for regular office visits and emergencies?
- How long is a typical office visit?
- Are your office hours compatible with our work schedules?
- Can an acutely ill child be seen the same day?
- How can we reach you in case of an emergency or after office hours?
- Who responds if you are not available?
- Do you return phone calls the same day?
- What sort of advice do you give parents who both work outside the home?
- Are you interested in preventive, developmental and behavioral issues?
- Do you provide written instructions for well-baby and sick-baby care?
- Do you support women in their efforts to breastfeed?
- What are your fees?
- Do your fees comply with our insurance?
- What is the nearest (to our home) emergency room or urgent-care center you would send us to?

**Analyzing Your Visit.** Some issues can be resolved only by analyzing your feelings *after* your visit. Below are some things you and your partner might want to discuss after you visit the pediatrician.

- Are the doctor's philosophies and attitudes acceptable to us, such as use of antibiotics and other medications, child-rearing practices or related religious beliefs?
- Did the doctor listen to us?
- Did he or she seem genuinely interested in our concerns?
- Is this a person we feel comfortable with?
- Is the office comfortable, clean and bright?
- Did the office staff seem cordial, open and easy to talk to?

By choosing someone to care for your baby before it is born, you have a chance to take part in deciding who will have that important task. If you don't, the doctor who delivers your baby, or the hospital personnel, will select someone. Another good reason for choosing someone ahead of time is if your baby has complications, you'll at least have met the person who will be treating him or her.

## Your Nutrition

You're getting close to the end of your pregnancy. You may be having a harder time with your food plan than you had earlier in your pregnancy. You may be bored with the foods you've been eating. Your baby is getting larger, and you don't seem to have as much room for food. Heartburn or indigestion may also be problems now.

Don't give up on good nutrition! It's important to continue to pay attention to what you eat. Be vigilant so you continue to provide your baby the best nutrition it needs before its birth.

Every day, try to eat one serving of a dark-green leafy vegetable, a serving of food or juice rich in vitamin C, and one serving of a food rich in vitamin A (many foods that are yellow, such as yams, carrots and cantaloupes, are good sources of vitamin A). Remember to keep up your fluid intake.

## You Should Also Know

### ᔈ *How Is Your Baby Presenting?*
At what point in your pregnancy can your doctor tell how baby is presenting for delivery—for example, if the baby's head is down or if the baby is breech? At what point will the baby stay in the position it is in?

Usually between 32 and 34 weeks of pregnancy, you can feel the baby's head in the lower abdomen below your umbilicus. Some women can feel different parts of the baby earlier than this. But the baby's head may not be hard enough yet to identify as the head.

Alignment of baby with head in pelvis before delivery. This is the preferable presentation.

Pelvis

The head gradually becomes harder as calcium is deposited in the fetal skull. Your baby's head has a distinct feeling. It is different from the feeling your doctor gets with a breech. A breech position has a soft, round feeling.

Beginning at 32 to 34 weeks, your doctor will probably feel your abdomen to determine how the baby is lying inside you. This position may have changed many times during pregnancy.

At 34 to 36 weeks of pregnancy, the baby usually gets into the position it's going to stay in. If you have a breech at 37 weeks, it's possible the baby can still turn to be head-down. But it becomes less likely the closer you get to the end of your pregnancy.

### ॐ *Packing for the Hospital*

Packing for the hospital can be unnerving. You don't want to pack too early and have your suitcase staring at you. But you don't want to wait till the last minute, throw your things together and take the chance of forgetting something important.

It's probably a good idea to pack about 3 or 4 weeks before your due date. Pack things you'll need during labor for you and your labor coach, items you and the baby will need after delivery and personal articles for your hospital stay.

There are a lot of things to consider, but the list below should cover nearly all of what you might need:

- completed insurance or preregistration forms and insurance card
- heavy socks to wear in the delivery room
- an item to use as a focal point
- 1 cotton nightgown or T-shirt for labor
- lip balm, lollipops or fruit drops, to use during labor
- light diversion, such as books or magazines, to use during labor
- breath spray
- 1 or 2 nightgowns for after labor (bring a nursing gown if you're going to breastfeed)
- slippers with rubber soles
- 1 long robe for walking in the halls
- 2 bras (nursing bras and pads if you breastfeed)
- 3 pairs of panties

- toiletries you use, including brush, comb, toothbrush, tooth-paste, soap, shampoo, conditioner
- hairband or ponytail holder, if you have long hair
- loose-fitting clothes for going home
- sanitary pads, if the hospital doesn't supply them
- glasses, if you wear contacts (you can't wear contacts during labor)

You may also want to bring one or two pieces of fruit to eat after the delivery. Don't pack them too early!

It's also a good idea to include some things in your hospital kit for your partner or labor coach to help you both during the birth. You might bring the following:

- a watch with a second hand
- talc or cornstarch for massaging you during labor
- a paint roller or tennis ball for giving you a low-back massage during labor
- tapes or CDs and a player, or a radio to play during labor
- camera and film
- list of telephone numbers and a long-distance calling card
- change for telephones and vending machines
- snacks for your partner or labor coach

The hospital will probably supply most of what you need for your baby, but you should have a few things:

- clothes for the trip home, including an undershirt, sleeper, outer clothes (a hat if it's cold outside)
- a couple of baby blankets
- diapers, if your hospital doesn't supply them

Be sure you have an approved infant car seat in which to take your baby home. It's important to start your baby in a car seat the very first time he or she rides in a car! Many hospitals will not let you take your baby home without one.

# Week 37

*Age of Fetus—35 Weeks*

## How Big Is Your Baby?

Your baby weighs almost 6½ pounds (2.95kg). Crown-to-rump length is 14 inches (35cm). Its total length is around 21 inches (47cm).

## How Big Are You?

Your uterus may stay the same size as measured in the last week or two. Measuring from the pubic symphysis, the top of the uterus is about 14¾ inches (37cm). From the bellybutton, it is 6½ to 6¾ inches (16 to 17cm). Your total weight gain by this time should be about as high as it will go at 25 to 35 pounds (11.3 to 15.9kg).

*Dad Tip* Let your partner know how she can reach you at work or when you're out. You may not understand how nervous she can be about getting in touch with you when she needs you. Carry a cell phone or a beeper with you all the time. This can comfort her and provide her with peace of mind.

# How Your Baby Is Growing and Developing

### *Is Your Baby's Head Down in Your Pelvis?*

Your baby is continuing to grow and to gain weight, even during these last few weeks of pregnancy. As discussed in Week 36, the baby's head is usually directed down into the pelvis around this time. However, in about 3% of all pregnancies, the baby's bottom or legs come into the pelvis first. This is called a *breech presentation*, which we discuss in Week 38.

## Changes in You

### ❧ *Pelvic Exam in Late Pregnancy*

About this time in your pregnancy, your doctor may do a pelvic exam. This pelvic exam helps your doctor evaluate the progress of your pregnancy. One of the first things he or she will observe is whether you are leaking amniotic fluid. If you think you are, it's important to tell your doctor.

Your doctor will examine your cervix during the pelvic exam. During labor, the cervix usually becomes softer and thins out. This process is called *effacement*. Your doctor will evaluate the cervix for its softness or firmness and the amount of thinning.

Before labor begins, the cervix is thick and is "0% effaced." When you're in active labor, the cervix thins out; when it is half-thinned, it is "50% effaced." Immediately before delivery, the cervix is "100% effaced" or "completely thinned out."

The dilatation (amount of opening) of the cervix is also important. This is usually measured in centimeters. The cervix is fully open when the diameter of the cervical opening measures 10cm. The goal is to be a 10! Before labor begins, the cervix may be closed. Or it may be open a little way, such as 1cm (nearly ½ inch). Labor is the stretching and opening of the cervix so the baby fits through it and can pass out of the uterus.

Your doctor also evaluates whether the baby's head, bottom or legs are coming first. (He or she may refer to a "presenting part.") The shape of your pelvic bones is also noted.

The station is then determined. Station describes the degree to which the presenting part of the baby has descended into the birth canal. If the baby's head is at a -2 station, it means the head is higher inside you than if it were at a +2 station. The 0 point is a bony landmark in the pelvis, the starting place of the birth canal.

Think of the birth canal as a tube going from the pelvic girdle down through the pelvis and out the vagina. The baby travels through this tube from the uterus. It's possible that you may dilate during labor but the baby doesn't move down through the pelvis. In this case, a C-section may be needed because the baby's head doesn't fit through the pelvic girdle.

**Information Your Doctor Learns.** When your doctor examines you, he or she may describe your situation in medical terms. You might hear you are "2cm, 50% and a -2 station." This means the cervix is open 2cm (about 1 inch), it is halfway thinned out (50% effaced) and the presenting part (baby's head, feet or buttocks) is at a -2 station.

Try to remember this information. It's helpful when you go to the hospital and are checked there. You can tell the medical personnel in labor and delivery what your dilatation and effacement were at your last checkup so they can know if your situation has changed.

## How Your Actions
## Affect Your Baby's Development

### ᕽ *Cesarean Delivery*
Most women plan on a normal vaginal birth, but a Cesarean delivery is always a possibility. With a Cesarean, the baby is delivered through an incision made in the mother's abdominal wall and uterus. The illustration on page 374 shows a Cesarean delivery. Common names for this type of surgery are *C-section, Cesarean section* and *Cesarean delivery*.

**Reasons for a C-Section.**  C-sections are done for many reasons. The most common reason for having a C-section is a previous Cesarean delivery. However, some women who have had C-sections can have a vaginal delivery with later pregnancies; this is called *vaginal birth after Cesarean (VBAC)*. See the discussion that begins on page 377. Discuss the matter with your doctor if you've had a C-section and believe you would like to attempt a vaginal delivery this time.

A Cesarean delivery may be necessary if your baby is too big to fit through the birth canal. This condition is called *cephalo-pelvic dispro-portion* (CPD). CPD may be suspected during pregnancy, but usually labor must begin before it can be confirmed. A C-section may be recommended if an ultrasound shows your baby is very large—9½ pounds or larger—and may not be easily delivered vaginally.

Fetal distress is another reason for a Cesarean section. Doctors use fetal monitors during labor to watch the fetal heartbeat and its response to labor. If the heartbeat indicates the baby is having trouble with labor contractions, a C-section may be necessary for the baby's well-being.

If the umbilical cord is compressed, a C-section may be necessary. The cord may come into the vagina ahead of the baby's head or the baby can press on part of the cord. This is a dangerous situation because a compressed umbilical cord can cut off the blood supply to the baby.

A C-section is usually necessary if the baby is in a breech presentation, which means the baby's feet or buttocks enter the birth canal first. Delivering the shoulders and the head after the baby's body may damage the baby's head or neck, especially with a first baby.

Placental abruption or placenta previa are also reasons for a Cesarean delivery. If the placenta separates from the uterus before delivery (placental abruption), the baby loses its supply of oxygen and nutrients. This is usually diagnosed when a woman has heavy vaginal bleeding. If the placenta blocks the birth canal (placenta previa), the baby cannot be delivered any other way.

**Rising Rate of Cesarean Deliveries.**  In 1965, only 4% of all deliveries were by C-section. Today, in the United States, Cesarean deliveries account

Delivery of a baby by Cesarean section.

for about 20% of all deliveries. In some areas, this percentage is even higher. In Canada, Cesarean deliveries account for almost 18% of all deliveries. This increase is related in part to more stringent monitoring during labor and safer procedures for C-sections. Another reason for more Cesarean deliveries is bigger babies. With bigger babies, a C-section is sometimes the only way to deliver. Researchers believe this increase in the size of babies is due to pregnant women eating a better diet, not smoking during pregnancy and being older when they deliver.

**How Is a C-Section Performed?**   You are often awake when a C-section is done. An anesthesiologist usually gives you an epidural or spinal anesthetic. (Types of anesthesia are discussed in Week 39.) If you're awake for the procedure, you may be able to see your baby immediately after delivery!

With a C-section, an incision is made through the skin of the abdominal wall to the uterus. The wall of the uterus is cut, then the amniotic sac containing the baby and placenta is cut. The baby is removed through the incision. Next, the placenta is removed. The uterus is closed in layers with sutures that absorb and do not have to be removed. The remainder of the abdomen is sewn together with absorbable sutures.

Most Cesarean deliveries done today are *low-cervical* Cesareans or *low-transverse* Cesareans. This means the incision is made low in the uterus.

In the past, a Cesarean was often done with a classical incision, in which the uterus is cut down the midline. This incision doesn't heal as well as a low-cervical incision. Because the incision is made in the muscular part of the uterus, it is more likely to pull apart with contractions (as in a vaginal birth after Cesarean). This can cause heavy bleeding and injure the baby. If you have had a classical Cesarean section in the past, you *must* have a C-section every time you have a baby.

A T-incision is another type of C-section incision. This incision goes across and up the uterus in the shape of an inverted T. It provides more room to get the baby out. If you have had this type of incision, you will need to have a Cesarean delivery with all subsequent pregnancies. It too is more likely to rupture than other types of incisions.

Advantages and Disadvantages of Having a C-Section.  There are advantages to having a C-section. The most important advantage is delivery of a healthy infant. The baby you are carrying may be too large to fit through your pelvis. The only safe method of delivery might be a C-section. Usually a woman needs to experience labor before her doctor will know if the baby will fit. It may be impossible to predict ahead of time.

The disadvantage is that a Cesarean section is a major operation and carries with it all the risks of surgery. Risks include infection, bleeding, shock due to blood loss and the possibility of blood clots and injury to other organs, such as the bladder or rectum.

In most areas, an obstetrician performs a C-section. In small communities, a general surgeon or a family practitioner may perform C-sections.

Will You Need a Cesarean?  It would be nice to know you're going to need a C-section before delivery so you wouldn't have to go through labor. Unfortunately, it's usually necessary to wait for labor contractions for a couple of reasons. You won't know ahead of time if your baby will be stressed by labor contractions. And it is often hard to predict if the baby will fit through your birth canal.

Some women believe that if they have a Cesarean, "it won't be like having a baby." They falsely believe they won't experience the entire birth process. That's not true. If you deliver by C-section, try not to feel this way. You haven't failed in any way!

Remember, having a baby has taken 9 long months. Even with a Cesarean delivery, you have accomplished an amazing feat.

After Your Cesarean Delivery.  After a C-section, you can hold the baby and perhaps even nurse. You may need pain relief for the incision. A new drug-pump system to deliver pain relief is available that may help you feel better without side effects for baby. Called the *ON-Q*, it sends a local painkiller to the *incision* area to help relieve pain. This system delivers medication to the pain site instead of sending it through your body, so very little, if any, medication can get to your baby through your breast milk. Ask your doctor about it at one of your prenatal visits.

You will probably stay in the hospital a couple of days longer than if you had a vaginal delivery. In the past, doctors usually recommended a woman have no solid food until 2 days after delivery. Recent research shows that this time can be cut from a few days to a *few hours* after the procedure. Why? In the past, many Cesarean deliveries required general anesthesia; food is not recommended after general anesthesia. However, today most C-sections require only regional anesthesia, so the same rules may not apply.

Recovery at home from a Cesarean section takes longer than recovery from a vaginal delivery. The normal time for full recovery from a C-section is usually 4 to 6 weeks.

### ↷ *Vaginal Birth after Cesarean (VBAC)*

Should you attempt a vaginal delivery after having had a C-section? Vaginal birth after Cesarean (VBAC) is becoming more common. Medically speaking, the method of delivery is not as important as the well-being of you and your baby.

Before you and your doctor make a final decision, you need to weigh the risks and the benefits to you and your baby with both types of delivery. In some cases, there may not be any choice in the matter. In other cases, you and your doctor may decide to let you labor for a while to see if you can deliver vaginally.

Some women like having a repeat Cesarean section. They request one because they don't want to go through labor only to end up with a Cesarean delivery anyway.

If you've had a previous C-section and want to try VBAC, you may need another C-section if you have gestational diabetes or other problems. Discuss it with your doctor if you have questions.

**Advantages and Risks of VBAC.** Advantages of a vaginal delivery include a decreased risk of problems associated with major surgery, which Cesarean birth is. Recovery after a vaginal delivery is shorter.

You can be up and about in the hospital and at home in a much shorter amount of time.

If you are small and the baby is large, you may need another C-section. Multiple fetuses may make vaginal delivery difficult or impossible without danger to the babies. Problems, such as high blood pressure or diabetes, may require a repeat C-section.

There is some risk that the internal surgical scar from an earlier C-section could stretch and pull apart, called *uterine rupture,* during subsequent labor and delivery, with serious consequences. Research has shown this is especially true if hormones are used to ripen the cervix and/or induce labor. In one study, it was shown that a woman's risk of uterine rupture increased *15 times* if topical hormones are applied to the cervix to ripen it. Researchers believe the contractions that are produced using this method are too strong for a uterus that is scarred by previous surgery. If an intravenous hormone is used to induced labor, such as oxytocin, the risk of rupture increases *5 times*.

In this case, a repeat C-section may be advised to avoid rupture of the uterus. However, if pregnancy and labor are closely monitored, a woman may be able to have a vaginal delivery.

Risk also increases for a woman who gets pregnant within 9 months of having a previous C-section. In this case, the uterus is *3 times* more likely to rupture during a Cesarean delivery. Researchers believe this might occur because it can take from 6 to 9 months for the uterine scar to heal (this is the scar on the uterus—not your abdomen). Until enough healing time has elapsed, the uterus may not be strong enough to stand up to the stress of a vaginal delivery. VBACs are safest when at least 18 months has passed between the previous C-section and the attempted vaginal delivery.

If you want to attempt VBAC, discuss it with your doctor in advance so plans can be made. During labor, you will probably be monitored more closely with fetal monitors. You may be attached to I.V.s, in case a Cesarean section becomes necessary.

Consider the benefits and risks in deciding whether to attempt a vaginal delivery after a previous Cesarean section. Discuss advantages and disadvantages at length with your doctor and your partner before making a final decision. Don't be afraid to ask your doctor his or her opinion of your chances for a successful vaginal delivery. He or she knows your health and pregnancy history.

## Your Nutrition

You and your partner have been invited to a big party. You've been diligent about your nutrition, and your pregnancy is almost over. Should you let yourself go, and eat and drink whatever you want? It's probably a good idea to maintain your good eating habits. You *can* party healthfully. Below are some suggestions to help you have a good time.

Eat food when it's fresh or hot—at the beginning of the party. As the party goes on, the food may not be chilled or heated enough to prevent bacteria from growing. So eat early or when dishes are refilled.

Eat something before you go to take the edge off your appetite. Or drink a large glass of water. It may be easier to avoid high-fat, high-calorie foods if you're not ravenous.

Avoid alcohol. Drink fruit juice "spiked" with ginger ale or lemon-lime soda. If it's the holiday season and they're serving eggnog, have a glass if it's pasteurized and alcohol-free.

Raw fruits and vegetables can be satisfying. Avoid raw seafood, raw meat and soft cheeses, such as Brie, Camembert and feta. They may contain listeriosis.

Stay away from the refreshment table if you can't resist the goodies. It may feel better to sit down (away from food), relax and talk with friends.

## You Should Also Know

### ✌ *Will You Have an Enema?*
Will you be required to have an enema when you arrive at labor and delivery? An *enema* is a procedure in which fluid is injected into the rectum for the purpose of clearing out the bowel.

Most hospitals offer an enema at the beginning of labor, but it is not always mandatory. However, there are certain advantages to having an enema early in labor. You may not want to have a bowel movement soon after your baby's delivery because of discomfort with an episiotomy. Having an enema before labor can prevent this discomfort.

*Tip for Week 37* Be prepared for delivery with bags packed, insurance papers filled out and available, and other important details taken care of.

An enema before labor can also make the birth of your baby a more pleasant experience. When the baby's head comes out through the birth canal, anything in the rectum comes out, too. An enema decreases the amount of contamination by bowel movement during labor and at the time of delivery. This can also help prevent possible infection.

Ask your doctor if an enema is routine or considered helpful. Tell him or her you'd like to know about the benefits of an enema and the reason for giving one. It isn't required by all doctors or all hospitals.

### ✎ What Is Back Labor?

Some women experience back labor. Back labor refers to a baby that is coming through the birth canal looking straight up. With this type of labor, you will probably experience lower-back pain.

The mechanics of labor work better if the baby is looking down at the ground so it can extend its head as it comes out through the birth canal. If the baby can't extend its head, its chin points toward its chest. This can cause pain in your lower back during labor.

This type of labor can also last longer. Your doctor may need to rotate the baby so it comes out looking down at the ground rather than up at the sky.

It may be difficult at times to tell the exact location of different parts of the baby. You may have a good idea according to where you feel kicks and punches. Ask your doctor to show you on your tummy how the baby is lying. Some doctors will take a marking pen and draw on your stomach to show you how the baby is lying. You can leave it so you can show your partner how your baby was lying when you were seen in the office that day.

### �ↄ Will Your Doctor Use Forceps or a Vacuum Extractor?

The use of forceps—metal instruments used in the delivery of babies—has decreased in recent years for a couple of reasons. One reason is the more frequent use of Cesarean delivery to deliver a baby that might be high up in the pelvis. A C-section may be much safer than a forceps delivery for the baby if it's not close to delivering on its own.

Another reason for the decrease in the use of forceps is the use of a *vacuum extractor.* There are two types of vacuum extractors. One has a plastic cup that fits on the baby's head by suction. The other has a metal cup that fits on baby's head. The doctor is able to pull on the vacuum cup to deliver baby's head and body.

The goal with every birth is to deliver the baby as safely as possible. If a large amount of traction with forceps is needed to deliver the baby, a Cesarean section might be a better choice.

If the possible use of a vacuum extractor or forceps causes you concern, discuss it with your physician. It's important to establish good communication with your doctor so you can communicate before and during labor about these concerns.

# Week 38

*Age of Fetus—36 Weeks*

## How Big Is Your Baby?

At this time, your baby weighs about 6¾ pounds (3.1kg). Crown-to-rump length hasn't changed much; it's still about 14 inches (35cm). Total length is around 21 inches (47cm).

## How Big Are You?

Many women don't grow larger during the last several weeks of pregnancy, but they feel very uncomfortable. The distance between your uterus and the pubic symphysis is about 14½ to 15¼ inches (36 to 38cm). From your bellybutton to the top of your uterus is about 6½ to 7¼ inches (16 to 18cm).

## How Your Baby Is Growing and Developing

### ꙮ Fetal Monitoring during Labor
You may wonder how your doctor can tell your baby is all right, especially during labor. In many hospitals, the baby's heart rate is moni-

tored throughout labor. Being able to detect problems early is important so they can be resolved.

Every time the uterus contracts during labor, less oxygenated blood flows from you to the placenta. Most babies are able to handle this stress without any problem. However, some babies are affected; this is called *fetal stress* or *fetal distress*.

There are two ways to monitor the baby's heartbeat during labor. *External fetal monitoring* can be used before your membranes rupture. A belt with a receiver is strapped to your abdomen. It uses a principle similar to ultrasound to detect the baby's heartbeat.

An *internal fetal monitor* monitors the baby's heartbeat more precisely. An electrode is placed on the baby's scalp and is connected by wires to a machine that records the fetal heart rate. Only women whose membranes are broken and who are dilated at least 1cm can be attached to an internal fetal monitor.

**Fetal Blood Sampling.** Doctors can also test your baby's blood pH to see how well baby is tolerating the stress of labor. Before this test can be done, your membranes must be ruptured, and you must be dilated at least 2cm.

An instrument is applied to the scalp of the baby to make a small nick in the skin. The baby's blood is collected in a small tube or pipette, and the pH (acidity) is checked. If the baby is having trouble with labor and is under stress, the pH level can help determine this. This test may be useful in making a decision as to whether labor can continue or if a C-section needs to be done.

## Changes in You

### ∾ *Postpartum Distress Syndrome*
After your baby is born, you may feel very emotional. You may even wonder if having a baby was a good idea. This is called *postpartum distress syndrome (PPDS)*. Most women experience some degree of postpartum distress syndrome. Many experts consider some degree of postpartum distress to be normal.

Up to 80% of all women have "baby blues." See the discussion below. It usually appears between 2 days and 2 weeks after the baby is born. Baby blues are temporary and usually leave as quickly as they come.

However, symptoms of postpartum depression may not appear until several months *after* delivery. They may occur when the woman starts getting her period again and experiences hormonal changes.

Postpartum distress syndrome can resolve on its own, but it can often take as long as a year. With more severe problems, treatment may relieve symptoms in a matter of weeks, and improvement should be significant within 6 to 8 months. Often medication is necessary for complete recovery.

**Different Degrees of Depression.**  The mildest form of postpartum distress is *baby blues*. This situation lasts only a couple of weeks, and symptoms do not worsen. See ways to handle baby blues on the opposite page.

A more serious version of postpartum distress is called *postpartum depression (PPD)*. It affects about 10% of all new mothers. The difference between baby blues and postpartum depression lies in the frequency, intensity and duration of the symptoms. PPD can occur from 2 weeks to 1 year after the birth. A mother may have feelings of anger, confusion, panic and hopelessness. She may experience changes in her eating and sleeping patterns. She may fear she will hurt her baby or feel as if she is going crazy. Anxiety is one of the major symptoms of PPD.

The most serious form of postpartum distress is *postpartum psychosis*. The woman may have hallucinations, think about suicide or try to harm the baby. Many women who develop postpartum psychosis also exhibit signs of bipolar mood disorder, which is unrelated to childbirth. Discuss this situation with your physician if you are concerned.

After you give birth, if you believe you are suffering from some form of postpartum distress, contact your doctor. Every postpartum reaction, whether mild or severe, is usually temporary and treatable.

In addition, if after 2 weeks of motherhood you are just as exhausted as you were shortly after you delivered, you may be at risk of developing postpartum depression. It's normal to feel extremely tired, especially after the hard work of labor and delivery and adjusting to the demands of being a new mom. However, if your exhaustion doesn't get better within 2 weeks, contact your physician.

**Causes of Postpartum Distress Syndrome.** A new mother must make many adjustments, and many demands are placed on her. Either or both of these situations may cause distress. We aren't sure what causes postpartum distress; not every woman experiences it. We believe a woman's individual sensitivity to hormonal changes may be part of the cause; the drop in estrogen and progesterone after delivery may contribute to postpartum distress syndrome.

Other possible factors include a family history of depression, lack of familial support after the birth, isolation and chronic fatigue. You may also be at higher risk of suffering from postpartum distress syndrome (PPD) if:

- your mother or sister suffered from the problem—it seems to run in families
- you suffered from PPD with a previous pregnancy—chances are you'll have the problem again
- you had fertility treatments to achieve this pregnancy—hormone fluctuations may be more severe, which may cause PPD
- you suffered extreme PMS before the pregnancy—hormonal imbalances may be greater after the birth
- you have a personal history of depression
- you have experienced any major life changes recently—you may experience a hormonal drop as a result

**Handling the Baby Blues.** One of the most important ways you can help yourself handle baby blues is to have a good support system near at hand. Ask family members and friends to help. Ask your mother or mother-in-law to stay for a while. Ask your husband to take some work leave, or hire someone to come in and help each day.

There are other things you can do to help relieve the symptoms. You might want to try any or all of the following.

• Rest when your baby sleeps.
• Find other mothers who are in the same situation; it helps to share your feelings and experiences.
• Don't try to be perfect.
• Pamper yourself.
• Do some form of moderate exercise every day.
• Eat nutritiously, and drink plenty of fluids.
• Go out every day.

Talk to your doctor about using antidepressants temporarily if the above steps don't work for you. About 85% of all women who suffer from postpartum depression require medication for up to 1 year.

**Dealing with the More Serious Forms of PPDS.** Beyond the relatively minor symptoms of baby blues, postpartum distress syndrome can be evidenced in two ways. Some women experience acute depression that can last for weeks or months; they cannot sleep or eat, they feel worthless and isolated, they are sad and they cry a great deal. For other women, they are extremely anxious, restless and agitated. Their heart rate increases. Some unfortunate women experience both sets of symptoms at the same time.

If you experience any of these symptoms, call your doctor immediately. He or she will probably see you in the office, then prescribe a course of treatment for you. Do it for you and your family.

## How Your Actions
## Affect Your Baby's Development

### ∽ *Breech Presentation*
As we've mentioned already, it's common for your baby to be in the breech presentation early in pregnancy. However, when labor starts, only 3 to 5% of all babies, not including multiple pregnancies, present as a breech. Do your actions determine how your baby presents?

Certain factors make a breech presentation more likely. One of the main causes is the baby's prematurity. Near the end of the second trimester, a baby may be in a breech presentation. By taking care of yourself, you may avoid going into premature labor. That gives your baby the best opportunity to change its position naturally.

Although we don't always know why a baby is in the breech position, we know breech births occur more often when:

- you have had more than one pregnancy
- you are carrying twins, triplets or more
- there is too much or too little amniotic fluid
- the uterus is shaped abnormally
- you have abnormal uterine growths, such as fibroids
- you have placenta previa
- your baby has hydrocephalus

There are different kinds of breech presentations. A *frank breech* occurs when the legs are flexed at the hips and extended at the knees. This is the most common

*Tip for Week 38* If your doctor suspects your baby is in a breech position, he or she may order an ultrasound to confirm it. It helps identify how the baby is lying in your uterus.

type of breech found at term or the end of pregnancy; feet are up by the face or head.

With a *complete breech presentation,* one or both knees are flexed, not extended. See the illustration on page 388.

**Delivering a Breech Baby.** There is some controversy in obstetrics over the best method of delivering a breech baby. For many years, breech deliveries were performed vaginally. Then it was believed the safest method was to deliver the baby by C-section, especially if it was a first baby. Today, most doctors believe a baby in the breech position can probably be delivered more safely by a Cesarean section performed during early labor or before labor begins.

Some doctors believe a woman can deliver a breech without difficulty if the situation is right. This usually includes a frank breech in a

Pelvis

Baby aligned in the pelvis bottom first, with knees flexed, is called a *complete breech presentation*.

mature fetus of a woman who has had previous normal deliveries. Most agree a *footling breech presentation* (one leg extended, one knee flexed) should be delivered by Cesarean section.

If your baby is breech, it's important to discuss it with your doctor. When you get to the hospital, tell the nurses and hospital personnel you have a breech presentation. If you call with a question about labor and you have a breech presentation, mention this information to the person you talk with.

**Turning Your Baby.** Attempts may be made to turn the baby from a breech to a head-down (vertex) presentation before your water breaks, before labor begins or in early labor. Using his or her hands, the doctor manually attempts to turn the baby into the head-down birth position. This procedure is called *external cephalic version (ECV)* or just *version*.

Problems can occur with ECV, and it's important to know about them. Talk with your physician about whether this procedure is an option for you. Possible risks include:

- rupture of membranes
- placental abruption
- affect on baby's heart rate
- onset of labor

More than 50% of the time, a doctor is successful in turning the baby. However, some stubborn babies shift again into a breech presentation. ECV may be tried again, but version is harder to perform as your delivery date draws closer.

**Other Types of Abnormal Presentations.** Another unusual presentation is a *face presentation*. The baby's head is hyperextended so the face comes into the birth canal first. This type of presentation is most often delivered by C-section if it does not convert to a regular presentation during labor.

In a *shoulder presentation*, the shoulder presents first. In a *transverse lie*, the baby is lying almost as if in a cradle in the pelvis. The

𝔇ad 𝒯ip   Ask your partner if there are things she would like you to bring to the hospital for her, such as special tapes or CDs and a player for the music. Discuss it ahead of time, and have things ready. If you take a tour of the hospital or birthing center, you might get other ideas of things you can do to help control the environment your new baby enters.

baby's head is on one side of your abdomen, and its bottom is on the other side. There is only one way to deliver these types of presentation, and that is by Cesarean section.

## Your Nutrition

You may not feel much like eating about this time, but it's important to keep eating a healthful diet. Snacks might be the answer. Instead of eating large meals, eat small snacks throughout the day to keep your energy levels up and to help avoid heartburn. You may be tired of the foods you've been eating. The list below offers some smart snacks for your healthy nutrition:

- bananas, raisins, dried fruit and mangoes to satisfy your sweet tooth and to provide you with iron, potassium and magnesium
- string cheese; it's high in calcium and protein
- fruit shakes made with skim milk and yogurt, ice milk or ice cream for calcium, vitamins and minerals
- crackers that are high in fiber; spread with a little peanut butter for taste and protein
- cottage cheese and fruit, flavored with a little sugar and some cinnamon, for tasty milk and fruit servings
- salt-free chips or tortillas with salsa or bean dip for fiber and good taste
- humus and pita slices for fiber and good taste
- fresh tomatoes, flavored with some olive oil and fresh basil; eat with a few thin slices of Parmesan cheese for a vegetable serving and dairy serving
- chicken or tuna salad (made from fresh chicken or tuna packed in water) and crackers or tortilla pieces for protein and fiber

## You Should Also Know

### ✌ *What Is a Retained Placenta?*

In most instances, the placenta is delivered within 30 minutes after the birth of your baby and is a routine part of the delivery. In some cases, a piece of placenta remains inside the uterus and does not deliver spontaneously. When this happens, the uterus cannot contract adequately, resulting in vaginal bleeding that can be heavy.

In other cases, the placenta does not separate because it's still attached to the wall of the uterus. This can be a very serious situation. However, this complication is rare.

Bleeding is usually severe after delivery, and surgery may be necessary to stop it. An attempt may be made to remove the placenta by D&C.

Reasons for an abnormally adherent placenta are many. It is believed a placenta may attach over a previous Cesarean-section scar or other previous incisions on the uterus. The placenta may attach over an area that has been scraped, such as with a D&C, or over an area of the uterus that was infected at one time.

Your doctor will pay attention to the delivery of your placenta while you are paying attention to your baby. Some people ask to see the placenta after delivery; you may wish to have your doctor show it to you.

### ✌ *Will You Need to Be Shaved?*

Many women want to know if they have to have their pubic hair shaved before the birth of their baby. It is not a requirement any longer. Many women are not shaved these days. However, some women who chose not to have their pubic hair shaved later said they experienced discomfort when their pubic hair became entangled in their underwear due to the normal vaginal discharge after the birth of their baby. So you might want to think about this procedure, and discuss it with your doctor.

# Week 39

*Age of Fetus—37 Weeks*

## How Big Is Your Baby?

Your baby weighs a little more than 7 pounds (3.25kg). By this point in your pregnancy, crown-to-rump length is about 14½ inches (36cm). The baby's total length is close to 21½ inches (48cm).

**Tip for Week 39** Don't take tags off shower gifts and other gifts until after your baby is born. You may need to exchange the gift if its size, color or "sex" isn't correct.

## How Big Are You?

The illustration on page 394 shows a side view of a woman with a large uterus and her baby inside it. She's about as big as she can get. You probably are, too!

If you measure from the pubic symphysis to the top of the uterus, the distance is 14½ to 16 inches (36 to 40cm). Measuring from the bellybutton, the distance is about 6½ to 8 inches (16 to 20cm).

You're almost at the end of your pregnancy. Your weight should not increase much from this point. It should remain between 25 and 35 pounds (11.4 and 15.9kg) until delivery.

# How Your Baby Is Growing and Developing

Your baby continues to gain weight, even up to the last week or two of pregnancy. It doesn't have much room to move inside your uterus. At this point, all the organ systems are developed and in place. The last organ to mature is the lungs.

### ᔈ *Can Your Baby Get Tangled in the Cord?*
You may have been told by friends not to raise your arms over your head or reach high to get things because it can cause the cord to wrap around the baby's neck. There doesn't seem to be any truth to this old wives' tale.

Some babies do get tangled in their umbilical cord and can get the cord tied in a knot or wrapped around their neck. However, nothing you do during pregnancy causes or prevents this from happening.

A tangled umbilical cord isn't necessarily a problem during labor. It only becomes a problem if the cord is stretched tight around the baby's neck or is in a knot.

# Changes in You

It would be unusual for you *not* to be uncomfortable and feel huge at this time. Your uterus has filled your pelvis and most of your abdomen. It has pushed everything else out of the way.

At this point in pregnancy, you may think you'll never want to be pregnant again because you're so uncomfortable. Or you may be sure your family is complete. At this point, some women consider permanent sterilization, such as tubal ligation.

### ᔈ *Tubal Ligation after Delivery?*
Some women choose to have a tubal ligation done while they are in the hospital after having their baby. Now is not the time to make the decision about having a tubal ligation if you haven't seriously considered it before.

Comparative size of the uterus at 39 weeks of pregnancy (fetal age—
37 weeks) with a baby that is close to full term.

Being sterilized following delivery of a baby has some advantages. You're in the hospital and won't need another hospitalization. However, there are disadvantages to having a sterilization at this time. Consider the procedure permanent and not reversible. If you have your tubes tied within a few hours or a day after having your baby, then change your mind, you may regret the tubal ligation.

If you have an epidural, it's possible to use the epidural as anesthesia for a tubal ligation. If you didn't have an epidural, it may be necessary to anesthetize you. This is often done the morning after you've had your baby. This doesn't usually lengthen the time you're in the hospital.

Different kinds of procedures are performed for permanent sterilization. Most common is a small incision underneath your bellybutton. The Fallopian tubes can be seen through this incision.

A piece of the tube can be removed, or a ring or clip can be placed on the tube to block it. This type of surgery usually requires 30 to 45 minutes to perform.

If you have second thoughts or are unsure about having it done, don't have the surgery. Tubal ligations can be reversed, but it's expensive and requires a hospital stay of 3 to 4 days. Reversals are about 50% effective, but pregnancy cannot be guaranteed.

## How Your Actions Affect Your Baby's Development

### ✑ *Is Breastfeeding Right for You and Your Baby?*

The discussion on the following pages actually concerns your actions *after* your baby is born —whether you breastfeed your baby. Your decision about breastfeeding is a personal one. One of the more compelling reasons to breastfeed is the bonding that occurs between mother and baby. This close relationship can begin as soon as the baby is born—some women breastfeed on the delivery table. It helps stimulate uterine contractions, which can prevent hemorrhage.

Breastfeeding encourages the natural intimacy of a newborn baby with its mother and the mother with her baby. The opportunity to breastfeed may be a relaxing time for you. It may give you a chance to spend some wonderful time with your new baby. However, if it doesn't work out, it's all right to stop and switch to formula.

**Benefits of Breastfeeding.** Both you and your baby benefit if you breastfeed. Mother's milk is good for your baby because it contains all the nutrients your baby needs during the first months of life. Commercial formulas have good mixtures of vitamins, protein, sugar, fat and minerals, but none can match your breast milk.

Another advantage of breastfeeding is you pass protection against infection (through antibodies) to your baby in your breast milk. Many people believe a breastfed baby is less likely to get colds and infections than a bottlefed baby.

Breastfeeding is also good for the baby because he or she will probably have to nurse more vigorously than is necessary with some bottle nipples. This encourages good tooth and jaw development. Breastfeeding may also help prevent SIDS (sudden infant death syndrome). One study showed that babies breastfed exclusively for 4 months or longer had a lower SIDS rate than babies who were breastfed for less than a month.

Nursing your baby may also protect him or her from high cholesterol levels in adulthood. Although a breastfed baby may have higher cholesterol levels as an infant, studies show that as an adult, cholesterol levels may be lower than those for other adults. In addition, one study reported breastfeeding may have positive effects on adult intelligence—your baby may be smarter as an adult if he or she is breastfed for at least 7 months.

Researchers have found an important reason to breastfeed your baby if he or she is born prematurely. A great deal of a preemie's protection from infections comes from your breast milk. Recently, outbreaks of an infection called *E. sakazakii* have been found in neonatal intensive care units and have been associated with milk-based powdered formulas. Based on these findings, the FDA recommends powdered infant formulas *not* be used for premature babies.

Another plus for breastfeeding—it's ecologically a better choice for the world! Producing infant formulas uses our resources, and the packaging of formulas adds greatly to our landfills.

Advantages for you include decreased cost as compared to buying formula. It's convenient to breastfeed; you don't have to carry bottles and formula with you for baby. Some women find breastfeeding makes it easier for them to regain their figure.

You may have noticed during pregnancy that your breasts have gotten larger and were probably tender at times. This happens because increased hormonal activity makes the alveoli in the breasts get larger. Milk in the breast is stored in small sacs of these alveoli.

Colostrum is the first milk that comes from the breasts. Regular breast milk usually arrives 2 or 3 days after delivery. Its arrival is initiated by stimulation from the baby suckling at your breast. The sucking sends a message to your brain to produce prolactin, a hormone that stimulates milk production in the alveoli.

**Learning to Breastfeed.** You may want to learn how to breastfeed while you're in the hospital. Ask the nurses to show you some of the tricks they've learned to help your baby catch on to it. Ask them any questions you have. What you learn may make the difference in keeping your baby happy with breastfeeding.

Breastfeeding requires a healthful nutrition plan for you, similar to the one you followed during pregnancy. You'll need at least 500 extra calories each day (compared to the extra 300 during pregnancy). Some doctors recommend you continue taking your prenatal vitamins after pregnancy, while you are nursing.

Be careful about what you eat and drink because things you eat can pass into your breast milk. Certain foods may not "sit" well with you or your baby. Spicy foods and chocolate you eat may cause an upset stomach in your baby! Caffeine can also pass to your baby. Any alcohol you drink passes to your baby through your breast milk, so be careful about your consumption of alcoholic beverages. The longer you breastfeed, the more you'll realize what you can (and cannot) eat and drink.

There may be times when you are away from the baby, but you want to continue to breastfeed. You can do this by using a breast pump and storing your breast milk. You can pump your breasts with battery-operated pumps, electrical pumps or manual pumps. Ask for suggestions before you leave the hospital.

Talk with your doctor during pregnancy about breastfeeding. Ask friends about their experiences and how much they enjoyed it. You may also want to contact the local La Leche League, an organization that encourages and promotes breastfeeding. It offers help to women who may be having trouble getting started with breastfeeding. Give them a call if you need information or support.

**Engorgement.**  A common breastfeeding problem for some women is *breast engorgement*. Breasts become swollen, tender and filled with breast milk. What can you do to relieve this problem?

- The best cure is to drain the breasts, if possible, as you do when breastfeeding. Some women take a hot shower and empty their breasts in the warm water.
- Ice packs may also help.
- Feed your baby from both breasts *each time* you feed. Don't feed on only one side.
- When you're away from your baby, try to express some breast milk to keep your milk flowing and breast ducts open. You'll also feel more comfortable.
- Mild pain medicines, such as acetaminophen, are often useful in relieving the pain of engorgement. Acetaminophen is recommended by the American Academy of Pediatrics as safe to use while breastfeeding.
- You might need to use stronger medications, such as acetaminophen with codeine, a prescription medication.
- Call your doctor if engorgement is especially painful. He or she will decide on treatment.

**Breast Infections.**  It is possible to get an infection in your breast while breastfeeding. If you think you have an infection, call your doctor. An infection may cause pain in the breast, and the breast may turn red and become swollen. You may have streaks of red discoloration on the breast; you may also feel as though you have the flu.

**Sore Nipples.**  Most nursing mothers have sore nipples at some point, particularly at first. You can take steps to lessen or to relieve the soreness. Try the following.

• Keep your breasts dry and clean.
• Do not air dry—it encourages scab formation and can take quite a while for a sore breast to heal.
• Moist healing is best. One brand of lanolin, called *Lansinoh,* does not contain pesticides or allergens. Cover the entire nipple area with lanolin every time baby finishes nursing.

Good news! Before too long—a few days to a few weeks—your breasts will become accustomed to breastfeeding, and problems will lessen.

**Inverted Nipples.**  Some women have trouble breastfeeding because of inverted nipples. This happens when the nipple retracts inward instead of pointing outward. If you have inverted nipples, it is still possible to breastfeed. Plastic breast shields are available to wear under clothing to help bring out an inverted nipple.

Some doctors also recommend pulling on the nipple and rolling it between the thumb and index finger. Talk about this situation at one of your prenatal appointments.

**Support Bras.**  Some women find wearing a support bra helpful in the last few weeks of pregnancy. A nursing bra is useful while nursing. Many doctors suggest wearing a nursing bra all the time, even when you sleep, to make you more comfortable. To prepare your breasts for nursing, however, expose them regularly to the air. Not wearing a bra now and then while you are wearing clothes allows your nipples to toughen slightly when they rub against the fabric of your clothes.

**Nursing with Silicone Breast Implants.**  Women have successfully nursed with breast implants; however, implants may make nursing more difficult. Doctors don't agree as to whether it is safe or possibly harmful to nurse with implants. If you are concerned, discuss the matter with your doctor; ask him or her for the latest information.

**The Bottlefeeding Option.**  It won't harm your baby if you choose to bottlefeed. We don't want any mother to feel guilty if she chooses bottlefeeding over breastfeeding. Statistics show that more women choose to bottlefeed than breastfeed their babies. We also know that with iron-fortified formula, a bottlefed baby receives good nutrition.

**Some Reasons You May Not Be Able to Breastfeed.**  You may be unable to breastfeed if you are extremely underweight or have some medical conditions, such as a prolactin deficiency, heart disease, kidney disease, tuberculosis or HIV/AIDS. Some infants have problems breastfeeding, or they are unable to breastfeed if they have a cleft palate or cleft lip. Lactose intolerance can also cause breastfeeding problems. Sometimes a woman cannot breastfeed because of a physical condition or problem.

Some women want to breastfeed and try to, but it doesn't work out. If breastfeeding doesn't work for you, please don't worry about it. Your baby will be OK.

**Advantages to Bottlefeeding.**  There are advantages to bottlefeeding.

- Some women enjoy the freedom bottlefeeding provides; others can help care for the baby.
- Bottlefeeding is easy to learn; it never causes the mother discomfort if it is done incorrectly.
- Fathers can be more involved in caring for baby.
- Bottlefed babies may go longer between feedings because formula is usually digested more slowly than breast milk.
- A day's supply of formula can be mixed all at once, saving time and effort.
- You don't have to be concerned about feeding your baby in front of other people.
- It's easier to bottlefeed if you plan to return to work soon after your baby is born.

- If you feed your baby iron-fortified formula, he or she won't need iron supplementation.
- If you use fluoridated tap water to mix formula, you may not have to give your baby fluoride supplements.

## Your Nutrition

### ↣ *If You Breastfeed*

If you're going to breastfeed your baby, you need to begin thinking about nutritional needs for the time you will nurse. You will probably be advised to eat about 500 extra calories each day during this time. A breastfeeding mother secretes 425 to 700 calories into her breast milk every day! The extra calories you take in will help you maintain good health. These calories should also be nutritious and healthy, like the ones you've been eating during pregnancy. Choose 9 servings from the bread/cereal/pasta/rice group and 3 servings from the dairy group. Fruit servings should number 4, and vegetable servings should number 5. The amount of protein in your diet should be 8 ounces during breastfeeding. Be particularly careful with fats, oils and sugars; limit intake to 4 teaspoons.

As previously discussed, you may have to avoid some foods because they can pass into breast milk and cause your baby some stomach distress. Avoid chocolate, foods that produce gas in you, such as Brussels sprouts and cauliflower, highly spiced foods and other foods you have problems with. Discuss the situation with your doctor and your pediatrician if you have questions and concerns.

In addition to the food you eat, you need to continue to drink lots of fluids. You need to drink at least *2 quarts* of fluid every day to make enough milk for your baby and for you to stay hydrated. You'll need more fluid in hot weather. Avoid caffeine-containing foods and drinks because caffeine can act as a diuretic. It can also pass to your baby through your breast milk. Although caffeine is out of your bloodstream in 3 to 5 hours, it can remain in a baby's bloodstream for up to 96 hours!

Keep up your calcium intake. It's important if you breastfeed. You might ask your doctor what kind of vitamin supplement you should take. Some mothers take a prenatal vitamin as long as they breastfeed.

### ❧ If You Bottlefeed

Even if you bottlefeed, it's important to follow a nutritious eating plan, such as the one you followed during pregnancy. Continue to eat foods high in complex carbohydrates, such as grain products, fruits and vegetables. Lean meats, chicken and fish are good sources of protein. For your dairy products, choose the low-fat or skim types.

If you bottlefeed, you need fewer calories than you would if you were breastfeeding. But don't drastically cut your caloric intake in the hopes of losing weight quickly. You still need to eat nutritiously to maintain good energy levels. Be sure the calories you eat are not from junk foods.

Following is a list of the types and quantities of foods you should try to eat each day: Choose 6 servings from the bread/cereal/pasta/rice group, and 3 servings of fruit. Eat 3 servings of vegetables. From the dairy group, choose 2 servings. Eat about 6 ounces of protein each day. We still advise caution with fats, oils and sugars; limit intake to 3 teaspoons. And keep up your fluid intake. You can also use the pregnancy nutrition plan as a reference; see Week 6.

## You Should Also Know

### ❧ Pain Relief during Labor

Labor is painful because your uterus has to change shape greatly so your baby can be born. You may request relief from this pain. Pain relief during labor is approached in many ways. When you take pain medication, remember there are two patients to consider—you and your unborn baby. It is best to find out in advance what is available for pain control. Then see how your labor goes for you before making a final decision.

A valuable part of your experience in labor and delivery is your preparation for it. This includes being aware of things that are happening to you, and why, and not being frightened by the pain you feel. You should have confidence in those taking care of you, including your doctor and the staff at the hospital.

An *anesthetic* is a complete block of all pain sensations and muscle movement. An *analgesic* is full or partial relief of pain sensations. Narcotic analgesics pass to your baby through the placenta and may decrease respiratory function in the newborn infant. They can also affect your baby's Apgar scores. These medications should not be given close to the time of delivery.

In many places, anesthesia for delivery is given by an injection of a particular medication to affect a particular area of the body. This is called a block, such as a *pudendal block*, an *epidural block* or a *cervical block*. Medication is similar to the type used to block pain when you have a tooth filled. The agents are xylocaine or xylocainelike medications.

Occasionally, it is necessary to use general anesthesia for delivery of a baby, usually for an emergency Cesarean delivery. A pediatrician attends the birth because it is possible the baby will be asleep following delivery.

**What Is an Epidural Block?** The epidural block is one of the most popular anesthetics used today for labor and delivery, and it is used frequently. It provides relief from the pain of uterine contractions and delivery. It should be administered only by someone trained and experienced in this type of anesthesia. Some obstetricians have this experience, but in most areas an anesthesiologist or nurse anesthetist must administer it.

A continuous epidural block is started while you are sitting up or lying on your side. The anesthesiologist numbs an area of skin over your lower back in the middle of your spinal cord. He or she then introduces a needle through the numbed area of the skin; anesthetic is placed around the spinal cord but not into the spinal canal. A plastic catheter is left in place.

Epidural pain medication may be given during labor with a pump. The anesthesiologist uses the pump to inject a small amount of medication at regular intervals or as needed. An epidural provides excellent relief from labor pain.

A combined spinal epidural block/walking epidural uses epidural and spinal techniques to relieve pain. There is often less numbness with this combination, so a woman may be able to walk around more easily. It is sometimes called a *walking epidural*.

You may have heard some confusing information about when you can receive an epidural, if you choose to have one. Most doctors believe an epidural block should be given during labor based on your level of pain. You may *not* be required to be dilated to a specific point before getting an epidural.

A problem with an epidural block is that it can make your blood pressure drop. Low blood pressure may affect blood flow to the baby. Fortunately, I.V. fluids administered with the epidural help reduce the risk of hypotension (low blood pressure). You may also have problems pushing during delivery. According to recent studies, no link between use of epidurals during labor and the experience of later back pain has been established.

**Other Pain Blocks.**  When contractions are regular and the cervix is beginning to dilate, uterine contractions may be uncomfortable. For pain in this early stage of labor, many hospitals use a mixture of a narcotic analgesic drug, such as meperidine (Demerol), and a tranquilizer, such as promethazine (Phenergen). This decreases pain and causes some sleepiness or sedation. Medication may be given through an I.V. or by injection into a muscle.

Spinal anesthesia may be used for a Cesarean section. With this anesthesia, pain relief lasts long enough for the Cesarean section to be performed. Today, spinal anesthesia is not used as often as epidural anesthesia for labor.

Another type of block used occasionally is a pudendal block. It is given through the vaginal canal and decreases pain in the birth canal itself. You still feel the contraction and tightening with pain in the uterus. Some hospitals use a paracervical block. It provides pain relief for the dilating cervix but doesn't relieve the pain of contractions.

Intrathecal anesthesia is a single dose of anesthesia into the area surrounding the spinal cord. It isn't a total block; the woman feels the contraction so she may push.

There is no perfect method for pain relief during labor and delivery. Discuss all the possibilities with your doctor, and mention any concerns. Find out what types of anesthesia are available and the risks and benefits of each.

**Anesthesia Problems and Complications.** There are possible complications from use of anesthesia. These include increased sedation of the baby with use of narcotics, such as Demerol. The newborn may have lower Apgar scores and depressed breathing. The baby may require resuscitation, or it may need to receive another drug, such as naloxone (Narcan), to reverse the effects of the first drug.

If a mother is given general anesthesia, increased sedation, slower respiration and a slower heartbeat may also be observed in the baby. The mother is usually "out" for more than an hour and is unable to see her newborn infant until later.

If you have an epidural or spinal block during delivery, you may experience various side effects after delivery. Some ways to help alleviate these discomforts include the following.

- If you experience itching, put pressure on the area with a towel or blanket. Ease discomfort by applying lots of lotion.
- If you have a headache, drink a beverage that contains caffeine, such as coffee, tea or a caffeinated soda.
- If you become nauseous, breathing deeply can help. Inhale through your nose, and exhale through your mouth.

It may be impossible to determine before you go into labor which anesthesia will be best for you. But it's helpful to know what's available and what types of pain relief you might be able to count on during your labor and delivery.

### ✂ Contraction of the Uterus after Delivery

After you deliver your baby, your uterus shrinks immediately from about the size of a watermelon to the size of a volleyball. When this happens, the placenta detaches from the uterine wall. At this time, there may be a gush of blood from inside the uterus signaling delivery of the placenta.

After the placenta is delivered, you may be given oxytocin (Pitocin). This helps the uterus contract and clamp down so it won't bleed.

Extremely heavy bleeding after vaginal delivery is called *postpartum hemorrhage*, which is bleeding more than 17 ounces (500ml). It can often be prevented by massaging the uterus and using medications to help the uterus contract.

The main reason a woman experiences heavy bleeding after delivering a baby is her uterus does not contract, called an *atonic* uterus. Your doctor, midwife or the nurse attending you may massage your uterus after delivery. They may show you how to do it so your uterus will stay firm and contracted. This is important so you won't lose more blood and become anemic.

## ๛ *Cord-Blood Banking*

Are you and your partner thinking about storing blood from your baby's umbilical cord? Researchers have found that stem cells, which are present in cord blood, have proved very successful in treating some diseases. *Cord blood* is blood left in the umbilical cord and placenta after a baby is born. In the past, the placenta and the umbilical cord were usually discarded following delivery.

There is a great deal of interest about saving cord blood after delivery. Umbilical-cord blood can be used to treat cancer and genetic diseases that are now treated by bone-marrow transplants. Cord blood has been used successfully to treat childhood leukemia, some immune diseases and other blood diseases. At present, research is being conducted in the United States and Europe to use cord blood for gene therapy in a number of diseases, including sickle-cell anemia, diabetes and AIDS.

Cord blood contains the same valuable cells that are found in bone marrow. These "stem cells" are the building blocks of the blood and immune systems. These special cells are undeveloped in cord blood. Because they are undeveloped, cord blood does not need to be matched as closely for a transplant as bone-marrow blood does. This feature can be especially important for members of ethnic minority groups or people with rare blood types. These groups traditionally have had more difficulty finding acceptable donor "matches."

Before their baby's birth, parents may request that the baby's cord blood be collected and "banked" for future use. The blood can be used by the child from whom it was collected, his siblings or parents.

Blood is collected directly from the umbilical cord immediately after delivery. There is no risk or pain to the mother or baby. The blood is transported to a banking facility where it is frozen and cryogenically stored.

Discuss this situation with your physician at a prenatal appointment—especially if your family has a history of certain diseases. Ask about how and where blood is stored and the cost of storing it. This is a decision you need to make with your partner, but first you need good information, such as the fact that at this time, blood storage is not usually covered by insurance.

The cost of cord-blood banking can include an initial fee of about $1,500, with about a $100-a-year storage fee. As more is learned about cord-blood banking and its use becomes more common, the cost may go down. Some health-insurance companies pay the fees for families at high risk of cancer or genetically based diseases. Cord-blood banking services may waive fees for at-risk families who are unable to afford them.

If you don't want to waste your baby's cord blood, think about donating it. A nonprofit bank can match it with someone who needs it. Ask your physician for information about cord-blood banking services and cord-blood donation in your area.

**Dad Tip** Who do you and your partner want in the delivery room? Having a baby is a unique and wonderful experience. Some couples choose the intimacy and privacy of being alone during the birth. Other couples want various family members and friends to share the experience with them. If you talk about it ahead of time, you can decide together what you both want. After all, it's your baby's birth.

# Week 40

*Age of Fetus—38 Weeks*

## How Big Is Your Baby?

Your baby weighs about 7½ pounds (3.4kg). Its crown-to-rump length is about 14¾ to 15¼ inches (37 to 38cm). Total length is 21½ inches (48cm). Your baby fills your uterus and has little room to move. See the illustration on page 410.

## How Big Are You?

From the pubic symphysis to the top of the uterus, you probably measure between 14½ and 16 inches (36 to 40cm). From your bellybutton to the top of your uterus is 6½ to 8 inches (16 to 20cm).

*Tip for Week 40* If you want to use a different labor position, massage, relaxation techniques or hypnotherapy to relieve labor pain, don't wait until you are in labor to ask about it. Discuss your concerns with your doctor at one of your prenatal visits.

By this time, you probably don't care an awful lot about how much you measure. You feel you're as big as you could ever be, and you're ready to have your baby. You may continue to grow and even to get a little bit bigger until you have your baby. But don't be discouraged—you'll have your baby soon.

## How Your Baby Is Growing and Developing

*Bilirubin* is a breakdown product from red blood cells. Before your baby is born, bilirubin is transferred easily across the placenta from the fetus to maternal circulation. Through this process, your body is able to get rid of the bilirubin from the baby. Once your baby is delivered and the umbilical cord is clamped, the baby is on its own to handle the bilirubin produced in its own body.

### ⌒ *Jaundice in a Newborn*
After birth, if your baby has problems dealing with bilirubin, it may develop high levels of it in the blood. Your baby may develop jaundice—yellowing of the skin and the whites of the eyes. Bilirubin levels typically increase for 3 or 4 days after the baby's delivery, then decrease.

Your pediatrician and the nurses in the nursery check for jaundice by observing your baby's color. Your baby may have a test to measure his or her bilirubin levels at the hospital or at your pediatrician's office.

A baby is treated for jaundice with *phototherapy,* which can be delivered in the hospital or at home with a freestanding device or a fiber-optic blanket. The light from the special device penetrates the skin and destroys the bilirubin. If high levels of bilirubin are present, the baby may undergo an exchange blood transfusion.

**Kernicterus in a Newborn.** Extremely high levels of bilirubin (hyperbilirubinemia) in a newborn infant cause doctors concern because a serious condition called *kernicterus* can develop. Kernicterus is seen more frequently in premature infants than in babies delivered at full term. If the baby survives the kernicterus, it may have neurological problems—spasticity, lack of muscle coordination and varying degrees of mental retardation. However, kernicterus in a newborn is rare.

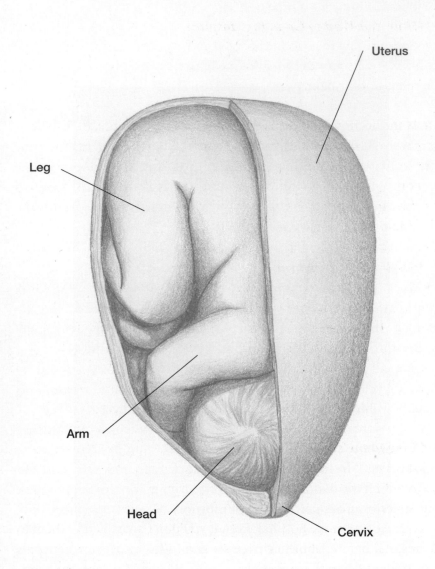

A full-term baby has little room to move. This is one reason fetal movements may slow down in the last few weeks of pregnancy.

## Changes in You

### ✌ *While You Wait to Go to the Hospital*

If you are waiting to go to the hospital and are experiencing pain, there are a few things you can do at home. The following actions may help you manage your pain.

- At the beginning of each contraction, take a deep breath. Exhale slowly. At the end of the contraction, again breathe deeply.
- Get up and move! It helps distract you and may relieve back pain.
- Ask your partner to massage your shoulders, neck, back and feet. It helps ease tension, and it feels good.
- Hot and/or cold compresses can help reduce cramping and various aches and pains. A warm shower or bath can feel very good.
- When a contraction begins, try to distract yourself with mental pictures of pleasant or soothing images.

## How Your Actions Affect Your Baby's Development

### ✌ *Going to the Hospital*

You may have preregistered at the hospital a few weeks before your due date. If you have, it will save time checking in, and it may help reduce your stress. You can preregister with forms you receive from the doctor's office or from the hospital. Even if you don't actually take them to the hospital before labor begins, it's a good idea to fill out the forms early. If you wait until you're in labor, you may be in a hurry and concerned with other things.

Take your insurance card or insurance information with you—have it readily at hand. It's also helpful to know your blood type and Rh-factor, your doctor's name, your pediatrician's name and the due date.

Ask your doctor how you should prepare to go to the hospital; he or she may have specific instructions for you. You might want to ask the following questions.

- When should we go to the hospital once I'm in labor?
- Should we call you before we leave for the hospital?
- How can we reach you after regular office hours?
- Are there any particular instructions for me to follow during early labor?
- Where do we go—to the emergency room or the labor-and-delivery department?

Many couples are advised to go to the hospital after an hour of contractions that are 5 to 10 minutes apart. However, leave sooner if the hospital is far away or hard to get to, or if the weather is bad.

The delivery of your baby is the event you've been planning for! If this is your first baby, you may be excited and a little apprehensive. Delivery of your baby is something you'll remember for a long time.

You need to decide who you want with you during delivery. Sometimes, family members assume they're invited to the delivery. Some couples choose to bring young children into the delivery room to see the birth of a new brother or sister. Discuss this with your doctor ahead of time, and get his or her opinion. The delivery of the baby might be exciting and special to you and your partner, but it may be frightening to a young child.

Many places offer special classes for older siblings to help prepare them for the new baby. This is a good way to help your older children feel they're part of the birth experience.

**The Labor Check.** When you get to the hospital, you may be sent home! This happens if labor hasn't really started or if it is early labor. When you arrive at the hospital, you will be evaluated for signs of labor. This is sometimes called a *labor check*.

If you are sent home, don't get frustrated, upset or mad. Understand that to determine if a woman is in labor she must often be seen and evaluated at the hospital. This is something that can't be determined over the phone!

The people who evaluate you know you want to get on with the birth process and that you don't want to go home. However, if you aren't in true labor, it *is* best to go home. If this happens to you, make the best of it. You'll be back when the time is right!

**In the Hospital.** When you are admitted to labor and delivery (or a birthing center), many things happen. You will probably be asked many questions when you check in. They may include the following.

- Have your membranes ruptured? At what time?
- Are you bleeding?
- Are you having contractions? How often do they occur? How long do they last?
- When did you last eat, and what did you eat?

Other important information for you to share includes medical problems you have and any medications you take or have taken during pregnancy. If you've had complications, such as placenta previa, tell medical personnel when you first come to labor and delivery. This is also the time to tell those taking care of you any information your doctor gave you about effacement, thinning of the cervix and station.

A copy of your office chart is usually kept on record in labor and delivery. It contains basic information about your health and pregnancy.

**Your Initial Exam.** A pelvic exam is performed to help determine what stage of labor you are in and to use as a reference point for future exams during labor. This exam and the vital signs are performed by a labor and delivery nurse (the nurse can be male or female). Only in unusual situations, such as in an emergency, will your doctor do this initial exam. In fact, it may be quite a while before you see your doctor, but rest assured the nurses are in close telephone contact with him or her. In many labors, the doctor does not arrive until close to delivery.

A brief pregnancy history is taken. Vital signs, including blood pressure, pulse, temperature and baby's heart rate, are noted.

**Once You Are Admitted.** If you are in labor and remain at the hospital, other things will happen. Your partner may have to admit you to the hospital if you haven't filled out pre-admittance papers. You may be asked to sign a release form or a permission slip from the hospital, your doctor and/or the anesthesiologist. This is done to ensure you are informed and aware of the procedures that will be done for you and any risks that are involved.

After you have been admitted, you may receive an enema, or an I.V. may be started. Blood will probably be drawn. Your doctor may want to discuss pain relief, or you may have an epidural put in place, if you have requested one.

If you have decided to have an epidural or if it looks as if labor will last quite awhile, an I.V. will be started. You may still be able to walk around. You can't eat, and you won't be allowed to have more than ice chips or small sips of water. During this time, you and your partner may be alone together, with nurses coming into the room to perform various tasks, then leaving. In most instances, a monitoring belt is placed on your abdomen to record your contractions and the baby's heartbeat. The monitoring record can be seen in the room and also by nurses at the nursing station.

Blood pressure is taken at regular intervals, and pelvic exams are performed to follow labor's progress. In most places, the doctor is notified upon your admission to labor and delivery; he or she is then called at regular intervals as labor progresses. Your doctor will also be called if any problem arises.

**When Your Doctor Isn't Available.** In some cases, when you get to the hospital you will learn your doctor is not available, and someone else will deliver your baby. If your doctor believes he or she might be out of town when your baby is born, ask to meet doctors that "cover" when your doctor is unavailable. Although your physician would like to be there for the birth of your baby, sometimes it is not possible.

### ❧ Keep Your Options Open during Labor and Delivery

An important consideration in planning for your labor and delivery is the method(s) you may use to get through the process. Will you have epidural anesthesia? Are you going to attempt a drug-free delivery? Will you need an episiotomy?

Every woman is different, and every labor is different. It's difficult to anticipate what will happen and what you will need during labor and delivery for pain relief. It's impossible to know how long labor will last—3 hours or 20 hours. It's best to adopt a flexible plan. Understand what's available and what options you can choose during labor.

During the last 2 months of your pregnancy, discuss these concerns with your doctor and become familiar with his or her philosophy about labor. Know what can be provided for you at the hospital you've chosen. Some medications may not be available in some areas.

### ❧ Pain Relief without Medication

Some women do not want medication during labor to relieve pain. They prefer to use different laboring positions, massage, breathing patterns, relaxation techniques or hypnotherapy to relieve their pain. Breathing patterns and relaxation techniques are usually learned in a childbirth-education class.

In some places, hypnosis to relieve pain during childbirth is used by some women. *HypnoBirthing* is a labor-pain management technique developed by Marie Mongan over 20 years ago. Ask your doctor about it at one of your prenatal visits if you are interested in trying it. Classes may be available in your area.

*Aromatherapy*, which consists of massage with certain aromatic oils, can be helpful for relaxation. *Birth pools* may be available in some hospitals. Some women experience a reduction in pain and increased relaxation in the water. The water also softens the perineal area, so it may stretch more easily. In some places, you have to get out of the pool to give birth. Discuss it with your physician if you are interested.

*Acupressure* uses pressure on specific parts of the body to help relieve pain and to relax you. It may give you a sense of well-being. However, for acupressure to work most effectively, it must usually be started at the beginning of labor.

### ✌ Laboring Positions

Different laboring positions may enable a woman and her partner (or labor coach) to work together during labor to find relief. This interaction can help you feel closer, and it lets you share the experience. Some women say that using these methods brought them closer to their partner and made the birth experience a more joyful one.

Most women in North America and Europe give birth in bed, on their backs. However, some women are trying different positions to find relief from pain and to make the birth of their baby easier.

In the past, women often labored and gave birth in an upright position that kept the pelvis vertical, such as kneeling, squatting, sitting or standing up. Laboring in this position enables the abdominal wall to relax and the baby to descend more rapidly. Because contractions are stronger and more regular, labor is often shorter.

Today, many women are asking to choose the birth position that is most comfortable for them. Freedom to choose the birth position can make a woman feel more confident about managing birth and labor. Women who choose their own methods may feel more satisfied with the entire experience.

If this is important to you, discuss the matter with your doctor. Ask about the facilities at the hospital you will use; some have special equipment, such as birthing chairs, squatting bars or birthing beds, to help you feel more comfortable. Positions you might consider for your labor are described below.

*Walking* and *standing* are good positions to use during early labor. Walking may help you breathe more easily and relax more. Standing in a warm shower may provide relief. When walking, be sure someone is with you to offer support (both physical and emotional).

*Sitting* can decrease the strength and frequency of contractions and can slow labor. Sitting to rest after walking or standing is acceptable; however, sitting can be uncomfortable during a contraction.

*Kneeling on hands and knees* is a good way to relieve the pain of back labor. *Kneeling against a support,* such as a chair or your partner, stretches your back muscles. The effects of kneeling are similar to those of walking and standing.

When you can't stand, walk or kneel, *lie on your side*. If you receive pain medication, you will need to lie down. Lie on your left side, then turn onto your right side.

Although *lying on your back* is the most common position used for labor, it can decrease the strength and frequency of contractions, which can slow the process. It can also make your blood pressure drop and cause your baby's heart rate to drop. If you lie on your back, elevate the head of the bed and put a pillow under one hip so you are not flat on your back.

Some women want to know if walking during labor makes labor easier and reduces the chance of a C-section. There has been some controversy about walking during labor. Some believe that walking helps move the baby into position more quickly, dilates the cervix faster and makes labor more pain free. Others note that walking puts the woman at risk of falling, and it doesn't allow for fetal monitoring, which can put the fetus at risk. A recent study of more than 1000 pregnant women demonstrated that walking had no effects, either way. We believe the bottom line is that it is a personal decision on your part, and you should be allowed to make the decision as to what feels best for you.

### ✎ Massage for Relief

Massage is a wonderful, gentle way to help you feel better during labor. The touching and caressing of massage helps you relax. One study showed that women who were massaged for 20 minutes every hour during active labor felt less anxiety and less pain.

Many parts of the body of a laboring woman can be massaged. Massaging the head, neck, back and feet can offer a great deal of comfort and relaxation. The person doing the massage should pay close attention to the woman's responses to determine correct pressure.

Different types of massage affect a woman in various ways. You and your partner may want to practice the two types of massage described below before labor for use during labor.

*Effleurage* is light, gentle fingertip massage over the abdomen and upper thighs; it is used during early labor. Stroking is light, but doesn't tickle, and fingertips never leave the skin.

Start with hands on either side of the navel. Move the hands upward and outward, and come back down to the pubic area. Then move the hands back up to the navel. Massage may extend down the thighs. It can also be done as a crosswise motion, around fetal-monitor belts. Move fingers across the abdomen from one side to the other, between the belts.

*Counterpressure massage* is excellent for relieving the pain of back labor. Place the heel of the hand or the flat part of the fist (you can also use a tennis ball) against the tailbone. Apply firm pressure in a small, circular motion.

## Your Nutrition

You won't be allowed to eat or drink anything during your labor. A woman often gets nauseated when she's in labor, which may cause vomiting. For your health and comfort, your doctor wants to avoid this problem, so you will be advised to keep your stomach empty during labor for your own safety.

Eating probably won't be of interest to you, but you may be thirsty. However, understand that you won't be allowed to drink anything during labor for the same reasons as stated above. You will be allowed sips of water or ice chips to suck on. You may even be offered a wet face cloth to suck on. If your labor is long, your body may be hydrated with fluids through an I.V. After your baby's birth, if everything is OK, you will be able to eat and drink.

## You Should Also Know

### ᷓ *Your Labor Coach*
In most instances, your partner is your labor coach. However, this isn't an absolute requirement. A close friend or relative, such as your mother or sister, can also serve as your labor coach. Ask someone ahead of time; don't wait until the last minute. Give the person time to prepare for the experience and to make sure he or she will be able to be there with you.

Not everyone feels comfortable watching the entire labor and delivery. This may include your partner. Don't force your partner or labor coach to watch the delivery if he or she doesn't want to. It's not unusual for a labor coach to get lightheaded, dizzy or pass out during labor and delivery. On more than one occasion, coaches or partners have fainted or become extremely lightheaded just from talking about plans for labor and delivery or a C-section.

Preparing ahead of time, as with prenatal classes, helps avoid some problems. In the past, you would have been alone with the nurses and doctor while your partner paced in the waiting room. Things have changed!

The most important thing about the labor coach is the support he or she gives you during pregnancy, labor, delivery and recovery following the birth of the baby. Choose this person carefully.

**Coaching Tips.** Once you arrive at the hospital, both of you may be nervous. Your coach can do the following to help you both relax:

- talk to you while you're in labor to distract you and to help you relax
- encourage and reassure you during labor and when it comes time for you to push
- keep a watch on the door and protect your privacy
- help relieve tension during labor
- touch, hug and kiss (If you don't want to be touched during labor, tell your coach.)
- reassure you it's OK for you to deal vocally with your pain
- wipe your face or your mouth with a washcloth
- rub your abdomen or back
- support your back while you're pushing
- help create a mood in the labor room, including music and lighting (Discuss it ahead of time; bring things with you that you would like to have available during labor.)
- take pictures (Many couples find still pictures taken of the baby after the delivery help them best remember these wonderful moments of joy.)

**What Can a Partner or Labor Coach Do?** Your partner or labor coach may be one of the most valuable assets you have during labor and delivery. He (or she) can help you prepare for labor and delivery in many ways. He can be there to support you as you go through the experience of labor together. He can share with you the joy of the birth of your baby.

An important role of the labor coach is to make sure you get to the hospital! Work out a plan during the last 4 to 6 weeks of pregnancy so you know how to reach your coach. It's helpful to have an alternate driver, such as a neighbor or friend, who is available in case you are unable to reach your labor coach immediately and need to be taken to the hospital. Before going to the hospital, your labor coach can time your contractions so you are aware of the progress of your labor.

It's all right for your labor coach to rest or to take a break during labor. This is especially true if labor lasts a long time. It's better if your coach eats in the lounge or hospital cafeteria.

Many couples do different things to distract themselves and to help pass time during labor. These include picking names for the baby, playing games, watching TV or listening to music. A labor coach should not bring work into the labor room—it is inappropriate and shows little support for the laboring woman.

Talk to your doctor about your coach's participation in the delivery, such as cutting the umbilical cord or bathing the baby after birth. Things like this vary from one place to another. Understand that the responsibility of your doctor is the well-being of you and your baby—don't make requests or demands that could cause complications.

Decide ahead of time about who needs to be called. Bring a list of names and phone numbers with you. There are some people you may want to call yourself. In most places, a telephone is available in the labor and delivery area.

Discuss showing the baby to those who are waiting with your labor coach. If you want to be with your partner when friends or relatives first see the baby, make it clear to him or her. Don't allow your baby to be taken out of the room unless that's what you want. In most instances, you need some cleaning up. Take some time for yourselves with your new baby. After that you can show baby to friends and relatives, and share the joy with them.

### ✎ *Vaginal Delivery of Your Baby*

We have already covered Cesarean delivery in Week 37. Luckily, most women don't have to have a Cesarean delivery—they have a vaginal birth.

There are three distinct stages of labor. In the first stage of labor, your uterus contracts with enough intensity, duration and frequency to cause thinning (effacement) and dilatation of the cervix. The first stage of labor ends when the cervix is fully dilated (usually 10cm) and sufficiently open to allow the baby's head to come through it.

The second stage of labor begins when the cervix is completely dilated at 10cm. Once full dilatation of the cervix is reached, pushing begins. Pushing can take 1 to 2 hours (first or second baby) to a few minutes (an experienced mom). This stage of labor ends with the delivery of the baby.

The third stage of labor begins after delivery of the baby. It ends with delivery of the placenta and the membranes that have sur-rounded the fetus. Delivery of the baby and placenta, and repair of the episiotomy (if you have one) usually takes 20 to 30 minutes.

Following delivery, you and the baby are evaluated. During this time, you finally get to see and to hold your baby; you may even be able to feed baby.

Depending on whether you deliver in a hospital or birthing center, you may deliver in the same room you have been laboring in (often called *LDRP* for labor, delivery, recovery and postpartum). Or you may be moved to a delivery room nearby. After the birth, you will go to re-covery for a short time, then move to a hospital room until you're ready to go home.

You will probably stay in the hospital from 24 to 48 hours after de-livery, if you have no complications. If you do have any complications, you and your doctor will decide what is best for you.

### ✎ *What Happens to Your Baby after It's Born?*

When your baby is delivered, the doctor clamps and cuts the umbilical cord, and the baby's mouth and throat are suctioned out. Then the baby is usually passed to a nurse or pediatrician for initial evaluation and attention. The Apgar scores (see page 422) are recorded at 1- and 5-minute intervals. An identification band is placed on the baby so there's no mix-up in the nursery.

It's important to keep the baby warm immediately after birth. To do this, the nurse will dry the baby and wrap it in warm blankets. This is done whether the baby is on your chest or attended to by a nurse or doctor.

If your labor is complicated, the baby may need to be evaluated more thoroughly in the nursery. The baby's well-being and health are of primary concern. You'll be able to hold and to nurse the baby, but if your child is having trouble breathing or needs special attention, such as monitors, immediate evaluation is the most appropriate procedure at this time.

Your baby will be taken to the nursery by a nurse and your partner or labor coach. In the nursery, the baby is weighed, measured and foot-printed (in many places). Drops to prevent infection are placed in the baby's eyes. A vitamin-K shot is given to help with the baby's blood-clotting factors. Your baby may receive the hepatitis vaccine, if you request it. Then the baby is put in a heated bassinet for 30 minutes to 2 hours. The time period varies, depending on how stable the baby is.

Your pediatrician is notified immediately if there are problems or concerns. Otherwise, he or she will be notified soon after birth, and a physical exam will be performed within 24 hours.

**Your Baby's Apgar Score.** After a baby is born, it is examined and evaluated at 1 minute and 5 minutes after delivery. The system of evaluation is called the *Apgar score.* This scoring system is a method of evaluating the overall well-being of the newborn infant.

In general, the higher the score, the better the infant's condition. The baby is scored in five areas. Each area is scored 0, 1 or 2; 2 points is the highest score for each category. The top total score is 10. Areas scored include the following.

**Heart rate of the baby.** If the heart rate is absent, a score of 0 is given. If it is slow, less than 100 beats per minute (bpm), a score of 1 is given. If it's over 100 bpm, 2 points are scored.

**Respiratory effort of the baby.** Respiratory effort indicates the newborn's attempts at breathing. If the baby isn't breathing, the score is 0.

If breathing is slow and irregular, the score is 1. If the baby is crying and breathing well, the score is 2.

**Baby's muscle tone.** Muscle tone evaluates how well the baby moves. If arms and legs are limp and flabby, the score is 0. If some movement is observed and the arms and legs bend a little, the score is 1. If the baby is active and moving, the score is 2.

**Reflex irritability of the baby.** Reflex irritability is scored 0 if the baby doesn't respond to stimulus, such as rubbing his or her back or arms. If there is a small movement or a grimace when the baby is stimulated, the score is 1. A baby who responds vigorously is scored with 2 points.

**Baby's color.** The baby's color is rated 0 if the baby is blue or pale. A score of 1 is given if the baby's body is pink and arms and legs are blue. A completely pink baby is scored at 2.

A perfect score of 10 is unusual. Most babies receive scores of 7, 8 or 9 in a normal, healthy delivery. A baby with a low 1-minute Apgar may need to be resuscitated. This means a pediatrician or nurse must help stimulate the baby to breathe and to recover from the delivery. In most cases, the 5-minute Apgar is higher than the 1-minute score because the baby becomes more active and more accustomed to being outside the uterus.

**𝔇ad 𝒯ip** Discuss your role in labor and delivery with your partner. Learn what you can do to assist your partner. You may be able to help maintain privacy. When people visit during or after labor, be sure they don't get too loud or it doesn't become too crowded. Let your partner rest and recuperate; be her knight in shining armor.

# Week 41

## When You're Overdue

Your due date has come and gone. You haven't delivered yet, and you're getting tired of being pregnant. You are anxious to get labor and delivery over and finally meet your baby.

You keep seeing the doctor, and he or she tells you, "I'm sure it'll be soon. Just sit tight." You feel ready to scream. But hang in there. It *will* be over soon—the wait just seems never-ending right now.

## What Happens When You're Overdue?

You've been anticipating the delivery of your baby. You counted the days to your due date—but that day has come and gone. And still no baby! As we've mentioned, not every woman delivers by her due date. Nearly 10% of all babies are born more than 2 weeks late.

A pregnancy is considered to be overdue (*postterm*) only when it exceeds 42 weeks or 294 days from the first day of the last menstrual period. (A baby that is 41½ weeks is *not* postterm!)

Your doctor will examine you and determine if the baby is moving around in the womb and if the amount of amniotic fluid is healthy and normal. If the baby is healthy and active, you are usually monitored until labor begins on its own.

Tests may be done as reassurance that an overdue baby is fine and can remain in the womb. These tests include a *nonstress test,* a *contraction stress test* and a *biophysical profile.* They are all discussed below. If signs of fetal stress are found, labor is often induced.

### ✐ Keep Taking Good Care of Yourself
It's often hard to keep a positive attitude when you're overdue. But don't give up yet!

Maintain good nutrition, and keep up your fluid intake. If you can do so without any problems, get some mild exercise, like walking or swimming.

One of the best exercises you can do at this point in your pregnancy is to exercise in the water. You can swim or do water exercises without the fear of falling or losing your balance. You can even just walk back and forth in the pool!

Rest and relax now because you're baby will be here soon, and you'll be very busy. Use the time to get things ready for baby so you'll be all set when you both come home from the hospital.

### ✐ Postterm Pregnancies
The majority of babies born 2 weeks or more past their due date are delivered safely. However, carrying a baby longer than 42 weeks can cause some problems for the fetus and the mother, so tests are done on these babies and labor is induced, when necessary.

While the fetus is growing and developing inside your uterus, it depends on two important functions performed by the placenta—respiration and nutrition. The baby relies on these functions for continued growth and development.

When a pregnancy is postterm, the placenta may fail to provide the respiratory function and essential nutrients the baby needs to grow, and an infant may begin to suffer nutritional deprivation. The baby is called *postmature.*

At birth, a postmature baby has dry, cracked, peeling, wrinkled skin, long fingernails and abundant hair. It also has less vernix covering its body. The baby appears almost malnourished, with decreased amounts of subcutaneous fat.

Because the postmature infant is in danger of losing nutritional support from the placenta, it's important to know the true dating of your pregnancy. This is one reason it's important to go to all of your prenatal visits.

## Tests You May Have

As we mentioned above, various tests may be done to reassure you and your doctor that your overdue baby is doing OK and can remain in the womb. In evaluating the baby, the doctor looks at various pieces of data to see how your baby is doing. For example, if you are having contractions, it's important to know how your baby is affected.

The tests are done on you to determine the health of your baby. One of the first tests you'll receive is a vaginal exam. Your doctor will probably do this test every week to see if your cervix has begun to dilate.

You may also be asked to record kick counts. See the discussion in Week 27. A weekly ultrasound may be performed to determine how big your baby is and how much amniotic fluid is present at any given time. It also helps to identify abnormalities in the placenta, which could cause problems for the baby.

Three other tests you may have will help determine fetal well-being inside the womb. These tests are often done when a baby is overdue. They are the nonstress test, the contraction stress test and the biophysical profile. They are discussed below.

### ᔾ *The Nonstress Test*
A nonstress test (NST) is performed in your doctor's office or in the labor and delivery department of a hospital. While you are lying down, a technician attaches a fetal monitor to your abdomen. Every time you feel your baby move, you push a button to make a mark on a strip of monitor paper. At the same time, the monitor records the baby's heartbeat.

When the baby moves, its heart rate usually goes up. Doctors use the findings from the NST to help them evaluate how well a baby is tolerating life inside the uterus. Your doctor will decide if further action is necessary.

## ✂ *The Contraction Stress Test*

A contraction stress test (CST) gives an indication of how the baby is doing and how well the baby will tolerate contractions and labor. If the baby doesn't respond well to contractions, it can be a sign of fetal stress. Some believe this test is more accurate than the nonstress test in evaluating the baby's well-being.

To perform a CST, a monitor is placed on your abdomen to monitor the baby. You are attached to an I.V. that dispenses small amounts of the hormone oxytocin to make your uterus contract. The baby's heartbeat is monitored to see its response to the contractions.

This test gives an indication of how well the baby will tolerate contractions and labor. If the baby doesn't respond well to the contractions, it can be a sign of fetal distress.

## ✂ *The Biophysical Profile*

A biophysical profile is a comprehensive test used to examine the fetus during pregnancy. It helps determine fetal health and is done when there is concern about fetal well-being. The test evaluates the well-being of your baby inside your uterus.

A biophysical profile uses a particular scoring system. The first four of the five tests listed below are made with ultrasound; the fifth is done with external fetal monitors. A score is given to each area. The five areas of evaluation are:

- fetal breathing movements
- fetal body movements
- fetal tone
- amount of amniotic fluid
- reactive fetal heart rate (nonstress test)

During the test, doctors evaluate fetal "breathing"—the movement or expansion of the baby's chest inside the uterus. This score is based on the amount of fetal breathing that occurs.

Movement of the baby's body is noted. A normal score indicates normal body movements. An abnormal score is applied when there are few or no body movements during the allotted time period.

Fetal tone is evaluated similarly. Movement, or lack of movement, of the arms and legs of the baby is recorded.

Evaluation of the volume of amniotic fluid requires experience in ultrasound examination. A normal pregnancy has adequate fluid around the baby. An abnormal test indicates no amniotic fluid or decreased amniotic fluid around the baby.

Fetal heart-rate monitoring (nonstress test) is done with external monitors. It evaluates changes in the fetal heart rate associated with movement of the baby. The amount of change and number of changes in the fetal heart rate differ, depending on who is doing the test and their definition of normal.

A normal score is 2; an abnormal score is 0 for any of these tests. A score of 1 in any of the tests is a middle score. From these five scores, a total score is obtained by adding all the values together. Evaluation may vary depending on the sophistication of the equipment used and the expertise of the person doing the test. The higher the score, the better the baby's condition. A lower score may cause concern about the well-being of the fetus.

If the score is low, a recommendation may be made to deliver the baby. If the score is reassuring, the test may be repeated at a later date. If results fall between these two values, the test may be repeated the following day. It depends on the circumstances of your pregnancy and the findings of the biophysical profile. Your doctor will evaluate all the information before making any decision.

## Inducing Labor

There may come a point in your pregnancy that your doctor decides to induce labor. If this happens, it might help you if you realize this is a fairly common practice. Each year, doctors induce labor for about 450,000 births. Labor is induced for overdue babies, but it is also used for a number of other reasons, including chronic high blood pressure in the mother, pre-eclampsia, gestational diabetes, intrauterine-growth restriction and Rh-isoimmunization.

As we've already discussed, when you see the doctor, you will probably have a pelvic exam. At this point in your pregnancy, it probably also includes an evaluation of how ready you are for an induction. Your doctor may use the *Bishop score* to help make this determination. It is a method of cervical scoring, used to predict the success of inducing labor. Scoring includes dilatation, effacement, station, consistency and position of the cervix. A score is given for each point, then they are added together to give a total score. This helps the doctor decide whether to induce labor.

## ✕ Ripening the Cervix for Induction

Today, doctors sometimes ripen the cervix before labor is induced. *Ripening the cervix* means medication is used to help the cervix soften, thin and dilate.

Various preparations are used for this purpose. The two most common are Prepidil Gel (dinoprostone cervical gel, 0.5mg) and Cervidil (dinoprostone, 10mg). Cervidil uses a controlled-release system.

In most cases, doctors use Prepidil Gel and Cervidil to prepare the cervix the day before induction. Both preparations are placed in the top of the vagina, behind the cervix. Medication is released directly onto the cervix, which helps it to ripen for induction of labor. Doctors do this procedure in the labor-and-delivery area of the hospital, so the baby can be monitored.

## ✕ Inducing Labor

If your doctor induces labor, you may first have your cervix ripened, as described above, then you will receive oxytocin (Pitocin) intravenously. This medication is gradually increased until contractions begin. The amount of oxytocin you receive is controlled by a pump, so you can't receive too much of it. While you receive oxytocin, you are monitored for the baby's reaction to your labor.

The oxytocin starts contractions to help you go into labor. The length of the entire process—ripening your cervix until the birth of your baby—varies from woman to woman.

It is important to realize that being induced or having an induction does not guarantee a vaginal delivery. In many instances, the induction doesn't work. In that case, a C-section is usually necessary.

# What Happens after Your Pregnancy?

*A*fter your baby is born, there will be a lot of changes in your life. Take a look at this overview so you'll have an idea of what to anticipate as you begin your life as a new mother.

## In the Hospital

- Muscles are sore from the effort of childbirth and labor.
- Your bottom is sore and swollen. If you had an episiotomy, it also hurts.
- Your incision may be uncomfortable, if you had a C-section or tubal ligation.
- Use the nurse-call button whenever necessary!

- Try different ways for you and your partner to bond with baby.
- Feeding (breast or bottle) the new miracle in your arms may be a little scary, but you'll soon be doing it like a pro!
- Heavy bleeding or passing blood clots larger than an egg can indicate a problem.
- High or low blood pressure may be a cause for further testing.

- Pain should be relieved by medication. If it isn't, tell the nurse.
- Fever over 101.5F (25.25C) may be a cause for concern.
- It's normal if you cry or feel emotional.
- Ask for the paperwork so you can get baby a social security number. Fill it out, and be sure to send it in.

- Try to rest. Ask to turn off your phone and to restrict visitors.
- Even though you just lost 10 to 15 pounds with baby's birth, it'll take awhile for the rest of your weight to come off.
- Eat nutritiously to keep up energy and for milk production, if you breastfeed.
- Write down thoughts and feelings about labor, delivery and the first hours with your new baby. Encourage your partner to do the same.
- Watch hospital videos about baby care. Ask staff for clarification or help.
- Get the name, address and telephone number of your pediatrician.
- Ask questions, and get help from the nurses and staff in the hospital.
- Ask your partner to take you for a walk outside your hospital room.
- Take time for you, your partner and your baby to bond as a family.

## 1st Week Home

- You'll still have painful uterine contractions, especially during nursing.
- It's normal for your breasts to be full of milk, engorged and leaking.
- The area of your episiotomy or tear is probably still sore.
- Muscles may also be sore.
- Maternity clothes may be the most comfortable clothes to wear.
- Your legs may still be swollen.
- You may leak urine or stool and can't control it.
- If bleeding gets heavier, or you pass blood clots, call your doctor.
- It may indicate a problem if you get red streaks or hard spots in your breasts.
- Call your doctor if you develop a fever.
- Take it easy; don't worry about the housework.
- It's normal to cry, sigh or laugh for no reason.
- Be sure to ask for help from friends and family.
- You may still look pregnant from the side.
- You still carry some of the extra weight you gained during pregnancy.
- Make baby's first appointment with the doctor.
- Have baby added to your insurance policy. There may be a time limit, so don't delay.
- Keep important "baby" documents together, such as the birth certificate, immunization record (when you get it at baby's first pediatrician's visit) and baby's social security card.
- Make your 6-week postpartum checkup appointment.
- Begin making plans for daycare arrangements, if you haven't started already.
- Give your partner a job or assignment to help you and to make him feel useful.
- Contact La Leche League, if you have any problems breastfeeding.

## 2nd Week Home

- Your breasts (whether or not you breastfeed) are full and uncomfortable.
- Hemorrhoids still hurt, but they should be getting better.
- With swelling and water retention diminishing, you can wear some of your clothes and shoes again.
- Feeding baby is starting to work better.
- When you cough, laugh, sneeze or lift something heavy, you may lose stool or urine and not be able to control it.
- You are probably fatigued. Taking care of baby requires a lot of time and energy.
- A foul odor or yellow-green vaginal discharge may indicate a problem; it should be decreasing at this point. If it isn't, contact your doctor.
- It's OK to let baby cry a little before checking on him or her.
- You can almost see your feet when you look down (your tummy is getting smaller).
- Write down any questions for your visit with your pediatrician.
- Keep your appointment with your doctor if you had a C-section or tubal ligation; you need your incision checked.
- Write down some of your thoughts and feelings in your journal.

## 3rd Week Home

- Swelling and soreness around your bottom are decreasing, but sitting for a long time still may not feel very comfortable.
- Swelling in hands decreases. If you took off your rings during pregnancy, try them on again.
- Baby doesn't know the difference between night and day, so your sleep patterns are also disturbed.
- Getting ready to go anywhere is like planning a major trip. It takes three times longer to get ready with baby.
- Call your doctor if you develop red streaks or tender, hard spots on your legs, particularly the back of the calves. It could be a blood clot.
- You may feel sad or depressed some of the time. You may even cry.
- You may have varicose veins, just like your mother! They'll get better as you recover from pregnancy and begin exercising again.
- Skin on your abdomen still looks stretched out when you stand up.
- Keep baby's first appointment with the pediatrician. You'll probably receive his or her immunization record at this visit. Put it in a safe place with baby's other important papers.
- Take lots of pictures and videos! You'll be amazed how quickly baby will change and grow.
- Keep your partner involved. Let him try his hand at caring for baby. Ask for his help with household chores.
- By this point, you've changed over 200 diapers—you're an expert.

## 4th Week Home

- Muscles feel better, and you can do more now. Be aware—it's easy to pull or to strain muscles you haven't used for a while.
- Control of urine and stool are improving. Doing your Kegel exercises is paying off.
- Baby is showing signs of adjusting to a regular schedule.
- Things that once were easy to do, such as bending over or lifting, may be harder now. Take things slowly, and allow yourself plenty of time for even the easiest chores.
- Your first menstrual period after delivery could happen at any time. If you don't breastfeed, your first period is usually 4 to 9 weeks after delivery, but it can happen earlier.
- Blood in your urine, dark or cloudy urine, or severe cramping or pain with urination may be symptoms of a urinary-tract infection (UTI). Call your doctor.
- You've been walking and doing light exercise, and it feels OK. Keep it up!
- Check on your 6-week postpartum appointment. Write down any questions you have as they come to you.
- A night out with your partner is a good plan. Grandparents, other family members and friends can babysit, if you ask them.
- Time with your new baby is precious. Soon you may be going back to work or returning to other activities.

## 5th Week Home

- As you get back to regular activities, sore muscles and a sore back may be expected.
- Bowel movements may still be uncomfortable in the area of your episiotomy or rectum from time to time.
- Bladder and bowel control have returned.
- You may be getting a little anxious to go back to work. You may have missed your friends and the work you do.
- It may be hard to go back to work and not be there for every moment with your baby.
- Plan for after-birth contraception. Decide on some type of birth control, and be ready to start it.
- Baby blues should be getting much better, if they haven't disappeared already.
- You may be a little nervous about going back to work.
- Clothes may still be snug, even if they were loose before pregnancy.
- Remind yourself that it took you 9 months of pregnancy to gain the weight you did. It will take awhile to return to your prepregnancy figure.
- Returning to work requires planning. Start now to put your "back-to-work" schedule into effect.
- Plans for daycare, tending, nursing and other things need to be in place soon. Family and friends can be an important ingredient.

## 6ᵗʰ Week Home

- Having a pelvic exam at your 6-week checkup isn't usually as bad as you might expect.
- In the 6 weeks since baby's birth, your uterus has gone from the size of a watermelon to the size of your fist; it now weighs about 2 ounces.
- At your 6-week postpartum appointment, plan to discuss several important subjects, such as contraception, your current activity level, limitations and future pregnancies.
- People in your OB's office have probably been helpful to you. Thank them, and ask if you can call with future questions.
- If you still have baby blues or feel depressed every day, tell your doctor.
- If you bleed vaginally or have a foul-smelling discharge, inform you doctor.
- If you have pain or swelling in your legs, or your breasts are red or tender, bring it up at your visit.
- Ask questions; make a list. Good questions include:

    *What are my choices for contraception?*

    *Do I have any limitations as far as exercise or sex?*

    *Is there anything I should know from this pregnancy and delivery if I decide to get pregnant again?*

- If you take baby with you to your postpartum checkup, take plenty of supplies. You may have to wait.
- If you're going back to work soon, double check on child-care arrangements.
- Continue to involve your partner as much as possible.
- Keep writing your thoughts and feelings in your journal. Encourage your partner to do the same.

## 3 Months

- Muscles may be sore from exercising—a little more than a month ago, you were given the OK to do any exercises you wanted.
- You may have your first period around this time. It could be heavier, longer and different from those before pregnancy.
- If you haven't done anything about contraception, do it now! (Unless you want to celebrate two birthdays in the same year.)
- It's OK to let baby cry when she's a little fussy and needs to soothe herself.
- Your pounds and inches may not be disappearing as quickly as you would like. Keep exercising and eating nutritiously. You'll get there!
- Write down baby's milestones as they happen; write them in baby's book or keep a journal.
- Look for things your partner can do to be involved in baby's care. Let him help out when he can.
- If you've stopped breastfeeding, let baby's dad give him a bottle.

## 6 Months

- Getting on the scale may still be a daunting task. But hang in there, and keep working hard on eating well and exercising!
- Your first period may occur around this time, if you are breastfeeding. It could be heavier, longer and different from those before pregnancy.

- Don't try to do it all yourself. Let your partner and others help.
- Baby's feeding schedule should be well established by now.
- Take time for yourself.
- Arrange time for regular activities, such as exercising, baby play groups and meeting with other new moms.
- You're starting to fit into some of your

clothing from before pregnancy.
- Share special baby moments with your partner.
- Record baby's noises, or take pictures. A tape recorder and videocamera are great for this!
- Find a friend with a baby, and trade child-care duties. It's a good way for each of you to find time for yourself.

## 1 Year

- All systems are go! It's taken time, energy and hard work, but your life is going smoothly now.
- Baby is on a schedule and sleeps through the night most of the time.
- Don't miss your yearly exam or your Pap smear.
- Your body is returning to its prepregnancy shape. Your tummy is flat, you've lost most of

the pregnancy weight and you feel great.
- Continue taking care of yourself. Eat nutritiously, get enough rest and exercise.
- Write down feelings about this time in your life. Encourage your partner to do the same.
- Sharing child care can be a good way to develop baby play groups. Interacting

with other children is good for baby.
- Baby's 1st birthday is just around the corner. Celebrate!
- Enjoy baby's first words, first steps and every other first that will happen.
- Continue taking pictures of baby.
- You may be considering another pregnancy.

# Resources

## General Information for Parents

For Adoptive Parents
*Good resource for adoption information*
www.adoption.com

American Academy of Pediatrics (AAP)
P.O. Box 927, Dept. C
Elk Grove Village, IL 60009-0927
www.aap.org

American Academy of Family Practitioners
(AAFP)
www.aafp.com

American College of Obstetricians and
Gynecologists (ACOG)
P.O. Box 4500
Kearneysville, WV 25430
800-762-2264
www.acog.com

American Psychological Association (APA)
202-336-5700
www.apa.org

Baby Doppler
*To buy a home-use doppler to hear baby's
heartbeat at home*
888-758-8822
www.babybeat.com

Birth Marker
*Product for marking infant in hospital so
baby mix-ups don't occur*
www.birth-mark.com

California Cryobank Cord Blood Services
*For information on storing baby's umbilical-
cord blood*
www.cryobank.com/baby

Car-Seat Installation
877-FIT-4-A-KID
www.fitforakid.com

Centers for Disease Control
*For up-to-date information on many
medical issues*
www.cdc.gov

Child Care Aware
800-424-2246

Children's Defense Fund
www.childrensdefense.org
COPE
37 Clarendon St.
Boston, MA 02116
617-357-5588

Home Testing for Pregnancy
*Compares various pregnancy tests*
www.kerouac.pharm.uky.edu/hometests/
pregnancy/ptoc.html

Intensive-Care Parenting magazine
ICU Parenting
RD #10, Box 176
Brush Creek Rd, Irwin, PA 15642

Internal Revenue Service
*For information on child-care expenses*
800-829-1040
www.irs.ustreas.gov

Juvenile Products Manufacturers Association
*For information on baby products, recalls
and other pertinent information*
236 Route 38 West, Suite 100
Moorestown, NJ 08057
www.jpma.org

## General Information for Parents *(continued)*

March of Dimes
*For information on various tests before and*
*during pregnancy*
888-663-4637
www.modimes.org

Military Families
*For families of military personnel*
www.4militaryparents.com

National Organization of Single Mothers
P.O. Box 68
Midland, NC 28107-0068
704-888-KIDS (704-888-5437)

On-line announcements
*Send on-line announcements and*
*invitations for almost every occasion*
www.senada.com
www.growingfamily.com

Parent's Resources
P.O. Box 107, Planetarium Sta.
New York, NY 10024
212-866-4776

Product Recalls
*For the latest baby-product recalls and*
*warnings*
www.childrecall.com
www.cpsc.gov
www.jpma.org

Sidelines
*For women experiencing complicated*
*pregnancies*
Candace Hurley, executive director:
714-497-2265
Tracy Hoogenboom: 909-563-6199

Social Security Administration
800-772-1213
www.ssa.gov

Spina Bifida Association of America
*For information on various tests before and*
*during pregnancy*
www.sbaa.org

StriVectin-SD
*Cream for treating stretch marks after*
*pregnancy*
888-340-1628
www.StriVectin.com

US Consumer Products Safety
Commission
800-638-2772
www.cpsc.gov

USDA
*For information on the food pyramid*
www.cnpp.usda.gov

Vaccines
*For information on vaccines from the*
*Children's Hospital of Philadelphia*
www.vaccine.chop.edu

Virtual Birth Center
*By state, lists obstetricians, midwives, birth*
*centers, doulas and other services*
www.virtualbirth.com

The Women's Bureau Publications
*For summary of state laws on family leave*
U.S. Department of Labor
Women's Bureau Clearing House
Box EX
200 Constitution Avenue, NW
Washington, DC 20210
800-827-5335
*Also see www.ecoc.gov/facts/fs-preg.html*

*Websites for further information*
www.americanbaby.com
www.babycenter.com
www.babyzone.com
www.bellycast.com
www.childmagazine.com
www.ibaby.com
www.ivillage.com
www.parenthoodweb.com

# At-Home Moms

F.E.M.A.L.E. (Formerly Employed Mothers
At the Leading Edge)
P.O. Box 31
Elmhurst, IL 60126
800-223-9399
www.femalehome.org

Miserly Moms
*Helps families save money by providing tips
for cooking, shopping, decorating and
gardening*
www.miserlymoms.com

Mothers At Home
800-783-4666
www.mah.org

MOMS (Mothers Offering Mothers Support)
25371 Rye Canyon Rd.
Valencia, CA 91355
805-526-2725

*Websites for further information*
www.momsonline.com
www.parentsplace.com
www.parentssoup.com
www.parenttime.com

# Breastfeeding Information

Avent
800-542-8368
www.aventamerica.com

Breastfeeding Basics
www.breastfeedingbasics.com

Breastfeeding Help
*For 24-hour breastfeeding support, referrals to
lactation consultants and helpful videos*
www.breastfeeding.com

Best Start
3500 E. Fletcher Avenue, Suite 519
Tampa, FL 33613
800-277-4975

FDA Hotline
800-332-4010

FDA Breast Implant Information Line
800-532-4440

International Lactation Consultant
Association
919-787-5181

La Leche League International
1400 North Meacham Road
Schaumburg, IL 60173-4840
800-LA-LECHE or check local telephone
directory
www.lalecheleague.org

Medela, Inc.
P.O. Box 660
McHenry, IL 60051
800-TELL-YOU (800-735-5968)

National Center for Nutrition and
Dietetics
*Consumer Nutrition Hotline*
800-366-1655

National Maternal and Child Health
Clearinghouse
2070 Chain Bridge Road, Suite 45
Vienna, VA 22182
703-821-8955, ext. 254

Wellstart
4062 First Avenue
San Diego, CA 92103
619-295-5192

*Websites for further information*
www.moms4milk.org
www.breastfeed.com

# Childbirth Information

American Academy of Husband-Coached
Childbirth (Bradley Method)
P.O. Box 5224
Sherman Oaks, CA 91413
800-422-4784
818-788-6662

American College of Nurse-Midwives
(ACNM)
818 Connecticut Avenue NW, Suite 900
Washington, DC 20006
202-728-9860

American Society for Pyschoprophylaxis in
Obstetrics (ASPO/Lamaze)
1200 19th Street NW, Suite 300
Washington, DC 20036-2422
800-368-4404

Association of Labor Assistants and
Childbirth Educators (ALACE)
P.O. Box 382724
Cambridge, MA 02238-2724
617-441-2500

Birth Centers
*Lists birthing centers in 37 states*
www.birthcenters.org

Doulas of North America
1100 23rd Avenue East
Seattle, WA 98112
FAX 206-325-0472
www.dona.com

Informed Home Birth
313-662-6852

International Cesarean Awareness Network
(ICAN)
1304 Kingsdale Avenue
Redondo Beach, CA 90278
310-542-6400

International Childbirth Education
Association
P.O. Box 20048
Minneapolis, MN 55420-0048
612-854-8660

Lamaze, *See American Society for
Pyschoprophylaxis in Obstetrics*

Midwives Alliance of North America
(MANA)
P.O. Box 175
Newton, KS 67114
316-283-4543

National Association of Childbearing
Centers (NACC)
3123 Gottschall Road
Perkiomenville, PA 18074
215-234-8068

Public Citizen's Health Research
*For information on C-sections and VBAC*
1600 20th Street NW
Washington, DC 20009

Video Prenatal Classes
*Great Expectations: Laugh and Learn about
Childbirth*
www.laughandlearn.com

# Child Care

Child Care Aware Hotline
800-424-2246

Department of Health and Human
Services; National Child Care Information
Center
800-616-2242

International Nanny Association
800-297-1477
www.nanny.org

National Association for the Education of
Young Children
www.naeyc.org

National Association of Child Care
Resource and Referral Agencies
800-424-2246
202-393-5501
www.childcarerr.org
www.naccrra.net

National Resource Center for Health and
Safety in Child Care
800-598-5437
www.nrc.uchsc.edu

Working Mother
www.workingmother.com

# Dads

At-Home Dad newsletter
61 Brightwood Avenue
North Andover, MA 01845
www.athomedad.com

Dad to Dad Network
Send self-addressed stamped envelope to:
13925 Duluth Court
Apple Valley, MN 55124
612-423-3705

Full-Time Dads
193 Shelley Ave.
Elizabeth, NJ 07208
908-355-9722
FAX 908-355-9723
www.fathersworld.com/fulltimedad

The Single & Custodial Father's Network
*For fathers who are primary caregivers, to connect with other fathers in similar situations*
www.single-fathers.org

*Websites for further information*
www.babycenter.com/dads
www.daddyshome.com
www.edads.com
www.fathersforum.com
www.fathersonline.com
www.fathersworld.com
www.infodad.com
www.manslife.com
www.newdads.com
www.portage.net/~rborelli/dads.html

# Financial Resources

BankRate
*For general financial information*
516-627-7330
www.bankrate.com

College Savings Plan Network
*For information on saving for college*
877-277-6496
www.savingforcollege.com

Consumer Credit Counseling Service
*For help with your budget*
888-775-0377

Consumer Federation of America
*For information on many consumer issues*
202-387-6121
www.consumerfed.org

Debtors Anonymous
*For debt-management services*
781-453-2743
www.debtorsanonymous.com

Easy Saver Plan
*For information on government savings bonds and how to buy them*
www.publicdebt.treas.gov

Health Insurance Association of America
*For information on health and disability insurance*
888-869-4078
www.hiaa.org

Insurance Information Institute
*For information on various types of insurance*
800-331-9146
www.iii.org

IntelliQuote Insurance Services
*For quotes to compare for various insurance policies*
888-622-0925
www.intelliquote.com

Internal Revenue Service
*For information on child-care expenses*
800-829-1040
www.irs.ustreas.gov

National Association of Personal Planners
*For help with your budget*
888-333-6659

National Foundation for Credit Counseling
*For debt-management services*
800-388-2227
www.nfcc.org

**Financial Resources** *(continued)*

National Insurance Consumer Helpline
*For answers to specific insurance questions*
800-942-4242

QuickQuote
*For a term life insurance quote*
800-867-2402
www.quickquote.com

Quotesmith
*For various insurance quotes*
800-431-1147
www.quotesmith.com

US Savings Bonds
800-4US-BONDS
www.savingsbonds.gov

*Websites for further information*
www.collegesavings.org
www.educationira.com
www.financenter.com
www.healthinsurancefinders.com
www.ihatefinancialplanning.com
www.insurance.com
www.localinsurance.com
www.mfea.com
www.morningstar.com
www.myvesta.org
www.naic.org/consumer.htm

# Mother's Health

All About Kegels
*Learn how to do kegel exercises correctly*
www.niddk.nih.gov/health/urolog/uibew/
exerc/exerc.htm

American Cancer Society
*For information on the dangers of passive
smoke*
800-ACS-2345

Chiropractic Care
*Discusses chiropractic care during pregnancy*
www.rlx.net/babycottage/pregnancy.htm

Depression after Delivery
P.O. Box 1282
Morrisville, PA 19067
800-944-4773 (answering machine only)

Group B Strep Association
P.O. Box 16515
Chapel Hill, NC 27516
919-932-5344

Inflammatory Breast Cancer
*For information about this type of breast cancer*
www.ibcsupport.com

Mom's Fitness
*For information and exercises to help
pregnant women and new moms*
www.fitmommies.com/pregnancy

Older Mothers to Be
*For information for older expectant mothers*
www.midlifemommies.com

Postpartum Support International
*For information and help with postpartum
distress syndrome*
805-967-7636
www.postpartum.net

Preggie Pops
*To help relieve morning sickness*
www.preggiepops.com

Sideline (for women on bed rest)
714-497-2265

SOS Morning Sickness
*For information on, and remedies for,
nausea and vomiting*
www.sosmorningsickness.com

# Multiples

Center for Loss in Multiple Birth
c/o Jean Kollantai
P.O. Box 1064
Palmer, AK 99645
907-746-6123

Center for Study of Multiple Births
333 E. Superior Street, Room 464
Chicago, IL 60611
312-266-9093

Mothers of Supertwins (M.O.S.T.) *(triplets
or more)*
P.O. Box 951
Brentwood, NY 11717
516-434-MOST
www.mostonline.org

Multiple Birth Resources
70 W. Sylvester Place
Highland Ranch, CO 80126
888-627-9519
www.expectingmultiples.com

Multiple Births Foundation
Queen Charlotte's and Chelsea Hospital
Goldhawk Road
London, England W6 OXG
081-748-4666, ext. 5201

National Online Fathers of Twins Club
www.member.aol.com/nofotc

National Organization of Mothers of
Twins Clubs, Inc.
P.O. Box 438
Thompson Station, TN 37179-0438
505-275-0955

Triplet Connection
P.O. Box 99571
Stockton, CA 95209
209-474-0885
www.tripletconnection.org

Twin Services
P.O. Box 10066
Berkeley, CA 94709
510-524-0863

Twin to Twin Transfusion Syndrome
(TTTS) Foundation
Mary Slaman-Forsythe, Executive Director
411 Longbeach Parkway
Bay Village, OH 44140
216-899-8887

The Twins Foundation
P.O. Box 6043
Providence, RI 02940-6043
401-729-1000

Twins Hope
*International center for twin-related diseases*
www.twinshope.com

Twins Magazine
5350 S. Roslyn Street, Suite 400
Englewood, CO 80111
800-328-3211

Twins World
*Good resource for couples expecting multiples*
www.twinsworld.com

# Nutrition Information

Beechnut Nutrition Hotline
800-523-6633

FDA Hotline
*For nutrition information*
800-332-4010

Food Guide Pyramid Brochure
USDA
P.O. Box 1144
Rockville, MD 20850
www.cnpp.usda.gov

# Premature Babies

Intensive-care Parenting magazine
ICU Parenting
RD #10, Box 176
Brush Creek Road
Irwin, PA 15642

Premature Infants
ECMO Moms and Dads
c/o Blair and Gayle Wilson
P.O. Box 53848
Lubbock, TX 79453
806-794-0259

# Safety for Your Baby

Auto Safety Hotline
888-327-4236

Back to Sleep
*For information on SIDS*
P.O. Box 29111
Washington, DC 20040
800-505-2742

The Danny Foundation
*For information on crib dangers*
3158 Danville Blvd.
P.O. Box 680
Alamo, CA 94507
800-833-2669

General Motors
"Precious Cargo: Protecting the Children
Who Ride with You" (free booklet)
800-247-9168

The International Association of Chiefs of
Police
Operation Kids
800-843-4227

Juvenile Products Manufacturers
Association
236 Route 38 West, Suite 100
Moorestown, NJ 08057
www.jpma.org

National Highway Traffic Safety
Administration
800-424-99393
www.nhtsa.dot.gov

National Lead Information Hotline and
Clearinghouse
800-424-LEAD

The National SAFE KIDS Campaign
800-441-1888
www.safekids.org

Nissan's Quest for Safety Campaign
Car Seat Safety (free booklet)
800-955-4500

Safety Alerts
*For information on recalls*
www.safetyalerts.com

SafetyBeltUSA
123 Manchester Blvd.
Inglewood, CA 90301
310 673 2666
www.carseat.org

US Consumer Products Safety
Commission
800-638-2772
www.cpsc.gov

# Glossary

## a

**Abdominal measurement**—Measurement taken of the growth of the baby in the uterus at prenatal visits. Measurement is from the pubic symphysis to the fundus. Too much growth or too little growth may indicate problems.

**Abruptio placenta**—See *placental abruption.*

**Acquired immune deficiency syndrome (AIDS)**—Debilitating, frequently fatal illness that affects the body's ability to respond to infection. Caused by the human immune deficiency virus (HIV).

**Active labor**—When a woman is dilated between 4 and 8cm. Contractions are usually 3 to 5 minutes apart.

**Aerobic exercise**—Exercise that increases your heart rate and causes you to consume oxygen.

**Afterbirth**—Placenta and membranes expelled after baby is delivered. See *placenta.*

**Alpha-fetoprotein (AFP)**—Substance produced by the unborn baby as it grows inside the uterus. Large amounts of AFP are found in the amniotic fluid. Larger-than-normal amounts are found in the maternal bloodstream if neural-tube defects are present in the fetus.

**Alveoli**—Ends of the ducts of the lung.

**Amino acids**—Substances that act as building blocks in the developing embryo and fetus.

**Amniocentesis**—Process by which amniotic fluid is removed from the amniotic sac for testing; fluid is tested for some genetic defects and for fetal lung maturity.

**Amniotic fluid**—Fluid surrounding the baby inside the amniotic sac.

**Amniotic sac**—Membrane that surrounds baby inside the uterus. It contains baby, placenta and amniotic fluid.

**Ampulla**—Dilated opening of a tube or duct.

**Anemia**—Any condition in which the number of red blood cells is less than normal. Term usually applies to the concentration of the oxygen-transporting material in the blood, which is the red blood cell.

**Anencephaly**—Defective development of the brain combined with the absence of the bones normally surrounding the brain.

**Angioma**—Tumor, usually benign, or swelling composed of lymph and blood vessels.

**Anovulatory**—Lack, or cessation, of ovulation.

**Anti-inflammatory medications**—Drugs to relieve pain or inflammation.

**Apgar scores**—Measurement of a baby's response to birth and life on its own. Taken 1 minute and 5 minutes after birth.

**Areola**—Pigmented or colored ring surrounding the nipple of the breast.

**Arrhythmia**—Irregular or missed heartbeat.

**Aspiration**—Swallowing or sucking a foreign body or fluid, such as vomit, into an airway.

**Asthma**—Disease marked by recurrent attacks of shortness of breath and difficulty breathing. Often caused by an allergic reaction.

**Atonic uterus**—Uterus that is flaccid; relaxed; lacking tone.

**Augmented labor**—When labor is "stalled" or progress is not being made during labor, medication (oxytocin) is given.

**Autoantibodies**—Antibodies that attack parts of your body or your own tissues.

# *b*

**Baby blues**—Mild depression in woman after delivery.

**Back labor**—Pain of labor felt in lower back.

**Beta-adrenergics**—Substances that interfere with transmission of stimuli. They affect the autonomic nervous system.

**Bilirubin**—Breakdown product of pigment formed in the liver from hemoglobin during the destruction of red blood cells.

**Biophysical profile**—Method of evaluating a fetus before birth.

**Biopsy**—Removal of a small piece of tissue for microscopic study.

**Birthing center**—Facility specializing in the delivery of babies. Usually a woman labors, delivers and recovers in the same room. It may be part of a hospital or a freestanding unit. Sometimes called *LDRP*, for labor, delivery, recovery and postpartum.

**Bishop score**—Method of cervical scoring, used to predict the success of inducing labor. Includes dilatation, effacement, station, consistency and position of the cervix. A score is given for each point, then they are added together to give a total score to help doctor decide whether to induce labor.

**Blastomere**—One of the cells the egg divides into after it has been fertilized.

**Blood pressure**—Push of the blood against the walls of the arteries, which carry blood away from the heart. Changes in blood pressure may indicate problems.

**Blood typing**—Test to determine if a woman's blood type is A, B, AB or O.

**Blood-pressure check**—Check of a woman's blood pressure. High blood pressure can be significant during pregnancy, especially nearer the due date. Changes in blood pressure readings can alert the doctor to potential problems.

**Blood-sugar tests**—See *glucose-tolerance test*.

**Bloody show**—Small amount of vaginal bleeding late in pregnancy; often precedes labor.

**Board certification (of physician)**—Doctor has received additional training and testing in a particular specialty. In the area of obstetrics, the American College of Obstetricians and Gynecologists offers this training. Certification requires expertise in care of women. FACOG following a doctor's name means he or she is a Fellow of the American College of Obstetricians and Gynecologists.

**Braxton-Hicks contractions**—Irregular, painless tightening of uterus during pregnancy.

**Breech presentation**—Abnormal birth position of the fetus. Buttocks or legs come into the birth canal before the head.

## C

**Canavan's disease screening**—Blood test performed on people of Ashkenazi Jewish background to determine if a fetus is affected with Canavan's disease.

**Cataract, congenital**—Cloudiness of the eye lens present at birth.

**Cell antibodies**—See *autoantibodies*.

**Cervical cultures**—To test for STDs; when a Pap smear is done, a sample may also be taken to check for chlamydia, gonorrhea or other STDs.

**Cervix**—Opening of the uterus.

**Cesarean section or delivery**—Delivery of a baby through an abdominal incision rather than through the vagina.

**Chadwick's sign**—Dark-blue or purple discoloration of the mucosa of the vagina and cervix during pregnancy.

**Chemotherapy**—Treatment of disease by chemical substances or drugs.

**Chlamydia**—Sexually transmitted venereal infection.

**Chloasma**—Increased pigmentation or extensive brown patches of irregular shape and size on the face (commonly has the appearance of a butterfly) or other parts of the body. They may be extensive. Also called *mask of pregnancy*.

**Chorion**—Outermost fetal membrane found around the amnion.

**Chorionic villus sampling (CVS)**—Diagnostic test that can be done early in pregnancy to determine pregnancy abnormalities. A biopsy of tissue is taken from inside the uterus through the abdomen or the cervix.

**Chromosomal abnormality**—Abnormal number or abnormal makeup of chromosomes.

**Chromosomes**—Thread in a cell's nucleus that contains DNA, which transmits genetic information.

**Cleft palate**—Defect in the palate, a part of the upper jaw or mouth.

**Colostrum**—Thin yellow fluid, which is the first milk to come from the breast. Most often seen toward the end of pregnancy. It is different in content from milk produced later during nursing.

Complete blood count (CBC)—Blood test to check iron stores and to check for infections.

Condyloma acuminatum—Skin tags or warts that are sexually transmitted. Also called *venereal warts.*

Congenital deafness screening—If a couple has a family history of inherited deafness, this blood test may identify the problem before baby's birth.

Congenital problem—Problem present at birth.

Conization of the cervix—Surgical procedure performed on premalignant and malignant conditions of the cervix. A large biopsy of the cervix is taken in the shape of a cone.

Conjoined twins—Twins connected at the body; they may share vital organs. Previously called *Siamese twins.*

Constipation—Bowel movements are infrequent or incomplete.

Contraction stress test—Test of fetal response to uterine contractions to evaluate fetal well-being.

Contractions—Uterus squeezes or tightens to push the baby out of the uterus during birth.

Corpus luteum—Area in the ovary where the egg is released at ovulation. A cyst may form in this area after ovulation. Called a *corpus luteum cyst.*

Crown-to-rump length—Measurement from the top of the baby's head (crown) to baby's buttocks (rump).

Cystitis—Inflammation of the bladder.

Cytomegalovirus (CMV) infection—Group of viruses from the herpes virus family.

# *d*

D&C (dilatation and curettage)—Surgical procedure in which the cervix is dilated and the lining of the uterus is scraped.

Developmental delay—Condition in which the development of the baby or child is slower than normal.

Diastasis recti—Separation of abdominal muscles.

Diethylstilbestrol (DES)—Nonsteroidal synthetic estrogen. Used in the past to try to prevent miscarriage.

Dilatation—Amount, in centimeters, the cervix has opened before birth. When a woman is fully dilated, she is at 10cm.

Dizygotic twins—Twins derived from two different eggs. Often called *fraternal twins.*

Doppler—Device that enhances the fetal heartbeat so the doctor and others can hear it.

Down syndrome—Chromosomal disorder in which baby has three copies of Chromosome 21 (instead of two); results in mental retardation, distinct physical traits and various other problems.

**Due date**—Date baby is expected to be born. Most babies are born near this date, but only 1 of 20 are born on the actual date.

**Dysuria**—Difficulty or pain urinating.

*e*

**Early labor**—When a woman experiences regular contractions (one every 20 minutes down to one every 5 minutes) for longer than 2 hours. The cervix usually dilates to 3 or 4cm.

**Eclampsia**—Convulsions and coma in a woman with pre-eclampsia. Not related to epilepsy. See *pre-eclampsia.*

**Ectodermal germ layer**—Layer in the developing embryo that gives rise to developing structures in the fetus. These include skin, teeth and glands of the mouth, the nervous system and the pituitary gland.

**Ectopic pregnancy**—Pregnancy that occurs outside the uterine cavity, most often in the Fallopian tube. Also called *tubal pregnancy.*

**ECV (External cephalic version)**—Procedure done late in pregnancy, in which doctor manually attempts to move a baby in the breech presentation into the normal head-down birth position.

**EDC (estimated date of confinement)**—Anticipated due date for delivery of the baby. Calculated from the first day of the last period, counting forward 280 days.

**Effacement**—Thinning of cervix; occurs in the latter part of pregnancy and during labor.

**Electroencephalogram**—Recording of the electrical activity of the brain.

**Embryo**—Organism in the early stages of development; in a human pregnancy from conception to 10 weeks.

**Embryonic period**—First 10 weeks of gestation.

**Endodermal germ layer**—Area of tissue in early development of the embryo that gives rise to other structures. These include the digestive tract, respiratory organs, vagina, bladder and urethra. Also called *endoderm* or *entoderm.*

**Endometrial cycle**—Regular development of the mucous membrane that lines the inside of the uterus. It begins with the preparation for acceptance of a pregnancy and ends with the shedding of the lining during a menstrual period.

**Endometrium**—Mucous membrane that lines inside of the uterine wall.

**Enema**—Fluid injected into the rectum for the purpose of clearing out the bowel.

**Engorgement**—Filled with fluid; usually refers to breast engorgement in a breast-feeding mother.

**Enzyme**—Protein made by cells. It acts as a catalyst to improve or cause chemical changes in other substances.

**Epidural block**—Type of anesthesia. Medication is injected around the spinal cord during labor or other types of surgery.

**Episiotomy**—Surgical incision of the perineum (area behind the vagina, above the rectum). Used during delivery to avoid tearing vaginal opening and rectum.

**Estimated date of confinement**—See *EDC*.

**Exotoxin**—Poison or toxin from a source outside the body.

**Expressing breast milk**—Manually forcing milk out of the breast.

# *f*

**Face presentation**—Baby comes into the birth canal face first.

**Fallopian tube**—Tube that leads from the uterine cavity to the area of the ovary. Also called *uterine tube*.

**False labor**—Tightening of uterus without dilatation of the cervix.

**Familial Mediterranean fever screening**—Blood test performed on people of Armenian, Arabic, Turkish and Sephardic Jewish background to identify carriers of the recessive gene. Permits diagnosis in a newborn so treatment can be started.

**Fasting blood sugar**—Blood test to evaluate the amount of sugar in the blood following a time period of fasting.

**Ferrous gluconate or sulfate**—Iron supplement.

**Fertilization**—Joining of the sperm and egg.

**Fertilization age**—Dating a pregnancy from the time of fertilization; 2 weeks shorter than gestational age. Also see *gestational age*.

**Fetal anomaly**—Fetal malformation or abnormal development.

**Fetal arrhythmia**—See *arrhythmia*.

**Fetal distress**—Problems with the baby that occur before birth or during labor; often requires immediate delivery.

**Fetal fibronectin (fFN)**—Test done to evaluate premature labor. A sample of cervical-vaginal secretions is taken; if fFN is present after 22 weeks, it indicates increased risk for premature delivery.

**Fetal goiter**—Enlargement of the thyroid in the fetus.

**Fetal monitor**—Device used before or during labor to listen to and to record the fetal heartbeat. Monitoring baby inside the uterus can be external (through maternal abdomen) or internal (through maternal vagina).

**Fetal period**—Time period following the embryonic period (first 10 weeks of gestation) until birth.

**Fetoscopy**—Test that enables doctor to look through a fetoscope (a fiber-optics scope) to detect subtle abnormalities and problems in a fetus.

**Fetus**—Refers to the unborn baby after 10 weeks of gestation until birth.

**Fibrin**—Elastic protein important in the coagulation of blood.

**Forceps**—Instrument sometimes used to deliver baby. It is placed around baby's head, inside the birth canal, to help guide baby out of the birth canal during delivery.

Frank breech—Baby presenting buttocks first. Legs are straight and knees extended.

Fraternal twins—See *dizygotic twins*.

Fundus—Top part of the uterus; often measured during pregnancy.

# *g*

Genes—Basic units of heredity. Each gene carries specific information and is passed from parent to child. A child receives half of its genes from its mother and half from its father. Every human has about 100,000 genes.

Genetic counseling—Consultation between a couple and specialists about genetic defects and the possibility of presence or recurrence of genetic problems in a pregnancy.

Genetic tests—Various screening and diagnostic tests done to determine whether a couple may have a child with a genetic defect. Usually part of genetic counseling.

Genital herpes simplex—Herpes simplex infection involving the genital area. It can be significant during pregnancy because of the danger to a newborn fetus becoming infected with herpes simplex.

Genitourinary problems—Defects or problems involving genital organs and the bladder or kidneys.

Germ layers—Layers or areas of tissue important in the development of the baby.

Gestational age—Dating a pregnancy from the first day of the last menstrual period; 2 weeks longer than fertilization age. Also see *fertilization age*.

Gestational diabetes—Occurrence or worsening of diabetes that occurs only during pregnancy (gestation).

Gestational trophoblastic disease (GTN)—Abnormal pregnancy with cystic growth of the placenta. Characterized by bleeding during early and middle pregnancy.

Globulin—Family of proteins from plasma or serum of the blood.

Glucose-tolerance test (GTT)—Blood test done to evaluate the body's response to sugar. Blood is drawn from the mother-to-be once or at intervals following ingestion of a sugary substance.

Glucosuria—Glucose (sugar) in the urine.

Gonorrhea—Contagious venereal infection, transmitted primarily by intercourse.

Grand mal seizure—Loss of control of body functions. Seizure activity of a major form.

Group-B streptococcal (GBS) infection—Serious infection occurring in the mother's vagina, throat or rectum. Infection can be in any of these areas.

Group-B streptococcus (GBS) test—Near the end of the pregnancy, samples may be taken from the expectant woman's vagina, perineum and rectum to check for GBS. A urine test may also be done. If the test is positive, treatment may be started or given during labor.

# h

**Habitual miscarriage**—Occurrence of three or more spontaneous miscarriages.

**Heartburn**—Discomfort or pain that occurs in the chest. Often occurs after eating.

**Hematocrit**—Determines the proportion of blood cells to plasma. Important in diagnosing anemia.

**Hemoglobin**—Pigment in red blood cells that carries oxygen to body tissues.

**Hemolytic disease**—Destruction of red blood cells. See *anemia*.

**Hemorrhoids**—Dilated blood vessels, most often found in the rectum or rectal canal.

**Heparin**—Medication used to thin the blood.

**Hepatitis-B antibodies test**—Test to determine if the pregnant woman has ever contracted hepatitis-B.

**High-risk pregnancy**—Pregnancy with complications that requires special medical attention, often from a specialist. Also see *perinatologist*.

**HIV/AIDS test**—Test to determine if a woman has HIV or AIDS (the test cannot be done without the woman's knowledge and permission).

**Homan's sign**—Pain caused by flexing the toes toward the knees when a person has a blood clot in the lower leg.

**Home uterine monitoring**—Contractions of a pregnant woman's uterus are recorded at home, then transmitted by telephone to the doctor (no special equipment is needed other than the monitor and a telephone). Used to identify women at risk of premature labor.

**Human chorionic gonadatropin (HCG)**—Hormone produced in early pregnancy; measured in a pregnancy test.

**Human placental lactogen**—Hormone of pregnancy produced by the placenta and found in the bloodstream.

**Hyaline membrane disease**—Respiratory disease of the newborn.

**Hydatidiform mole**—See *gestational trophoblastic disease*.

**Hydramnios**—Increased amount of amniotic fluid

**Hydrocephalus**—Excessive accumulation of fluid around the brain of the baby. Sometimes called *water on the brain*.

**Hyperbilirubinemia**—Extremely high level of bilirubin in the blood.

**Hyperemesis gravidarum**—Severe nausea, dehydration and vomiting during pregnancy. Occurs most frequently during the first trimester.

**Hyperglycemia**—Increased blood sugar.

**Hypertension, pregnancy-induced**—High blood pressure that occurs during pregnancy. Defined by an increase in the diastolic or systolic blood pressure.

**Hyperthyroidism**—Elevation of the thyroid hormone in the bloodstream.

**Hypoplasia**—Defective or incomplete development or formation of tissue.

**Hypotension**—Low blood pressure.

**Hypothyroidism**—Low or inadequate levels of thyroid hormone in the bloodstream.

# *i*

**Identical twins**—See *monozygotic twins.*

**Imaging tests**—Tests that look inside the body, including X-rays, CT scans (or CAT scans) and magnetic resonance imaging (MRI).

**Immune globulin preparation**—Substance used to protect against infection with certain diseases, such as hepatitis or measles.

**In utero**—Within the uterus.

**Incompetent cervix**—Cervix that dilates painlessly, without contractions.

**Incomplete miscarriage**—Miscarriage in which part, but not all, of the uterine contents are expelled.

**Induced labor**—Labor started using a medication. See *oxytocin.*

**Inevitable miscarriage**—Pregnancy complicated with bleeding and cramping. Usually results in miscarriage.

**Insulin**—Peptide hormone made by the pancreas. It promotes the use of glucose.

**Intrauterine-growth restriction (IUGR)**—Inadequate growth of the fetus during the last stages of pregnancy.

**Iodides**—Medications made up of negative ions of iodine.

**Iron-deficiency anemia**—Anemia produced by lack of iron in the diet; often seen in pregnancy.

**Isoimmunization**—Development of specific antibody directed at the red blood cells of another individual, such as a baby in utero. Often occurs when an Rh-negative woman carries an Rh-positive baby or is given Rh-positive blood.

# *j-k*

**Jaundice**—Yellow staining of the skin, sclera (eyes) and deeper tissues of the body. Caused by excessive amounts of bilirubin. Treated with phototherapy.

**Ketones**—Breakdown product of metabolism found in the blood, particularly from starvation or uncontrolled diabetes.

**Kick count**—Record of how often a pregnant woman feels her baby move; used to evaluate fetal well-being.

**Kidney stones**—Small mass or lesion found in the kidney or urinary tract. Can block the flow of urine.

# *l*

**Labor**—Process of expelling a fetus from the uterus.

**Laparoscopy**—Minor surgical procedure performed for tubal ligation, diagnosis of pelvic pain or diagnosis of ectopic pregnancy.

Leukorrhea—Vaginal discharge characterized by a white or yellowish color. Primarily composed of mucus.

Lightening—Change in the shape of the pregnant uterus a few weeks before labor. Often described as the baby "dropping."

Linea nigra—Line of increased pigmentation that often develops during pregnancy; line runs down the abdomen from bellybutton to pubic area.

Lochia—Vaginal discharge that occurs after delivery of the baby and placenta.

## *m*

Malignant GTN—Cancerous change of gestational trophoblastic disease. See *gestational trophoblastic disease.*

Mammogram—X-ray study of the breasts to identify normal and abnormal breast tissue.

Mask of pregnancy—Increased pigmentation over the area of the face under each eye. Commonly has the appearance of a butterfly.

McDonald cerclage—Surgical procedure performed on an incompetent cervix. A drawstring-type suture holds the cervical opening closed during pregnancy. Also see *incompetent cervix.*

Meconium—First intestinal discharge of the newborn; green or yellow in color. It consists of epithelial or surface cells, mucus and bile. Discharge may occur before or during labor or soon after birth.

Melanoma—Pigmented mole or tumor. It may or may not be cancerous.

Meningomyelocele—Congenital defect of the central nervous system of the baby. Membranes and the spinal cord protrude through an opening or defect in the vertebral column.

Menstrual age—See *gestational age.*

Menstruation—Regular or periodic discharge of endometrial lining and blood from the uterus.

Mesodermal germ layer—Tissue of the embryo that forms connective tissue, muscles, kidneys, ureters and other organs.

Metaplasia—Change in the structure of a tissue into another type that is not normal for that tissue.

Microcephaly—Abnormally small development of the head in the developing fetus.

Microphthalmia—Abnormally small eyeballs.

Miscarriage—Termination or premature end of pregnancy; giving birth to an embryo or fetus before it can live outside the womb, usually defined as before 20 weeks of pregnancy.

Missed miscarriage—Failed pregnancy without bleeding or cramping. Often diagnosed by ultrasound weeks or months after a pregnancy fails.

Mittelschmerz—Pain that coincides with release of an egg from the ovary.

**Molar pregnancy**—See *gestational trophoblastic disease.*

**Monilial vulvovaginitis**—Infection caused by yeast or monilia. Usually affects the vagina and vulva.

**Monozygotic twins**—Twins conceived from one egg. Often called *identical twins.*

**Morning sickness**—Nausea and vomiting, with ill health, found primarily during the first trimester of pregnancy. Also see *hyperemesis gravidarum.*

**Morula**—Cells resulting from the early division of the fertilized egg at the beginning of pregnancy.

**Mucus plug**—Secretions in the cervix; often released just before labor.

**Multiple-markers test**—See *quad-screen test* and *triple-screen test.*

**Mutations**—Change in the character of a gene. Passed from one cell division to another.

# n

**Natural childbirth**—Labor and delivery in which the mother has as few interventions as possible. This may include no medication or monitoring. The woman usually has taken classes to prepare her for labor and delivery.

**Neural-tube defects**—Abnormalities in the development of the spinal cord and brain in a fetus. Also see *anencephaly; hydrocephalus; spina bifida.*

**Nonstress test**—Test in which movements of the baby felt by the mother or observed by a healthcare provider are recorded, along with changes in the fetal heart rate. Used to evaluate fetal well-being.

**Nuchal translucency screening**—Detailed ultrasound that allows the doctor to measure the space behind baby's neck. When combined with blood test results, can measure a woman's probability of her baby having Down syndrome.

**Nurse-midwife**—Nurse who has received extra training in the care of pregnant patients and the delivery of their babies.

# o

**Obstetrician**—Physician who specializes in the care of pregnant women and the delivery of their babies.

**Oligohydramnios**—Lack or deficiency of amniotic fluid.

**Omphalocele**—Presence of congenital outpouching of the umbilicus containing internal organs in the fetus or newborn infant.

**Opioids**—Synthetic compounds with effects similar to those of opium.

**Organogenesis**—Development of the organ systems in the embryo.

**Ossification**—Bone formation.

**Ovarian cycle**—Regular production of hormones from the ovary in response to hormonal messages from the brain. The ovarian cycle governs the endometrial cycle.

**Ovulation**—Cyclic release of an egg from the ovary.

**Ovulatory age**—See *fertilization age.*

**Oxytocin**—Medication that causes uterine contractions; used to induce or augment labor. It may be called by its brand name *Pitocin.* Also the hormone produced by pituitary glands.

# *p*

**Palmar erythema**—Redness of palms of the hands.

**Pap smear**—Routine screening test that evaluates presence of premalignant or cancerous conditions of the cervix.

**Paracervical block**—Local anesthetic to relieve pain of cervical dilatation.

**Pediatrician**—Physician who specializes in the care of babies and children.

**Pelvic exam**—Physical examination by the doctor who feels inside the pelvic area to evaluate the size of the uterus at the beginning of pregnancy and to help the doctor determine if the cervix is dilating and thinning toward the end of pregnancy.

**Percutaneous umbilical-cord blood sampling (PUBS, cordocentesis)**—Test done on the fetus to diagnose Rh-incompatibility, blood disorders and infections. Also called *cordocentesis.*

**Perinatologist**—Physician who specializes in the care of high-risk pregnancies.

**Perineum**—Area between the rectum and vagina.

**Petit mal seizure**—Attack of a brief nature with possible short impairment of consciousness. Often associated with blinking or flickering of the eyelids and a mild twitching of the mouth.

**Phosphatidyl glycerol (PG)**—Lipoprotein present when fetal lungs are mature.

**Phospholipids**—Fat-containing phosphorous; the most important are lecithins and sphingomyelin, which are important in the maturation of fetal lungs before birth.

**Phototherapy**—Treatment for jaundice in a newborn infant. Also see *jaundice.*

**Physiologic anemia of pregnancy**—Anemia during pregnancy caused by an increase in the amount of plasma (fluid) in the blood compared to the number of cells in the blood. Also see *anemia.*

**Placenta previa**—Low attachment of the placenta, very close to, or covering, the cervix.

**Placenta**—Organ inside the uterus that is attached to the baby by the umbilical cord. Essential during pregnancy for growth and development of the embryo and fetus. Also called *afterbirth.*

**Placental abruption**—Premature separation of the placenta from the uterus.

**Pneumonitis**—Inflammation of the lungs.

**Polyhydramnios**—See *hydramnios.*

**Postmature baby**—Baby born 2 weeks or more past its due date.

Postterm birth—Pregnancy of 42+ weeks gestation.

Postpartum—The 6-week period following a baby's birth. Refers to the mother, not the baby.

Postpartum blues—Mild depression after delivery.

Postpartum distress syndrome (PPDS)—A range of symptoms including baby blues, postpartum depression and postpartum psychosis.

Postpartum hemorrhage—Bleeding greater than 17 ounces (450ml) at time of delivery.

Pre-eclampsia—Combination of significant symptoms unique to pregnancy, including high blood pressure, edema, swelling and changes in reflexes.

Pregnancy diabetes—See *gestational diabetes.*

Premature delivery—Delivery before 38 weeks gestation.

Preterm premature rupture of membranes (PPROM)—Rupture of fetal membranes before 37 weeks of pregnancy.

Prenatal care—Program of care for a pregnant woman before the birth of her baby.

Prepared childbirth—Woman has taken classes so she knows what to expect during labor and delivery. She may request pain medication if she needs it.

Presentation—Describes which part of the baby comes into the birth canal first.

Propylthiouracil—Medication used to treat thyroid disease.

Proteinuria—Protein in urine.

Pruritis gravidarum—Itching during pregnancy.

Pubic symphysis—Bony prominence in the pelvic bone found in the middle of a woman's lower abdomen. Landmark from which the doctor often measures the growing uterus during pregnancy.

Pudendal block—Local anesthesia during labor.

Pulmonary embolism—Blood clot from another part of the body that travels to the lungs. Can close passages in the lungs and decrease oxygen exchange.

Pyelonephritis—Serious kidney infection.

# *q–r*

Quad-screen test—Measurement of four blood components to help identify problems. The four tests include alpha-fetoprotein, human chorionic gonadotropin, unconjugated estriol and inhibin-A.

Quickening—Feeling the baby move inside the uterus.

Radiation therapy—Method of treating various cancers.

Radioactive scan—Diagnostic test in which radioactive material is injected into a particular part of the body and scanned to find a problem within that part of the body.

Rh-factor—Blood test to determine if a woman is Rh-negative.

Rh-negative—Absence of rhesus antibody in the blood.

Rh-sensitivity—See *isoimmunization.*

RhoGAM—Medication given during pregnancy and following delivery to prevent isoimmunization. Also see *isoimmunization.*

Round-ligament pain—Pain caused by stretching the ligaments on the sides of the uterus during pregnancy.

Rubella titers—Blood test to check for immunity against rubella (German measles).

Rupture of membranes—Loss of fluid from the amniotic sac. Also called *breaking of waters* or *water breaking.*

## S

Seizure—Sudden onset of a convulsion.

Sexually transmitted disease (STD)—Infection transmitted through sexual contact or sexual intercourse.

Sickle-cell anemia—Anemia caused by abnormal red blood cells shaped like a sickle or a cylinder.

Sickle-cell trait—Presence of the trait for sickle-cell anemia. Not sickle-cell disease itself.

Sickle crisis—Painful episode caused by sickle-cell disease.

Silent labor—Painless dilatation of the cervix.

Skin tag—Flap or extra buildup of skin.

Sodium—Element found in many foods, particularly salt. Ingestion of too much sodium may cause fluid retention.

Sonogram or sonography—See *ultrasound.*

Spina bifida—Birth defect in which membranes of the spinal cord and the spinal cord itself protrude outside the protective bony canal of the spine. Can cause paralysis or malfunctioning of lower extremities.

Spinal anesthesia—Anesthesia given in the spinal canal.

Spontaneous miscarriage—Loss of pregnancy during the first 20 weeks of gestation.

Stasis—Decreased flow.

Station—Estimation of the baby's descent into the birth canal in preparation for birth.

Stillbirth—Death of a fetus before birth, usually defined as after 20 weeks gestation.

Stress test—Test in which mild contractions of the mother's uterus are induced; fetal heart rate in response to the contractions is noted.

Stretch marks—Areas of the skin that are torn or stretched. Often found on the abdomen, breasts, buttocks and legs.

Syphilis test—To test for syphilis; if a woman has syphilis, treatment will be started.

# t

Teratology—Study of abnormal fetal development.

Term—Baby is considered "term" when it is born after 38 weeks. Also called *full term.*

Transition—Phase after active labor during which the cervix fully dilates. Contractions are strongest during this stage.

Trimester—Method of dividing pregnancy into three equal periods of about 13 weeks each.

Triple-screen test—Measurement of three blood components to help identify problems. The three tests include alpha-fetoprotein, human chorionic gonadotropin and unconjugated estriol.

# u

Ultrasound—Noninvasive test that shows a picture of the fetus inside womb. Sound waves bounce off fetus to create a picture.

Umbilical cord—Cord that connects the placenta to the developing baby. It removes waste products and carbon dioxide from baby and brings oxygenated blood and nutrients from mother through the placenta to baby.

Urinalysis and urine cultures—To test for any infections and to determine the levels of sugar and protein in the urine.

Uterus—Organ an embryo/fetus grows in. Also called a *womb.*

# v

Vacuum extractor—Device sometimes used to provide traction on fetal head during delivery; used to help deliver a baby.

Vagina—Birth canal.

Varicose veins—Blood vessels (veins) that are dilated or enlarged.

Vena cava—Major vein in the body that empties into the right atrium of the heart. It returns unoxygenated blood to the heart for transport to the lungs.

Venereal warts—See *condyloma acuminatum.*

Vernix—Fatty substance made up of epithelial cells that covers fetal skin inside the uterus.

Vertex—Head first.

Villi—Projection from a mucous membrane. Most important within the placenta in the exchange of nutrients from maternal blood to the placenta and fetus.

# *w*

**Weight check**—Weight is checked at every prenatal visit; gaining too much weight or not gaining enough weight can indicate problems.

**Womb**—See *uterus.*

# *y-z*

**Yeast infection**—See *monilial vulvovaginitis; thrush.*

**Zygote**—Cell that results from the union of a sperm and egg at fertilization.

# Index

*Page numbers in italics indicate boxed information.*

ALSO BY GLADE B. CURTIS, M.D., M.P.H., OB/GYN
AND JUDITH SCHULER, M.S.

*Bouncing Back
After Your Pregnancy*
ISBN: 0-7382-0606-7

*Your Baby's First Year,
Week by Week*
ISBN: 1-55561-232-6 (paper)
1-55561-257-1 (cloth)

*Your Pregnancy Journal
Week by Week*
ISBN: 1-55561-343-8

*Your Pregnancy
for the Father to Be*
ISBN: 0-7382-1002-1

*Your Pregnancy After 35*
ISBN: 0-7382-1004-8

*Your Pregnancy
Questions and Answers*
ISBN: 0-7382-1003-X

*Your Pregnancy:
Every Woman's Guide*
ISBN: 0-7382-1001-3

Da Capo Lifelong Books are available wherever books are sold and at special discounts for bulk purchases in the U.S. by corporations, institutions, and other organizations. For more information, please contact the Special Markets Department at the Perseus Books Group, 11 Cambridge Center, Cambridge, MA 02142, or call (800) 255-1514, or e-mail specialmarkets@perseusbooks.com.